Metaverse

Peter Hoffmann

Metaverse

The fusion of reality and virtuality in the Next Generation Internet

Second Edition

Peter Hoffmann
Rorschach, Switzerland

ISBN 978-3-658-49376-9   ISBN 978-3-658-49377-6   (eBook)
https://doi.org/10.1007/978-3-658-49377-6

Translation from the German language edition: "Metaversum" by Peter Hoffmann, © Der/die Herausgeber bzw. der/die Autor(en), exklusiv lizenziert an Springer Fachmedien Wiesbaden GmbH, ein Teil von Springer Nature 2025. Published by Springer Fachmedien Wiesbaden. All Rights Reserved.

This book is a translation of the original German edition "Metaversum," 2nd edition, by Peter Hoffmann, published by Springer Fachmedien Wiesbaden GmbH in 2025. The translation was done with the help of an artificial intelligence machine translation tool. A subsequent human revision was done primarily in terms of content, so that the book will read stylistically differently from a conventional translation. Springer Nature works continuously to further the development of tools for the production of books and on the related technologies to support the authors.

© The Editor(s) (if applicable) and The Author(s), under exclusive license to Springer Fachmedien Wiesbaden GmbH, part of Springer Nature 2026

This work is subject to copyright. All rights are solely and exclusively licensed by the Publisher, whether the whole or part of the material is concerned, specifically the rights of translation, reprinting, reuse of illustrations, recitation, broadcasting, reproduction on microfilms or in any other physical way, and transmission or information storage and retrieval, electronic adaptation, computer software, or by similar or dissimilar methodology now known or hereafter developed.
The use of general descriptive names, registered names, trademarks, service marks, etc. in this publication does not imply, even in the absence of a specific statement, that such names are exempt from the relevant protective laws and regulations and therefore free for general use.
The publisher, the authors and the editors are safe to assume that the advice and information in this book are believed to be true and accurate at the date of publication. Neither the publisher nor the authors or the editors give a warranty, expressed or implied, with respect to the material contained herein or for any errors or omissions that may have been made. The publisher remains neutral with regard to jurisdictional claims in published maps and institutional affiliations.

This Springer imprint is published by the registered company Springer Fachmedien Wiesbaden GmbH, part of Springer Nature.
The registered company address is: Abraham-Lincoln-Str. 46, 65189 Wiesbaden, Germany

If disposing of this product, please recycle the paper.

Preface to the 2nd, Updated and Expanded Edition

Not even a year and a half has passed since the (official) publication of the first edition of this book. Nevertheless, it seemed reasonable to begin revising and updating it almost immediately after its release. Computer science and the world of IT are incredibly fast-moving—and the world of the metaverse even more so.

Not only are techniques and technologies continuously evolving, but these new methods are also giving rise to ever more application areas. All of these developments needed to be taken into account in this second edition. A real challenge!

Listing every single revision in the respective sections here would clearly go beyond the scope—virtually no chapter remained completely untouched. However, the rapid pace of development has led to the addition of several entire chapters. These are, in detail:

- Section 2.7—The Metaverse as an Information-Centric Web
- Section 3.6.1—The Real-Life Connector—Foundation for New Interaction Paradigms (while this chapter is not entirely new, it has undergone a significant expansion through a new perspective on convergence)
- Section 3.6.2—Physical Convergence
- Section 4.5—A Contemporary Form of Modusage: D2A Commerce
- Section 4.6.8—The Metaverse and the World of Work
- Section 4.6.15—The Banker Role
- Section 4.6.16—A Social Metaverse?
- Section 4.6.17—Politics and Administration
- Chapter 5—The Metaverse vs. Current Trends
- Chapter 6—More Relevant Than Ever: Artificial Intelligence in the Metaverse?

Overall, this update has resulted in an increase of more than 50 pages in length.

Enjoy reading and exploring :-)

At this point, I would like to extend my **sincere thanks** to all those who have shared my enthusiasm for immersive worlds and the concept of the metaverse. First and foremost, these are the many students at the

- FHV—Vorarlberg University of Applied Sciences in Dornbirn and the
- FOM University of Applied Sciences for Economics and Management at the Munich Study Center

with whom I was able to discuss many of the aspects mentioned above, sometimes quite controversially, and who were not discouraged by these discussions but instead chose to write term papers in the context of the metaverse. I am even more grateful to those students who went on to write their theses in the broader context (and in some cases continue to work on the topic).

Special thanks are also due to my colleagues at the (aforementioned) FHV—Vorarlberg University of Applied Sciences in Dornbirn, with whom I have repeatedly engaged in stimulating discussions in, around, and about the metaverse.

And last but certainly not least, special mention must go to:

- Steffi, who puts up with my nerdy obsession for this strange metaverse and
- my two iTigers, Oskar and Paul, who serve as models and counter-models for real reality and who often pulled me back from the highly immersive world of writing into the real world.
- And who made me realize that cats, cat pictures, and cat videos will likely continue to play a significant role in the next generation of the Internet, too.

Rorschach, Switzerland   Peter Hoffmann

Contents

1	**Metaverse?**	1
	References	5
2	**Where from … Where to … or: What is it Anyway**	7
	2.1 Reality	9
	2.2 Virtuality	9
	2.3 Augmented Reality	13
	2.4 Augmented Virtuality	15
	2.5 Mixed and Other Realities	17
	2.6 And the Metaverse?	20
	2.7 The Metaverse as an Information-Centric Web	23
	References	26
3	**The Merging of Worlds and … Verses**	29
	3.1 Sensory Fusion	32
	3.2 Spatial Merging	35
	3.3 Semantic Merging	37
	3.4 Temporal Merging	42
	3.5 The Merging of Interaction	48
	3.6 All-together – The Path to Socio-cultural Convergence	53
	3.6.1 The Real-Life Connector – Foundation for New Interaction Paradigms	54
	3.6.2 Physical Fusion	59
	3.6.3 Social and Societal Convergence	65
	3.6.4 Fusion in Everyday Life: Leisure, Culture, Art …	71
	3.6.5 The Fusion in Everyday Life: The World of Work	79
	3.6.6 Or the Opposite: The Defusion of	80
	References	81
4	**Another Dimension: Economic Merging**	91
	4.1 The Analog Economy of the "Classical Value Chain"	94
	4.2 Early Ideas of Convergence: Prosumerism	95
	4.3 The Fusion in the Web Economy: Produsage	98

	4.4	The Merged Cross-Economy of the Metaverse: Modusage	100
	4.5	A Contemporary Form of Modusage: D2A-Commerce	103
	4.6	The Digital 49ers: New Business Models and Application Areas	106
		4.6.1 Advertising & Marketing	113
		4.6.2 Shopping	116
		4.6.3 Gaming & Games	119
		4.6.4 Art & Culture	120
		4.6.5 Social Events	122
		4.6.6 Tourism	126
		4.6.7 Education	128
		4.6.8 The Metaverse and the World of Work	131
		4.6.9 The Metaverse and Medicine	132
		4.6.10 The Business Internal Metaverse	135
		4.6.11 Metaverse Service Providing	138
		4.6.12 Back into the Real World	140
		4.6.13 The "God Role"	141
		4.6.14 DAOs and the Metaverse	143
		4.6.15 The Banker Role	145
		4.6.16 A Social Metaverse?	146
		4.6.17 Politics and Administration	147
		4.6.18 The yet to be Imagined	150
	4.7	And how is that Supposed to Work?	151
	4.8	A Success Story?	155
	4.9	(Not Only) Economic Concerns: Metaverse-Hopping!	158
		4.9.1 A Unified Metaverse?	159
		4.9.2 Diverse Metaverses?	161
	4.10	The Extended Economic Environment	164
	References		170
5	**The Metaverse vs. Current Trends**		185
	5.1	The Metaverse—Another Attempt at a Definition	186
	5.2	The Metaverse vs. Web3	186
	5.3	The Metaverse vs. Fediverse	189
	5.4	The Metaverse vs. IoT & Embedded Systems	190
	5.5	The Metaverse vs. Spatial Computing	193
	5.6	The Metaverse vs. Synthetic Media & Social Media	194
	5.7	Overview of Differences and Similarities	196
		5.7.1 Metaverse, Web3, Fediverse	196
		5.7.2 Metaverse, IoT, Embedded Systems	198
		5.7.3 Metaverse, Spatial Computing	199
		5.7.4 Metaverse, Synthetic Media, Social Media	201
	References		202

6	More Relevant than ever: Artificial Intelligence in the Metaverse?	205
	References	211
7	**What must not be Missing: Criticism**	215
	7.1 The General Themes of Criticism	216
	7.2 The merging of the political world?	219
	7.3 Or Rather the Division of the Political World?	220
	7.4 But: A View from a Different Perspective	222
	References	224
8	**The Real Vision**	227
	8.1 The Institutional Perspective on the Metaverse	227
	8.1.1 ITU and IEEE	228
	8.1.2 World Wide Web Consortium W3C	230
	8.1.3 World Economic Forum	231
	8.1.4 Metaverse Standards Forum	233
	8.2 The Perspective of Professionals and Users	235
	8.2.1 Matthew Ball	236
	8.2.2 Cathy Hackl	239
	8.2.3 Amy Webb	241
	8.2.4 Steve Mann	242
	8.3 The Metaverse – the Operating System of the Future?	244
	References	248
9	**Now is the time to Build!**	253
	References	254
10	**The Current Addendum 1—Still Relevant: Is the Hype Already over?**	257
	References	260
Glossary		263

Abbreviations

AAL	Ambient Assisted Living
AR	Augmented Reality
AV	Augmented Virtuality
BIM	Building Information Modeling
CAD	Computer Aided Design
CAVE	Cave Automatic Virtual Involvement
CGI	Computer-Generated Imagery
CMO	Chief Metaverse Officer
DAO	Decentralized Autonomous Organization
DID	Decentralized Identifier
D2A	Direct-to-Avatar
EU	European Union
GAN	Generative Adversarial Network
GPT	Generative Pre-trained Transformer
GUI	Graphical User Interface
HCI	Human-Computer Interaction
HMD	Head-mounted display
III/I3	Immersive Interactive Information Space
KI/AI	Artificial Intelligence
ML	Machine Learning
MR	Mixed Reality
MSP	Metaverse Service Providing
MUI	Metaverse User Interface/Interaction
NFT	Non-Fungible Token
NPC	Non-Player Character (NPC)
NLP	Natural Language Processing
NUI	Natural User Interface
PVR	Persistent Virtual Reality
P2P	Peer-to-peer
RVK	Reality–Virtuality Continuum

VC	Verifiable Credential
VR	Virtual Reality
WEF	World Economic Forum (WEF)
WIMP	Window, Icon, Menu, Pointer (interaction paradigm)
WWW	World Wide Web
XR	Extended Reality

List of Figures

Fig. 2.1	The Reality-Virtuality Continuum according to Milgram and Kishino. (Adapted from [MIL95]).	8
Fig. 2.2	The extreme of pure reality in the RVC. (Adapted from [MIL95])	9
Fig. 2.3	The extreme of pure virtuality in the RVK. (Adapted from [MIL95])	10
Fig. 2.4	Patent drawing of the Sensorama by Morton Heilig. (Morton Heilig: The Sensorama, from U.S. Patent #3050870).	11
Fig. 2.5	Difference in VR presentation: Headset vs. CAVE. (Own illustration: Peter Hoffmann, Invisible Cow)	12
Fig. 2.6	Augmented Reality (AR) in the RVK. (Original illustration: Peter Hoffmann, Invisible Cow)	13
Fig. 2.7	Simplified system architecture for AR. (Original illustration: Peter Hoffmann, Invisible Cow)	15
Fig. 2.8	Augmented Virtuality (AV) in the RVC. (Own illustration: Peter Hoffmann, Invisible Cow)	16
Fig. 2.9	Screenshot from the VR live concert by Lindsey Stirling [STI19]	17
Fig. 2.10	Classification scheme for head-mounted displays: top left: monocular, see-through; bottom left: binocular, see-through; top right: monocular, non-see-through; bottom right: binocular, non-see-through. (Original illustration: Peter Hoffmann, Invisible Cow).	19
Fig. 2.11	Digital artifacts vs. the real world: Mixed Reality. (Original illustration: Peter Hoffmann, Invisible Cow).	21
Fig. 2.12	The positioning of the metaverse within the RVC. (Own illustration: Peter Hoffmann, Invisible Cow)	23
Fig. 3.1	Logic and suspense of the narrative vs. freedom of interaction. (Own illustration: Peter Hoffmann, Invisible Cow)	31
Fig. 3.2	The dimension of narrative reality (N) – narratem (atomic narrative unit); (P) presentation object; (A) (user) action. (Own illustration: Peter Hoffmann, Invisible Cow)	31

Fig. 3.3	Technical sub-aspects of fusion. (Adapted from [BIT22])	32
Fig. 3.4	A systematics of perception in HCI. (Original illustration: Peter Hoffmann, Invisible Cow).	33
Fig. 3.5	Semantic fusion as a location-based service. (Original illustration: Peter Hoffmann, Invisible Cow).	38
Fig. 3.6	Screenshots of the mobile apps from DB and SBB.	39
Fig. 3.7	Sub-aspects of context formation. (Original illustration: Peter Hoffmann, Invisible Cow)	40
Fig. 3.8	Multimodal interaction: "Put that there" [BOL80]	51
Fig. 3.9	The Real Life Connector. (Original illustration: Peter Hoffmann, Invisible Cow).	55
Fig. 3.10	Immersion of interaction paradigms: Metaverse User Interaction (MUI). (Original illustration: Peter Hoffmann, Invisible Cow).	60
Fig. 3.11	Differences in the characteristics of avatars, NPCs, and digital twins. (Original illustration: Peter Hoffmann, Invisible Cow).	61
Fig. 3.12	The Decentraland Metaverse Music Festival 2022. (Screenshots: DMMF 2022, Peter Hoffmann, Invisible Cow)	75
Fig. 4.1	Web 1–2–3. (After [SCHm21a]).	92
Fig. 4.2	Simplified value chain. (Own illustration: Peter Hoffmann, Invisible Cow).	94
Fig. 4.3	Feedback as an extension of the simplified value chain: Prosumerism. (Original illustration: Peter Hoffmann, Invisible Cow).	96
Fig. 4.4	The transformation of the value chain: Produsage. (Own illustration: Peter Hoffmann, Invisible Cow)	98
Fig. 4.5	The value chain in the metaverse: Modusage. (Original illustration: Peter Hoffmann, Invisible Cow).	101
Fig. 4.6	Degree of digitalization vs. value chain model. (Original illustration: Peter Hoffmann, Invisible Cow).	103
Fig. 4.7	Industry activities in the RVC. (Own illustration: Peter Hoffmann, Invisible Cow).	107
Fig. 4.8	Revised business models around the metaverse. (Own illustration: Peter Hoffmann, Invisible Cow)	113
Fig. 4.9	Consumer expectations for the future of shopping. (Based on [PAV23])	118
Fig. 4.10	Travel in the future metaverse. (Adapted from [BIT22b])	126
Fig. 4.11	Hotels in the metaverse (here: M Social). ([MUL23, TEO22])	127
Fig. 4.12	M-Social Vacay Phuket.	128
Fig. 4.13	The metaverse and relevant technologies. (Based on the Gartner Hype Cycle [PER22]).	157

List of Figures

Fig. 5.1	Chronology of related terms. (Own illustration: Peter Hoffmann, Invisible Cow)	186
Fig. 5.2	Embedded Systems–IoT–Metaverse	192
Fig. 8.1	Seven rules for the metaverse. (Adapted from: Tony Parisi [PAR21])	236
Fig. 8.2	The flow of information in the wearable computing paradigm. (Adapted from [MAN98])	244
Fig. 8.3	An architectural diagram for the metaverse. (Adapted from [JAB22, DED09])	246

Metaverse? 1

The Metaverse—a term that is widely known and used by many people. Nevertheless, discussions often reveal that each user has their own individual understanding of what the term actually means. For this reason, it is essential to define the term Metaverse precisely, as well as all related concepts such as Virtual Reality (VR), Augmented Reality (AR), Mixed Reality (MR), and Extended Reality, and to examine them in detail.

One of the main reasons for the popularity of the term Metaverse is likely that marketing departments of both large and small companies quickly jumped on this new buzzword without truly understanding what it entails. These companies are now attempting to leverage the term for their own purposes, which is understandable given its significance, but this also complicates the use and discussion of the term and the topic as a whole.

There have been many attempts to describe the essence of the Metaverse. Such descriptions usually sound catchy and intriguing, but upon closer inspection, they are at best imprecise and often simply incorrect:

> "The Metaverse is the moment when our digital life is worth more than our physical life" states Shaan Puri, tech founder and former Twitch manager [ERL23].

What a statement! However, the question arises as to whether, as physical beings, we actually want to leave our physical lives behind in order to exist solely in the digital world. While such definitions may be useful for a philosophical discussion of the Metaverse, they are not necessarily helpful for its practical realization. At the very least, they are ambiguously phrased. What Puri means is that "in the next ten to twenty years," users' attention will increasingly shift from the real world to the digital world. This is because users will work or live in front of screens even more than they do today. In many cases, however, it seems that a maximum threshold has already been reached, as the use of social media on mobile devices such as smartphones and tablets already often causes people to lose awareness of their surroundings.

> "The Metaverse is one of the most popular virtual worlds available today. It allows users to create their own avatars and explore many different environments. The platform offers hundreds of games for users to play, as well as thousands of different shops where they can purchase unique items."

Such definitions, which are clearly developed from a marketing perspective, are also unhelpful for implementation purposes and are inaccurate in terms of content.

Describing the Metaverse as one of the most popular virtual worlds can certainly be criticized, as it does not yet exist as a standalone entity. There are only a few independent virtual worlds, such as Fortnite, World of Warcraft, and others, which enjoy great popularity. Moreover, the features attributed to the Metaverse, such as the ability to create avatars and explore environments, are not unique but have long been established in numerous virtual 3D platforms.

The claim that the Metaverse offers hundreds of games and thousands of shops should also be viewed critically, as this cannot be considered a real distinguishing feature. These possibilities have long been available simply through the Internet.

It should be noted, in all fairness, that it is not only marketing departments that are appropriating the term "Metaverse." Both small and large technology companies are jumping on the bandwagon and often hastily claim that they are now and will be in the future "Metaverse companies," working to create Metaverses in order to improve or expand people's digital and physical realities. Of course, these companies must also achieve economic success, and that is their prerogative. However, upon closer examination, it becomes apparent that these companies were already active in the fields of 3D computing, virtual reality, or related areas, and are merely adding a new label to their portfolio. While this is permissible, they must now also face criticism that, in doing so, they are not advancing the definition of the Metaverse in any meaningful way.

Undoubtedly, many more similarly inadequate definitions and perspectives could be identified that treat the term in an equally vague manner. However, to enable reliable communication and discussion on the topic, the following sections will first attempt to define the context of this planned Metaverse. The goal is to ultimately present a concrete, tangible, and enduring definition.

To do so, however, it is necessary to first take a step back—a step that leads us back to today's Internet.

The Internet is one of the most widespread innovations of recent history on a global scale. Conceived in the 1960s by ARPA, an agency of the US Department of Defense, as a decentralized and fail-safe communications network, it began in 1969 in the academic research sector. The original ARPANET served as a platform for the exchange of scientific results and was gradually expanded with additional nodes, communication protocols, and applications. In the 1980s, ARPANET evolved into a global communications network. With the development of the World Wide Web by Tim Berners-Lee in 1989 and its subsequent commercialization, the Internet became an omnipresent phenomenon. Over the years, the Internet has undergone various phases of development and has been continuously expanded with new applications, such as user-generated content and social networks. The next revolutionary stage of development remains to be seen [BRA10]. Perhaps it is just around the corner with "the Metaverse." Compared to the current Internet, which gradually built up its economic, social, and cultural relevance over a period of three decades, the Metaverse is also undergoing a steady and ongoing evolution. It could well be the Trojan horse that enables well-known technologies to break through into a novel virtual world in a new form [SCHm21a].

But is this new virtual world, which will be even more interconnected and tangible than today's, truly desirable? A comparison with the transformation of our geopolitical world may be helpful here. Comparing the current younger generations of European citizens reveals that they do not know a life without the European Union (EU) and a united Europe. Although the EU is certainly not perfect, it has nonetheless created a significant economic and social space composed of interconnected yet very different individual worlds. In the EU, it is possible to travel from Hamburg to Lisbon or to shop in Rome, Dublin, or Athens without paying customs duties or passing through border controls. The common currency is valid both at the northernmost point of Finland and in a mountain tavern in Crete. The Schengen Agreement has helped create an economic ecosystem that is greater than the sum of its parts.

The old, fragmented Europe with border posts, countless currencies, and complex customs regulations is almost unimaginable for younger generations. The same is true of today's Internet. Services such as Amazon, Google, Zoom, Twitter (now X), Netflix, Minecraft, and many others are simply used, but these applications, like the member states of the EU, each stand alone and are separate from one another. For each of these places, we need a new digital identity and mostly use the two-dimensional space of our screens.

The concept of the Metaverse aims to connect these various isolated elements and to develop an Internet capable of seamlessly linking the real and virtual worlds. The Metaverse is intended to exist in real time and in parallel with the physical world. In addition, it is envisioned to have its own economic system that enables an unprecedented degree of personal development. Furthermore, it is to become a platform where digital data and goods can be exchanged without restrictions and regardless of borders.

This raises the question of what this should mean in practice. Cathy Hackl, who will be mentioned more frequently below, has formulated a thought experiment using the example of a young woman as a user of the near-future Metaverse. In her vision, Hackl sees the young woman being awakened in the morning by her virtual, voice-based assistant. She then begins her morning routine. Afterwards, she goes to her closet and looks at her volumetric representation in the form of an avatar or hologram. She tries on clothes virtually by using the volumetric model, which takes all her measurements into account, and then selects what she wants to wear that day. The actual clothing she puts on her physical self has a digital component that is transferred to her digital likeness. Depending on the virtual environment she is in, she can adjust the appearance of her outfit. Perhaps even digital, haptic nanoparticles are embedded in her lipstick, allowing her to greet her partner, who is traveling in another country, and feel his embrace.

There are many such—and similar—visions of life in and with the metaverse. The interesting question, therefore, is how these visionaries actually arrive at these ideas. It is possible that they are simply parroting, without reflection, the statements of other vocal consultants and agencies, such as Axel Springer's hy [SCHm21a]:

> "Five characteristics are particularly important. The metaverse is defined above all by the following [...] characteristics:
> 1. reality and virtuality are seamlessly connected,
> 2. the metaverse operates continuously and in real time, synchronized with the physical world,
> 3. it spans its own economic system across both the analog and digital worlds,
> 4. it enables individual fulfillment as never before, and
> 5. digital data and assets can be transferred seamlessly across all boundaries."

However, such vague statements unfortunately leave unanswered what this actually means both technically and socially.

At least, there also seems to be a grounded counter-euphoria that takes a somewhat more sober look at the metaverse of the future: "A visit to one of the many NFT galleries may sound interesting at first, but once there, it quickly becomes clear that two-dimensional artworks simply do not benefit from the 3D world. In the end, JPGs and AVIs are simply displayed much more sensibly on a website. Even a virtual bar opened by the US brewery Miller Lite in Decentraland for the Super Bowl works at best as a curiosity. After five minutes at the latest, the walkable commercial has been explored, and even virtual free beer is not a truly convincing reason to spend even a minute longer in the surprisingly dingy dive" [RIX22].

However, such harsh criticism of the use of the term "metaverse" does not mean that this context should be viewed only negatively. Technology is constantly evolving. Therefore, this introductory section should conclude with a statement by Yu Yuan, the current director of the IEEE, as a positive transition to the following considerations [BAL22]:

> "In the narrow sense, the metaverse can simply be defined as Persistent Virtual Reality (PVR). In the broader sense, the metaverse is the advanced stage and the long-term vision of digital transformation."

This is precisely why it is so important to engage with the concept, the theory, and the possible practical implementation of the metaverse.

References

[BAL22] Ball, Matthew; Furness, Thomas; Inbar, Ori; Kalinowski, Caitlin; Lange, Danny; Lebaredian, Rev; Mann, Steve; Miralles, Evelyn; Rosedale, Philip; Trevett, Neil; Yuan, Yu (14.06.2022): Metaverse decoded by top experts. In: Versemaker: Metaverse Lands-cape & Outlook Series. Online: https://versemaker.org/download (Retrieved: 10.05.2023).

[BRA10] Braun, Torsten (2010). Geschichte und Entwicklung des Internets. Informatik-Spektrum: Vol. 33, No. 2. Berlin Heidelberg: Springer-Verlag. (pp. 201–207). https://doi.org/10.1007/s00287-010-0423-9.

[ERL23] Erl, Josef; Bastian, Matthias (03.09.2022): Hier sind 10 Metaverse-Definitionen, sucht euch eine aus. In: mixed.de. Online: https://mixed.de/metaverse-definitionen/ (Retrieved: 10.05.2023).

[RIX22] Rixecker, Kim (23.02.2022): Metaverse-Selbstversuch: Wir waren da – und schwer gelangweilt. In: t3n. Online: https://t3n.de/news/metaverse-selbstversuch-decentraland-1451407/ (Retrieved: 17.05.2023).

[SCHm21a] Schmidt, Cord (2021): Wie das Internet zum Metaverse wird. In: hy – the Axel Springer Consulting Group. Online: https://hy.co/2021/12/01/into-the-metaverse-oder-die-naechste-aera-des-internets/#1 (Retrieved: 10.05.2023).

Where from … Where to … or: What is it Anyway 2

The term "post-Internet era" is often used to describe the metaverse. However, the term "post-Internet" does not refer to a time after the Internet, but rather to our current era, in which the Internet has become so ubiquitous and commonplace that people hardly notice it anymore. The metaverse represents an innovation that enables the creation of online spaces where users can interact with each other multidimensionally. Instead of passively consuming digital content, users are meant to become visitors to the metaverse, immersing themselves in a world where the digital and the physical merge into an entirely new experience [SMA20].

Although the concept of the metaverse is still relatively new, it is, first and foremost, merely an evolution of augmented reality, virtual reality, and other technologies. In contrast to these technological approaches, however, the metaverse offers a new space for play, movement, or interaction for humanity, advancing to a higher level of the virtual [JIA22].

The enthusiasm surrounding the metaverse is not due to the person who first coined the term. In fact, the term "metaverse" originally comes from the science fiction novel "Snow Crash," written by Neal Stephenson in 1992 [STE92]. However, even though this book introduced the term, it did not trigger the hype we are witnessing today in connection with the metaverse. Rather, it is statements such as those by Mark Zuckerberg, who describes the metaverse as the future "embodied internet" and predicts that, in the future, the distinction between the real and the virtual world in the metaverse will no longer be discernible. This would mean a fusion of reality and virtuality. However, before accepting such statements at face value, it is important to first examine how users actually perceive real and virtual worlds. Without such an understanding, the intended merging of these worlds can hardly be successfully achieved [BIT22].

"There is consensus in all discussions that the metaverse represents a form of virtual world or virtual experience."

It is important to note, however, that the nature and self-concept of virtual worlds are currently undergoing change. These virtual worlds have existed for quite some time. Computer games are a good example of this. However, it would be a mistake to assume that the metaverse is simply the next computer game. Especially among the younger generation, virtual worlds such as Minecraft, Fortnite, or Roblox have long since taken on new significance. They serve not only as entertainment media but also as social meeting places. It is not uncommon for people to arrange to meet in Minecraft to work together on a project, such as building a train station for Oberursel, as demonstrated by the "Oberurselcraft" platform [BOGoJ, KOM17, OBE20].

An approach that may prove helpful here, and which is deliberately referenced in this context, is the Reality-Virtuality Continuum (RVC) developed and presented by Paul Milgram and Akira Kishino in 1994, as shown in Fig. 2.1 [MIL95]. Milgram—who should not be confused with the well-known psychologist Milgram—uses this model to describe, from the perspective of human-computer interaction, human perception and the spectrum of this perception. He distinguishes between the extremes of 100% reality and 100% virtuality, which are separated by a broad spectrum of transitions between these two aspects. This describes how humans perceive their respective environments and what this means in relation to the relevant technology and techniques.

Therefore, before focusing further on the metaverse itself, it is first necessary to consider how humans—and, by extension, technology—perceive their respective environments. At this point, the frequently mentioned immersiveness of virtual worlds is not yet the focus; this will be addressed later, once the foundational concepts introduced here have been established.

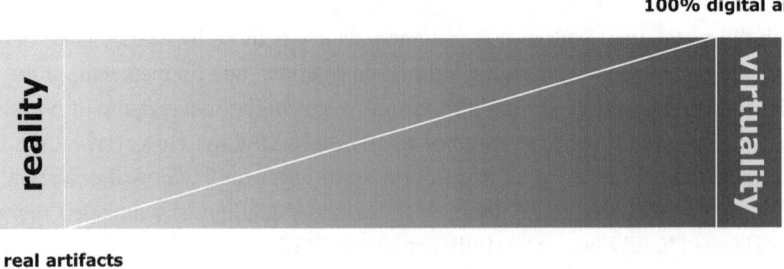

Fig. 2.1 The Reality-Virtuality Continuum according to Milgram and Kishino. (Adapted from [MIL95])

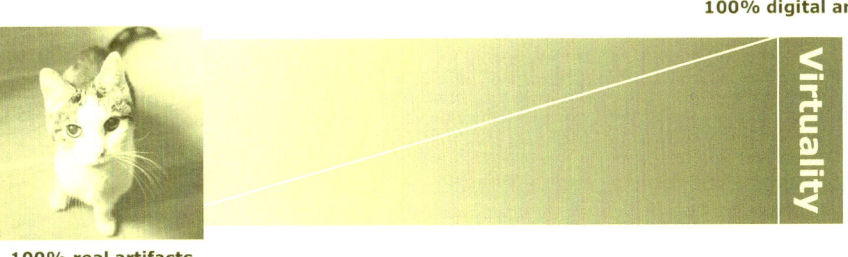

Fig. 2.2 The extreme of pure reality in the RVC. (Adapted from [MIL95])

2.1 Reality

The continuum established by Milgram and Kishino has an extreme at each end. One of these extremes is reality. In this context, the term does not refer to a philosophical debate about the nature of reality, but rather, within the framework of the Reality-Virtuality Continuum, to the current perception of humans and their environment.

Reality, as defined by Milgram and Kishino's continuum, means that a person receives only real artifacts through all available sensory channels (see Fig. 2.2). At this point, one could certainly consider which sensory channels are available to humans for perceiving their environment and how these could be mapped to technical applications. However, this will be addressed later in Sect. 3.1.

2.2 Virtuality

At the other end of the continuum, according to Milgram, lies the exact opposite extreme: 100% virtuality. Here, too, it is meant that a person perceives only virtual or digital artifacts through all available sensory channels. That is, on this side of the continuum, a person sees only digitally generated and rendered objects and hears only digitally produced audio information. However, this is only a small part of this extreme perspective; rather, the idea must be extended to include the person also feeling, smelling, and tasting only digitally generated impressions. Such an extreme view leads to the conclusion that a person's perception is completely and entirely disconnected from the real environment.

While the extreme of reality is technically very easy to achieve—for example, simply by switching off all digital devices—the technical effort required for the extreme of virtuality is exceptionally high, as can be seen in Fig. 2.3. Although images and sound can be artificially generated in high quality and even in so-called real time, this does not apply to all other sensory channels. It is certainly conceivable, for example, to present an

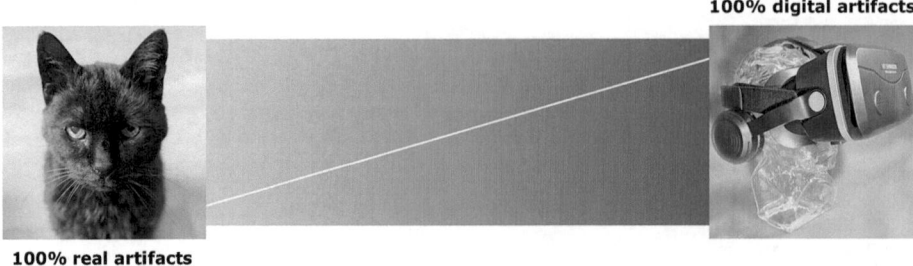

Fig. 2.3 The extreme of pure virtuality in the RVK. (Adapted from [MIL95])

artificially generated scent to a user by using essential oils delivered to the nose [LIU23, SCH23a]. And it is also theoretically conceivable to address the human sense of taste by technically stimulating the taste receptors on the tongue and in the mouth area. However, whether such a technical implementation would be accepted by users is highly questionable. In fact, there are currently very few projects that even attempt to address this problem. Of course, the potential for future sensory activation via brain interfaces is excluded from this discussion. But even in this case, the question remains whether users would accept such forms of interaction devices. Furthermore, the ethical questions arising in the development of brain interfaces are far from being fully discussed.

By contrast, the haptic sensory channels are much easier to address. Data gloves and even full-body data suits that convey mechanical or tactile impressions have been available for quite some time. In fact, the development of such technical devices is currently experiencing significant momentum. New materials now make it possible to greatly miniaturize what were until recently rather bulky devices, thereby significantly improving the comfort of wearing them. This, in turn, is likely to increase user acceptance. Such suits can also be easily integrated with heating and cooling elements, so that human temperature perception can also be artificially or technically stimulated.

However, there is still one sensory channel that, at least for now, cannot be artificially replicated: the perception of gravity, which is unlikely to be altered by technical devices in the foreseeable future. Again, the potential technical possibility of using the brain interfaces mentioned above is explicitly excluded here.

Targeted stimulation of human sensory modalities is only possible with intensive technical support. To achieve one hundred percent virtuality, numerous technical devices must be integrated into a single system. Known under the umbrella term "Virtual Reality," the high degree of technological sophistication might suggest that the idea and its technical realization are novel. However, this is a misconception, as the first ideas can be traced back to the early 20th century.

Not only the ideas, but also the implementations of virtual reality systems are much older. As early as 1957 to 1962, Morton Heilig, a filmmaker and cinema technician,

2.2 Virtuality

developed the so-called "Sensorama," the precursor to all virtual reality systems known today [WIKoJ,HEI62]. However, this system was both far too bulky and of too low a display quality to become a real success on the mass market (see Fig. 2.4).

Since then, there have been several attempts to make virtual reality suitable for the mass market. Especially in the 1980s and 1990s, well-known companies such as Sony presented a range of devices intended to conquer the home computer and personal

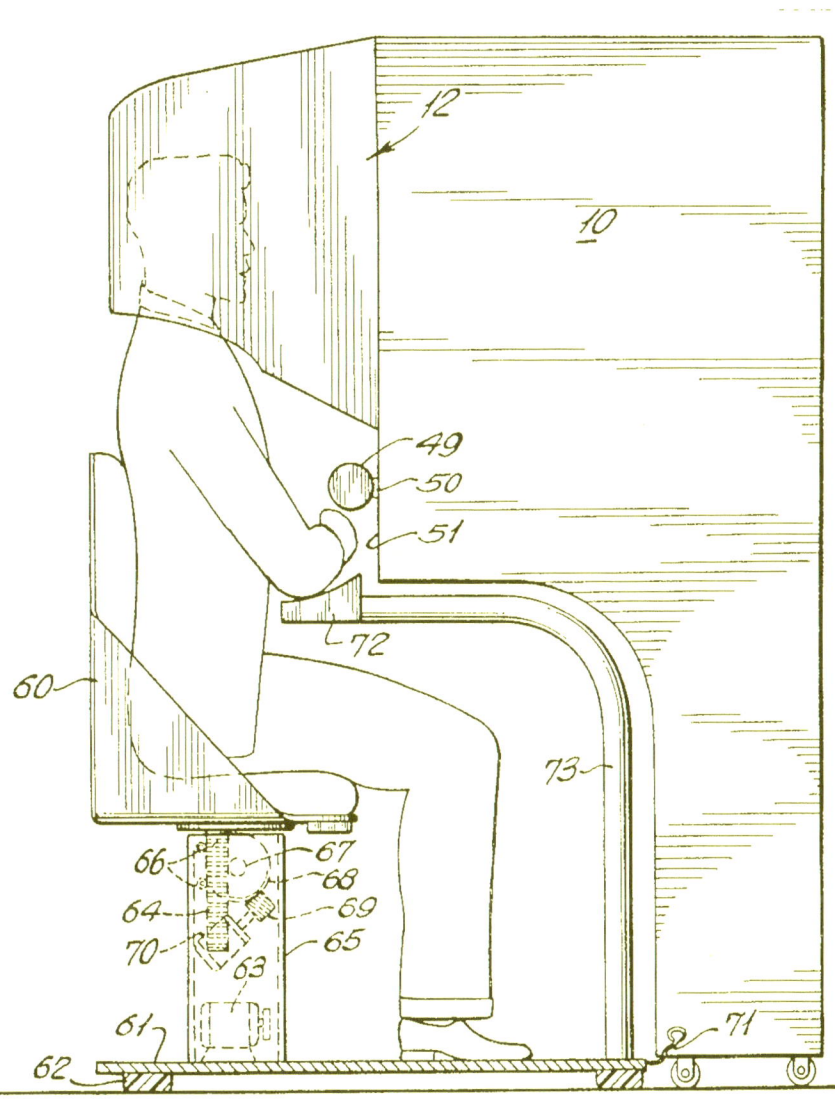

Fig. 2.4 Patent drawing of the Sensorama by Morton Heilig. (Morton Heilig: The Sensorama, from U.S. Patent #3050870)

computer markets. However, none of these attempts were truly successful. In the professional sector, on the other hand, a variety of virtual reality solutions were developed for specific applications, proving their suitability and stability. Nevertheless, their overall distribution remained quite limited.

Whether the current new wave with devices such as the Oculus Rift, Quest, or others will be successful on the mass market this time remains to be seen. The market still appears to be a difficult one, as a glance at the shelves of major electronics and media retailers shows. Typically, not a single VR headset is available for sale there.

A further technical distinction must also be made here (see Fig. 2.5). On the one hand, there is the approach of achieving one hundred percent virtuality through devices such as the aforementioned Oculus Rift and similar products, known as "VR headsets," which address only the senses of the head. In combination with a suit for the bodily senses, this could indeed be a way to achieve virtuality as defined by Milgram. On the other hand, there is the approach of the so-called CAVE [CRU92,CRU93], which was first introduced in 1992.

The name CAVE, an acronym for "Cave Automatic Virtual Involvement," is descriptive. Much like in a real cave, the user is located in a fully enclosed space, with artificially generated visual information projected onto all six interior surfaces. The user can move freely within this space without having to wear bulky and movement-restricting technical devices as with a headset. While this is certainly comfortable for the user, it seems rather unlikely that CAVE technology will become established in the consumer and mass market, since it would have to be integrated into people's living environments, which is much more complex and challenging than using a VR headset.

The example of the CAVE clearly illustrates, however, that one hundred percent virtuality automatically entails the near-complete decoupling of humans from their real environment.

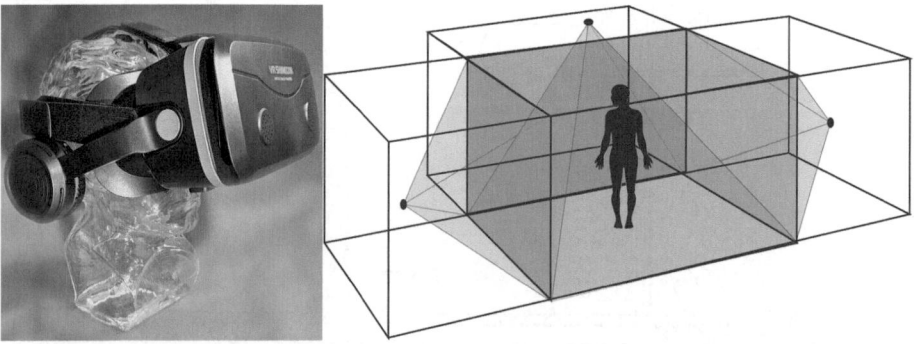

Fig. 2.5 Difference in VR presentation: Headset vs. CAVE. (Own illustration: Peter Hoffmann, Invisible Cow)

2.3 Augmented Reality

Between the two extremes of perception—on the one hand, exclusively real artifacts, and on the other, exclusively digital artifacts—Milgram and Kishino left ample room in their continuum for a broad spectrum of different, fluid gradations. Starting from the extreme of one hundred percent reality, perception is increasingly overlaid and enriched by digital artifacts, as illustrated in Fig. 2.6.

Milgram and Kishino divide this middle part of the continuum into two areas. The better-known of these is the area of augmented reality, in which real impressions and artifacts predominate over digital ones in perception. The significance that can or should be attributed to the digital artifacts is not taken into account here. In their description, Milgram and Kishino simply assume that the perception of reality is enriched by artificially generated digital or virtual information and artifacts.

The concept of the reality-virtuality continuum presented here is therefore closely linked to the concept of augmented reality as it is understood today in computer science. Although the history goes back further, the technical foundations were first described by Ronald T. Azuma in 1993 [AZU93]. According to his definition, augmented reality means that digital objects are precisely inserted into the human user's field of view. In this context, "precisely" means that an inserted object blends seamlessly and without any discernible transition into the perception of the otherwise real environment. Azuma is particularly referring to three-dimensionally modeled digital objects [AZU95, AZU97].

Based on this idea, the concept of accuracy must be specified:

- Geometric accuracy refers to the digital object itself, as it must match reality in shape and size.
- Geographic accuracy, which is derived from geometric accuracy, refers to the position of the object to be inserted. It must not only fit in terms of shape and size, but also be placed exactly where the user expects it or where logic dictates.

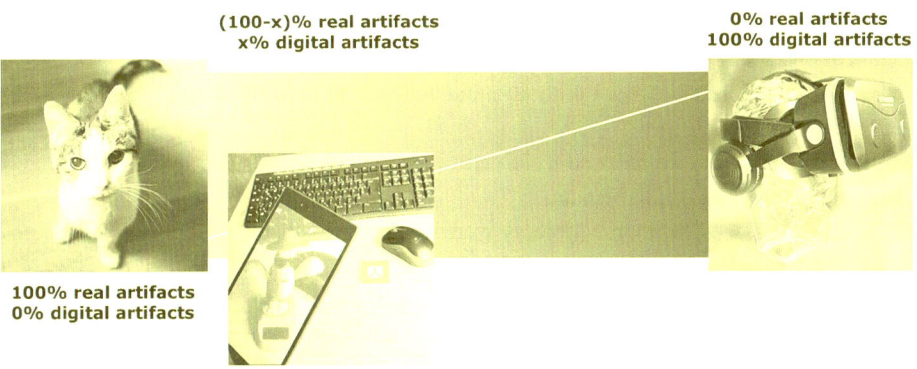

Fig. 2.6 Augmented Reality (AR) in the RVK. (Original illustration: Peter Hoffmann, Invisible Cow)

- Geographic accuracy leads directly to a third point, as the position, perspective, and (viewing) angle of the user must also be taken into account. This is particularly important because Azuma assumes that the user is looking into reality through glasses, and the digital augmentation or enrichment takes place within the glasses. These glasses move with the user and their head, meaning that body movement and posture influence the orientation of the displays in the glasses.
- Temporal accuracy, or more simply, the synchronization of the rendering of the digital artifact with the user's movement and perception. This is influenced by two aspects: on the one hand, the position and posture of the user must be captured at high speed; on the other hand, the rendering of the object to be added must be computed just as quickly.

Even the slightest deviation in any aspect of the above-mentioned accuracies can easily lead to user irritation and thus to a loss of acceptance. This can be well compared to the perception of films or videos in which, for example, the compositing of an actor into a scene is not optimally achieved, or in which a temporal asynchrony between the video and audio track of a film leads to a loss of lip synchronization.

An interesting idea regarding "augmented" reality is the negation of this understanding. Typically, it is assumed that AR extends perception with digital artifacts. However, this can also be thought of in the opposite way. If a digital artifact is placed at a fixed coordinate in perception, this simultaneously means that a part of reality is overlaid and thus no longer perceived. This idea leads to the concept of diminished reality. While this may initially sound like a joke, it takes on a serious dimension, especially in terms of safety-related issues. For example, what could be the consequences if a step in the user's path is obscured by a digital artifact [HER10, MAN01].

The idea of augmented reality presented by Azuma in 1994 requires the use of powerful technical systems. This is illustrated by a simplified system architecture in Fig. 2.7. This is probably one of the reasons why augmented reality was initially unable to gain widespread adoption. Nevertheless, the concept of enriching real perception with digital artifacts seems so significant that many approaches have been explored to overcome the technical obstacles in other ways.

The main performance requirements could be reduced in fairly simple ways.

- First, 3D objects were reduced to 2D artifacts, which significantly decreased the geometric complexity of the objects.
- In a further step, geometric objects were often replaced by simple text fragments, which meant a further reduction in complexity.
- Finally, geographic precision was reduced, and the requirement for pixel-accurate augmentation was replaced by merely location-based augmentation.

2.4 Augmented Virtuality

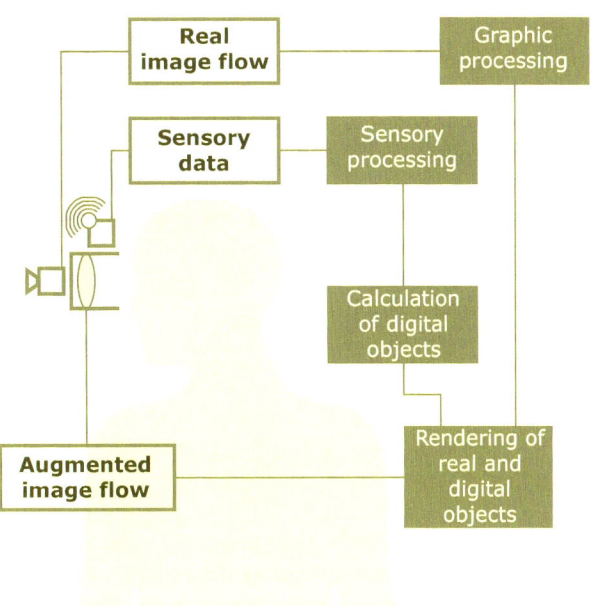

Fig. 2.7 Simplified system architecture for AR. (Original illustration: Peter Hoffmann, Invisible Cow)

In other words, the idea of augmented reality was further developed and transferred into what are now established location-based services, also known as Location Based Services. This aspect will be revisited in Sect. 3.2.

Even though today's computers are, of course, significantly more powerful than those of the 1990s, current systems—especially mobile systems such as smartphones and similar devices—still often reach their technical limits when implementing augmented reality as described by Azuma. Nevertheless, there are now numerous examples of successful 3D-based augmented reality applications. These are found primarily in professional settings, such as industrial maintenance or assembly. However, it is foreseeable that, as the performance of computer systems continues to increase, more and more application examples for the private sector will be realized.

2.4 Augmented Virtuality

Milgram and Kishino developed the concept of the reality-virtuality continuum to describe the spectrum of mixed realities, ranging from the real world to the fully virtual world. Within this spectrum, the domain of Augmented Virtuality (AV) represents another subcategory of augmentation (see Fig. 2.8). In their continuum, Augmented Reality is positioned closer to the real world, while Augmented Virtuality is more closely aligned with the virtual world. In contrast to AR, perception in AV consists of a computer-generated virtual world that is enhanced with real objects and data. In this

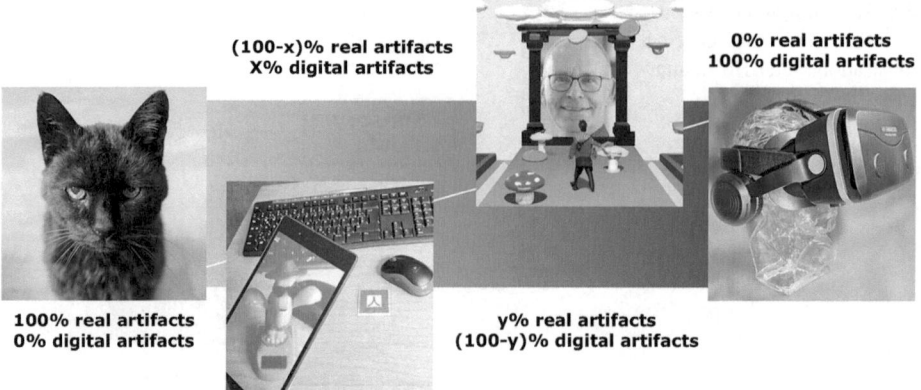

Fig. 2.8 Augmented Virtuality (AV) in the RVC. (Own illustration: Peter Hoffmann, Invisible Cow)

case, digital artifacts numerically outweigh the real artifacts perceived by the user. Milgram and Kishino thus refer to Augmented Virtuality when reality recedes behind virtuality. However, the transition between AR and AV is fluid, as it is ultimately impossible to precisely measure when and in what quantity each form of artifact appears in perception, and the notion of predominance is highly subjective.

The significance of Augmented Virtuality lies in the fact that it represents an intermediate step between Augmented Reality and Virtual Reality. While Virtual Reality aims for complete immersion in an artificial, computer-generated environment, Augmented Virtuality enables the integration of real-world artifacts into this virtual environment. This further blurs the boundaries between reality and virtuality, while still maintaining a sense of reality.

Distinguishing between AV and AR is therefore useful for better understanding the spectrum of possible augmentations of perception and for classifying the respective applications and technologies.

The idea of Augmented Virtuality is currently still a relatively rare concept. Nevertheless, there are indeed use cases for this area of the reality-virtuality continuum.

- One clear example is the entertainment and gaming sector, where, for instance, a player can immerse themselves in a 3D-rendered game environment and communicate with real teammates via another sensory channel, such as the auditory channel. Real teammates can also be integrated into the rendered game world via camera images.
- However, this form of telepresence of real people in virtual worlds can also be applied outside of gaming environments. Concepts for implementation have been described in the fields of medical applications as well as engineering applications [GERoJ, ROS22, SHE19].

2.5 Mixed and Other Realities

Fig. 2.9 Screenshot from the VR live concert by Lindsey Stirling [STI19]

- Telepresence can also open up exciting opportunities in the entertainment sector. For example, violinist Lindsey Stirling performs live concerts in virtual environments (see Fig. 2.9) and enhances them with real-time chats, allowing the audience, who attend the concert in the real world, to interact with the artist in a multimedia fashion [CRA19,STI19].
- A promising application scenario also appears to be the field of human-robot interaction [LI19, LEE21]. Here, potential applications range from remote control of machines and robots to the acquisition and visualization of sensor data and images.

With the continued development of the metaverse concept, the number of examples and implementations of Augmented Virtuality will certainly increase significantly, as AV enables enhanced interaction between real and virtual elements, thereby intensifying the desired immersive experiences.

2.5 Mixed and Other Realities

Milgram and Kishino subsume the concepts of Augmented Reality and Augmented Virtuality under the overarching concept of Mixed Reality. However, this is where terminological difficulties begin. Both the transition between Augmented Reality and Augmented Virtuality and the entire domain of Mixed Reality are highly fluid. These terminological issues are further exacerbated by the fact that many companies now use the term Mixed Reality as a product name or marketing buzzword.

The definition of the term Mixed Reality becomes even more problematic because, in everyday language, Mixed Reality is often extended toward the extreme of complete virtuality and is taken to include it. This makes it significantly more difficult to provide a precise definition of Mixed Reality.

A comprehensible and practical approach is presented by Bellalouna et al. [BEL22]. This approach builds on the work of Milgram and Kishino and defines Mixed Reality as the area between the two extremes of complete reality and complete virtuality [MIL95], but distinguishes it from what is known as Extended Reality (XR). Thus, the scope of Mixed Reality according to Milgram and Kishino remains unchanged. However, as soon as Virtual Reality is added to Mixed Reality, Bellalouna et al. refer to this as Extended Reality. For understanding the concept of the metaverse, this approach appears quite reasonable, as will become clear later when the merging of the real and virtual worlds comes into focus.

The term Mixed Reality alone does not significantly contribute to understanding the metaverse. Much more interesting, therefore, is the concept of Extended Reality as outlined above. According to Bellalouna, Extended Reality encompasses everything that is in any way augmented by digital artifacts, and thus also includes Virtual Reality. In a strict interpretation of Mixed Reality according to Milgram and Kishino, Virtual Reality was previously excluded. This now results in a continuous spectrum that begins with the first digital artifact introduced into perception.

Unfortunately, as already mentioned above, the term Mixed Reality has now been used by many companies purely as a marketing term, most notably by Microsoft, which has almost entirely appropriated the term with its HoloLens. Upon closer examination, especially considering Milgram's continuum, it becomes apparent that Microsoft's marketing interprets the term Mixed Reality at least differently than Milgram originally described.

This becomes evident when comparing the HoloLens with the definitions of Mixed Reality found in Microsoft's own publications. For example, it is stated that Mixed Reality encompasses any kind of augmentation up to and including full Virtual Reality. However, aside from the conflict with the reality-virtuality continuum, it is not actually possible to achieve this complete augmentation in the form of Virtual Reality with the HoloLens itself, since it is a device from the class of so-called see-through devices.

Furthermore, the same publications about the HoloLens also claim that it is a holographic display, which, according to general technical definitions, is also not correct. The HoloLens actually falls into the category of "binocular see-through head-mounted displays." To better understand the various display devices, the typical categorization for such head-mounted displays (HMDs) is presented here, which distinguishes between monocular and binocular devices on the one hand, and see-through and non-see-through devices on the other. This categorization is illustrated in Fig. 2.10.

What Microsoft has implicitly created with the term Mixed Reality—namely, the extension beyond the augmented domains of AR and AV toward the inclusion of complete Virtual Reality—was, as described above, already anticipated by Bellalouna

2.5 Mixed and Other Realities

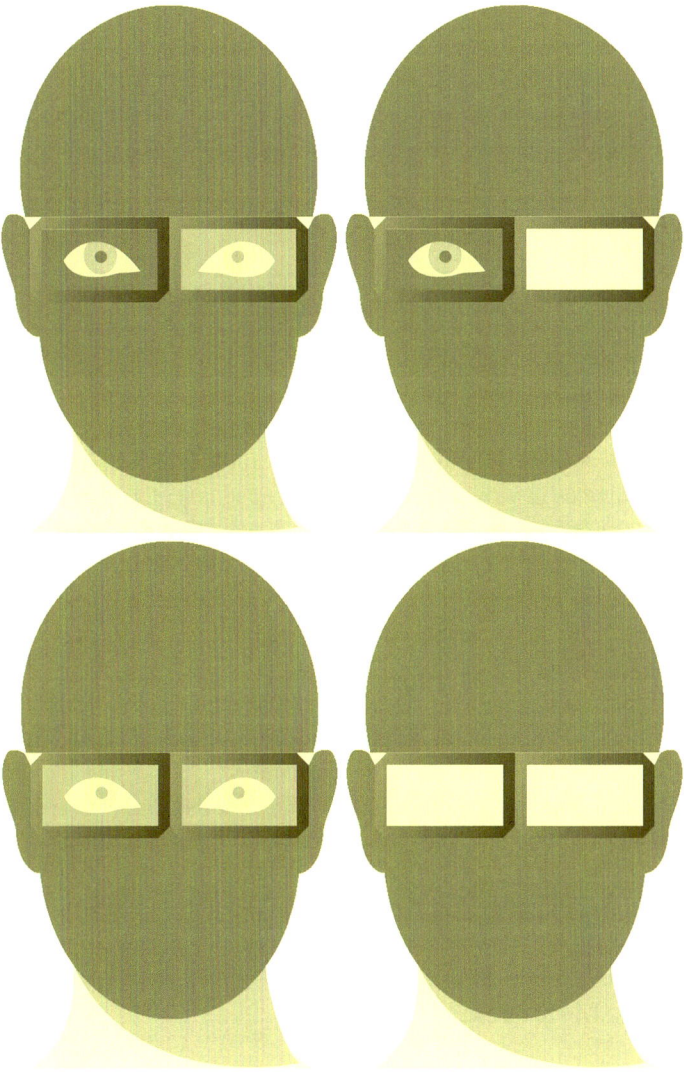

Fig. 2.10 Classification scheme for head-mounted displays: top left: monocular, see-through; bottom left: binocular, see-through; top right: monocular, non-see-through; bottom right: binocular, non-see-through. (Original illustration: Peter Hoffmann, Invisible Cow)

et al., who then no longer called it Mixed Reality but Extended Reality. However, this approach to extension is not the only definition of XR. In fact, some definitions go a considerable technical step further.

According to the classical definitions, both Augmented Reality and Augmented Virtuality require that 3D artifacts be integrated into visual perception. These 3D objects are geometrically modeled and anchored at a location with a fixed spatial coordinate.

However, a few modeling approaches allow for 3D artifacts not only to be anchored at a fixed coordinate but also to move along the three spatial axes.

While this type of modeling is certainly complex in itself, it is relatively straightforward in that the modeling describes only the digital, artificial, or virtual object and its behavior. An interesting approach to expanding the concept of Mixed Reality is the following idea:

What happens when a digitally generated and modeled coffee cup augments reality and is positioned on a real, physical table?

In the context of Augmented Reality, and thus within the context of Mixed Reality as defined by the Milgram and Kishino continuum, a viewer can now walk around the real table and see the precisely inserted digital cup from all perspectives, for example, through their see-through device.

However, if the viewer bumps into the table during their walk and moves it in the real world, this has no effect on the position of the digital cup. It remains unchanged at its assigned coordinates in virtual space. In the extreme case, the viewer might move the table so far that the cup leaves the table and, much like Wile E. Coyote in his pursuit of the Road Runner, remains suspended in mid-air. The difference from the real, physical world becomes very clear here. In the real world, either the cup would be moved along with the table, or, if the table were suddenly pulled out from under it, the cup would fall to the floor and likely shatter (see also Fig. 2.11).

The reason for this is that there is no sensor-actuator connection between the real and digital artifacts in Mixed Reality. One idea for extending MR to Extended Reality is to establish a connection between real and digital artifacts so that the digital artifacts behave just like real objects. The digital cup would therefore either be moved along with the table or would fall off the table. This approach will be revisited and further elaborated in Sect. 3.2, where the modeling of the physical behavior of digital objects will also be discussed in more detail.

2.6 And the Metaverse?

Milgram's reality-virtuality continuum thus represents a highly effective descriptive tool that explains the possibilities of information systems and how they are perceived by users. This is especially true when this tool is viewed and applied as a dynamic instrument, allowing for its further extension. Bellalouna et al., and, albeit only implicitly, Microsoft, expand the originally defined inner segment of the continuum known as Mixed Reality to also include the extreme of Virtual Reality, thereby creating what is referred to as Extended Reality.

The scope of consideration now extends from a purely real perception, which encompasses only physical artifacts, through all possible combinations of real and virtual elements, up to the perception of exclusively digital artifacts. However, what Milgram and Kishino did not sufficiently address—or at least did not describe in detail—is that this

2.6 And the Metaverse?

Fig. 2.11 Digital artifacts vs. the real world: Mixed Reality. (Original illustration: Peter Hoffmann, Invisible Cow)

also applies to every manifestation of the media form of digital artifacts. Perception can be enriched either by a single media form, for example, only static images, or by a comprehensive media mix.

With regard to the metaverse, the question now arises as to where exactly the metaverse itself is situated within this continuum. At this point, the focus is not on the definitions later formulated and established for the metaverse by Matthew Ball or Tony Parisi, but rather on the approach predicted by Mark Zuckerberg. He described the metaverse as the internet of the future, and in the present context even more precisely as the "embodied internet"—that is, the embodied internet that emerges from the fusion of the real and virtual worlds. Ultimately, the immediate concern here is to integrate the metaverse into the user's spectrum of perception, interaction, and action.

Various modeling approaches follow Mike Boland, who tends to distinguish between a VR metaverse and an AR metaverse [BOL22a, BOL22b]. While this may simplify the modeling process, it contradicts the characteristics of the metaverse emphasized by Matthew Ball and Tony Parisi, who explicitly state that there is only one metaverse [BAL22, PAR21]. It seems more appropriate to view the metaverse as a reflection of the fluid spectrum within the reality-virtuality continuum. This implies that, under this approach, the extreme of perception focused exclusively on real and physical artifacts is excluded, as this cannot be part of the interpretation of Zuckerberg's and others' ideas of what the metaverse is intended to be.

Although many of the scenarios presented exhibit a high degree of three-dimensionality, the extreme of one hundred percent virtuality, while certainly possible, will likely remain an exception. This is because, in all the ideas and scenarios discussed here, the interplay between real objects and people and their digital counterparts is central. The following sections will take this aspect into account. It is assumed that the metaverse will offer the possibility for …

- … real people to communicate, interact, and collaborate with other real people via the metaverse.
- Likewise, real people can communicate and interact with digital representations of other real people.
- Furthermore, real people can interact with digital objects, just as …
- … digital representations of real people can interact, collaborate, and communicate with digital representations of other real people.
- Finally, digital representations of real people can also communicate and interact with digital objects.

The transitions within the reality-virtuality continuum are fluid and influence one another. There are overlaps between the various stages, which make it possible to link them and thereby create new applications and innovations, such as the development of augmented virtuality from the concept of augmented reality (see also Fig. 2.12). At the same time, this also opens up the potential to create hybrid environments that combine "the best of both worlds" in order to develop innovative and immersive learning or working environments. Moreover, the fusion of virtual and real environments can also be used for novel forms of entertainment and art.

However, linking the different levels of the continuum also brings challenges. Data protection and security aspects are of particular importance when combining virtual and real environments. The integration of technologies also requires close cooperation between different industries and the joint development of standards to ensure smooth integration and interoperability.

Another issue regarding the connection of the various levels is the complexity and unpredictability of the technology. When introducing new technologies to the market, it is always difficult to predict how they will interact with existing technologies. Likewise, it is hard to foresee the impact of this integration on the user experience and on society as a whole.

2.7 The Metaverse as an Information-Centric Web

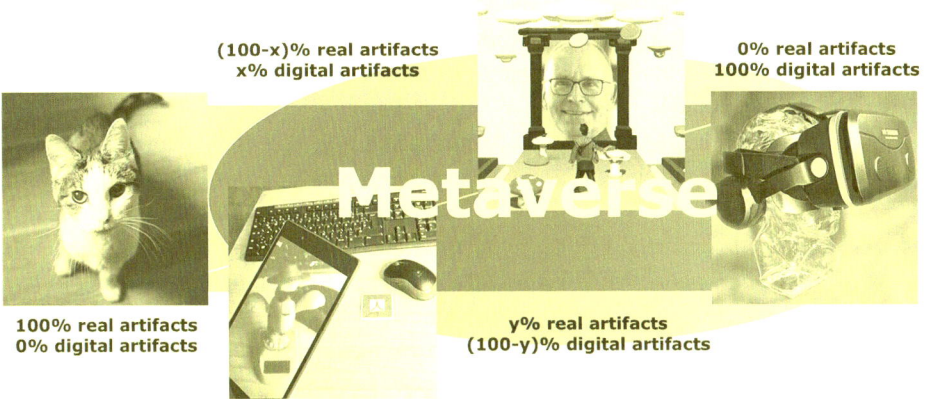

Fig. 2.12 The positioning of the metaverse within the RVC. (Own illustration: Peter Hoffmann, Invisible Cow)

2.7 The Metaverse as an Information-Centric Web

The current perspective on the WWW originates from what Tim Berners-Lee sought to achieve with its development, namely to create connections between initially independent documents [BER89]. By defining connections, i.e., links, between such documents, a coherent new (hyper-) document was to be created. However, this perspective must also change in light of the transformation occurring as the WWW evolves toward an embodied Internet in the sense described by Zuckerberg. One might argue that the documents forming the WWW are now becoming objects or bodies. However, this approach is too limited. It is more appropriate to view the WWW in the future not as document-centric, but rather as information-centric, and to expand the boundaries from the web "page" toward a spatial concept.

The difference between a document-centric web and such an information-centric, interactive, immersive space lies in the fundamental approaches to the representation of information, its organization, and the ways users interact with it.

As previously mentioned, the web in its current form is primarily document-centric. It focuses on static content interconnected by hyperlinks. The structure is either hierarchical or networked, based on HTML documents and web pages. Users navigate this system by clicking links or using search engines to move from one information source to the next. Classic examples include web pages, blogs, PDFs, or articles.

In contrast, an increasingly information-centric, interactive, and immersive space is emerging, where information is no longer presented solely in text and images, but is embedded in three-dimensional, dynamic environments. Here, the structure follows a spatial and often non-linear organization. Information is represented by virtual worlds, avatars, or interactive objects within these virtual worlds. Examples include virtual spaces in the metaverse, interactive 3D models, or simulations. Access is provided via devices such as VR/AR headsets and corresponding controllers, allowing users to interact with the environment directly through gestures, indirectly via controlled avatars, or by using voice commands.

Unsurprisingly, the representation of information also differs fundamentally. In the document-centric web, content is typically organized two-dimensionally and consists of text, images, videos, and occasionally interactive elements such as forms. Navigation is sequential via hyperlinks, guiding users from one information source to the next. In immersive spaces, by contrast, information is presented three-dimensionally and is often embedded in objects, avatars, or virtual environments. The content is dynamic, responds to user input in real time, and can be combined with additional sensory dimensions such as haptic feedback, sound, or motion.

Interactivity also differs between the two approaches. In the document-centric web, user interaction is mainly limited to clicking links, filling out forms, and consuming content. In contrast, immersive spaces enable far more extensive interaction. Users can manipulate, move, or alter objects, trigger simulated processes, or interact with other users in real time via avatars. Furthermore, immersive technologies enable physical and sensory interactions, for example through gesture control, VR controllers, or voice commands.

The user experience in the document-centric web is primarily cognitive. Content is consumed linearly and sequentially, with a focus on reading, understanding, and navigating. Immersive spaces, on the other hand, offer multisensory experiences that combine visual, auditory, and haptic stimuli. Interaction is often personalized, as content objects are dynamically adapted in form and behavior to user preferences or real-time data.

Technologically, the classic web is based on HTML, CSS, and JavaScript, and can be easily accessed via web browsers on computers or mobile devices without the need for specialized hardware. Immersive environments, by contrast, use more advanced technologies such as VR and AR platforms, 3D rendering engines like Unity or Unreal Engine, and often already integrate IoT and AI applications.

As a result, the organization and access to information are also changing. In the document-centric web, information is structured in files and pages that are accessible via search engines or hyperlinks. As previously described, access is mostly sequential and text-based. Immersive spaces, on the other hand, organize information in virtual worlds, where users discover content through direct interaction with objects or environments. Access to information occurs through gestures, voice commands, or direct manipulation of virtual elements.

Ultimately, the differences between the two approaches are also evident in their respective applications. While Wikipedia, online shops, or news portals are typical examples of the document-centric web (WWW), virtual museums, educational simulations, or metaverse platforms offer "innovative" opportunities for interactive and immersive experiences in an "III/I3." For example, users can view artworks in 3D, experience chemical reactions in a virtual environment, or navigate digital cities to obtain information through direct interaction with objects or avatars. While the document-centric web is geared more toward the passive consumption of information, the information-centric, immersive space aims to enable active, multisensory, and dynamic engagement with the content provided.

	WWW	III/I3
Approach and Structure	Focus on documents and static content, connected by hyperlinks. Structure is hierarchical or networked.	Focus on embedded information in three-dimensional, dynamic environments. Spatial and often non-linear structure.
Information Representation	Information is presented in text, images, videos, and interactive elements. Navigation is sequential via links.	Information is embedded in 3D objects or virtual worlds. Content responds to user input in real time and includes multisensory aspects.
Interactivity	Interaction is limited to clicking links, filling out forms, and consuming content. Mostly passive or reactive interaction.	Users can manipulate objects, trigger simulated processes, and interact with other users in real time. Interaction via gestures, VR controllers, or voice.
User Experience	Linear, cognitive experience through reading and navigation. Less personalized and immersive interaction.	Immersive, multisensory experience with personalized content. Combination of visual, auditory, and haptic stimuli.
Technology	Technologies such as HTML, CSS, and JavaScript. Access via web browsers on computers or mobile devices, no special hardware required.	Technologies such as VR/AR, 3D rendering engines, IoT, and AI. Access via immersive devices such as VR headsets, AR glasses, or haptic vests, higher hardware requirements.
Information Organization and Access	Information is organized in files and pages, accessed textually via search engines or hyperlinks.	Information is organized spatially; users discover it through interaction with objects and environments.
Example Applications	Wikipedia (articles with links), online shops (product categories), news portals (linear content).	Virtual museums (3D art viewing), educational simulations (chemical reactions, physical processes), metaverse platforms (virtual cities, interactive avatars).

References

[AZU93] Azuma, Ronald T. (1993). Tracking Requirements for Augmented Reality. In: Communications of the ACM 36, 7 (July 1993), 50–51.

[AZU95] Azuma, Ronald T. (1995). Predictive Tracking for Augmented Reality. Ph.D. dissertation. UNC Chapel Hill Department of Computer Science technical report TR95-007 (February 1995).

[AZU97] Azuma, Ronald (1997). "A Survey of Augmented Reality" (PDF). Presence: Teleoperators and Virtual Environments. MIT Press. 6 (4): 355–385. https://doi.org/10.1162/pres.1997.6.4.355.S2CID469744 . Retrieved 2 June 2021.

[BAL22] Ball, Matthew; Furness, Thomas; Inbar, Ori; Kalinowski, Caitlin; Lange, Dan-ny; Lebaredian, Rev; Mann, Steve; Miralles, Evelyn; Rosedale, Philip; Trevett, Neil; Yuan, Yu (14.06.2022): Metaverse decoded by top experts. In: Verse-maker: Metaverse Lands-cape & Outlook Series. Online: https://versemaker.org/download (Retrieved: 10.05.2023).

[BEL22] Bellalouna, Fahmi; Langebach, Robin; Stamer, Volker; Zipperling, Franco (2022). Use Cases für industrielle Anwendungen der Augmented Reality Technologie (Use Cases for Industrial Applications of Augmented Reality Technology). In: HMD Praxis der Wirtschaftsinformatik. 59. https://doi.org/10.1365/s40702-021-00824-x .

[BER89] Berners-Lee, Tim (1989). Information Management: A Proposal. In: CERN, W2C. Online: https://www.w3.org/History/1989/proposal.html (Retrieved: 23.05.2023).

[BIT22] Bitkom (2022). Wegweiser in das Metaversum – Technologische und rechtliche Grundlagen, geschäftliche Potenziale, gesellschaftliche Bedeutung. In: Bitkom e. V., AG Metaverse Forum, Projektleitung: Dr. Sebastian Klöß. Online: https://www.bitkom.org/Bitkom/Publikationen/Wegweiser-Metaverse (Retrieved: 10.05.2023).

[BOL22a] Boland, Mike (January 25, 2022). Predictions: Metaverse Mania Wanes. AR-Insider. Online: https://arinsider.co/2022/01/25/2022-predictions-metaverse-mania-wanes/ . (Retrieved: 14.02.2025).

[BOL22b] Boland, Mike (February 18, 2022). XR Talks: The Race to Build the Metaverse. Online: https://arinsider.co/2022/02/18/xr-talks-the-race-to-build-the-metaverse/ . (Retrieved: 14.02.2025).

[BOGoJ] Bogatzki, Josef Heinrich (o.J.). Oberurselcraft. Online: https://thejocraft.de/obuc/ (Retrieved: 17.05.2023).

[CRA19] Craig, Emory (August 25, 2019). Violinist Lindsey Stirling to do Live Performance in VR. In: Digital Bodies – Learning and Living in AR, VR ans AI. Online: https://www.digitalbodies.net/violinist-lindsey-stirling-to-do-live-performance-in-vr/ . (Retrieved: 14.02.2025).

[CRU92] Cruz-Neira, Carolina; Sandin, Daniel J.; DeFanti, Thomas A.; Kenyon, Robert V.; Hart, John C. (1 June 1992). "The CAVE: Audio Visual Experience Automatic Virtual Environment". Commun. ACM. 35 (6): 64–72. https://doi.org/10.1145/129888.129892 [Titel anhand dieser DOI in Citavi-Projekt übernehmen]. ISSN 0001-0782. S2CID 19283900.

[CRU93] Cruz-Neira, C., Sandin, D. J., & DeFanti, T. A. (1993). Surround-screen projection-based virtual reality: The design and implementation of the CAVE. Proceedings of the 20th Annual Conference on Computer Graphics and Interacti-ve Techniques, 135–142.

[GERoJ] Geriatronics (o.J.). Forschungszentrum Geriatronik der TUM, München. Online: https://geriatronics.mirmi.tum.de/ (Retrieved 17.05.2023).

[HEI62] Heilig, Morton (1962). The Sensorama. US Patent #3,050,870.

References

[HER10]	Herling, Jan; Broll, Wolfgang (2010). Advanced self-contained object removal for realizing real-time Diminished Reality in unconstrained environments. International Symposium on Mixed and Augmented Reality. 207–212. https://doi.org/10.1109/ISMAR.2010.5643572 .
[JIA22]	Jiaxin, Li; Gongjing, Gao (2022). Socializing in the Metaverse: The Innovation and Challenge of Interpersonal Communication. In: Advances in Social Science, Education and Humanities Research, volume 664. Proceedings of the 2022 8th International Conference on Humanities and Social Science Research (ICHSSR 2022).
[KOM17]	Kommune 21 (31.08.2017). Oberursel: Stadtentwicklung mit Minecraft. Online: https://www.kommune21.de/meldung_27130_Stadtentwicklung+mit+Minecraft.html (Retrieved: 17.05.2023).
[LEE21]	Lee, Lik-Hang; Braud, Tristan; Zhou, Pengyuan; Wang, Lin; Xu, Dianlei; Lin, Zijun; Kumar, Abhishek; Bermejo, Carlos; Hui Pan (2021): All One Needs to Know about Metaverse: A Complete Survey on Technological Singularity, Virtual Ecosystem, and Research Agenda. In: Journal of LaTex Class Files, Vol. 14, No. 8, September 2021 1.
[LI19]	Li, Yang; Huang, Lin; Tian, Feng; Wang, Hong-An; Dai, Guo-Zhong (2019). Gesture interaction in virtual reality. In: Virtual Reality & Intelligent Hardware, Volume 1, Issue 1, 2019, Pages 84–112. ISSN 2096-5796, https://doi.org/10.3724/SP.J.2096-5796.2018.0006 .
[LIU23]	Liu, Yiming; Yiu, Chun, Zhao, Zhao; Park, Wooyoung; Shi, Rui; Huang, Xingcan; Zeng, Yuyang; Wang, Kuan; Wong, Tsz; Jia, Shengxin; Zhou, Jingkun; Gao, Zhan; Zhao, Ling; Yao, Kuanming; Li, Jian; Sha, Chuanlu; Gao, Yuyu; Zhao, Guangyao; Huang, Ya; Yu, Xinge (2023). Soft, miniaturized, wireless olfactory interface for virtual reality. Nature Communications. 14. https://doi.org/10.1038/s41467-023-37678-4 .
[MAN01]	Mann, Steve; Fung, James (14.03.2001). VideoOrbits on Eye Tap devices for deliberately Diminished Reality or altering the visual perception of rigid planar patches of a real world scene. In: International Symposium on Mixed Reality ({ISMR} 2001).
[MIL95]	Milgram, Paul; Takemura, Haruo; Utsumi, Akira; Kishino, Akira (1995). Augmented reality: a class of displays on the reality-virtuality continuum. In: Proceedings of SPIE 2351, Telemanipulator and Telepresence Technologies. 21. December 1995, pp. 282–292.
[OBE20]	Oberursel im Dialog (28.08.2020). Oberurselcraft Wettbewerb. Jetzt mitmachen! Von: Stadt Oberursel (Taunus). Online: https://www.oberurselimdialog.de/post/oberurselcraft-wettbewerb-jetzt-mitmachen (Retrieved: 17.05.2023).
[PAR21]	Parisi, Tony (22.10.2021). The Seven Rules oft he Metaverse – A framework for the coming immersive reality. In: Medium. Online: https://medium.com/metaverses/the-seven-rules-of-the-metaverse-7d4e06fa864c (Retrieved: 22.5.2023).
[ROS22]	Rosenberg, Louis (24.07.2022). Medicine and the metaverse: New tech allows doctors to travel inside of your body. In VentureBeat. Online: https://venturebeat.com/datadecisionmakers/medicine-and-the-metaverse-new-tech-allows-doctors-to-travel-inside-of-your-body/ (Retrieved: 17.05.2023).
[SCH23a].	Schlott, Karin (10.05.2023). Wenn die Computerblume duftet. In: Spektrum.de. Online: https://www.spektrum.de/news/virtuelle-realitaet-wenn-die-computerblume-duftet/2137641 (Retrieved: 17.05.2023).

[SHE19]	Sherman, W. R.; Craig A. B. (2019). Chapter 1 – Introduction to Virtual Reality. In: Sherman WR, Craig AB (eds) Understanding Virtual Reality (Second Edition), Second Edition. Morgan Kaufmann, Boston, pp 4–58.
[SMA20]	Smarzoch, Raphael (22.02.2020). „Miss Anthropocene" von Grimes: Verlorene Zukunft. In: Deutschlandfunk: Raphael Smarzoch im Kollegengespräch mit Fabian Elsäßer. Online: https://www.deutschlandfunk.de/miss-anthropocene-von-grimes-verlorene-zukunft-100.html (Retrieved: 10.05.2023).
[STE92]	Stephenson, Neal (1992). Snow Crash. Blanvalet, München 1995. ISBN 978-3-442-23686-2, Kap. 37. Englisches Original: Snow Crash. New York, 1992.
[STI19]	Lindsey Stirling Virtual Concert (2019). Youtube. Online: https://www.youtube.com/watch?v=mK5Jb1vgrgw . (Retrieved: 14.02.2025).
[WIKoJ]	Wikipedia (o.J.). Sensorama. Online: https://en.wikipedia.org/wiki/Sensorama (Retrieved: 10.05.2023).

3 The Merging of Worlds and ... Verses

During the presentation announcing the renaming of the Facebook corporation to "Meta," Marc Zuckerberg made a statement that triggered the hype surrounding the topic of the metaverse [BLU21]:

> "You can think of the metaverse as an embodied internet, where you are not just viewing content—you are in it and you are immersed in it."

In order to "immerse" oneself in content or to "be in it," the perceptual aspects discussed above, ranging from reality to virtuality, must be linked to an additional aspect not considered in the RVK: immersion!

The term "immersion" originates from the Latin word "immersio," which can generally be translated as "immersion" or "submersion." Typically, the concept of immersion is primarily addressed in the field of communication studies and characterizes the sensation of being deeply absorbed in media content. More recently, however, immersion has also gained increasing importance for and within interactive systems [DER19]. Without explicitly referring to the term immersion, Ludwig Kapeller, a journalist for the magazine UHU, described the "broadcasting of tomorrow" in 1926 as a comprehensive, multimedia sensory experience [DER19]. In this context, he illustrated his personal impressions and the potential he recognized in the then-emerging television transmission technology.

In a more contemporary context, immersion is regarded as a kind of quality criterion for video games. Jan-Noël Thon, Professor of Media Studies at the Norwegian University of Science and Technology, developed a model of immersion that describes four distinct types of immersion in video games [ASC12]:

- *Spatial immersion*: This refers to an effect in computer games where the player's attention gradually shifts from their real environment to the fictional game world presented by the game. In this process, the player assumes the role of an avatar representing them and gains direct access to the events within the game [THO06].

- *Ludic immersion*: Here, too, the focus is on the player's complete concentration on the presented gameplay. In contrast to spatial immersion, the emphasis here is on interaction with the virtual environment, control of the avatar, and the challenges posed by the game. A balanced level of challenge is the decisive factor for the emergence of ludic immersion. Overwhelming the player can quickly lead to frustration, while insufficient challenge results in boredom [THO06].
- *Narrative immersion*: The integration of additional sequences of events between different phases of the game can lead to a more compelling design of the fictional game environment. If this successfully generates suspense and focuses the player's attention on the progression of the story and its characters, this is referred to as narrative immersion [THO06].
- *Social immersion*: While narrative immersion primarily concerns single-player games, multiplayer games further promote the emergence of social immersion. By bringing avatars together in virtual environments, players have the opportunity to interact with other participants. To enable this, online games typically offer communication features such as text chat or voice transmission [THO06].

However, immersion is not only a goal in the context of games. More generally, immersion as a concept is gaining importance for (multi-)media systems focused on storytelling. The particular challenge in this context is that the narrative must be both logically coherent and engaging for the individual audience, while at the same time granting the user the highest possible degree of freedom of interaction. These different dimensions often stand in direct opposition to each other, which complicates the development and production of such systems [HOF10]. This is illustrated in Fig. 3.1.

With strong immersion, a narrative reality can be embedded within a virtual reality, as shown in Fig. 3.2. In this case, the user is not only technically and interactively immersed in the virtual world. Rather, supported by the interactive freedom offered, the user becomes immersed in the narrative events within the virtual world [HOF10].

To develop a workable definition of the metaverse, the reality-virtuality continuum provides a good starting point. From a marketing perspective, as already mentioned, Mark Zuckerberg explains that the metaverse represents the embodied internet of the future. However, the central question remains how the user is supposed to and can perceive this new embodied internet.

The term "embodied internet" indicates that in the metaverse, the physical world of the body and the digital world of the internet are to be brought together into a new world of applications and information, and in the extreme case, even merge. The continuum introduced by Milgram can serve as a helpful foundation for this. Between the two extremes of pure reality and pure virtuality, the continuum addresses the enrichment of each world with artifacts from the opposite domain.

It is precisely this fusion in its original form, especially with the extension through the introduction of the term Extended Reality, that helps to situate the idea of the metaverse within the human perceptual world and should do so. However, a complete fusion of

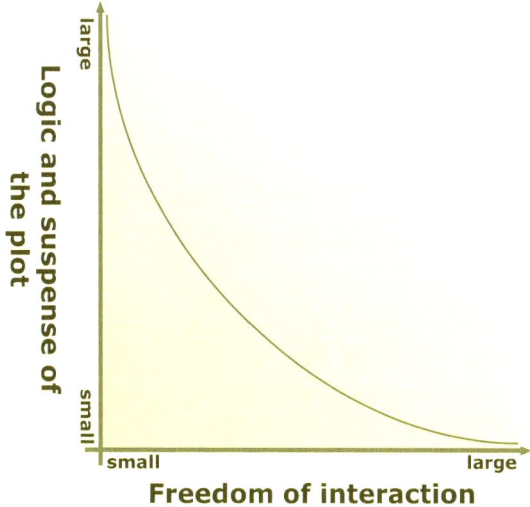

Fig. 3.1 Logic and suspense of the narrative vs. freedom of interaction. (Own illustration: Peter Hoffmann, Invisible Cow)

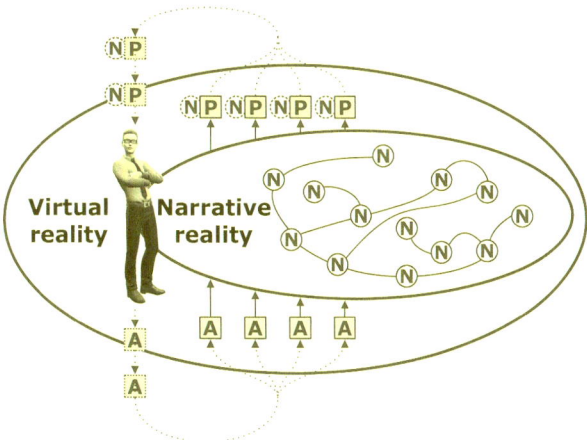

Fig. 3.2 The dimension of narrative reality (N) – narratem (atomic narrative unit); (P) presentation object; (A) (user) action. (Own illustration: Peter Hoffmann, Invisible Cow)

virtuality and reality, as would be required for a true embodiment of the internet, is by no means achieved by the perceptual focus of the continuum alone.

Rather, a whole range of other perspectives emerge in which the physical and digital worlds can, or even must, merge in order to fully realize this embodied Internet. In addition to perception, aspects such as the following must also be incorporated into the overall picture:

- Sensory fusion as the basis for perception.
- Spatial fusion, as already suggested in the context of Extended Reality.
- Semantic, that is, content-based fusion, which builds on perception, sensor technology, and spatiality.

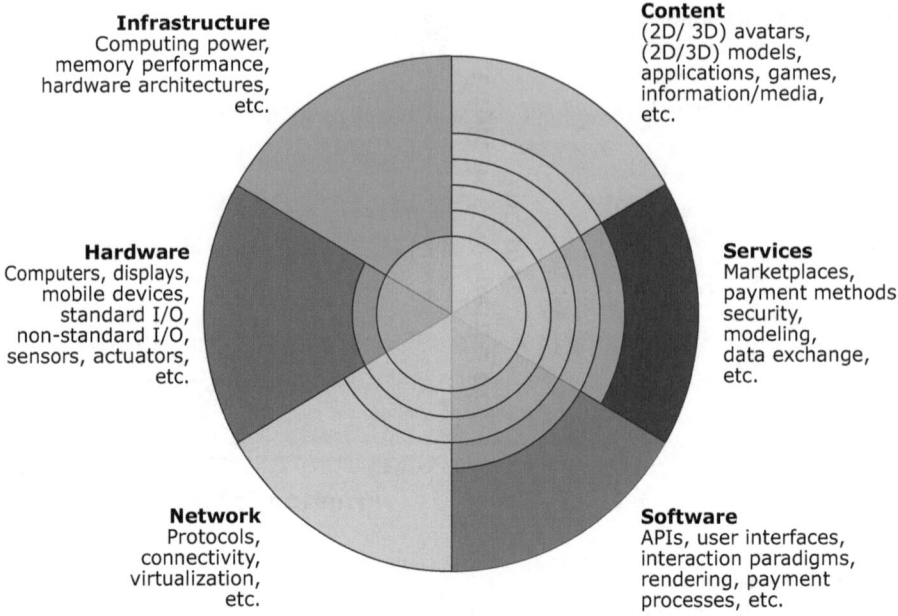

Fig. 3.3 Technical sub-aspects of fusion. (Adapted from [BIT22])

- Derived from this, the fusion of interactions in the physical and digital worlds into a combined new form of interaction, also in reference to the concept of Extended Reality.
- Temporal fusion, aiming for the synchrony of actions and behaviors of artifacts in the physical and digital worlds.
- As well as sociocultural fusion, when digital twins of real people communicate, interact, and collaborate with other digital twins of real people or with the individuals themselves.

All these aspects, which are also listed in Fig. 3.3, will first be considered individually in the following sections and discussed in terms of their impact and challenges. Subsequently, they will be brought together to create, in its entirety, a new embodied medium. In doing so, the technical challenges will also be taken into account.

3.1 Sensory Fusion

If the foundation of the metaverse is to be understood as the fusion of the perception of reality and digitality, or virtuality—as can indeed be inferred from Milgram's continuum—then the first essential step must be to analyze through which sensory channels humans perceive or are able to perceive their environment. This applies both to the real, physical environment and to the digital, virtual environment.

The basis for perceiving the real physical environment relies on human sensory channels (see Fig. 3.4). The classic modalities typically include the visual, auditory, haptic-tactile, olfactory, and gustatory channels. This traditional perspective is often supplemented by additional sensory modalities. For example, in this context, Ayres also includes the vestibular and proprioceptive channels—that is, the sense of balance and deep sensation [AYR13, AYR79]. Furthermore, she expands the consideration of the tactile modality by attributing surface sensitivity to this channel as well. Finally, nociception, or pain perception, also belongs to this area. However, this aspect has so far—and hopefully will continue to be—largely disregarded in the use of the metaverse or digital environments in general. A rare exception, aside from research presumably conducted in the military sector, is the entertainment industry, as illustrated by the so-called Painstation [MOR01] or more recently by the "Feelbelt" [DAN21].

What already applies to the general design of interaction must also be applied to fusion with the goal of the metaverse—namely, the transfer of human modalities to their digital and technical counterparts. For example, visual media are required so that human users can perceive artificial or virtual graphic and visual information, just as auditory media are needed for the perception of artificial soundscapes and audio environments. Moreover, it is necessary to find such equivalents for all other sensory channels as well. As already suggested, this is easily achievable for the visual and auditory channels, since there are numerous modeling approaches as well as established media and data formats that can describe, store, and transmit content in these forms. Established here means that a very large number of technical standards already exist and are available in this area.

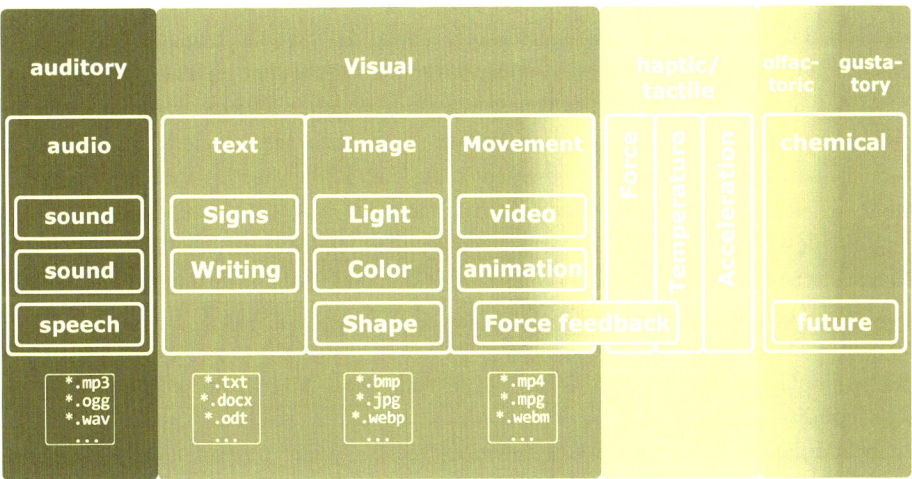

Fig. 3.4 A systematics of perception in HCI. (Original illustration: Peter Hoffmann, Invisible Cow)

However, the situation is more problematic for the haptic-tactile channel. On the one hand, there are numerous applications, especially in the entertainment sector, that demonstrate that haptic and tactile information can indeed be artificially generated and transmitted. Examples include tactile feedback in many games, experienced via joystick or gamepad, or even more so, tactile feedback in professional simulation environments, such as the three-axis trainers used in the aerospace industry. What these approaches have in common, however, is that there are no widely established standards; instead, each individual solution pursues its own proprietary approach. They also share the fact that they are technically extremely complex.

Technically, the stimulation of the gustatory and olfactory sensory channels is considerably less complex, since, for example, the use of aromatic oils, which can be vaporized near the nose or mouth, would suffice. There are also research projects and individual solutions for these approaches which, although not particularly demanding technically, have so far not achieved widespread adoption or become established [LIU23, SCH23a].

The previous discussion has tacitly assumed that the technical infrastructure—that is, the computer systems used—would be supplemented by technical extensions. However, if the concept of the embodiment of the internet is taken literally, this implicit assumption could also be expanded or even reversed, so that it is not the technical system or infrastructure that is extended, but rather the human being, thus expanding their immediate biological-human sensory capabilities.

Although this may sound extreme, this process actually began some time ago, not least through the constant presence of devices such as smartphones or devices from the field of wearable computing. Especially in this context, the human user perceives not only their immediate sensory environment, but also the digital environment through the digital senses of their accompanying devices. The term "environment" should initially be understood metaphorically here and will only be examined in more detail in the following Sect. 3.2. Nevertheless, through these technical devices, the human user perceives things and information that do not originate from their immediate physical perception.

A look at the course of technical development, as well as human creativity and willingness, suggests that the supplementation with additional devices accompanying humans as accessories will not be the end of the line. Rather, there are trends toward the much-debated concept of the cyborg. Research and developments by reputable scientists, such as Steve Mann and Thad Starner, show that it is already technically possible for humans to have technical devices implanted for perception and later interaction [KRE13, MAN13]. Ultimately, this is just another logical step, as the example of technical development reveals. For a long time, people have had devices such as pacemakers or insulin pumps implanted, and prosthetics have also made great advances in supporting people with mobility impairments.

In addition to such reputable approaches for the direct support and assistance of humans, there is also research and development in many areas on the so-called direct brain interface. At this point, no philosophical or ethical discussion of these developments will be initiated, although this would certainly be justified—and interesting. That this is not the realm of fiction is demonstrated by examples from the field of so-called transhumanism, such as the artist Stelarc or, even more strikingly, Neil Harbisson. The ultimate fusion of sensory input from the real physical and digital virtual worlds is evident in his non-removable implant, which provides him with a new sensory channel. In this way, color information that Harbisson cannot perceive due to his color blindness is converted into haptic-tactile information [DON17]. It must be emphasized here that such an extreme case as Neil Harbisson's will certainly remain a rare exception of sensory fusion and human augmentation in the near future. It can be assumed that the metaverse will be accessible and usable for the average human user even without such extreme interventions. Whether this will change in the distant future cannot be said with certainty today.

3.2 Spatial Merging

Engagement with the metaverse reveals, at certain points, characteristics that can be considered schizophrenic or at least inconsistent. On the one hand, as in earlier discussions, it is claimed that the metaverse will be the embodied Internet and will therefore merge the digital and physical worlds. On the other hand, upon closer examination, some sources state exactly the opposite. Statements such as [THEoJ] can be found:

> "A new cult is born, the digital world is coming, and we are no longer bound to physical space."

This view is, at first glance, unrelated to any merging, as digitality and physical reality are clearly separated here. However, this has no impact on the discussions initiated in the previous Sect. 3.1 regarding sensing and perception. Ultimately, whether merged or not, both domains must be perceived and sensed by the user. Clearly, two definitional approaches are in contradiction here.

Things become particularly interesting—and even amusing—when, as a brief preview of later sections, potential business models are already considered here. On the vast majority of platforms that describe themselves as metaverse platforms, users can only become truly active once they acquire a plot of land located in the digital world of the respective platform. Thus, we leave the physical space to act in the digital space, separate but parallel, using equally spatial metaphors such as plot sizes and distances. This type of marketing argument is taken even further in statements like [STO22]:

> "Compared to the physical world, virtual worlds are not bound by the laws of physics. [...] Logistics, travel time, waste, or environmental pollution do not exist in the metaverse."

Waste and environmental pollution in terms of sustainability will not be further discussed here. However, the claim that logistics and travel time are irrelevant is ultimately a fallacy. If there are plots with spatial dimensions, these dimensions and distances must also be traversed. Certainly, one could now argue that the metaverse is intended to be the Internet of the future and thus naturally inherits the characteristics of today's Internet, where all information is just a click away—with a single click, one can go from the Tokyo Dome in Japan to the Tuileries in Paris and to the Statue of Liberty in New York [HOF21]. However, this characteristic renders the concept of distance associated with the notion of plots absurd, and this conceptual misdirection goes even further. The user's representation in the virtual world of the metaverse is the avatar, which moves on or between plots. If the avatar moves in the same way as a person does in the physical world, then the supposedly saved travel time suddenly becomes crucial again.

This raises the question of how spatial merging is actually supposed to take place, and whether it should or must be a genuine goal in the development of the metaverse.

A central challenge in merging the spatial properties of real and virtual worlds lies in linking the movements of objects in both worlds. A typical example, often presented as a possible realization of the metaverse, is the virtual world "Oasis" from the novel [CLI11] and the film "Ready Player One" [SPI18]. In this world, the protagonist assumes the role of a player who aims to achieve a goal in the Oasis. To do so, he controls an avatar in the virtual game world. He does this by wearing a full-body data suit in the real world, which transfers the human user's movements to the avatar. This works both in the book and film, as well as in real-world applications, since such data suits do exist and are practically usable. However, the use cases are quite specialized [LEE20b], and the price of these suits will not be considered here, as it far exceeds what is reasonable for the general consumer market.

Such a suit enables the transfer of the human user's full-body movements to a three-dimensional avatar in a virtual world. This also applies to the avatar's movement: the user's walking movements can likewise be transferred to the avatar to move it from one place to another.

The intriguing question now is how avatar and human are actually linked or merged in the virtual and real worlds. Today, people move on so-called treadmills, similar to a running belt, on a movable platform or inside a sphere, without changing their actual position in the real world, while the avatar changes its location in the virtual world [WEH20]. This means that there is no merging connection from real to virtual. Nor is there such a connection in the opposite direction, from virtual to real, since any movement of an avatar in the virtual world and the associated change of position or location has no effect in the real world: the user remains standing where they were before. Therefore, it cannot be said that a true merging occurs here.

Apart from the lack of connection between the virtual avatar and the real human, the idea of spatial merging between avatar and human user poses a significant potential risk for the user in the real world. The fundamental question is: to what extent do the real and virtual worlds correspond?

- If both are in complete and precise alignment, the risk to the user in the real world would likely be rather low. For example, if the avatar wants to cross a street, the process should hopefully be similar to that in the real world: the avatar approaches the street, waits until it is clear, and then crosses without being hit by a (virtual) vehicle.

- However, if the real and virtual worlds are not aligned and the avatar crosses a large open area, one can only hope that this large open area also exists in the physical world and that the user's path does not intersect with that of a car on a street.

Addressing and resolving this spatial merging represents a significant challenge for the acceptance of the metaverse. Although there is frequent talk of the so-called digital twin of the user, of other real objects, or even of digital twins of entire manufacturing plants and cities, if there is indeed to be a walkable, 3D-modeled world, this will be just one of many application scenarios. It is more likely that 3D-modeled worlds will be designed very differently from the real world in terms of their dimensions, distances, and especially their structure. The metaverse will not represent the real world as a 3D model, since the goal is to create new worlds in which innovative solutions and interaction possibilities can be modeled and presented.

Although the previous discussion of the merging of spatial properties of the physical and virtual worlds has tended to be critical, it must be acknowledged that this aspect of merging will be a fundamental aspect of the future metaverse. After all, even today, internet-based services routinely respond, for example, to the user's current location. This must also be ensured in the future metaverse. If, for example, a user moves from one place to another, such as from one store to the next in a city center pedestrian zone, their avatar, as their digital twin, should be informed of this change in position. Only in this way can location-based services and transactions be initiated or used in the virtual world. Without some form of spatial merging—whatever it may ultimately look like—the metaverse as the embodied Internet of the future would be inconceivable.

3.3 Semantic Merging

It is easy to claim that the features of merging the spatial, physical world with the digital, virtual world, as described at the end of the previous Section 3.2, have already been solved for some time. For a long while now, users have been accompanied on their journey through the physical world by mobile devices. In most cases, the user's current location is now captured, transmitted, analyzed, and used to trigger transactions—usually without the user's explicit consent, even though, for security reasons, it would certainly be better from the user's perspective to decide for themselves.

In addition, the user is provided with up-to-date data and information relevant to their current location, as illustrated in Fig. 3.5. Examples include mobile apps for public transportation that display the nearest stop and list the departure times at that stop.

It is true that this type of content-based or semantic support has long been known and available as location awareness. The example above, which enriches the real world with location-based information such as the nearest public transport stops or information about surrounding retail stores, illustrates this (see Fig. 3.5).

Fig. 3.5 Semantic fusion as a location-based service. (Original illustration: Peter Hoffmann, Invisible Cow)

However, a closer look at the real-world situation depicted reveals something else: typically, it is individual applications that respond to the user's current location as positional information. Moreover, these individual applications operate exclusively in a selective and highly limited manner. The application's response is always based on a single piece of information about the user—their location. Only a few apps incorporate additional information to provide more precise recommendations.

For example, if a user is walking through the city center and has installed a public transport app, this app will not help if the user suddenly craves a local delicacy. Even within their own application context, such as public transportation, these apps quickly reach their limits. Most of these applications do internally, and more or less transparently for the user, list recent or preferred stops, as shown in the screenshot of the DB and SBB apps in Fig. 3.6. However, they generally do not proactively suggest how the user can get from the Obernstraße stop in downtown Bremen to the Weserstadion or the Fallturm at the University of Bremen. Such assistive information cannot be extracted from location data alone. Instead, a wide range of additional contextual information would need to be linked and combined.

The challenge of context formation is already evident in everyday use of the Internet. Here, too, attempts are often made to recognize context in order to support or unobtrusively assist the user, for example in web-based e-commerce applications. However, such information is often limited to aspects that are only marginally helpful. In a virtual bookstore, it may still make sense to present potential customers with information such as "Readers who bought this book also bought the following." But if, based on a user's

3.3 Semantic Merging   39

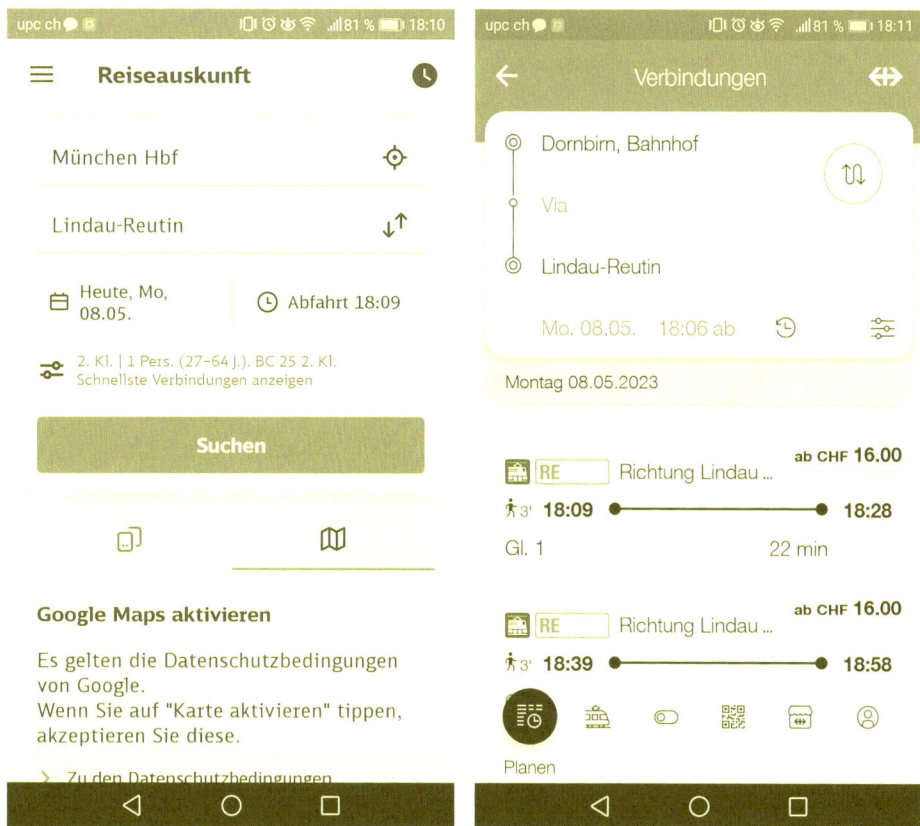

Fig. 3.6 Screenshots of the mobile apps from DB and SBB

purchase history, a suggestion is generated to buy another set of winter tires right after they have just purchased a set for their vehicle, this can hardly be considered helpful assistance or good context recognition. The difficulty of recognizing user context on the web has already been demonstrated by Ziegler, Lohmann et al. [ZIE05].

Context initially consists of three distinct semantic domains (see Fig. 3.7). The fundamental component is, of course, the technical system. This is also the area from which information for context recognition can most easily be derived. The system knows itself, its general functions, and the functionalities currently available. Ultimately, all of this information can be obtained from the system's self-monitoring and kept continuously up to date.

The other two subdomains, which influence each other, are the human and the physical environment in which the human user moves and acts. To establish an accurate action and assistance context, it is first necessary to determine the current state of the human user. This includes general information such as location, but often also medical and other data. In the broadest sense, this also encompasses parameters such as hunger or thirst.

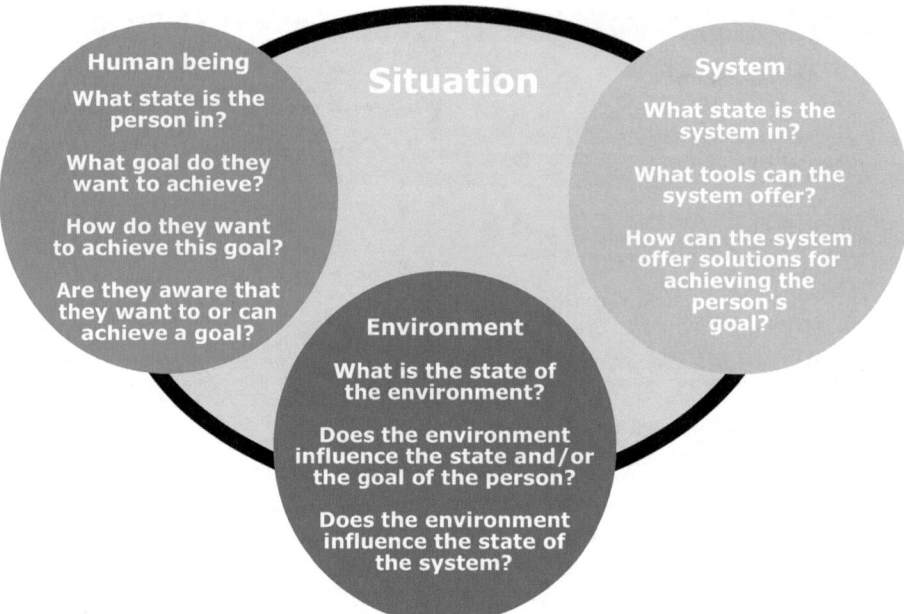

Fig. 3.7 Sub-aspects of context formation. (Original illustration: Peter Hoffmann, Invisible Cow)

To add further complexity, this also includes data about the user's mental state, such as current stress factors or the user's present stress level. Many mobile devices, including a wide range of wearable devices, are capable of recording medical data. For example, smartwatches and similar devices can already measure pulse, blood pressure, and in some cases even blood sugar levels and similar parameters. The accuracy of these measurements will not be considered here, as the focus is not on preventive medical objectives. However, by combining such values, it is possible to obtain a limited but useful assessment of the user's mental state and, for example, to infer the stress level mentioned above.

The third domain is the environment in which both the human and the system are situated. The state of the environment has a significant impact on how the current context is constructed. The information underlying this domain is even more heterogeneous than that of the human subdomain. The latter generally consists of the two aforementioned subcomponents: medical and mental. In contrast, the state of the environment can depend on a wide variety of parameters, starting with simple meteorological factors such as temperature, air pressure, rain, and sunshine. In addition, the current traffic situation and the number of people actively present in the vicinity may also play a role. Noise, odors, general hustle and bustle caused by nearby people, and many other factors must be considered to obtain an overall impression and assessment of the environment.

3.3 Semantic Merging

Individually, this information is certainly tangible. While meteorological data can be collected through simple sensor-based methods, other information, such as traffic conditions or more advanced insights, may require less accessible sources. For example, traffic density could be determined by aggregating information from many individual devices available at the location. The heterogeneity of information sources on the one hand, and data privacy concerns on the other, pose significant challenges for context acquisition of this kind.

As is often the case, capturing the state of the human, system, and environment domains in this approach is merely a simplified representation, since each aspect has so far been considered in isolation. In reality, however, the situation is much more complex, as the three domains are in constant and close interaction with one another.

The system may, in this context, have to process the least influence from the other two domains. In contrast, human and environment are closely interconnected; the state of the human is closely dependent on the state of the environment. Intense heat, heavy traffic, or a high level of activity among nearby people can easily lead to an increase in an individual's stress level. Similarly, the state of the system can also cause such a rise in stress—who is not familiar with the often aggressive reactions when a technical system or application once again fails to respond as the user expects?

This means that, in order to capture the entire context from the three domains, a description must be found that shows how these three domains are interconnected and mutually influence each other.

At this point, another aspect must be considered as a fourth domain: the temporal, or situational, aspect. The detection of the state of each domain and their respective evaluation must be carried out continuously, in temporal synchronization and up-to-date. The circumstances and states of the individual domains can change significantly over time. Neglecting temporal synchronization could easily result in an incorrect context being assembled. From a technical perspective, this requirement also presents a major challenge for the acquisition and generation of contextual information.

The central aspect of assistive support for the user has so far not been sufficiently addressed, despite the complex construction of context through the situational and synchronous interplay of the three domains. The fundamental question for assistive support is what task the user is currently pursuing or what goal they aim to achieve with their activities. It can be assumed that the user will not actively communicate their goal to the system. Rather, the system must be able to recognize it autonomously. This requires further analysis of the already examined "human" domain. It is neither effective nor sufficient to attempt to infer the user's goal solely from historical data. Instead, a wide range of information sources must be integrated in order to identify such a goal precisely and accurately.

Without sophisticated context recognition, the semantic merging of the digital and physical worlds is doomed to fail from the outset. The overarching goal, already pursued with the Internet and even more so with the metaverse, is ultimately for the user to immerse themselves in this metaverse not just figuratively, but literally. This, in turn, means that the user does not want to be distracted by constantly having to provide input to inform the system of their current state or immediate goal. It must be acknowledged that this is not just a specific problem of the metaverse and its implementation, but ultimately the fundamental challenge for all active and proactive assistance systems.

3.4 Temporal Merging

The aspect of semantic merging examined in the previous Sect. 3.3 is likely the central point when it comes to how the physical and virtual worlds can be combined and to what extent they should merge. Within the semantic perspective, the synchronization of the three domains—system, human, and environment—is the core issue. This synchronization, in turn, is part of another perspective on merging. If the physical and digital worlds are to merge, this process must also be temporally synchronized as a whole. Therefore, it is important to consider how the temporal behaviors of the real and digital worlds can be brought into a synchronous relationship. In this context, at least three different approaches exist:

- The first perspective concerns the synchronization of the temporal behavior of physical and virtual objects, taking into account whether, in certain situations or contexts, an asynchronous temporal relationship may be possible.
- Building on this is the second perspective on the temporal behavior of merged physical and virtual worlds: the continuous temporal flow of both realities. In the real world, the state changes continuously through interactive and proactive behavior as well as through the autonomous behavior of objects, even when an individual human is not present as part of this world. For example, a bus travels from stop A to stop B regardless of whether a human passenger is on board. This second perspective also raises the question of whether, in certain contexts or situations, an interruption of the respective continuous temporal flow can or even must or should occur.
- The third perspective in examining temporal behavior does not concern the flow of time itself, but rather raises the question of whether temporal sequences could be shifted relative to one another. This approach aims to allow certain events in the virtual world to be revisited or re-experienced as a replay, as is familiar from video or film. This goes so far as to enable past events to be represented again by decoupling the temporal sequences between the real and virtual worlds. Such possibilities would be of particular interest, for example, for teaching and learning purposes or for simulations.

The Internet can be understood as a document-centric network. Ultimately, it can be regarded as a large, interconnected document or medium. Although this document is being continuously edited in countless places, resulting in constant changes to its content

3.4 Temporal Merging

and state, these changes are, relative to the scope and size of the overall content, negligibly small [HOF21]. Changes occur in two ways:

- The first approach is to add or remove a domain or subdomain on the Internet, or to add or remove a document to or from a subdomain or domain. This represents the classic method of editing the Internet.
- The second approach concerns the editing of an individual document. This can be seen as a characteristic feature of what is known as Web 2.0, that is, the web with user-generated content.

Although the proportion of user-generated content has increased significantly in recent years, as can easily be seen, for example, from the growth in YouTube upload numbers [STA23], the volume of such content remains considerably smaller than the static portion. Even when taking into account social media platforms such as YouTube or Instagram, changes on the Internet occur only in a limited segment, which hardly affects the rest. As a result, the Internet and its content change little or not at all during a user's absence. Of course, it can happen that a document is no longer accessible after a user's absence because it has been deleted, or that the content of a document has changed due to editing by another user. However, when these changes are considered in relation to the unchanged content, this confirms the initial assertion that the classic Internet is document-centric and can be treated as such.

From this, it can be concluded that the Internet can be regarded as a network primarily consisting of static content. Temporal aspects play only a subordinate role here, as there is no need for comprehensive temporal synchronization between the user's real world and the virtual world of document contents. However, this static perspective changes in the context of the metaverse. The metaverse can be seen as an actor-centered network. Drawing on software development and the tools used therein, such as UML, the entirety of the metaverse emerges from the interaction of a wide variety of actors. These actors can be divided into six groups:

- The first group consists of human users, who are anchored in the physical world.
- The second group comprises avatars, which serve as digital twins of the human users and are anchored in the digital world.
- The third group encompasses the real physical world with its objects.
- The fourth group is made up of digital twins of real-world objects. Like avatars, these digital twins are also anchored in the digital world.
- A fifth group of actors includes objects that exist solely in the virtual world. These can be further subdivided into …
    - … objects that describe the digital world, such as a door serving as a portal to another virtual space, or a chair on which the virtual avatar can sit, as well as …
    - … information objects, which are comparable to documents in the classical Internet.

- The sixth group of actors includes objects that serve exclusively for communication between the virtual and physical worlds and vice versa. These can be distinguished according to their primary communication direction into …
  - … communication objects for communication from the digital to the real world, and …
  - … those for communication from the real to the digital world.

In particular, group 5b can be compared to the classical Internet in terms of its content. The actors within this group exhibit no or only extremely minimal change over time, much like documents in the classical Internet, which also do not change over time.

This temporal behavior can be transferred to some of the actors in group 5a. Certainly, the aforementioned chair, on which the avatar does not normally sit by itself, will also not move, change, or disappear on its own. This means that such objects exhibit no or only extremely minimal change over time. Nevertheless, there may also be objects or actors in group 5a that change autonomously, without requiring any physical or virtual user interaction. The most illustrative example of this is probably a vehicle or a virtual animal that exists solely in the virtual world and does not have a real-world counterpart.

Even within this subgroup of group 5a, it becomes clear that, when merging the physical and virtual worlds into a metaverse, the different temporal flows must be taken into account. Groups 3 and 4 also contain objects that do not change over time, as well as those that exhibit their own dynamics or interaction-driven dynamics and thus change over time accordingly.

Although the third and fourth groups of actors are listed separately, they are closely connected, as each group represents the respective twin of individual objects in the other world. There will certainly also be objects that have no inherent dynamics and are thus static actors in their respective worlds. However, a look at the physical world shows that such static objects are rather rare, since the aspect of dynamics concerns not only characteristics such as position or size, but all states in which individual objects can exist in each world. Such state changes also leave traces in the temporal flows of the respective world, regardless of whether it is physical or virtual.

It becomes evident that there is a necessity for temporal synchronization in groups 1 and 2, as these involve humans as actors. In group 1, the human user, through their own behavior and motivation, compels their digital twin as an actor in group 2 to change. However, the reverse causal relationship is also conceivable, namely from the digital twin as an actor in group 2 to the human user as an actor in group 1. For example, the digital twin in its virtual environment could be addressed or otherwise influenced by another actor, regardless of that actor's group affiliation. In this case, the virtual actor from group 2 must transmit this influence or its consequences to its twin actor in group 1 in order to trigger a reaction in group 1.

3.4 Temporal Merging

		Entity	Anchored in the …	Role	Change/Example
1		Human user	physical world	The independently acting user	Self-initiated change of all kinds of states (position, movement, gestures, information seeking, etc.)
2		Digital twin of a human user (avatar)	virtual world	The representative of the physical user in the virtual world	Driven by its physical twin
					Can also be driven by its own autonomous behavior
3	a	Physically existing object	physical world	As a physical twin, represents a digital object in the virtual world	Can be static
					Can be externally triggered to change their own state in any way (size, position, own behavior, etc.)
					Can independently change their own state in any way (size, position, own behavior, etc.)
	b	Physically existing object	physical world	Exists exclusively in the physical world without a digital twin	
4	a	Digital object	virtual world	As a digital twin, represents a real object in the physical world	Can be static
					Can be externally triggered from the physical world to change their own state in any way (size, position, own behavior, etc.)
					Can be externally triggered from the virtual world to change their own state in any way (size, position, own behavior, etc.)
					Can independently change their own state in any way (size, position, own behavior, etc.)

		Entity	Anchored in the ...	Role	Change/Example
	b	Digital object	virtual world	Exists exclusively in the virtual world without a physical twin	
5	a	World-describing objects	virtual world	Contribute to the construction and understanding of the virtual world. Usually have no representative in the "other" world	No inherent drive to change state (e.g., digital chair in a virtual room);
					Low inherent drive to change state (e.g., a cup falling from a table)
					Autonomous change of state even without physical or virtual interaction by users or other objects (e.g., an autonomous virtual vehicle or a virtual living being)
	b	Information objects (documents)	virtual world	Present static and dynamic media and their informational content	e.g., virtual screens without the ability to change themselves
6	a	Communication objects	physical world	Communication from the physical to the virtual world	e.g., physical devices for interaction such as keyboard, mouse, etc.
	b		virtual world	Communication from the virtual to the physical world	e.g., virtual tools for communication such as chats, etc.

The examples mentioned above make it clear that synchronization of temporal processes and flows is absolutely essential. For instance, if a virtual actor wishes to initiate communication with a real user via the digital twin of that user, this must necessarily occur in temporal synchrony. This is because it is generally assumed that communication between avatars and their "real twins" will take place in the form of a conversation, rather than asynchronously, as in a text chat or an email exchange.

The example of communication just used illustrates the discussion from the perspective of Viewpoint 1. Communication between human users, avatars, or interactions between humans and avatars can occur either synchronously or asynchronously. However, synchronous communication necessarily requires the simultaneous presence or at least the availability of the involved actors.

The email exchange, as an example of asynchronous communication, departs from Viewpoint 1 and leads to Viewpoint 2. Of course, both actors involved in the communication can be present at the same time and still communicate asynchronously. However,

3.4 Temporal Merging

it is also possible for the actors not to be present in their respective worlds at the same time. The temporal progression in the respective world nevertheless continues, even if the communication flow is currently in a state of static pause. The state of the respective world also continues to change continuously, even when the communication process or flow is not currently changing.

Even if it may not be immediately obvious, both Viewpoints 1 and 2 require an extremely sophisticated technical implementation of the metaverse. The technical hurdles and challenges arising from Viewpoint 1 were already addressed in the earlier Sect. 2.5 during the analysis of the concept of Mixed Reality. The example given there was the virtual coffee cup placed on a table. The idea of Mixed Reality was interpreted such that if the real table moves out from under the virtual cup, the virtual cup does not float in space, but instead, just like its analog twin, falls in the virtual world. This is also an aspect of temporal merging, since naturally the virtual cup should only fall once the real table has moved out from under it, and not before. However, it should also not remain suspended in virtual air for several seconds before accelerating toward the ground in the virtual world. To realize this temporal merging in such a synchronous form, it must be known where and in what state of motion both the table in the real world and the virtual cup in the virtual world are located.

In the case of the virtual cup, one could argue that this is, of course, part of the cup's data model. However, this also leads to the requirement that the state in the cup's data model must always be persistently stored and retrievable. This is a purely data-driven problem. The real table in the real world, however, poses significantly higher technical demands. While it can also be said here that the position and movement information of the table, in addition to its shape, size, and color, must be stored as other characteristics in its data model, the real challenge lies elsewhere: How or who observes the table, records its position and movement, and stores this information? Is it the table itself, which is a smart table and monitors its own state in the physical world via sensors? Or is it the world itself that observes the objects within it, including the table? Both approaches require an immense technical infrastructure, which is theoretically solvable. This is certainly an aspect considered in the broad research field of the Internet of Things. However, implementation presents an exceptionally high technical hurdle. Ultimately, every real object that is to have a twin in the virtual world must either be observed or be smart and intelligent itself. Whether and to what extent this meets the newly demanded requirements of sustainability will not be discussed here.

The technical requirements and challenges hinted at above, which already arise in Viewpoints 1 and 2, become particularly apparent in Viewpoint 3. In this context, the focus is on the fact that the temporal progressions of the real and virtual worlds can be shifted relative to each other. However, this implies that, at least for the timeline to be shifted, comprehensive information about the historical states of the involved actors must be available. Otherwise, it would not be possible to restart the temporal progression and take into account the individual time-dynamic behaviors of the actors.

In this context, the term "historical" remains vague, as do the requirements for data quality. If only the last communication exchange is to be repeated, both the amount of information and the temporal scope are comparatively small. However, if actual historical events are to be reconstructed, such as the Battle of Waterloo or the first moon landing, this requires a significant leap along the timeline in terms of history, as well as in the amount and quality of data needed to describe the respective situation. For the depiction of the first moon landing, information about the Eagle lander and the two astronauts Neil Armstrong and Edwin "Buzz" Aldrin is initially sufficient. In contrast, a realistic reenactment of the Battle of Waterloo would require a vastly greater amount of information, for example, about as many of the participating soldiers as possible, their weapons, movements, as well as the state of the environment, landscape, and buildings. However, it is unlikely that such data on the Battle of Waterloo exists or can even be generated, since not all participating soldiers and their movements and behaviors are known. Similar information is often unavailable even for more recent historical moments or situations. Thus, we encounter both technical and data-related limitations here.

3.5 The Merging of Interaction

Section 3.1 has already examined the sensor technology necessary to generally capture the environment. In the first step, it does not matter whether the environment to be captured is virtual or real. However, since the metaverse aims to merge virtuality and reality, it is not sufficient to consider only the two extremes of one hundred percent reality and virtuality, as discussed in Sect. 2.6 during the discussion and positioning of the metaverse within the reality-virtuality continuum. There, it was important to first conduct a more detailed examination of the perception channels. This approach should and must now be continued in this section, which addresses the question of how the user should interact with and within the combined environment in the metaverse.

The term "interaction" is defined and used very differently across various disciplines. In the context of the present considerations of the metaverse, various aspects of interaction are to be brought together. First, it is important to clarify the possible forms of interaction for the human user: How can they actively intervene in their environment? Typically, the focus here is on the "actuators" of the human user. However, it must not be overlooked whether interaction refers to social interaction, such as communication with other people, or to influencing objects or the surrounding world.

In a fully real environment, without digital artifacts, humans have various tools available for interaction.

- The most powerful tools are undoubtedly the hands in combination with the arms. They serve both as gripping tools to touch, move, and alter objects in the real world, and for communication, such as through pointing gestures.

3.5 The Merging of Interaction

- Additional human interaction tools are the feet and legs, which are used for locomotion.
- However, humans do not interact solely with their limbs; they also use their face and sometimes their entire body for communication and interaction with their social environment. Gestures, facial expressions, and body posture serve to convey a wide range of information.
- Not to be forgotten is speech, arguably the most powerful form of communication.

It is already apparent here that interaction should never be considered in isolation. Rather, it is always necessary to take into account the context and the goal that is to be achieved through an interaction. From the list of interaction channels, three different target areas can therefore be derived:

1. Changing the environment and the objects within it.
2. Adjusting the position of the person within the environment.
3. Direct and indirect communication with the environment, especially with other human interaction partners.

Naturally, this discussion merely forms the general foundation for human interaction with technical devices and environments. However, it is even more relevant for the design of human interaction with information technology devices. Unlike the classic machines of the analog and physical world, computers are not just tools for work, but also instruments for communication between people. Moreover, they are increasingly evolving into proactive communicative partners and thus autonomous interaction partners, as can be seen in numerous more or less intelligent chatbots. Furthermore, the approach of merging reality and virtuality reduces the distance between humans and their digital tools.

With the completion of the final step—full immersion—this distance disappears entirely. The computer and the application become independent interaction and communication partners, ideally behaving autonomously as well. However, this means that new approaches must be found for designing interaction, since traditional interaction paradigms still separate the entities of human and computer. For the goal of a merged metaverse, it therefore seems highly relevant to follow Steve Mann's proposal and not merely design Human Computer Interfaces (HCI), but rather to consider this interface from the perspective of Humanistic Intelligence. This should not be confused with the typical concepts of Artificial Intelligence (AI). With this term, Mann aims to emphasize that the distinction between human and machine will not be helpful in future IT systems. Incidentally, the term, which Mann first coined in 1998 in the context of wearable computing, also shows that the idea of merging reality and digitality is not as new as it is often described today [MAN91,MIN13].

Designing the metaverse requires the development of at least one new interaction paradigm for IT, since, as previously discussed, existing paradigms are insufficient for this purpose. In contrast to previous paradigms, this new interaction paradigm will focus less on technical capabilities and characteristics of the interface. Instead, this novel interaction paradigm will be multidimensional, integrating various aspects:

- The discussion at the beginning of this section, which was also used in the context of sensor technology, initially focused on examining individual interaction channels. In the real, natural world, however, human interaction typically does not occur through a single channel; rather, people usually interact using a combination of different channels simultaneously. In computer science, this phenomenon is referred to as "multimodal interaction." As early as 1978, an example of this was presented at MIT (Fig. 3.8), the so-called "Put-that-there" scenarios, in which pointing gestures were combined with voice commands [BOL80].
- The next challenge in developing the new paradigm is to combine the dimension of multimodality so that it can be effective both synchronously "cross-media" and, beyond that, "across worlds." An interaction in the physical world may refer exclusively to the physical environment or may also affect the virtual environment. At the same time, an interaction in the virtual environment may refer exclusively to that virtual environment or may also influence the physical environment. In this context, the physical and digital worlds are considered as different modalities.
- In addition, another challenge for the new paradigm is emerging. The merging of reality and digitality also leads to a merging of application domains, processes, and transactions. Traditional interaction paradigms always refer exclusively to a single application or process. An interaction is initiated in the context of an application and refers solely to it. While these applications may vary in complexity, they remain self-contained. An example is interaction within a word processor, which modifies textual information or, at most, saves this information. Other information, however, is not addressed. This perspective can also be applied to the context of operating systems, since launching or closing an application occurs within the context of the operating system. In the traditional application world, direct influence of one application on another at the same level, for example within the ISO-OSI model, is still quite rare. In the context of the future metaverse, however, this will become the norm. Interactions performed in a virtual space will influence the physical environment or other virtual spaces, as well as the transactions and events occurring there.

An example will illustrate this. If the avatars of two people are facing each other and one avatar points to an accessory of the other avatar and says, "*That is a nice bag. Hello, metaverse, I would like to have one for myself as well.*", this affects a whole range of different applications running in the background:

- First, the multimodal interaction of pointing and speaking in the current virtual space must be correctly interpreted. It must be recognized which accessory—in this case, the bag—is being referred to and in which store this bag can be purchased.

3.5 The Merging of Interaction   51

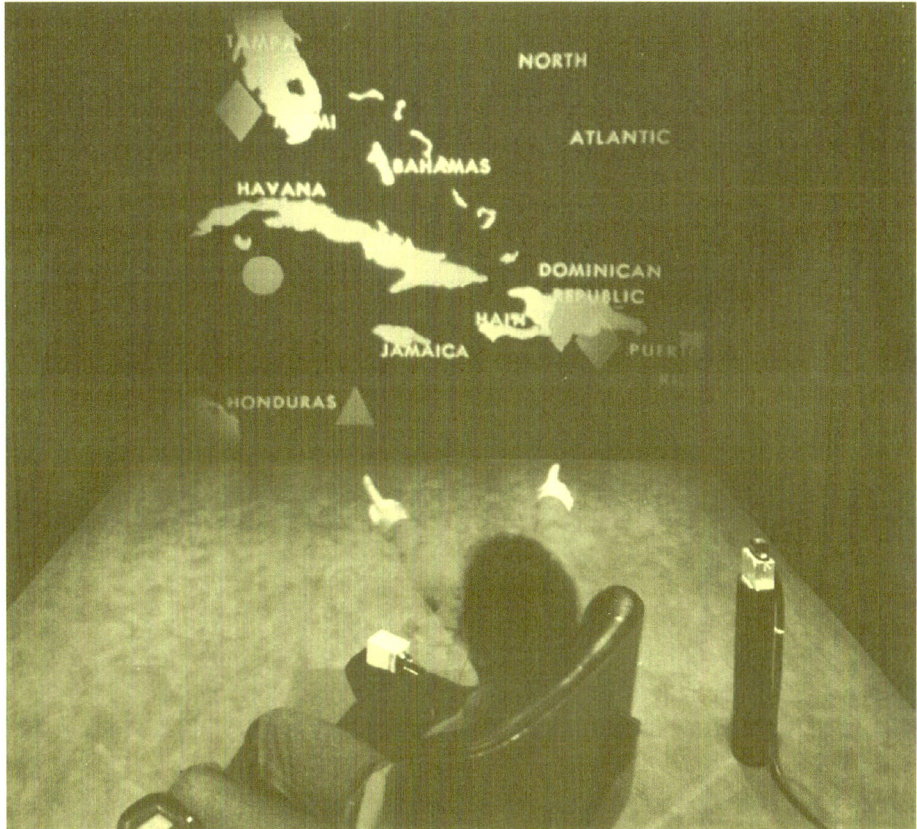

Fig. 3.8 Multimodal interaction: "Put that there" [BOL80]

- The purchase transaction must then be initiated in this store.
- This also requires virtual inventory management and virtual payment to be processed in the store.
- This, in turn, means that banking sub-transactions must also be processed.
- Finally, the newly acquired virtual bag must be added to the avatar of the purchasing person.

This collaboration between the various processes and transactions must occur automatically, without requiring individual confirmation of each transition between transaction threads. Otherwise, the immersion of the real person in the virtual environment would be negatively affected.

- The final challenge for the new interaction paradigm lies in its technical implementation. Ultimately, it must be possible to initiate the interaction itself as well as all subsequent processes on a wide variety of devices and device types. In current web design, this approach is known as responsive design. However, responsiveness in the context of the metaverse will be significantly more complex. While classic web design mainly needs to account for different screen sizes and orientations, the goal for the metaverse is to cover the entire reality-virtuality continuum. This means that both traditional, display-based devices such as smartwatches, smartphones, tablets, laptops, and desktop PCs, as well as VR devices, smart glasses, CAVEs, and all augmented reality or augmented virtuality devices must be taken into account.

The above discussion aims to combine and ideally synchronize the effects of interaction in the physical and virtual worlds. The temporal effects that must be considered in this context were already addressed in the previous section 3.4. However, this is only one of the objectives of such a new interaction paradigm. Another aspect, which ultimately underlies all other interaction paradigms, is to provide the user with the simplest possible way to interact with a machine, an application, or the entire world. In some contexts, this is referred to as a Natural User Interface (NUI) [BLA13,JAI11].

On the one hand, this certainly offers advantages for users, as the more natural an interaction is designed, the more intuitive and easier it will be to understand. However, whether this can actually be achieved remains to be seen, since every time a new technology enters the market, it takes time for people to adopt it. For example, the introduction of graphical user interfaces (GUIs) following the WIMP paradigm, along with Douglas Engelbart's first mouse in the late 1960s, was impressive but not necessarily successful [ENG65].

Apart from the insufficient computing power for such interaction systems at the time, users faced an immense mental challenge. Understanding that moving a real physical object on the desk would cause a graphical pointer to move correspondingly on the screen required a high level of abstraction. For users of these early computer systems, this was a hurdle that was simply too high. Similar obstacles appeared with every subsequent new interaction paradigm or interaction technique. Only when users become accustomed to or are willing to adapt to a new paradigm does it spread throughout society and eventually become the new normal [NEXoJ].

Currently, it can be observed that, in the case of the metaverse, the foundation for a metaverse-related interaction paradigm has been laid by the now widely available VR and AR applications, as well as by the many games that utilize these technologies. However, it must also be noted that users who are already accustomed to these technologies mainly come from a few rather narrow niches, such as gaming or specific design domains, and the mass market has not yet truly been reached.

Another exciting challenge, especially for interaction designers, will be usability, or more precisely, user experience. Both of these aspects are influenced by the merging of reality and virtuality. It is no longer just about designing the user interface beyond the digital boundary; rather, usability must be considered across boundaries. People move in the physical world and initiate actions in the digital world. As Tauziet puts it [TAU16]:

"The higher a person has to raise their arm to perform an interaction, the faster this interaction should be to avoid fatigue."

From this seemingly simple statement, Tauzier derives a series of challenges [TAU16]:

- Fatigue from raising the arm without elbow support
- Challenges when interacting with moving user interfaces (e.g., watches), especially during rapid actions
- Difficulties in visually perceiving depth; this requires time and practice since (as yet) VR object manipulation is often unfamiliar
- Grasping objects while seated close to the virtual body can become problematic
- Visually realistic hands can cause discomfort, especially in cases of errors such as penetrating physical objects
- Familiar objects provide cues for handling, e.g., the expectation that weapon-shaped props can be used for aiming
- Different physics are required for physical objects; for example, should a pen pass through a table or bounce off it instead?
- Loss of awareness of the real environment when in VR; hand movements could lead to collisions or loss of controllers

Examples of possible technical solutions may come from the broad field of telepresence [LEE20a]. Particularly illustrative examples include ActiTouch [ZHA19] and PocketThumb [DOB17].

The ultimate challenge arises from the interplay of the merging of interaction PLUS the merging of sensing PLUS inclusion AND accessibility. As described in the visionary design of human-city interaction [LEE20a], the design of mobile AR/MR user interaction in urban environments should take into account various stakeholders. The metaverse should also include all members of the community, regardless of race, gender, age, or religion, including children, the elderly, people with disabilities, and so on. Different types of content may appear in the metaverse, and it must be ensured that these are suitable for a wide range of user groups. Furthermore, it is important to consider personalized content presentation for users [LAM21] and to promote the fairness of recommendation systems in order to reduce biased content and thus influence user behavior and decision-making [LAN18].

3.6 All-together – The Path to Socio-cultural Convergence

According to the vision of its driving forces, the metaverse is intended to become an even more central component of future human life than the internet has ever been. Whether the end result will actually resemble what Neal Stephenson described in "Snow Crash" [STE92], Ernest Cline in "Ready Player One" [CLI11], or William Gibson in

"Neuromancer" [GIB84] remains to be seen. A look at history impressively demonstrates that new technologies, and especially new forms of media, can influence the social and societal environment of humans—from the first media revolution initiated by Johannes Gutenberg and the introduction of the movable-type printing press in the 15th century, to the advent of electrically powered media and communication technologies such as the telegraph, telephone, radio, and television at the beginning of the 20th century, and finally to the not-so-distant introduction of the PC, internet, and World Wide Web. Each of these new media and communication technologies has, to a greater or lesser extent, radically changed the way people communicate, how information is conveyed, and ultimately also societal structures and social interactions [MCL64]. A similar development can therefore be expected from the metaverse, provided it is realized in the intended form.

3.6.1 The Real-Life Connector – Foundation for New Interaction Paradigms

The significance of the convergence of the virtual and real worlds has been exemplified in the preceding sections. The focus has always been on individual aspects, each considered and evaluated separately. The possibilities of each individual aspect alone are already impressive, at times perhaps daunting, and certainly technically demanding overall. However, it is important to recognize that these aspects will not exist in isolation. Rather, it is to be expected that they will continue to develop in parallel, albeit at different rates. To gain at least a somewhat realistic perspective on the future possibilities and impacts of the metaverse, it is necessary to connect these individual aspects—a process that will be examined more closely in this section.

The world is neither monomedia nor monomodal—this holds true for both the real and the virtual world. For this reason, it is necessary to unite the various aspects discussed above. Therefore, a Real Life Connector will be systematically developed here, as presented in Fig. 3.9, with the aim of achieving the most comprehensive representation possible of the fusion between the virtual and real worlds.

- *Step 1*: Since the metaverse is, at its core, also a computer-controlled application, it is essential in this context that the user has the ability to interact with the metaverse just as they would with any other application.

At this point, it should be noted that the term "user" as a designation for someone visiting the metaverse may not be optimally chosen. It remains questionable whether it is truly accurate to say that someone "uses" the metaverse. Other terms might be more appropriate, but each comes with its own difficulties. For example, instead of "user," the term "spectator" could be used, but this implies a passivity that excludes other activities and thus does not do justice to the active experience of the metaverse. The most fitting alternative term would probably be "visitor," as this best reflects the intended immersion

3.6 All-together – The Path to Socio-cultural Convergence

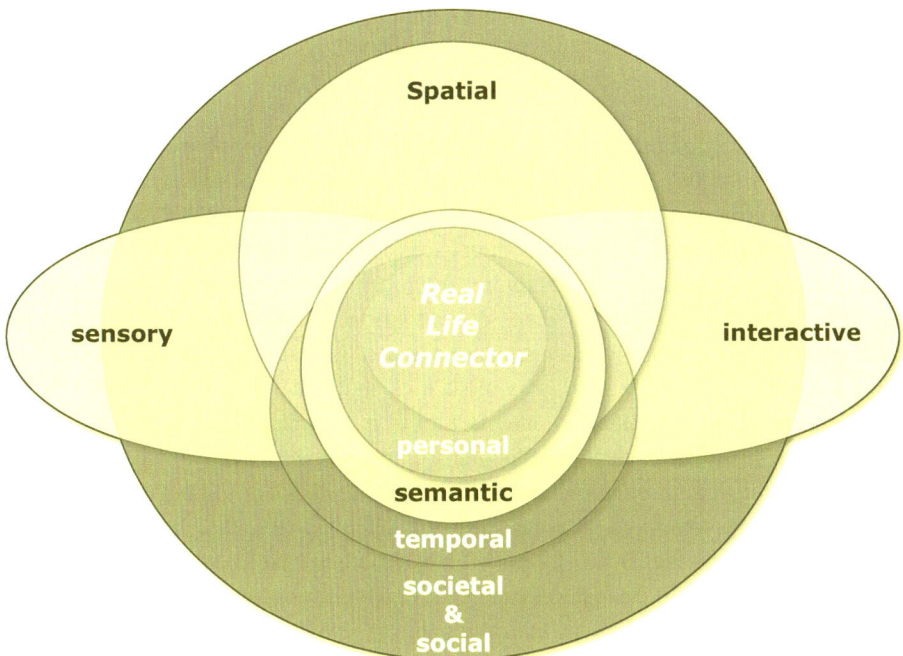

Fig. 3.9 The Real Life Connector. (Original illustration: Peter Hoffmann, Invisible Cow)

in the metaverse or a virtual world. However, due to this terminological issue and the widespread use of the term in IT, the term "user" will continue to be used here.

In order to enable the user to actively participate in the "metaverse" application, it must be ensured that they can not only perceive the metaverse but also take action themselves. This must also be taken into account by the intended Real Life Connector. Therefore, the first step is to consider the fusion of sensing and interaction, as detailed in Sections 3.1 and 3.5. Without perception of the real world synchronized with perception of the virtual world, the user remains anchored solely in their real environment. Mere perception, however, would push the user into the aforementioned passivity and make them a spectator. For this reason, the possibility of interaction in the real world must be combined, on the same level, with the possibility of interaction in the virtual world, in synchronization. Only in this way can the user actively participate in both worlds. The technical challenge at this lower level of the Real Life Connector is thus the bidirectional synchronization of these two aspects.

- *Step 2*: In the first step, it was ensured that the user can both perceive the two sub-worlds—reality and virtuality—sensory-wise and simultaneously interact with the available real and virtual artifacts. The second step must therefore aim to link the possibilities for perception and interaction with the user both spatially and temporally.

Currently, it is unclear whether separating spatial from temporal coupling is meaningful, which is why both aspects should be considered together in the first generation of the Real Life Connector's description.

The spatial coupling of perception and interaction to the user in the metaverse is fundamental, since in the real world both perception and interaction are always related to the user's immediate surroundings: we see the things that surround us at our current location and interact with those that allow for interaction. This also applies in the context of the metaverse for the virtual world. Therefore, the results of sensory and interactive fusion must necessarily be linked to the user's current spatial location. In terms of perception, this is probably not a major challenge, since the user will always want to perceive both reality and virtuality through all sensory modalities: in the real world, we do not normally switch off our visual perception at one place to turn it on at another, unless special circumstances or disturbances require it. Similarly, in the virtual world, we will try to receive information through all available sensory channels at any place and at any time. For interaction, this may be somewhat different, as it is quite conceivable that the possibilities for interaction depend on the current position. Simply because the interactable artifacts vary at different locations, it is often necessary in the real world to use different tools for interaction. For example, one might switch from voice to keyboard input if it is too loud at a particular location for the application to correctly capture the user's speech. Thus, sensory and interactive fusion are directly linked to the user and their spatial position.

Sensory and interactive fusion are also closely coupled from the user's temporal perspective. It can be assumed that it is normal for the user to perceive the current situation in both the virtual and real environments. Likewise, it is likely that the user wants to interact with the artifacts currently surrounding them. In a normal situation, it would be rather unusual for the user to interact with an artifact that was present or accessible at the current location at an earlier time. Certainly, examples could be found for such states, for instance if a previous state of a digital artifact is made available. In this case, however, the user would need to be informed about the earlier state of the digital artifact. This means, with respect to the user, that sensory and interactive fusions are bound both spatially and temporally to the user, their position, and possibly also to their current state.

However, spatial and temporal fusions can be extended further, as they do not only relate to the user but also to all other artifacts. It is entirely conceivable that artifacts exist independently of the user in both the real and virtual worlds and act proactively or interactively. In such cases, the perception and interaction of these artifacts must be synchronized both spatially and temporally.

In addition to the combined spatial and temporal coupling, it is also conceivable that sensory and interactive fusions are coupled either only spatially or only temporally.

- *Step 3*: In steps 1 and 2, the focus was on fusion and coupling directly related to the user and artifacts, considering them as objects. These objects were reduced to their individual significance, which arose from the object itself. However, taking into account the spatial and temporal connections between user and artifacts can expand this self-reference. In this way, semantic meaning can be assigned or emerge from the object itself. Nevertheless, such semantic meaning is not conceivable without the situational, i.e., the temporal and spatial level. Likewise, for this semantic meaning, there must be a perception that takes into account the state of the world and the current situation. Interaction can, but does not necessarily have to, play a role at this semantic level.

In many use cases, a further step is required. These are the use cases that take the final step toward the "Embodied Internet" in the sense of a "walk-in Internet," as described by Kreutzer and Klose [HUS24]. The user now merges, in the truest sense of the word, personally with their avatar.

- *Step 4*: In this final step, the focus is on the fusion of the user with their digital representation in the virtuality of the metaverse. Even today, sensory and, even more so, interactive fusion is used for the direct control of avatars as representatives of the user in virtual environments. However, there are already signs that direct control of avatars by the user will not remain the norm. Whereas today the avatar in the virtual world becomes inactive when the user in the real world turns to other things, the avatars of the future will become entities that act autonomously on behalf of the user in the virtual sphere of the metaverse and will continue to perform activities even when the user is not directly controlling the avatar.

With steps 1 to 3 and the integration of sensory, interactive, semantic, as well as spatial and temporal fusion, a technical foundation for the Real Life Connector has initially been established. It is now important to review the prevailing interaction paradigms to determine whether they meet the requirements arising from the convergence of these various aspects. Given the particularity that the metaverse is intended to be both highly interactive and highly immersive, these two aspects must be incorporated into the requirements for the Real Life Connector. From the dimension of immersion, three distinct levels of immersion can be identified for the metaverse:

- If the metaverse is viewed as a classic internet, it corresponds to typical desktop applications.
- If the metaverse is regarded as pure virtual reality, technical VR manifestations apply here, such as access via VR headset or access using a CAVE.
- Between these two extremes lies the domain of augmentation, which encompasses AR and AV and is characterized by the user experiencing a perception of reality enriched by digital artifacts.

Regardless of the dimension of immersion, there are currently three well-known interaction paradigms for the dimension of interaction:

- The most widespread interaction paradigm at present is terminal or WIMP interaction using keyboard, mouse, or, depending on the implementation, possibly also touch input or stylus. This paradigm predominates in desktop workstation scenarios.
- From some specialized workplace situations, but especially from entertainment and gaming applications, the paradigm of direct interaction is known. Here, interaction does not occur via a writing tool such as the keyboard or pointing devices like a mouse or touchpad; instead, the user takes control of digital artifacts using specialized controllers. In its most technically advanced form, this can extend to data gloves or even a full data suit. Compared to WIMP and terminal, this second paradigm is significantly less common.
- It is also possible that the currently increasing prevalence of voice interaction could be adopted as an additional interaction paradigm in the future.

The task now is to reconcile these two dimensions to determine whether current interaction paradigms can meet the requirements of the metaverse. The question arises as to whether the current, predominant interaction paradigms are sufficient to cover the broad spectrum of immersion necessary for effective interaction with the metaverse:

- Terminal and WIMP were specifically developed for the desktop environment and have always been oriented toward it.
- Direct interaction in the desktop environment is only possible with significant limitations. Of course, one could argue that entering and editing text or image files on the desktop constitutes direct interaction with these texts and images. However, this is more of an exceptional form of direct interaction. Direct manipulation of a three-dimensional digital artifact, on the other hand, is very difficult or even impossible using a keyboard or traditional mouse, which typically only moves in the two-dimensional plane of the desktop.
- However, terminal and WIMP are unsuitable for both augmented reality (AR) and virtual reality (VR). Immersion in VR would be significantly disrupted by the need to focus attention on a keyboard to perform an interaction. This applies equally, if not even more, to AR, since here the user is situated in the physical world and is usually not at a desktop. Of course, as in the often-cited example of Tom Cruise in Minority Report, a keyboard could be projected into the user's field of view [SPI02]. Nevertheless, even in this case, immersion would be disrupted by the need to focus attention on the keyboard.
- Just as terminal and WIMP were developed for the desktop environment, the paradigm of direct interaction is specifically designed for use in virtual realities.
- For augmented reality, direct interaction is at least partially fundamental, since the display of digital artifacts, which are bound to a spatial situation and position, directly depends on the position and viewing vector from which the user perceives the digital artifact. If the user changes their position or viewing direction, the display also

changes. A direct relationship between user and artifact is therefore essential here. However, whether the user can actually "touch" or "manually manipulate" the digital artifact is not necessarily guaranteed.

It can currently be stated that some aspects of interaction and immersion are technically feasible, but there are still significant gaps in many areas and across all levels of immersion. Therefore, it seems necessary to develop a new, independent interaction paradigm for the metaverse as a fused medium. What this paradigm will look like can probably only be described once the requirements for and of the fused metaverse are known. Such a new interaction paradigm must incorporate the known advantages and disadvantages of previous interaction paradigms. For some time now, studies have been conducted on the well-known GUI as the embodiment of the WIMP interaction paradigm, analyzing how the use of keyboard and mouse influences cognitive processes in our brains, particularly with regard to interaction with the environment and other people [DOU01]. The underlying idea is that human cognitive development is fundamentally shaped by physical and social interactions with objects and living beings. The findings of such studies broaden the concept of paradigms.

For some time now, the term Reality-Based Interaction, coined by Jacob et al. [JAC08], has been in use, and in their description they also incorporated approaches from so-called multimodal interaction, which was already introduced in 1978. Although Jacob et al., with Reality-Based Interaction, remain technically focused like other interaction paradigms, some developments—such as Reiterer's Blended Interaction—go a significant step further by leaving the purely technical context [DOU01] and also considering how workflows, business processes, or practices in the entertainment sector influence the design of interactions.

Numerous foundations have thus already been laid for a new, let us call it fused, interaction paradigm tailored to the coming metaverse (see Fig. 3.10).

It is therefore fundamentally necessary for the development of a Metaverse User Interaction Paradigm (MUI) to consider both technical and user-oriented aspects, such as the integration of business processes into the design process and context. Furthermore, the novel interaction must not only be accepted by users but, above all, also understood. It is essential to incorporate all insights from interaction design that are common in the fields of user interaction design or usability. These can generally be traced back to Don Norman and his seminal work "The Design of Everyday Things" [NOR02], although, of course, many others have contributed to this field as well.

3.6.2 Physical Fusion

The fourth step of convergence outlined above signifies the attainment of the embodied Internet. In this context, it is first necessary to consider the three concepts of avatar, NPC, and digital twin, which influence the extent to which this embodiment is achieved

Fig. 3.10 Immersion of interaction paradigms: Metaverse User Interaction (MUI). (Original illustration: Peter Hoffmann, Invisible Cow)

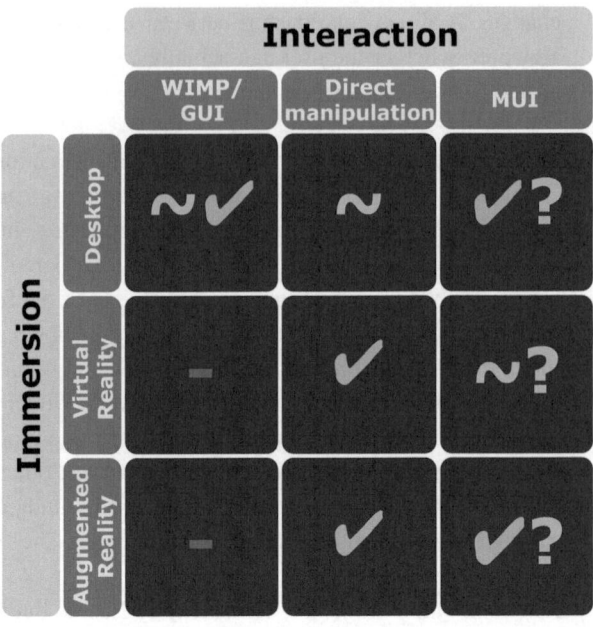

and ultimately accepted by users. The question of acceptance will be crucial for future applications of the metaverse, as it involves a form of personification and identification that touches users in a very direct—or perhaps even intimate—way. Figure 3.11 attempts to illustrate this as an approximation.

- Avatars are digital representations of users that enable them to be physically present in virtual environments [BAI04]. This embodiment can be both visual and interactive, ranging from simple 2D images to highly complex 3D characters with realistic movement capabilities [SCHroe02]. Modern technologies such as motion capture systems and haptic technologies enhance the sense of physical presence by enabling real-time synchronization between body movements and avatar actions [LEE06].
- NPCs are non-player-controlled characters that operate in virtual environments and assume a pre-programmed or AI-driven role. They serve to enable interactions, advance narratives, and make the digital world more believable [LAI01]. Advances in artificial intelligence (AI) increasingly allow NPCs to exhibit realistic behaviors and even interact with avatars in personalized ways [DU25]. This leads to a stronger fusion of reality and virtuality, especially when NPCs are connected to adaptive learning systems [RUS20].
- The concept of the digital twin goes beyond mere virtual representation by enabling real-time coupling between a physical object or person and its digital counterpart [GRI15]. This connection makes it possible to transfer physical interactions into digital simulations and vice versa [TAO18]. In fields such as healthcare, industry, and smart cities, a digital twin can serve as the digital embodiment of real people, enabling a deep intertwining of reality and virtuality [FUL20].

3.6 All-together – The Path to Socio-cultural Convergence

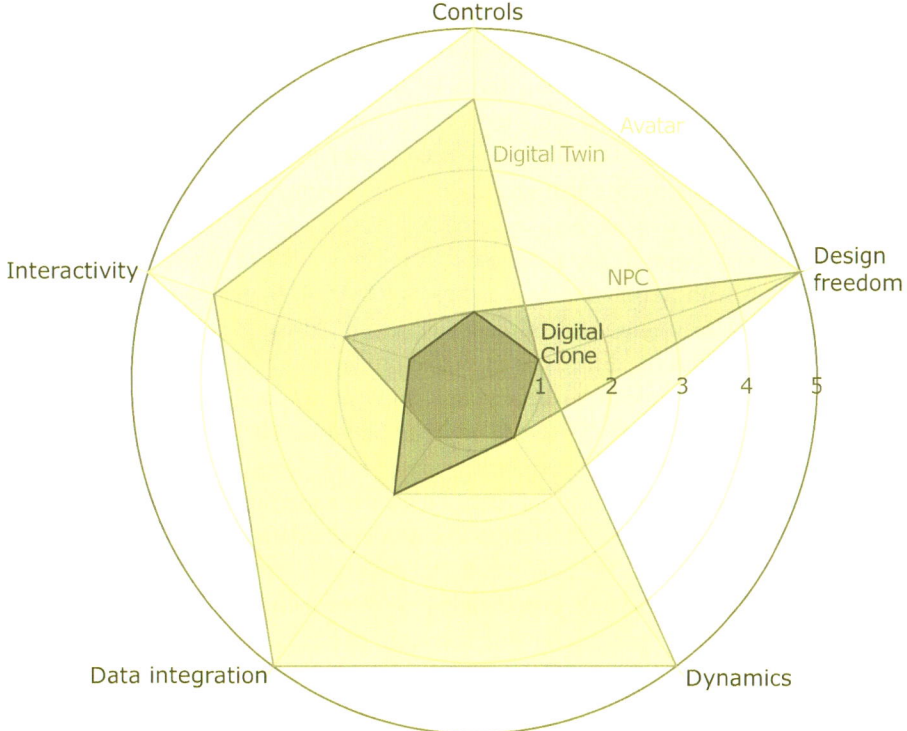

Fig. 3.11 Differences in the characteristics of avatars, NPCs, and digital twins. (Original illustration: Peter Hoffmann, Invisible Cow)

Avatars as digital representations of real people in virtual worlds and the metaverse are now an established concept. As mentioned above, avatars are created and controlled by users to interact, act, or present themselves in virtual worlds [BAI18]. These digital identities are an essential component of virtual environments, enabling users to express themselves in various digital spaces and engage in social interactions.

Avatars now play a central role in the direct-to-avatar (D2A) model, especially when the avatar is addressed as the direct consumer of digital goods and services. Instead of the traditional B2C or D2C model, in which brands interact directly with the real customer, companies in the D2A approach target the users' avatars directly. This includes digital products such as virtual clothing, accessories, animations, or even virtual real estate. Through this direct access to users' digital identities, companies can create personalized and immersive shopping experiences that are deeply integrated into digital ecosystems [KIM23,RIV23,WIE23].

A prominent example of the D2A model is the purchase of virtual luxury goods within metaverse platforms such as Roblox or Decentraland. For instance, the luxury brand Gucci offers digital clothing items that can be purchased and worn exclusively by avatars. A user can, for example, buy a virtual Gucci coat for their avatar to represent their digital status within the platform. Such digital consumer goods are becoming increasingly important, as they allow users to emphasize their individuality in virtual spaces while opening up new business models for companies [HUS24].

Non-player characters (NPCs) have long been known, especially in the world of gaming. These are computer-controlled characters used in virtual environments to populate them, provide information, or perform specific tasks. They are not controlled by real users. Instead, they typically operate based on pre-programmed algorithms that define their interactions with the environment and users [CAS00]. In more recent applications, implementation increasingly involves the integration of AI-based behaviors. In the D2A model, which describes the direct sale of digital products to avatars of real users, NPCs generally do not play a role as buyers or target audience. Instead, they serve as supporting elements, for example as salespeople or guides in virtual shops, providing users with product information or presenting products.

In theory, it seems possible to integrate NPCs as consuming entities into the D2A model, but this would require a re-evaluation of both the definition and function of the model, as well as the terms NPC and D2A. In current practice, NPCs are not buyers of digital products, as they have no consumption needs of their own [KIM23]. Moreover, sales to NPCs generate neither economic nor social value, since there is no real person behind the transaction [CAS06]. These factors make NPCs an unsuitable target group for D2A models now and likely in the future, as these models focus on direct interaction between brands and avatars of real users.

Nevertheless, there are potential scenarios in which NPCs could act as consumers. In virtual economic simulations, for example, they could act as buyers to replicate realistic consumer behavior and intensify interaction with real users [MOR23c]. In this context, NPCs would help increase immersion in the virtual environment by simulating economic dynamics. NPCs could also be deliberately used as consuming characters in brand storytelling. For example, it is conceivable that NPCs could wear digital fashion and thus act as virtual influencers, inspiring real users to make purchases [KAP20]. In gamified metaverse environments, NPCs could also play a role as buyers by purchasing certain products to support game mechanics or foster interactivity with users [TAY15]. Another conceivable scenario is the targeted use of NPCs to stabilize internal economies within virtual worlds by generating artificial demand for digital goods.

Although these approaches offer potential, integrating NPCs as consumers presents several challenges. A key issue is the authenticity of the D2A model. Purchases by NPCs could be perceived as artificial, which could undermine users' trust in the economic system of the metaverse [LAN17]. It also remains questionable whether NPC transactions are economically relevant, as they do not generate direct financial value for companies as long as there is no real person behind the purchases. Furthermore, implementing realistic consumption logic for NPCs requires advanced AI systems capable of making authentic purchasing decisions, thereby meaningfully enhancing the user experience [BRY14].

3.6 All-together – The Path to Socio-cultural Convergence

Despite these challenges, NPCs could still provide added value as consuming entities in certain contexts. For example, they could enhance immersion in virtual worlds by creating a more lively and interactive environment. Additionally, they could be used as part of marketing strategies, acting as brand ambassadors and increasing the incentive for real users to make purchases [HOL04]. In virtual economic systems with their own economies, NPCs could also play a stabilizing role by offsetting cyclical fluctuations in demand.

With the advancement of artificial intelligence and the increasing complexity of virtual economies, NPCs could play a greater role as consuming entities in the future. Highly developed AI models could equip NPCs with realistic decision-making and consumption patterns, allowing them to integrate into the economic system of the metaverse. In autonomous virtual economies, it is conceivable that NPCs could act as consumers to drive economic processes. Furthermore, users could be given the ability to individually customize NPCs in their environment and equip them with digital goods they have acquired themselves.

Digital twins and the metaverse are closely related, as both concepts are based on the fusion of physical and virtual worlds. While the metaverse creates an immersive, interactive digital environment, digital twins serve as a bridge between the real world and these virtual experiences. The combination of both technologies enables deeper integration and interaction between physical and digital systems, giving rise to new applications in various fields [GRI17].

A digital twin is a virtual representation of a physical object, system, or process that is synchronized in real time with data from the real world. This data is often collected by IoT sensors or other data acquisition systems and continuously updated [TAO19]. Digital twins are used in numerous application areas, including industrial manufacturing, urban planning, healthcare, and architecture. For example, machines in a factory can be modeled as digital twins to optimize maintenance, cities can be planned more efficiently using virtual models, and in healthcare, digital twins enable more precise diagnoses and therapy planning through simulation-based approaches [BAR19].

A key feature of digital twins is real-time data integration, which enables continuous synchronization between the physical and digital worlds. This technology makes it possible to accurately simulate physical processes and optimize them more efficiently through data-driven improvements. In addition, digital twins offer a high degree of interactivity, as users can interact with them in virtual environments to conduct simulations or test predictions, for example [FUL20].

The integration of digital twins into the metaverse opens up far-reaching possibilities, particularly through the realistic mapping of the physical world in virtual spaces. Cities, buildings, or machines can be transferred into the metaverse as 1:1 models, enabling a detailed and interactive reproduction of the real world. Real-time data integration makes these models dynamic and responsive, so that changes in the physical world can be immediately reflected in the metaverse. This offers significant advantages, especially for industries such as urban planning, manufacturing, healthcare, and architecture [YAQ23].

In urban planning, digital twins could be used to simulate urban developments and develop more sustainable transportation concepts. Through virtual models of production facilities, companies can optimize and make their manufacturing processes more efficient. In healthcare, the combination of digital twins with the metaverse enables more precise diagnoses and individualized therapy planning. For example, digital twins of patients could be used to plan surgical procedures in a virtual environment before they are performed in reality. In architecture, digital twins offer an innovative way to visualize and analyze construction projects or renovations in an immersive virtual environment before implementation [BET19].

The interactivity and simulation enabled by the combination of digital twins and the metaverse is a decisive advantage of these technologies. Users can interact with digital twins to conduct simulations, analyze problems, and test decisions based on realistic models. For instance, an engineer could analyze the performance of a machine in the metaverse and make optimizations before these changes are implemented in the real world. Such simulations help companies and research institutions minimize risks and test innovations more efficiently [JON20].

The combination of digital twins with the metaverse also offers significant advantages in visualization, collaboration, and real-time monitoring. The metaverse enables immersive, three-dimensional visualization of digital twins, making it possible to capture and analyze complex data more intuitively. At the same time, this technology opens up new opportunities for location-independent collaboration, as users worldwide can work together on digital twins. This is particularly relevant for international projects in architecture, urban planning, or industrial manufacturing, where experts from different countries can simultaneously work on virtual models [SCHwir24].

Another significant advantage lies in the simulation of scenarios enabled by digital twins in the metaverse. For example, in the field of disaster management, various crisis scenarios can be simulated and optimization strategies tested. Similarly, digital twins can be used in economic simulations to predict market changes or analyze production processes. Through real-time monitoring and control of physical systems, digital twins can also be utilized to monitor critical processes in real time and make adjustments as needed [LU20].

	Avatars	NPCs	Digital Twins
Definition	Digital representations of real people in virtual worlds.	Computer-controlled characters that populate virtual environments and provide information.	Virtual representations of physical objects, systems, or processes with real-time data integration.
Control	Created and controlled by real users	Controlled by algorithms or artificial intelligence	Automated control via IoT sensors or data systems.

	Avatars	NPCs	Digital Twins
Function in the Metaverse	Serve for interaction, communication, and self-representation in digital spaces.	Can serve as salespeople, guides, or storytelling elements.	Used for simulation, optimization, and real-time monitoring of physical systems in the metaverse.
Interaction with Users	High, as they are controlled by users.	Limited, primarily via scripts or AI-driven responses.	Possible, as users can interact with them to conduct simulations or tests.
Role in the D2A Model	Central consumers of digital products and services.	Not direct consumers, but potentially usable as brand ambassadors or for simulating economic dynamics.	Not intended as consumers, but essential for data-driven decisions and optimization of real-world processes.
Examples of Applications	Purchasing virtual goods (e.g., Gucci fashion in Roblox or Decentraland).	Virtual shop assistants, AI-driven assistants, potentially as digital influencers.	Virtual cities for traffic planning, digital twins of machines for process optimization, simulation of medical diagnoses.
Potential Future Developments	Expansion of customization options, deeper integration into digital economic systems.	Ability to simulate consumer behavior or act as economic stabilizers in virtual economies.	Deeper integration into the metaverse for real-time control and optimization of physical systems.

3.6.3 Social and Societal Convergence

As previously emphasized, the current analysis of convergence focuses on individual, independent aspects. Such isolated considerations are initially helpful, as they are easier to manage. However, they are not sufficient if the metaverse is to be implemented as the future embodied internet and thus as the future form of human life and coexistence [JIA22]. Instead, what is needed is something referred to above as the "Real Life Connector," in which the various aspects are brought together. It is important to note that this involves not only technical aspects, but also human and social dimensions. The metaverse, as currently conceived, is intended to enable a new experience of virtual realities in connection with "real reality." This includes not only individual experiences, but also social interaction and various areas of users' lives, such as learning, travel, or cultural experiences [BIT22]. To avoid a purely virtual parallel world that merely represents another perspective of today's mobile internet, the metaverse must instead be a logical evolution of it. This can only succeed if the integration of the various aspects is successfully achieved.

Naturally, the entire concept is initially based on the premise that each individual aspect can in fact be implemented and exist independently. This means that methods must first be developed to perceive the new combination of physical and virtual reality at all, as well as approaches to enable interaction with these new combinations of reality. At this stage, the technical aspects are the primary focus.

Regardless of sensor and interaction technology, solutions must be developed to combine the spatial sub-aspects and challenges of both realities, so that, for example, the movement of objects can take place across all combined sub-realities.

At this point, the need to move beyond a purely technical perspective on convergence becomes clear. As mentioned in the previous section 3.6.1, the area of interaction encompasses not only direct interaction with visible objects in the various realities, but also the interaction of applications with each other in terms of a process- or transaction-oriented approach. While technical interfaces are required for these cross-process interactions, what is fundamentally needed first is a basic process understanding of the interrelationships within the metaverse itself [BAL20].

Even at this initial stage, a combination occurs in that the states of both physical and digital reality must be considered together. Achieving the connection between sensing and interaction with respect to spatiality is generally only possible if temporal aspects are also taken into account.

It is this holistic integration that will ultimately characterize the metaverse. Multimodal interaction alone is no more the metaverse than multimodal sensing alone. Only the interplay of all aspects will lead to an innovative medium that can meet the expectations currently associated with the idea of the metaverse.

At the latest at this point, the question must certainly be asked: What is all this for? Why do we need such an elaborate, technologically complex network?

To begin with, we can return to the thread introduced above. The future metaverse is intended to be open to everyone and, not least, to help shape all the barriers we face in everyday life—such as in daily mobility, at work, and in leisure—in such a way that no one is actually excluded. The major goal here is practical accessibility. What at first seems like a contradiction—that many different aspects must be considered and combined, which will of course require immense technical and technological effort—is in fact not a contradiction at all. It is precisely through this extensive combination that accessibility will become significantly easier to achieve.

The limitations people experience due to their varying abilities—such as vision and hearing, mobility, or mental and cognitive perception—can be compensated for by combining different synchronous channels to create redundancy. The challenges here lie in the diversity of these limitations and the lack of universally recognized standards. While there are numerous frameworks for accessible web design, these are rarely used, and when they are, they are often not applied consistently or thoroughly. The number of accessible solutions for VR is even lower. The number of accepted, established standards in this area is limited. As for AR, it is hardly worth mentioning, as the number of publications from practical projects in this field is virtually zero.

3.6 All-together – The Path to Socio-cultural Convergence

In addition to this technically driven, practical, or user-centered approach intended to enable the metaverse, there is another, potentially equally practical approach. Looking at the technical developments to date, with a focus on the Internet, it is obvious and undeniable that the introduction of the Internet, and especially the World Wide Web, has significantly changed the way people live. Both the world of work and the way information is obtained and handled, as well as leisure activities, are fundamentally different today than they were just a few decades ago. Certainly, other technologies have contributed to this, such as mobile telephony. Ultimately, however, even this technology has converged into today's mobile Internet and shapes our current way of life. How, then, could a metaverse, considering the converging aspects discussed so far, influence our way of life in the future? Cathy Hackl, a well-known blogger and journalist in the fields of IT, the web, and the metaverse, has provided a vivid example [HAC21]:

At the beginning of this example, it should be noted that the reader of this book is likely somewhat older than the main character in the example. But every reader can undoubtedly remember their first concert. It does not matter whether it was a small local band in a neighborhood venue or a large multi-day festival. We all remember what it felt like to stand in reality, body to body with other euphoric people, in front of the stage—seeing, hearing, and feeling the band, and perhaps even smelling the person next to us. This matches Cathy Hackl's memories, but she recounts the first concert experience of her ten-year-old son. He attended a performance by Lil Nas X, which, due to the ongoing coronavirus pandemic, did not take place in a real venue but in the virtual world of Fortnite. Unlike the crush of the mosh pit in front of a real stage, Cathy Hackl's son enjoyed the concert from home using a VR headset. Although it was a purely digital experience, it was no less real for the young man.

This is further illustrated by another example from Cathy Hackl. During the pandemic, she organized a birthday party for her son in the virtual world of Roblox [HAC21]. Just as almost every (not only) teenager would do in the real world, Cathy Hackl's son placed great importance on how his avatar would appear at the party. The design and appearance of his avatar were just as important to him as a shirt or blouse would be to guests in the real world.

Such examples highlight an important insight: VR, AR, or MR are not the essential core components of the emerging metaverse. Rather, the central element is the possibility for social interaction within the virtual world. If this option is not implemented and made available to users, the coming metaverse would be nothing more than an ordinary virtual world, as known from classic entertainment and gaming environments or as depicted in numerous dystopias. The most popular example of such a dystopian implementation is the frequently mentioned "Ready Player One" [CLI11], in which people immerse themselves in the OASIS primarily to experience better living conditions. However, this also shows that the OASIS cannot be considered a true implementation of the metaverse. Users lose themselves in the OASIS and simultaneously escape reality, which fundamentally contradicts the definition of the metaverse.

The fact that technology recedes into the background while social and cultural aspects come to the fore presents a major challenge for users. If the metaverse is actually realized in the merged form envisioned here, significant impacts on users' social interactions are to be expected, and substantial changes will be initiated. Such changes are well known from the history of computers, the Internet, and especially the World Wide Web. Both the computer itself and the Internet initially carried a stigma when they were introduced. The general public regarded the use of computers and later the Internet as mostly wasted and even antisocial time. The destigmatization of both computers/PCs and the Internet took a very long time. Even today, about 30 years after the introduction of the Internet, the use of this medium is still viewed critically in some quarters—which is certainly justified to some extent.

This is exactly what can be expected for the new metaverse—perhaps even more so than for the classic Internet, since the typical user—the surfer in media worlds—is usually not isolated from their environment when using the Internet. Typically, they sit in front of a screen and are generally approachable, even if they are peering into cyberspace through the window of their monitor [BAL22]. In the metaverse, however, there is a risk that users will actually disconnect from the real world through the use of devices such as VR headsets and similar equipment, and thus may no longer be directly approachable.

Early adopters may soon be confronted with this stigma. However, it is possible that the period until this negative perception of the metaverse shifts to a neutral or even positive perspective will be shorter than it was for the Internet. After all, the metaverse is already familiar to many users and to society in general, as numerous people are already active in VR or 3D worlds when they immerse themselves in gaming environments [BAL21b].

The real challenge arising from this convergence is therefore not technical, but sociocultural in nature. On the one hand, the emerging metaverse and its users must be reconciled with pure real-world reality, because only if broad acceptance is achieved can the metaverse become successfully established. However, other sociocultural observations from the World Wide Web can be transferred to the coming metaverse. It is now undisputed [DÖR10,FRI09] that the establishment of the Internet has had, and continues to have, a significant impact on society and social interaction. Behaviors, forms of expression, and expectations regarding communication and communication structures have changed compared to the paper-based analog era, not least due to the media discontinuity. But even within the medium of the Internet or the WWW, new social forms have emerged. For example, the conventions in social media differ from those in the classic forums of the early Internet. Even within social media, there are different forms of communication and interaction. Communication on channels such as Twitter or Telegram is characterized by a high degree of directness, which, for example, is not found on professional platforms like LinkedIn. This aspect also applies to other media forms such as wikis, which are shaped by collaboration, and even more so to media forms like gaming platforms. While these involve competition, it often takes place within social structures such as gaming clans and similar groups.

3.6 All-together – The Path to Socio-cultural Convergence

If, even in the "classic" Internet—where there is not yet a fusion of digitality and reality—pseudo- or partial societies and sociocultural trends emerge, it is highly likely that new sociocultural trends will also arise in the context of a new medium that specifically focuses on and seeks this fusion. The major challenge is that, in this metaverse, there is no longer any way to rely on physical experiences as people have previously had in and through the real environment and their social surroundings. Even if it is unpopular, it is a deeply human behavior to automatically categorize others based solely on the first visual and auditory impression. People who appear Eurasian are attributed different character traits than those who appear African or Asian. Of course, such initial categorizations are not always accurate and are usually corrected through longer interaction. However, in the fully merged environment of the metaverse, users can no longer rely on such perceptions in any way.

Users immerse themselves in the metaverse, typically using avatars that they can design with complete freedom. This applies not only to the avatar's appearance but also to its behavior, which can likewise be scripted. This raises the question of how we should categorize, for example, a gorgon covered in purple plush, standing before us on one of its seven legs, brandishing a giant axe. How do we communicate with an avatar that exhibits such an absurd and certainly unnatural form, shape, and possibly behavior? In the real world, we would likely be extremely cautious and reserved in such a situation, assuming that this being might not be well-disposed toward us. Who can say what might happen if our digital counterpart suddenly decides to swing its axe and injure or even kill our avatar, which—as mentioned above—serves as our digital twin? After all, as real persons, we are fused with our digital avatars. Such situations can have a range of effects, not only on personal behaviors and patterns but also more generally on the structure and behavior of individuals within social groups. If we think positively, we might hope that the metaverse will allow us to leave behind all these prejudiced ways of thinking and mental structures. Where it might lead if we think negatively, the reader is invited to imagine for themselves.

Problems related to sociocultural fusion in the metaverse can also emerge from another perspective. In the future, it will likely be uncommon, or perhaps not occur at all, for us to enter the metaverse and find that the virtual world we are entering is a digital clone or twin of our real world. Of course, such applications will exist; for example, in the tourism industry, it would be highly desirable to have a digital twin of a vacation paradise, as will be discussed in Sect. 4.6.6. In these cases, we could immerse ourselves not only from home but also on-site, enriching our perception with virtual information. Typical examples include classic augmented reality projects, such as visiting an archaeological site where AR can be used to bring the ruins back to life.

In the metaverse, commercially operated platforms will emerge that present innovative virtual worlds independent of the real world, accessible from anywhere on Earth. Here, too, we can draw a comparison to our experiences in the real world: when we board a plane and travel to a remote location in a different cultural context—be it the

Nepalese highlands or a distant Polynesian island—we have some idea, upon disembarking, of the cultural world we are entering. Based on this, we usually infer how we should or should not behave. In a freely designed virtual world, however, such as in the case of the aforementioned gorgon avatar, we cannot make such inferences. Strictly speaking, when we enter such a freely designed virtual world, we are stepping into the creator's imagination. In such a world, the typical laws of the real world do not necessarily apply. The term "laws" here refers not only to sociocultural norms but also to actual legal regulations. Furthermore, it includes physical and other scientific laws. Indeed, a visitor in such a freely designed virtual world cannot be certain whether …

- … the laws of nature, such as gravity or similar principles, also apply in this virtual world, …
- … what the spatial structure of the world is like and how the visitor can orient themselves within it, and …
- … how the avatars present will ultimately respond to their presence and behavior.

For this reason, the user is initially helpless, lacking any information, and must explore the world and its rules on all levels. While some users find this easy, being more open or playful by nature, the initial helplessness can be problematic for others and may prevent them from easily accessing this world.

The integration of the real world with virtual worlds, especially in the area of sociocultural fusion but also in other domains such as economic integration—which will be examined in more detail in the following major Chap. 4—poses significant challenges for the legislative, judicial, and executive branches. The foundations for these challenges can already be observed and derived from current dealings with the Internet. However, these challenges will be far greater in the metaverse. For example, the question arises as to which legal rules actually apply in a virtual world. Let us consider a thought experiment: two avatars meet in the digital world and both perform the same action. In the physical origin of one avatar's real-world counterpart, this action is permitted, while in the physical origin of the other's, it is prohibited. What are the implications for the virtual world? Which rules and laws apply here?

The term "action" has been deliberately chosen in this context, as it can refer to both a social action and any other type of action, such as an economic transaction, as previously indicated. Henz describes this issue very vividly [HEN22]:

"Even if a metaverse platform is used globally, users must comply with the laws of their physical region. This is important because crimes can also occur in virtual reality, such as harassment, stalking, theft, elimination, or kidnapping of an avatar. If potential perpetrators and victims come from different countries, additional laws may apply. This depends on the extent to which a country is able to extend its legal system internationally. The avatar can be perceived as a unique part of the user; any form of violence against it would have relevant effects on the person, even if it were committed while the user was offline and the avatar was acting semi-autonomously. The perceived safety of being in the metaverse, as well as the consequences in the physical world, is essential to encourage users to stay."

3.6.4 Fusion in Everyday Life: Leisure, Culture, Art …

While the previous Sect. 3.6.3 examined the user both individually and from a societal perspective as a social being, this section focuses on the practical, everyday world of this social being. The range of individual topics that arise here is, of course, so broad that a single book would not suffice to explore each in depth. Nevertheless, this section aims to provide at least a brief impression and insight into various areas of daily life. As examples, one application domain will be presented for each of the three major everyday topics: leisure, art, and culture.

A close look at leisure activities reveals that technologies such as VR and AR have become increasingly established in this area. For example, there is a growing number of offerings that further develop the now well-established leisure activities such as escape rooms and laser tag arenas. These are often based on the CAVE concept, where, as previously described, the visitor enters a squash court-like space in which a VR world is projected onto every wall, as well as the floor and ceiling. The visitor is thus literally standing in the middle of the VR world. Before entering, the visitor puts on equipment fitted with sensors that enable the detection of their movements and translate them into positional changes and interactions. The visitor is therefore not merely passive but can move freely within the projected world and interact with various digital artifacts. However, since the projection is limited to the walls surrounding the user, interaction with the artifacts is still relatively restricted. A further technical approach involves the visitor also entering a room, but the projection of the virtual world is delivered via a VR headset, which the visitor wears in addition to the sensor-equipped gear. This scenario is actually similar to what many gamers already experience at home when they enhance their gaming consoles with a VR headset. However, professional leisure installations offer a significant added value in that users can actually move around within the installation—something that is often impossible or highly problematic at home due to limited space. Moreover, in these professional environments, the powerful computer systems installed make it possible to experience the selected VR world collaboratively. This often closely resembles the frequently cited example of OASIS from Ready Player One. The aim here is either action games or escape room scenarios, which can be offered in various themes suitable for almost all age groups.

The leisure activities just mentioned are entirely based on virtual reality. However, when discussing the merging of virtual and real worlds, especially in the leisure sector, it is important not to overlook another trend that is much older than the VR offerings described above. This involves the genuine integration of digital leisure activities into real-life presence, in the form of digital or virtual games that are played in the real world.

The most well-known example of this form of merging, with a focus on leisure, is likely Pokémon Go, developed by Niantic and published by Nintendo in 2015. In a very short time, the game became a huge success, prompting hundreds of thousands of players worldwide to chase after virtual Pokémon characters. Thus, Pokémon Go was the first game to successfully merge the real world with a digital game world and virtual content, and to become widely known to the public [MAR15]. There were already some predecessors, such as the game Ingress, on which Pokémon Go is actually based, but these were primarily technical feasibility studies and not games intended for a broad audience.

For example, in November 2021, Pokémon Go entered into a special collaboration with British singer-songwriter Ed Sheeran. As part of an event, an exclusive video of Sheeran performing several of his hits—including "Perfect," "Bad Habits," and "Shivers"—was presented in the Pokémon Go app. Accompanying this, an in-game event took place in which water-type Pokémon appeared more frequently—a tribute to Sheeran's fondness for water-type starter Pokémon in the main series games. In addition, the popular sunglasses-wearing Squirtle returned, available both in the wild and through field research tasks. With this collaboration, Sheeran expressed his long-standing enthusiasm for the Pokémon series, while also creating a successful connection between music and gaming. Through such events, Pokémon Go manages to incorporate cultural phenomena and continuously expand the gaming experience for its community [POK21].

The idea of combining virtual worlds, familiar from computer games, with the real world is, however, much older than Pokémon Go, as demonstrated by the example of PacManhattan from 2004, initiated by the Tisch School of the Arts at New York University. In this urban game, the rectangular layout of Manhattan's streets served as the basis for transferring the Pac-Man game into the real world. In this version, a human player took on the role of Pac-Man, while other players acted as the hostile Pac-Man ghosts chasing the player. These ghosts received instructions on where to run from a central command, where the positions of the human players in the real environment were managed and decisions were made about the ghosts' movements. Although the degree of digitization was relatively low, the level of merging between the real world and the game world was quite high. This is evidenced not only by video recordings but also by reports on the game [LANoJ,LAN09].

But even PacManhattan is not the first example of merging the real and digital worlds. As early as 1996, an attempt was made—with a significantly higher degree of digitization—to integrate a virtual game world into the real world. Students at the School of Computer and Information Science at the University of South Australia attempted to transfer the then-popular shooter game Quake to the university parking lot using augmented reality. Considering the computing power available at the time, the results are still quite impressive even by today's standards [PIEoJ,PIE02].

It seems highly relevant to use the merging of real and virtual worlds not only for the acquisition and processing of information, but also with the aim of experiencing games in this way. This is currently evident on an even larger scale in the entertainment sector. Here, not only the VR-based installations presented above, but also renowned amusement parks are increasingly relying on this merging. The brand term "Coastality" hints at the goal of these efforts [COAoJ], namely to further enhance the experience of roller coaster rides with VR technologies. Passengers sit in the coaster train and wear VR headsets during the ride. As a result, they are visually disconnected from the real environment and immersed in a virtual world. The other sensory modalities remain unaffected, meaning the physical sensations of a typical roller coaster ride—such as acceleration, wind, and the laughter and screams of fellow riders—originate from the real world and are perceived as such [PLOoJ].

For passengers, it may be a physical challenge to wear a VR headset of the current size and weight during the accelerations of a roller coaster ride. However, the required registration of the passenger is significantly lower compared to AR games such as the aforementioned AR Quake. Here, registration can be accomplished by installing sensors on the ride itself, tailored to the specific environment. This increases the accuracy of registration. In addition, the graphical representation—that is, the rendering of virtual artifacts—is much simpler in this context. Since the entire world into which the passenger is immersed is rendered, there is no need to precisely insert virtual artifacts into the passenger's visual perception. The world's first ride experience enhanced in this way was the Galaxy Express at the Space Center Bremen, introduced in 2003. This was an indoor steel roller coaster, where the ride was supported by screens embedded in the passenger cars that rendered the VR effect. The result was reportedly quite impressive, although this can no longer be verified, as the Space Center in Bremen closed after only a short time [AIR14].

Although the Galaxy Express was not successful, the technology it was based on served as a foundation for further developments. The developer and manufacturer Mack GmbH & Co. KG has been designing and building roller coasters since 1921 and has been closely associated with Europa-Park in Rust since 1975, which was also founded by the Mack family. The area around this park has now become a hub for the integration of VR, AR, and amusement park technologies. In addition to virtually enhanced roller coasters in the park, there are also dedicated VR experiences in the immediate vicinity, where research and development in this field are conducted and transferred into application and operation. Some of these developments and attractions are technically connected beyond today's standard, such as the possibility of experiencing VR in and under water during a virtual snorkeling and diving trip.

The enhancement of roller coasters and other rides with VR and AR technologies is not only interesting for passengers, but also represents a significant economic factor for operators. Equipping an existing ride with VR technology makes it possible to change the experience for the passenger without altering the mechanical construction. Typically, such rides also have a limited period of acceptance and must be replaced by new or different rides at regular intervals to maintain their appeal. VR technology offers the possibility of exchanging the virtual world in which the ride is embedded around the real-world construction, thereby offering a novel ride experience. However, there are still no long-term studies on how much the operational lifespan of mechanical constructions can be extended through the use of VR and AR.

In the realm of cultural entertainment, particularly in pop culture, there is a growing number of active examples indicating that the merging of virtual and real worlds is becoming increasingly relevant in this domain as well. However, the approaches differ. One such example is Cathy Hackl's thought experiment, in which artists from the real world perform in virtual environments. A long list of artists now perform in virtual worlds such as Fortnite, Decentraland, and Roblox. Ariana Grande's 2021 concert in Fortnite reportedly attracted around 78 million viewers [WEB21] and generated revenues of approximately €20 million [DAI21]. Various video recordings on YouTube and other video platforms [MEI21] also show a considerable number of active avatars during the virtual performance. Even though 78 million avatars are not clearly visible, the event can still be considered a success. Although not every virtual concert event can be regarded as such a success, the Ariana Grande event demonstrates that success is indeed possible. However, this does not apply to every virtual concert. Opinions on the success or failure of the Decentraland Metaverse Music Festival 2022, which is shown again in Fig. 3.12, differ significantly. While the platform operator describes the event as a success in company-affiliated blogs and publications, citing high virtual attendance and revenue, other sources are far more critical. For example, around 100 students from the Computer Science, Business Informatics, and Digital Transformation programs at FOM University in Munich were asked to participate in the event [HOF22]. The feedback collected and discussed afterwards ranged from incomprehension to dismay regarding the quality of the graphical rendering and the small number of visible user avatars. None of the students—who, given their technical background and age, are considered a target audience for such platforms and events—rated the event positively or indicated that they could imagine attending music festivals in this way in the future. Reports from established magazines such as Metal Hammer point in the same direction [GER22].

The aforementioned Decentraland Metaverse Music Festival 2022 clearly highlights the challenges of such events, especially in comparison to events like the previously mentioned Ariana Grande concert in Fortnite. Due to the small number of avatars present, it was impossible to create the typical festival atmosphere familiar to attendees of events like Rock am Ring or Wacken Open Air. The olfactory and haptic sensations that are characteristic of festivals were absent. Moreover, the technical execution of this event was questionable. Decentraland must therefore consider whether it is truly necessary to model and implement a three-dimensional virtual venue if only YouTube videos or livestreams are being shown on virtually installed screens. Would it not have been better to simply show these videos on a regular screen? This example also demonstrates that big names alone do not guarantee success. The well-known Ozzy Osbourne attempted to market his renowned metal festival Ozzfest as part of DMMF 2022 in a virtual format. A dedicated virtual festival venue was modeled and implemented for this purpose. However, here too, mainly videos of famous metal bands were shown. The marketing for this virtual Ozzfest did go a step further, as in addition to the videos, Ozzy Osbourne himself and the late Lemmy Kilmister of Motörhead appeared as avatars on the virtual

3.6 All-together – The Path to Socio-cultural Convergence

Fig. 3.12 The Decentraland Metaverse Music Festival 2022. (Screenshots: DMMF 2022, Peter Hoffmann, Invisible Cow)

stage. Yet even these virtual performances cannot be considered successful. The modeling of the avatars was reminiscent of the graphics quality of early computer games, and the avatars' movements were limited and not synchronized with the music or vocals [GER22,HOF22].

At this point, another issue must be mentioned, one that is independent of the DMMF events and the platform itself. The question arises as to the extent to which interaction devices such as VR headsets impair immersion, even if the graphical rendering and photorealistic modeling of the musicians' avatars were of the highest quality. Despite good wearing comfort, the weight of these devices is noticeable and affects users' mobility. It can be assumed that typical physical behaviors associated with music genres like metal are hindered. Headbanging with a VR headset will likely only become a reality when these devices become significantly smaller and lighter than they are today.

In addition to the technical points of discussion and criticism raised in connection with the implementation of virtual music events such as the DMMF, some of the visitors surveyed subsequently initiated a more ethical debate. The serious question was raised as to whether it is acceptable to have deceased artists, who did not give their consent, appear posthumously as avatars, especially for commercial purposes. While Ozzy Osbourne's real-life counterpart was still alive at the time of DMMF 2022, Lemmy Kilmister had already passed away in December 2015. It is likely that this question cannot be answered universally. However, there are now a number of events in which deceased artists perform together with living musicians before a real audience in the real world. Examples include the hologram shows of Ronnie James Dio [BAK21,BLI19], Michael Jackson [FEE14,VIB23], and other artists. The main argument for this merging of real worlds with virtual artifacts is often that it allows younger people to experience concerts with these artists. Hologram technology creates an impressive experience, especially since it engages not only the visual and auditory modalities, as is the case with virtual concert experiences, but also provides a concrete and real concert experience.

A brief look at the film industry also reveals the growing importance of digital technologies in reviving deceased actors. A prominent example is the film "Rogue One: A Star Wars Story" from 2016, in which Peter Cushing, who died in 1994, was digitally reconstructed as Grand Moff Tarkin. To achieve this, the Lucasfilm production team used a combination of computer-generated imagery (CGI) and motion-capture technology to project Cushing's face and expressions onto the body of actor Guy Henry. However, this digital resurrection raised ethical and legal concerns, particularly regarding the posthumous use of an actor's likeness without their explicit consent. theguardian.com [PUL17].

Similarly, in 2019's "Star Wars: The Rise of Skywalker," the character Leia Organa was brought back to life using CGI and previously unreleased footage of Carrie Fisher, who passed away in 2016. Although these techniques make it possible to maintain character continuity in film series, they also raise questions about authenticity and respect for the legacy of deceased actors [SAR16].

The practice of using avatars or CGI in general to depict deceased actors has sparked a broader debate about the ethical implications of such technologies, both within the film industry and beyond. While some argue that these methods can preserve the artistic integrity and legacy of actors, others see them as potential exploitation and a violation of posthumous personality rights. There is also concern that the increasing sophistication of these technologies could lead to the replacement of living actors with digital avatars, raising fundamental questions about the future of the acting profession [LEF23].

In this way, not only can deceased artists be brought back to the screen and stage, but it is also possible to experience living artists in action through such means. A truly impressive example of this is the Swedish group ABBA, which in 2022 had its own concert hall built in London, where the so-called "Abbatars" perform in a show as virtual twins of the band members [ABB23,ASW23]. Interestingly, in this case, the digital twins were de-aged and do not correspond to the actual age of the real individuals. This broadly aligns with the idea of temporal fusion discussed in Sect. 3.4, where the temporal progression between the real and virtual worlds is first altered and only then merged.

Similar to ABBA, the rock band KISS has also found the use of digital avatars interesting enough to expand their musical presence beyond traditional live performances. In collaboration with Industrial Light & Magic (ILM) and Pophouse Entertainment, the Swedish company also behind ABBA's "Voyage" show, KISS plans to use digital likenesses of its members for future performances after the conclusion of the "End of the Road" tour and their farewell to live stage shows. These avatars were first introduced at the band's farewell concert in December 2023 at Madison Square Garden, where they were presented as larger-than-life holographic projections with spectacular effects such as flying and fire-breathing [HEL23].

The technology behind these avatars is based on current motion-capture techniques, in which the movements of the band members are recorded in special suits and digitally reproduced. Gene Simmons, bassist and co-founder of KISS, emphasized that these digital representations allow the band to "stay forever young and iconic" and to bring their performances to places that were previously unimaginable [BAU23]. While ABBA primarily uses their avatars to reproduce classic performances, KISS plans to equip their digital likenesses with additional superpowers and effects to create an even more intense experience. Paul Stanley, guitarist and co-founder of KISS, described the planned project as a mix of "KISS and Cirque du Soleil on steroids" and emphasized that the avatars will look "insanely realistic."

The idea of merging real and virtual elements can be taken even further by completely dispensing with human participation on stage. The successful and usually sold-out concert events of Hatsune Miku are an excellent example of this. Originally designed in 2007 as a drawn mascot for a software synthesizer, this character quickly evolved—thanks to the artificially synthesized singing voice of the software—into a singer who released singles and albums in the J-Pop genre that achieved considerable success [REH21]. Barely a year after the first album release, Hatsune Miku performed live for the first time—virtually on a video screen—at Japan's largest anime music concert. The positive response to the concert and music releases led to Hatsune Miku performing every year since 2013 in August in Japan as a hologram before a real audience under the name Magical Mirai, and she now also tours worldwide as Miku Expo [CLI20].

At this point, the circle is undoubtedly completed, which began with Cathy Hackl's concert description in the previous Sect. 3.6.3: The fusion of virtual and real worlds in the field of concert events can now be considered established and successful. However, the limits of creativity and possibilities have certainly not yet been reached. Further developments are emerging in the highly dynamic pop culture of South Korea. In the K-Pop business, the Korean counterpart to J-Pop, the metaverse is deliberately addressed and considered in the planning and design of new groups. There are now a number of bands in South Korea that, like Hatsune Miku, are purely virtual. For example, the K-Pop girl group Eternity, introduced in 2021, consists of 11 members, all of whom are virtual characters [BBC22]. In contrast to the manually modeled avatars of Lemmy Kilmister and Ozzy Osbourne mentioned above, the characters in this group are photorealistic thanks to AI rendering. The founding of such bands, at least in the case of Eternity, is not artistically motivated. Rather, it is argued that, especially in the K-Pop industry, human stars often reach their physical and mental limits, as the demands of perfectly choreographed performances and the number of events these groups must attend are extreme. Virtual characters have clear advantages over human performers in this regard [BUS23,MUR22,NOO22,YOU23]. While these purely virtual groups are widely accepted by audiences, even the industry leaders and creators behind these groups admit that they would probably still prefer real groups [BBC22]:

> "Honestly, if someone asks me, 'Do you want to watch Billlie on the metaverse for 100 minutes or in real life for ten minutes?', I'll choose to see Billlie for ten minutes in real life."

A different approach to merging real and virtual presence is pursued by the South Korean label SM Entertainment with the group aespa. This group consists of four real members, for whom digital twins were developed and presented at the time of the group's formation. In various ways, the human members interact with their digital counterparts. The possibility is also utilized that the virtual twins can represent the group independently of the human members, thereby helping to reduce the physical and mental strain on individual members [STEoJ]. In addition, these digital band members are also interesting from a business perspective, as they can serve as the basis for collectible and merchandise strategies.

The creation of 3D worlds itself, and especially that of 3D avatars—regardless of whether they are produced using AI-assisted tools or entirely manually by traditional means—requires not only extensive technical knowledge and skills. In fact, many examples of such 3D models are characterized by a high level of artistic ambition. Digital art has now become an established genre within the art world. This reveals an intersection with renowned computer artists such as Herbert W. Franke [FRA01], Frieder Nake [DIE86], and others, who already in the early days of computer development sought to establish a connection between new technology and art. This ever-closer relationship between art and technology has been observable since 1979 at Ars Electronica, which has since become one of the leading platforms and annual events for electronic art in the broadest sense [ARSoJ,FORoJ].

A brief look at the artworks and performances presented over time shows that, in this environment, artistic engagement and exchange with the metaverse and its associated technologies have been taking place for quite some time. The examples range from exploiting the interactive possibilities between visitors and artistic artifacts, to proactive 3D installations, and even to augmenting the real world with digital art objects. Interestingly, even before the term metaverse was introduced, artistic experimentation with the fusion aspects described above was already underway. This extends to artworks that play with the temporal relationship between visitor and artwork. This artistic environment provides a space where things and ideas can simply be tried out, without needing to fulfill any direct economic or other purpose. It can also be seen as a playground for technical ideas that may eventually find their way into serious applications at some undetermined point in the future.

It is hardly surprising that, in examining the connection between the art world and the metaverse, the current metaverse—much like its predecessor Second Life about 20 years ago—is regarded by many exhibitors and museums as a potentially significant venue for future presence. However, developments in the context of the metaverse go far beyond what was possible in Second Life [SECoJ,HUA14]. While in Second Life, museums and exhibitions were almost exclusively designed by their real-world counterparts, i.e., museums in the physical world, the metaverse, through its openness and the much simpler possibilities for creating custom worlds on numerous platforms, now offers anyone interested the opportunity to design their own virtual museum or exhibition. For this purpose, there are dedicated platforms such as Spatial.io, which pursue exactly this goal [SPAoJ].

3.6.5 The Fusion in Everyday Life: The World of Work

Another fundamental aspect of everyday human life is undoubtedly the world of work. In this area as well, the concept of the metaverse will gain increasing significance in the future. However, it should be emphasized that the integration of the metaverse and the workplace is already an established and widespread application.

Although the term "metaverse" has not yet been frequently mentioned in this context, the associated technologies have been the subject of research and development for use in the workplace for some time. There are numerous examples of the implementation and use of virtual reality for a wide range of applications, as well as for the use of augmented reality. In addition, it has been common practice for many years for production lines and manufacturing halls to have a digital twin. These digital twins are used to analyze the installation of equipment and production machinery, as well as workflows and potential hazard areas. For this reason, this area will not be explored further here; instead, reference is made to the extensive publications by, for example, Bitkom and other industry associations and research institutions.

At this point, it is also deliberately questioned whether the vision of future workplaces so impressively presented by Mark Zuckerberg during the announcement of Facebook's rebranding to Meta is actually realistic. Only future work scenarios will reveal whether typical office workplaces—where people work with ERP systems, spreadsheets, or word processing—are suitable environments that can be transferred into the metaverse or at least transformed through AR and VR. This also applies to other workplaces, situations, and industries. The same question likely arises for retail or skilled trades such as hairdressers or electrical work. Ultimately, it will depend on how the term metaverse is defined in the future. The support of work through augmented and virtual reality technologies can certainly be successful in the future. However, whether this will actually be the case remains uncertain for now, even though numerous research projects are active in this area.

3.6.6 Or the Opposite: The Defusion of ...

If fusion is such a central element in the establishment of a metaverse, which can be viewed from various perspectives as outlined above, the question arises whether the opposite—a "defusion," and thus a deliberate separation of certain aspects—is also conceivable and might even be advantageous in some situations.

The first thought that likely comes to mind in this context is that the user sends their digital twin into the metaverse with a task to complete independently. A vivid example of this is again the concert scenario. The user wants to spontaneously attend a metaverse concert that includes both real and virtual elements but does not yet have a ticket. While making their way to the real venue in the physical world, they instruct their avatar in the virtual space to independently visit the virtual concert location and purchase tickets there. This allows the user to focus on traffic and transportation in the real world without having to worry about buying tickets themselves. Ultimately, this idea is not new but rather an evolution of the already existing assistance solutions in the workplace.

However, this defusion does not have to be limited to the separation of virtual and real artifacts. In fact, it can be particularly useful to deliberately introduce the idea of separation within the virtual environment itself. Here again, the concert scenario provides a clear example. According to the organizers, the Ariana Grande concert on Fortnite mentioned in Section 3.6.4 was attended by about 78 million guests [WEB21,WIC21]. Even today's supercomputers are not capable of allowing each of these guests to bring their own virtual avatar to such an event, as registration and rendering are highly computationally intensive. The IT infrastructure would quickly reach its limits. Moreover, even in the virtual world, each avatar needs a space to occupy, just as a human guest in the real world needs a place from which to view the concert. One of the largest concerts in the real world was the Rolling Stones' 2006 performance in Rio de Janeiro during their "Bigger Bang" world tour. Approximately 1.5 million visitors are said to have gathered at Copacabana Beach for the event [ROH06]. They were spread out along the roughly 4 km long beach. Assuming that an avatar in the metaverse requires about as much space as a person in the real world, one can imagine the scale of a concert venue that would need to accommodate 78 million guests. For this reason, both due to computing capacity and user experience, it makes sense to split the event and hold the concert in several parallel sessions. That this works and is accepted by attendees is demonstrated by the concert of the artist Marshmello, which also took place in Fortnite in 2019. Although only 11 million guests attended this concert in the metaverse, computing power and virtual space would still have posed a challenge to a high-quality concert experience. Fortnite divided this concert into 100,000 instances, each with only about 100 attendees. Users accepted this situation and this defusion, even though they could see and interact with only a few of the other guests. Nevertheless, the concert itself was an enjoyable experience for every attendee [RUB19,WEB19].

In addition to the technical and practical considerations already mentioned, there are certainly further aspects that can be considered separately. In some situations, it might be interesting or simply advantageous to implement a temporal defusion, placing the human and the digital twin on separate timelines. On the digital twin's timeline, the sequence of events could then be accelerated or slowed down. Ultimately, this idea moves in the direction of the previously considered virtual assistance.

References

[ABB23]	ABBA (2023). Voyage. Online: https://abbavoyage.com/ (Retrieved: 19.05.2023).
[AIR14]	Airtimers (03.08.2014). Galaxie Express [2003/04] Space Center Bremen. In: Airtimers. Online: http://forum.airtimers.com/index.php?/topic/3807-galaxie-express-200304-space-center-bremen/ (Retrieved: 22.05.2023).
[ARSoJ]	Ars Electronica (o.J.). Ars Electronica. Online: https://ars.electronica.art (Retrieved: 10.05.2023).
[ASC12]	Ascher, Franziska (27.08.2012). Immersion – Die Faszinationskraft virtueller Welten. In: Paidia Zeitschrift für Computerspielforschung. Online: https://www.paidia.de/immersion (Retrieved: 17.05.2023).
[ASW23]	Aswad, Jem (02.05.2023). ABBA's 'Voyage' Virtual Concert to Go on Tour 'Around the World'. In: Variety. Online: https://variety.com/2023/music/news/abba-voyage-virtual-concert-tour-1235541368/ (Retrieved: 19.05.2023).
[AYR13]	Ayres, Anna Jean (2013). Bausteine der kindlichen Entwicklung – Sensorische Integration verstehen und anwenden. Heidelberg: Springer, 5. Auflage.
[AYR79]	Ayres, Anna Jean (1979). Sensory Integration and the Child. Los Angeles: Western Psychological Services.
[BAI04]	Jeremy N. Bailenson; James Blascovich (2004). Avatars. In: Encyclopedia of Human-Computer Interaction. ABC-CLIO, Santa Barbara.
[BAI18]	Jeremy Bailenson (2018). Experience on Demand: What Virtual Reality Is, How It Works, and What It Can Do. W. W. Norton & Company, New York. ISBN-13: 978-0393253696.
[BAR19]	Barbara Rita Barricelli; Elena Casiraghi; Daniela Fogli (2019). A Survey on Digital Twin: Definitions, Characteristics, Applications, and Design Implications. In: IEEE Access, vol. 7, pp. 167653–167671, 2019, https://doi.org/10.1109/ACCESS.2019.2953499.
[BAK21]	Baker, Danica (05.04.2021). Ronnie James Dio's hologram for 'Dio Returns' cost $2.6 million. In: Tone Deaf. Online: https://tonedeaf.thebrag.com/widow-reveals-price-of-dio-hologram/ (Retrieved: 19.05.2023).
[BAL20]	Ball, Matthew (13.01.2020). What It Is, Where to Find it, and Who Will Build It. Online: https://www.matthewball.vc/all/themetaverse (Retrieved: 17.05.2023).
[BAL21b]	Ball, Matthew (28.06.2021). Evolving User + Business Behaviors and the Metaverse. In: The Metaverse Primer. Online: https://www.matthewball.vc/all/userbehaviorsmetaverse (Retrieved: 17.05.2023).

[BAL22] Ball, Matthew; Furness, Thomas; Inbar, Ori; Kalinowski, Caitlin; Lange, Danny; Lebaredian, Rev; Mann, Steve; Miralles, Evelyn; Rosedale, Philip; Trevett, Neil; Yuan, Yu (14.06.2022): Metaverse decoded by top experts. In: Versemaker: Metaverse Lands-cape & Outlook Series. Online: https://versemaker.org/download (Retrieved: 10.05.2023).

[BAU23] Kristina Baum (03.12.2023). Hier verwandeln sich Kiss in Avatare. Rolling Stone. Online: https://www.rollingstone.de/hier-verwandeln-sich-kiss-avatare-video-2678055/. (Retrieved: 14.02.2025).

[BBC22] BBC (12.12.2022). K-pop: The rise of the virtual girl bands. In BBC Asia. Online: https://www.bbc.com/news/world-asia-63827838 (Retrieved: 19.05.2023).

[BET19] Bettels, Lutz (15.12.2019). Der digitale Zwilling—Die nächste Evolutionsstufe der BIM-Methode. Deutsche BauZeitschrift. Bauverlag BV GmbH. Online: https://www.dbz.de/artikel/dbz_Der_digitale_Zwilling-3472174.html (Retrieved: 20.05.2025).

[BIT22] bitkom (2022). Wegweiser in das Metaversum – Technologische und rechtliche Grundlagen, geschäftliche Potenziale, gesellschaftliche Bedeutung. In: Bitkom e. V., AG Metaverse Forum, Projektleitung: Dr. Sebastian Klöß. Online: https://www.bitkom.org/Bitkom/Publikationen/Wegweiser-Metaverse (Retrieved: 10.05.2023).

[BLA13] Blake Joshua (12.08.2013). Einführung in natürliche Benutzeroberflächen (NUI) und Kinect – Kinect für Windows: Blog für Entwickler. In: Microsoft Shows. Online: https://learn.microsoft.com/de-de/shows/k4wdev/introduction-to-natural-user-interfaces-nui-kinect (Retrieved: 21.05.2023).

[BLI19] Blistein, Jon (09.04.2019). Ronnie James Dio Hologram to Tour U.S. In: Rolling Stone. Online: https://www.rollingstone.com/music/music-news/ronnie-james-dio-hologram-us-tour-dates-820040/ (Retrieved: 19.05.2023).

[BLU21] Blug, Finn (14.10.2021). Immersion: Eintauchen ins Metaverse. In: ada. Online: https://ada-magazin.com/de/immersion-eintauchen-ins-metaverse (Retrieved: 17.05.2023).

[BOL80] Bolt, Richard A. (1980). Put that there: Voice and gesture at the graphics interface. In: SIGGRAPH '80: Proceedings of the 7th annual conference on Computer graphics and interactive techniques; July 1980 Pages 262–270. https://doi.org/10.1145/800250.807503.

[BRY14] Erik Brynjolfsson; Andrew McAfee (2014). The Second Machine Age: Work, Progress, and Prosperity in a Time of Brilliant Technologies. W. W. Norton & Company, New York. ISBN: 978-0-393-35064-7.

[BUS23] Buse, Keskin (16.03.2023). Metaverse K-pop girl band MAVE goes viral on social media. In: Reuters, Daily Sabah. Online: https://www.dailysabah.com/life/science/metaverse-k-pop-girl-band-mave-goes-viral-on-social-media (Retrieved: 19.05.2023).

[CAS00] Justine Cassell; Henry Jenkins (2000). From Barbie to Mortal Kombat: Gender and Computer Games. MIT Press, Cambridge. ISBN-13: 978-0262531689.

[CAS06] Edward Castronova (2006). Synthetic Worlds: The Business and Culture of Online Games. University of Chicago Press, Chicago. ISBN-13: 978-0226096278.

[CLI11] Cline, Ernest (2011). Ready Player One. Blanvalet Verlag, München 2014, ISBN 978-3-442-38030-5.

[CLI20] Cliff, Aimee (12.01.2020). Hatsune Miku review – hologram star fires up crowdsourced power pop. In: The Guardian. Online: https://www.theguardian.com/music/2020/jan/12/hatsune-miku-review-london-02-academy-brixton-london (Retrieved: 19.05.2023).

References

[COAoJ]	Coastiality (o.J.). Coastiality – Entdecke neue unglaubliche Welten. Online: https://coastiality.com/ (Retrieved: 19.05.2023).
[DAI21]	Daily Local (04.08.2021). Ariana Grande to earn more than „$20m" for virtual Fortnite concert. In: Daily Local News. Online: https://www.dailylocal.com/2021/08/04/ariana-grande-to-earn-more-than-20m-for-virtual-fortnite-concert/ (Retrieved: 19.05.2023).
[DAN21]	Danneberg, Benjamin (19.09.2021). Feelbelt im Test: Zwischen Sound-Wucht und Haptikbrei. In: Mixed. Online: https://mixed.de/feelbelt-test/ (Retrieved: 20.05.2021).
[DER19]	Dernbach, Beatrice; Godulla, Alexander; Sehl, Annika (08.01.2019). Komplexität im Journalismus. Springer Fachmedien Wiesbaden GmbH, ein Teil von Springer Nature. https://doi.org/10.1007/978-3-658-22860-6_8.
[DIE86]	Dietrich, Frank (1986). Visual Intelligence: The First Decade of Computer Art (1965–1975). In: Leonardo, vol. 19, no. 2, 1986, pp. 159–69. JSTOR, https://doi.org/10.2307/1578284. (Retrieved: 19.05.2023).
[DOB17]	Dobbelstein, David; Winkler, Christian; Haas, Gabriel; Rukzio, Enrico. (2017). PocketThumb: a Wearable Dual-Sided Touch Interface for Cursor-based Control of Smart-Eyewear. Proceedings of the ACM on Interactive, Mobile, Wearable and Ubiquitous Technologies. 1. 1–17. https://doi.org/10.1145/3090055. Online: https://www.researchgate.net/publication/318071779_PocketThumb_a_Wearable_Dual-Sided_Touch_Interface_for_Cursor-based_Control_of_Smart-Eyewear (Retrieved: 17.05.2023).
[DON17]	Donahue, Michelle Z. (09.11.2017). Ein farbenblinder Künstler wurde zum ersten Cyborg der Welt. In: National Geographic. Online: https://www.nationalgeographic.de/wissenschaft/2017/04/ein-farbenblinder-kuenstler-wurde-zum-ersten-cyborg-der-welt (Retrieved: 21.05.2023).
[DÖR10]	Döring, Nicola (2010). Sozialkontakte online: Identitäten, Beziehungen, Gemeinschaften. Handbuch online-kommunikation 1 (2010): 159–183.
[DOU01]	Dourish, P. (2001). Where The Action Is: The Foundations of Embodied Interaction. MIT Press, Cambridge, MA, USA.
[DU25]	Du, Haodong. (2025). The Progress and Trend of Intelligent NPCs in Games. In: Applied and Computational Engineering. 133, 158–164. https://doi.org/10.54254/2755-2721/2025.20635.
[ENG65]	Engelbart, Douglas C.; English, W. K.; Huddart. B. (1965). Computer-aided display control Final report. In: NASA Technical Documents, 1965.
[FEE14]	Feeney, Nolan (19.05.2014). Watch a Michael Jackson Hologram Moonwalk at the Billboard Music Awards. In: Time. Online: https://time.com/104725/michael-jackson-hologram-billboard/ (Retrieved: 19.05.2023).
[FORoJ]	Forum OÖ Geschichte (o.J.). Ars Electronica Festival. Online: https://www.ooegeschichte.at/archiv/themen/kunst-und-kultur/musikgeschichte-oberoesterreichs/musikforschung-und-musikpflege/ars-electronica-festival (Retrieved: 10.05.2023).
[FRA01]	Franke, Herbert W. (2001). Wege zur Computerkunst – ein Rückblick In: Murnau Manila Minsk – 50 Jahre Goethe-Institut. 2001, ISBN 3-406-47542-6.
[FRI09]	Frieling, J. (2009). Zielgruppe Digital Natives: Wie das Internet die Lebensweise von Jugendlichen verändert: Neue Herausforderungen an die Medienbranche. Diplomica Verlag.
[FUL20]	Aidan Fuller; Zhong Fan; Charles Day; Chris Barlow (2020). Digital Twin: Enabling Technologies, Challenges and Open Research. In: IEEE Access, Vol. 8, pp. 108952–108971, 2020. https://doi.org/10.1109/ACCESS.2020.2998358.

[GIB84]   Gibson, William (1984). Neuromancer. Ace.
[GER22]   Gerber, Lothar (15.11.2022). Das Ozzfest im Metaverse: was für ein überflüssiges Event. In: Metal-Hammer. Online: https://www.metal-hammer.de/das-ozzfest-im-metaverse-was-fuer-ein-ueberfluessiges-event-1992083/ (Retrieved: 19.05.2023).
[GRI15]   Michael Grieves. Digital Twin: Manufacturing Excellence through Virtual Factory Replication. White Paper. Online: https://www.researchgate.net/publication/275211047_Digital_Twin_Manufacturing_Excellence_through_Virtual_Factory_Replication. (Retrieved: 14.02.2025).
[GRI17]   Michael Grieves; John Vickers (2017). Digital Twin: Mitigating Unpredictable, Undesirable Emergent Behavior in Complex Systems. In: Kahlen, J., Flumerfelt, S., Alves, A. (eds) Transdisciplinary Perspectives on Complex Systems. Springer, Cham. https://doi.org/10.1007/978-3-319-38756-7_4.
[HAC21]   Hackl, Cathy (27.10.2021). The metaverse is coming. Cathy Hackl explains why we should care. In: Freethink. Online: https://www.freethink.com/hard-tech/building-the-metaverse-cathy-hackl-gives-us-a-glimpse-of-the-future (Retrieved: 21.05.2023).
[HEL23]   Burt Helm (12-03-2023). Kiss exits the stage and leaves its avatar band to rock and roll all night, forever. Fastcompany. Online: https://www.fastcompany.com/90989900/kiss-final-concert-avatar-virtual-band-pophouse. (Retrieved: 14.02.2025).
[HEN22]   Henz, Patrick (2022). The societal impact of the metaverse. In: Discov Artif Intell 2, 19. https://doi.org/10.1007/s44163-022-00032-6 (Retrieved: 19.05.2023).
[HOF10]   Hoffmann, Peter (01.12.2010). „Narrative Realitäten": Informationspräsentation über multimediales, programmiertes Geschichtenerzählen. In: Berichte aus der Informatik. Shaker, Düren.
[HOF21]   Hoffmann, Peter (04.12.2021). Beyond Hypermedia – Interaktion in Hypermedia neu gedacht. bifop-Verlag, Bremen. ISBN: 978-3-948773-27-4.
[HOF22]   Hoffmann, Peter (16.11.2022). Lemmy würde …! Virtual Headbanging beim #DLMVMF Ozzfest. In 1E9, Community #Metaverse. Online: https://1e9.community/t/lemmy-wuerde-virtual-headbanging-beim-dlmvmf-ozzfest/18268 (Retrieved: 19.05.2023).
[HOL04]   Douglas B. Holt (2004). How Brands Become Icons: The Principles of Cultural Branding. Harvard Business Review Press, Brighton. ISBN-13: 9781578517749.
[HUA14]   Huang, Yu-Chun; Han, Sooyeon (2014). An Immersive Virtual Reality Museum via Second Life Extending Art Appreciation from 2D to 3D. Communications in Computer and Information Science. 434. https://doi.org/10.1007/978-3-319-07857-1_102.
[HUS24]   Muhammad Hussain; Shahid Khalil; Raza Hasan; Muhammad Khuram Khalil (2024). The Metaverse Marketing Revolution: How Virtual Worlds Are Redefining Digital Advertising and Paving the Way for Corporate Success. In: AI-Driven Marketing Research and Data Analytics (pp. 360–377), IGI Global. https://doi.org/10.4018/979-8-3693-2165-2.ch020.
[JAC08]   Jacob, Robert; Girouard, Audrey; Hirshfield, Leanne; Horn, Michael; Shaer, Orit; Solovey, Erin; Zigelbaum, Jamie (2008). Reality-based interaction: A framework for post-WIMP interfaces. CHI '08: Proceeding of the Twenty-Sixth Annual SIGCHI Conference on Human Factors in Computing Systems, Florence, Italy, 5–10 April 2008, ACM, New York, NY, pp 201–210.
[JAI11]   Jain, Jhilmil; Lund. Arnold; Wixon, Dennis (07.05.2011). The future of natural user interfaces. In: CHI EA '11: CHI '11 Extended Abstracts on Human Factors in Computing Systems May 2011 Pages 211–214. https://doi.org/10.1145/1979742.1979527.
[JIA22]   Jiaxin, Li; Gongjing, Gao (2022). Socializing in the Metaverse: The Innovation and Challenge of Interpersonal Communication. In: Advances in Social Science, Education and Humanities Research, volume 664. Proceedings of the 2022 8th International Conference on Humanities and Social Science Research (ICHSSR 2022).

References

[JON20]	David Jones; Chris Snider; Aydin Nassehi; Jason Yon; Ben Hicks (2020). Characterising the Digital Twin: A systematic literature review. In: CIRP Journal of Manufacturing Science and Technology. 29.https://doi.org/10.1016/j.cirpj.2020.02.002.
[KAP20]	Jean-Noël Kapferer; Vincent Bastien (2020). The Luxury Strategy: Break the Rules of Marketing to Build Luxury Brands. Kogan Page, London. ISBN-13: 978-0749464912.
[KIM23]	Kim, Se (2023). Virtual fashion experiences in virtual reality fashion show spaces. Frontiers in Psychology. 14. https://doi.org/10.3389/fpsyg.2023.1276856.
[KRE13]	Kress, Bernard; Starner, Thad (2013). A review of head-mounted displays (HMD) technologies and applications for consumer electronics. In: Proceedings of SPIE – The International Society for Optical Engineering. 8720. 87200A. 10.1117/12.2015654.
[LAI01]	John Laird; Michael van Lent (2001). Human-level AI's killer application: Interactive computer games. In: AI Magazine, 22(2), 15–26. https://doi.org/10.1609/aimag.v22i2.1558.
[LAM21]	Lam, Kit Yung; Lee, Lik Han; Hui, Pan (21). A2w: Context-awarerecommendation system for mobile augmented reality web browser. InACM International Conference on Multimedia, United States, October2021. Association for Computing Machinery (ACM).
[LAN09]	Lantz, Frank. (2009). PacManhattan. https://doi.org/10.1007/978-3-7643-8415-9_94.
[LAN17]	Jaron Lanier (2017). Dawn of the New Everything: Encounters with Reality and Virtual Reality. Henry Holt and Company, New York. ISBN-13: 978-1627794091.
[LAN18]	Lanette, Simone; Chua, Phoebe K.; Hayes, Gillian; Mazmanian, Melissa (2018). How much is 'too much'? the role of a smartphone addictionnarrative in individuals' experience of use. Proc. ACM Hum.-Comput. Interact., 2(CSCW), November 2018.
[LANoJ]	Lantz, Frank (o.J.). Pacmanhattan. In: New York University NYU ITP/ IMA. Online: https://www.pacmanhattan.com/about.php (Retrieved: 22.05.2023).
[LEE06]	Kwan Min Lee (2006). Presence, Explicated. In: Communication Theory, Volume 14, Issue 1, 1 February 2004, Pages 27–50. https://doi.org/10.1111/j.1468-2885.2004.tb00302.x.
[LEE20a]	Lee, Lik-Hang; Braud, Tristan; Hosio, S.; Hui, Pan (2020). Towards augmented reality-driven human-city interaction: Current research and futurechallenges. ArXiv, abs/2007.09207, 2020.
[LEE20b]	Lee, Shaun; Teh, Pei-Lee (2020). "Suiting Up" to Enhance Empathy Toward Aging: A Randomized Controlled Study. Frontiers in Public Health. 8. 376. https://doi.org/10.3389/fpubh.2020.00376.
[LEF23]	Lauren Leffer (2023). Ersetzt künstliche Intelligenz bald Schauspieler?. Spektrum.de. Online: https://www.spektrum.de/news/ersetzt-kuenstliche-intelligenz-bald-schauspieler/2166312. (Retrieved: 14.02.2025).
[LIU23]	Liu, Yiming; Yiu, Chun, Zhao, Zhao; Park, Wooyoung; Shi, Rui; Huang, Xingcan; Zeng, Yuyang; Wang, Kuan; Wong, Tsz; Jia, Shengxin; Zhou, Jingkun; Gao, Zhan; Zhao, Ling; Yao, Kuanming; Li, Jian; Sha, Chuanlu; Gao, Yuyu; Zhao, Guangyao; Huang, Ya; Yu, Xinge (2023). Soft, miniaturized, wireless olfactory interface for virtual reality. Nature Communications. 14. https://doi.org/10.1038/s41467-023-37678-4.
[LU20]	Yuqian Lu; Chao Liu; Kevin Wang; Huiyue Huang; Xun Xu (2019). Digital Twin-driven smart manufacturing: Connotation, reference model, applications and research issues. In: Robotics and Computer-Integrated Manufacturing. 61. https://doi.org/10.1016/j.rcim.2019.101837.

[MAN13] Mann, Steve (01.03.2013). My „Augmediated": Life What I've learned from 35 years of wearing computerized eyewear. In: IEEE Spectrum. Online: https://spectrum.ieee.org/view-from-the-valley/consumer-electronics/portable-devices/steve-mann-the-man-who-invented-wearable-computing (Retrieved: 21.05.2023).

[MAN91] Mann, Steve; Wyckoff, Charles (1991). Extended Reality, MIT 4-405, 1991, Online: http://wearcam.org/xr.htm (Retrieved: 17.05.2023).

[MAR15] Marshall, Cain (10.092015). Pokémon go is brought up into the real world through iOS and Android. In: GeekSnack. Online: https://web.archive.org/web/20150912184201/http://www.geeksnack.com/2015/09/10/pokemon-go-is-brought-up-into-the-real-world-through-ios-and-android/ (Retrieved: 21.05.2023).

[MCL64] McLuhan, Marshall (1964). Understanding Media: The Extensions of Man. McGraw-Hill, New York.

[MEI21] MeinMMO (07.08.2021). Fortnite: So lief das Ariana Grande Konzert ab – Lasst es euch nicht entgehen. In:. MeinMMO. Online: https://mein-mmo.de/fortnite-so-lief-das-ariana-grande-konzert-ab-lasst-es-euch-nicht-entgehen/ (Retrieved: 19.05.2023).

[MOR01] Morawe, Volker; Reiff, Tilman (2001). Painstation. In: Kunsthochschule für Medien zu Köln. Online (Memento des Originals vom 28. September 2007 im Internet Archive): https://web.archive.org/web/20070928103548/http://www.khm.de/~morawe/painstation/PainStation_ger.pdf (Retrieved: 20.05.2021).

[MIN13] Minsky, Marvin; Kurzweil, Ray; Mann, Steve (2013). „The society of intelligent veillance." 2013 IEEE International Symposium on Technology and Society (ISTAS): Social Implications of Wearable Computing and Augmediated Reality in Everyday Life. IEEE, 2013.

[MOR23c] Roberto Moro-Visconti; Andrea Cesaretti (2023). Digital Token Valuation Cryptocurrencies, NFTs, Decentralized Finance, and Blockchains. Springer. ISBN-13: 978-3-031-42970-5.

[MUR22] Murray, Sean (28.01.2022). South Korea Is Planning A 'K-Pop Metaverse' With Full Government Support. In: The Gamer. Online: https://www.thegamer.com/south-korea-k-pop-metaverse/ (Retrieved: 19.05.2023).

[NEXoJ] Next Meet (o.J.). Will Metaverse Change How People Interact With The World l Metaverse The Technology Of Future. Online: https://nextmeet.live/people-interacting-in-metaverse-metaverse-the-technology-of-future/ (Retrieved: 17.05.2023).

[NOR02] Norman, Donald A. (2002). The Design Of Everyday Things. Basic Books (Perseus).

[NOO22] Noor, Jasmine; Putri, Andhreta (04.03.2022). A World Beyond: Metaverse and the K-pop Industry. In: Center for Digital Society. Online: https://cfds.fisipol.ugm.ac.id/2022/03/04/a-world-beyond-metaverse-and-the-k-pop-industry/ (Retrieved: 19.05.2023).

[PIE02] Piekarski, Wayne & Thomas, Bruce. (2002). ARQuake: The Outdoor Augmented Reality Gaming System. Commun. ACM. 45. 36–38. https://doi.org/10.1145/502269.502291.

[PIEoJ] Piekarski, Wayne (o.J.). The Wearable Computer Lab at the School of Computer and Information Science, University of South Australia. In: tinmith. Online: https://www.tinmith.net/arquake/ (Retrieved: 22.05.2023).

[PLOoJ] Ploog, Keno (o.J.). Die Entwicklung von VR in Freizeitparks. In: Coasterfriends. Online: https://coasterfriends.de/joomla/magazin/15-sonstige/2934-die-entwicklung-von-vr-in-freizeitparks (Retrieved: 19.05.2023).

[POK21] Pokemon Go Live (2021). A brand-new collaboration event with Ed Sheeran! Online: https://pokemongolive.com/post/ed-sheeran-collab/. (Retrieved: 14.02.2025).

References

[PUL17]	Andrew Pulver (Mon 16 Jan 2017 15.13 CET). Rogue One VFX head: 'We didn't do anything Peter Cushing would've objected to'. The Guardian. Online: https://www.theguardian.com/film/2017/jan/16/rogue-one-vfx-jon-knoll-peter-cushing-ethics-of-digital-resurrections. (Retrieved: 14.02.2025).
[REH21]	Rehagen, Tony (05.05.2021). One of Japan's most beloved pop stars is a hologram. In: experience magazine. Online: https://expmag.com/2021/05/one-of-japans-most-beloved-pop-stars-is-a-hologram/ (Retrieved: 19.05.2023).
[RIV23]	war [WIE22] Giuseppe Riva; Brenda Wiederhold; Fabrizia Mantovani (2023). Searching for the Metaverse: Neuroscience of Physical and Digital Communities. In: Cyberpsychology, behavior and social networking. 27. 10.1089/cyber.2023.0040.
[ROH06]	Rohter, Larry (19.02.2006). The Stones Rock 1.5 Million in Rio Days Before Carnival. In: The New York Times. Online: https://www.nytimes.com/2006/02/19/world/americas/the-stones-rock-15-million-in-rio-days-before-carnival.html (Retrieved: 10.05.2023).
[RUB19]	Rubin, Peter (05.02.2019). Fortnite's Marshmello Concert Is the Future of the Metaverse. In: Wired. Online: https://www.wired.com/story/fortnite-marshmello-concert-vr-ar-multiverse/ (Retrieved: 10.05.2023).
[RUS20]	Stuart Russell; Peter Norvig (2020). Artificial Intelligence: A Modern Approach. Pearson, 4. Auflage. ISBN-13: 978-0134610993.
[SAR16]	Samit Sarkar (Dec 27, 2016, 10:30 PM GMT+1). Rogue One filmmakers explain how they digitally recreated two characters. The Polygon. Online: https://www.polygon.com/2016/12/27/14092060/rogue-one-star-wars-grand-moff-tarkin-princess-leia. (Retrieved: 14.02.2025).
[SCH23a].	Schlott, Karin (10.05.2023). Wenn die Computerblume duftet. In: Spektrum.de. Online: https://www.spektrum.de/news/virtuelle-realitaet-wenn-die-computerblume-duftet/2137641 (Retrieved: 17.05.2023).
[SCHroe02]	Ralph Schroeder (2002). Social Interaction in Virtual Environments: Key Issues, Common Themes, and a Framework for Research. In: Schroeder, R. (eds) The Social Life of Avatars. Computer Supported Cooperative Work. Springer, London. https://doi.org/10.1007/978-1-4471-0277-9_1.
[SCHwir24]	Martin Schwirn (2024). The future of collaboration in virtuality. In: Computer Weekly. Online: https://www.computerweekly.com/feature/The-future-of-collaboration-in-virtuality. (Retrieved: 14.02.2025).
[SECoJ]	Second Life (o.J.). Museen. In: Second Life. Online: https://secondlife.com/destinations/learning/museums (Retrieved: 10.05.2023).
[SPAoJ]	Spatial.io (o.J.). Unlock Your Imagination. Online: https://www.spatial.io/ (Retrieved: 10.05.2023).
[SPI02]	Spielberg, Steven (Regie) (2002). Minority Report. 20th Century Fox.
[SPI18]	Spielberg, Steven (Regie) (2018). Ready Player One. Warner Bros. Pictures.
[STA23]	Staista (2023). Hours of video uploaded to YouTube every minute as of February 2022. In: Statista. Online: https://www.statista.com/statistics/259477/hours-of-video-uploaded-to-youtube-every-minute/ (Retrieved: 21.05.2023).
[STE92]	Stephenson, Neal (1992). Snow Crash. Blanvalet, München 1995. ISBN 978-3-442-23686-2, Kap. 37. Englisches Original: Snow Crash. New York, 1992.
[STEoJ]	Stern, Bradley (o.J.). aespa Is Leading Us Into the Metaverse. Get in loser, we're going to the SMCU. In: MuuMuse. Online: https://muumuse.com/2021/11/aespa-metaverse-sm-entertainment.html/ (Retrieved: 19.05.2023).
[STO22]	Stoyanov, Nadine; Moser, Christian; Kwiatkowski, Marta (2022). Extended Retail – Die Zukunft des Handels ist grenzenlos. Zühlke und GDI/Studie zu «Extended

	Retail». Von: – Zühlke Engineering AG. Online: https://www.zuehlke.com/de/extended-retail-die-zukunft-des-handels-ist-grenzenlos (Retrieved: 17.05.2023).
[SUN23]	Sun T, He X, Li Z. Digital twin in healthcare: Recent updates and challenges. In: Digit Health, Jan. 2023. https://doi.org/10.1177/20552076221149651.
[TAO18]	Fei Tao; He Zhang; Ang Liu; Andrew Y. C. Nee (2018). Digital Twin in Industry: State-of-the-Art. In: IEEE Transactions on Industrial Informatics. 15. 2405–2415. https://doi.org/10.1109/TII.2018.2873186.
[TAO19]	Fei Tao; He Zhang; Ang Liu; Andrew Y. C. Nee (2019). Digital Twin in Industry: State-of-the-Art. In IEEE Transactions on Industrial Informatics, vol. 15, no. 4, pp. 2405–2415, April 2019. https://doi.org/10.1109/TII.2018.2873186.
[TAU16]	Tauziet,Christophe (15.12.2016). Designing for Hands in VR – The next step in buil-ding natural human-machine interactions. In: Design at Meta, Medium. Online: https://medium.com/designatmeta/designing-for-hands-in-vr-61e6815add99 (Retrieved: 17.05.2023).
[TAY15]	T. L. Taylor (2015). Raising the Stakes: E-Sports and the Professionalization of Computer Gaming. MIT Press, Cambridge. ISBN-13: 978-0262527583.
[THEoJ]	The Fabricant x DapperLabs (o.J.): Iridescence. Online: https://www.thefabricant.com/iridescence (Retrieved: 10.05.2023).
[THO06]	Thon, Jan-Noël (2006). Immersion revisited. Varianten von Immersion im Comput-erspiel des 21. Jahrhunderts. In: Christian Hißnauer/Andreas Jahn-Sudmann (Hg.): Medien – Zeit – Zeichen. Beiträge des 19. Film- und Fernsehwissenschaftlichen Kolloquiums. Marburg: Schüren 2006. S. 125–132. Online: https://www.academia.edu/3414149/Immersion_revisited_Varianten_von_Immersion_im_Computerspiel_des_21_Jahrhunderts (Retrieved: 17.05.2023).
[WEB19]	Webster, Andrew (21.02.2019). Fortnite's Marshmello concert was the game's biggest event ever. In: The Verge. Online: https://www.theverge.com/2019/2/21/18234980/fortnite-marshmello-concert-viewer-numbers.
[WEB21]	Webster, Andrew (09.08.2021). Ariana Grande's Fortnite tour was a moment years in the making. In: The Verge. Online: https://www.theverge.com/2021/8/9/22616664/ariana-grande-fortnite-rift-tour-worldbuilding-storytelling (Retrieved: 10.05.2023).
[WEH20]	Wehden, Lars-Ole; Reer, Felix; Janzik, Robin; Tang, Wai Yen; Quandt, Thorsten (17.04.2020). The Slippery Path to Total Presence: How Omnidirectional Vir-tual Reality Treadmills Influence the Gaming Experience. In: Media and Com-munication (ISSN: 2183-2439) 2021, Volume 9, Issue 1, Pages 5–16. https://doi.org/10.17645/mac.v9i1.3170.
[WIC21]	Wickes, Jade (09.08.2021). Inside Ariana Grande's Fortnite virtual concert. In: The Face. Online: https://theface.com/music/ariana-grande-fortnite-rift-tour-performance-gaming-vr-mac-miller-travis-scott-lil-nas-x (Retrieved: 10.05.2023).
[WIE23]	war [WIE22] Brenda, Wiederhold, Brenda (2023). (Mental) Healthcare Consumer-ism in the Metaverse: Is There a Benefit? In: Cyberpsychology, behavior and social networking. 26. 145–146. https://doi.org/10.1089/cyber.2023.29269.editorial.
[VIB23]	Vibe (05.05.2023). Michael Jackson Most Requested Artist for a Hologram Con-cert in Canada. In: Vibe. Online: https://www.mjvibe.com/michael-jackson-most-requested-artist-for-a-hologram-concert-in-canada/ (Retrieved: 19.05.2023).
[YAQ23]	Ibrar Yaqoob; Khaled Salah; Latif U. Khan; Raja Jayaraman; Ala Al-Fuqaha; Mohammed Omar (2023). Digital Twins for Smart Cities: Benefits, Enabling Tech-nologies, Applications, and Challenges. https://doi.org/10.1109/FNWF58287.2023.10520349.

[YOU23]	Young, Jin Yu; Stevens, Matt (29.01.2023). Will the Metaverse Be Entertaining? Ask South Korea. In: The New York Times. Online: https://www.nytimes.com/2023/01/29/business/metaverse-k-pop-south-korea.html (Retrieved: 19.05.2023).
[ZHA19]	Zhang, Yan; Kienzle, Wolf; Ma, Yanjun; Ng, Shiu S.; Benko, Hrvoje; Harrison, Chris (2019). ActiTouch: Robust Touch Detection for On-Skin AR/VR Interfaces. In: UIST '19: Proceedings of the 32nd Annual ACM Symposium on User Interface Software and Technology, October 2019, Pages 1151–1159. https://doi.org/10.1145/3332165.3347869.
[ZIE05]	Ziegler, Jürgen; Lohmann, Steffen; Kaltz, J. Wolfgang (2005). Kontextmodellierung für adaptive webbasierte Systeme. In: C. Stary (Hrsg.): Mensch & Computer 2005: Kunst und Wissenschaft – Grenzüberschreitungen der interaktiven ART. München: Oldenbourg Verlag. 2005, S. 181–189.

4 Another Dimension: Economic Merging

If the metaverse is viewed as an evolution of the Internet, its technical development can be traced back to 1968, when the ARPANET was created. However, the theory underlying the Internet, and especially today's World Wide Web, has roots that go back even further [REDoJ]. As early as 1945, Vannevar Bush presented the theoretical idea of a networked information management and retrieval system in his article "As We May Think" in The Atlantic magazine [BUS45]. At that time, his considerations were still based on static documents, presented two-dimensionally as text and images. Nevertheless, Bush already recognized the need not only to store the documents themselves, but also to preserve the work performed on them for future research purposes. The user interface he envisioned would still be compatible with modern systems, but the Memory Expander, or "Memex," could not be technically realized at that time. Nevertheless, the theoretical concept was revolutionary for its era.

It remains unproven whether or to what extent Vannevar Bush's Memex was considered in the conception of the ARPA network. However, the goal and content of the ARPA network corresponded to the Memex concept, as it aimed to create a decentralized network for communication and data exchange between U.S. universities and research institutions. In 1972, the first email was sent via the ARPA network, which gradually evolved into a precursor of today's Internet. Although only 400 computers were connected to the network in 1983, the number increased significantly thereafter, until the Internet was opened for commercial use in 1989/1990 [HRZoJ].

Around the same time, Tim Berners-Lee at CERN in Zurich began his hypertext project, which was ultimately released in 1991 as the WWW and developed into today's World Wide Web. It thus forms the theoretical and technical foundation for the future metaverse. Interestingly, the development of the WWW parallels the current debate about the metaverse [BER89]. While technology enthusiasts supported and advanced the idea, others dismissed it as a useless hype that would not last. In the case of the WWW, there were voices such as Bill Gates and Ron Sommer who believed that the Internet and the WWW were merely passing trends that would play no role for their companies. Similar opinions can be found in the current discussion about the metaverse.

In the early days of the World Wide Web, the focus was on documents and information. There was an idealistic notion that the web would facilitate access to information and thereby improve access to education and political information, strengthening democratic structures (see also Fig. 4.1). However, it soon became apparent that the web also offered economic potential. The possibility of consumption was integrated into the network, and paper catalogs were transferred into electronic form. Although placing an order initially required overcoming a media discontinuity—order-relevant information had to be sent by phone, fax, or email—this did not hinder the rapid establishment of commercial use of the web. In fact, the situation at the time, in which all information, including catalog content, was freely accessible and retrievable, laid the foundation for the development and success of the web.

At the beginning of the 2000s, the web underwent a significant transformation compared to its earlier version. Thanks to new technologies, programming languages, and concepts, the originally static web was further developed into an interactive medium under the label Web 2.0. The development of wikis played a central role in this process. Although users could already post contributions in forums in the early web, applications such as wikis greatly expanded users' ability to interact with web content. In Web 2.0, users could now work directly with content, for example by editing texts in a wiki or uploading their own content to share with others. The static web, which had served only for content consumption or order processing, was transformed into an interactive web in which every user could participate directly. The economic potential of this participation was quickly recognized, and attempts began to monetize content. However, this proved difficult due to the technology, as digital artifacts and information as content of Web 2.0 could not truly be protected, and users were accustomed to accessing web content free of charge. This "free mentality" remains deeply ingrained among users, and it is still

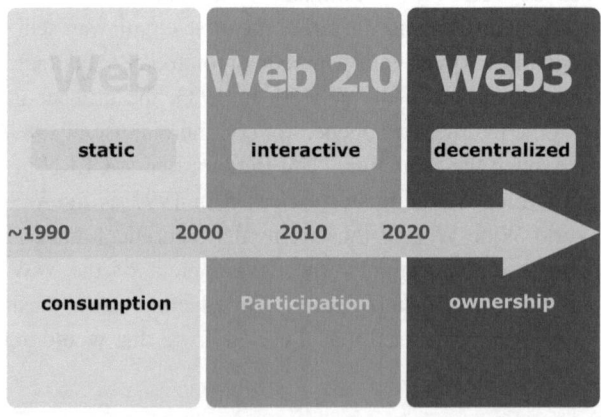

Fig. 4.1 Web 1–2–3. (After [SCHm21a])

extremely difficult to persuade them to pay for content even in Web 2.0. This aspect will be revisited in the following sections.

The original idealistic goals of the early Internet have obviously not been fully realized. The freedom of access to all information is now restricted and controlled from many sides. Furthermore, the underlying technology is a point of criticism and a security risk for certain users, as it is often difficult or even impossible to operate on the Internet without disclosing personal data. In addition, it is gradually being recognized that not all content can be free of charge. The production of media and high-quality journalistic content requires compensation for the effort and work involved. For this reason, since the early 2020s, efforts have been underway to develop a decentralized Internet based on the concept of ownership, intended to replace the interactive Web 2.0. This development is accompanied by new technological approaches such as blockchain, smart contracts, and NFTs, and is expected to form the foundation for the metaverse.

In the metaverse, a significant aspect revolves around the ownership and trade of virtual goods and artifacts. Therefore, it is essential to establish the concept of copyright and intellectual property in virtual spaces to enable ownership and property rights [BIT22]. This contrasts with the common understanding that digital artifacts can be infinitely duplicated, as is typically possible through copy & paste. Blockchain and NFTs now offer at least initial approaches to assign a unique owner to digital objects. This is particularly fundamental in the realm of cryptocurrencies, as the simple duplication of payment units would be economically disastrous. The same applies to digital artifacts such as virtual artworks. Without economic security, the metaverse cannot develop into an independent economic system.

	Web	Web 2.0	Web3
Presentation	• Web browser (WIMP paradigm)	• Web browser • mobile web	• Web browser • mobile web • immersive web
Technology	• HTML • early JavaScript	• HTML • CSS • ECMAScript, TypeScript	• HTML • CSS • ECMAScript, TypeScript • specialized APIs and applications (e.g., Unity)
Data	• Static data • mostly text files with a small proportion of images	• Static data • Dynamic data • User generated content • increasing share of images and video	• Static data • Dynamic data • User generated content • NFT & smart contracts • growing share of synthetic media

	Web	Web 2.0	Web3
Usage	• Communication and linking of documents	• Communication and linking of documents • Application in/for work environments • Social media	• Communication and linking of documents • Application in/for work environments • Social media • Networked ecosystems

According to Chris Dickson of Andreessen Horowitz, it is essential for the metaverse to develop into a fully-fledged economic system that corresponds to our physical lives [SCHm21a]. In this context, users should have the ability to create, acquire, own, sell, or otherwise manage digital artifacts. The example of Second Life demonstrates that paid work is also possible in such a context [SEC19, LAY07]. Therefore, it is absolutely necessary that applications in a metaverse or in various parallel metaverses exhibit the highest degree of interoperability, including interoperability between technical platforms, commercial applications, and the digital and physical worlds [BAL20].

4.1 The Analog Economy of the "Classical Value Chain"

If the metaverse is viewed as an economic system that connects the real and digital economies, the value chain must be adapted to this new environment. Even on the internet, an independent economy has emerged, which, particularly through the widespread adoption of social media and platforms, has evolved into a platform economy. If these are also to play a significant role in the metaverse, individual transactions and business models must be able to merge across the boundary between the real and virtual worlds. The German industry association Bitkom emphasizes in its "Guide to the Metaverse" that the roles of market participants will change, to the point where separate roles can be assumed by a single company or even a single person [BIT22].

To better understand these changes within the value chain in the metaverse, the following sections will first adopt a highly simplified view of this value chain, as shown in Fig. 4.2, and then compare and expand this with existing theories and models from business administration and economics. The aim is to at least provide a basic understanding of the new value chain in the metaverse. The simplification consists in reducing the value chain to three participants:

- the producer, who offers a product or service,
- the consumer, who wishes to consume the product or service, and
- the distributor as intermediary.

Fig. 4.2 Simplified value chain. (Own illustration: Peter Hoffmann, Invisible Cow)

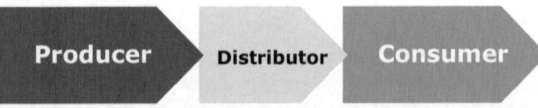

4.2 Early Ideas of Convergence: Prosumerism

While the roles and tasks of producer and consumer will also change, it is the role of the distributor and their responsibilities that will undergo a much more significant transformation and gain central importance.

In the value chain considered here, which is reduced to the essentials, the situation of the classical economy is depicted.

- The role of the producer, as already indicated, is clearly defined in its objectives: the producer aims to manage a product on the market and offer it to the consumer. Despite the strong simplification in this representation, the producer's tasks are extensive. They include both production planning and the procurement of raw materials, operating resources, and especially production equipment. The automotive industry can serve as an example here, where the producer designs a car and also sets up and operates the assembly lines for production.
- In this still classical view of the value chain, the distributor is responsible for transport and sales. Sales is particularly important here, as it establishes the communicative link to the consumer.
- Although the value chain described would not exist without the consumer, their functional role in this context is the least pronounced. It consists merely in purchasing and utilizing the offering provided by the producer.

A closer look at the flow of communication reveals both an advantage and a disadvantage of this simplified chain. The advantage is undoubtedly that the producer can focus on their core competencies and delegate all activities broadly associated with distribution to the distributor. However, this delegation also leads directly to the disadvantage that there is no direct connection between consumer and producer. This means that information about the consumer's expectations, wishes, and behavior does not reach the producer, or only does so if the distributor, in addition to their primary tasks, establishes a feedback channel between consumer and producer. By taking on this additional task, the distributor becomes an infomediary, communicating both towards the consumer and towards the producer.

For the real world, with exclusively physical products and services that revolve around these physical products, this perspective is sufficient. The roles presented in this context remain within their clearly defined areas of responsibility and only rarely cross these boundaries.

4.2 Early Ideas of Convergence: Prosumerism

The reduced value chain of classical economics introduced in the previous Sect. 4.1 was established over a long period on the basis of limited communication and the absence of industrial mass production. Only with the advent of automated manufacturing methods and a significant increase in production volumes were consumers able to choose from a growing number of producers and their products. From this point at the latest, it became increasingly important for manufacturers to establish a communicative feedback channel to their customers. Henry Ford's simple statement from 1909 regarding his Model T [CRO22]

> "You can have it in any color you want as long as it's black"

was no longer sufficient for successful market activity. Instead, it became ever more important for producers to understand the needs and expectations of consumers. During the early days of industrial mass production, this feedback channel was still very weak, but with the introduction of electrical and later digital means of communication, consumers and producers came into ever closer communicative contact. As a result, the role of the distributor also began to change, as its importance as an infomediary or communication channel between consumers and producers declined significantly. New, especially digital, communication channels enabled almost direct communication between customers and manufacturers (see Fig. 4.3), making the distributor's role in information transfer just one of many possible channels.

The American futurist Alvin Toffler was one of the first to recognize the significance of these developments in economic systems and attributed great potential to them for the future. In his 1980 book "The Third Wave" [TOF80], he predicted the phenomenon now known as Industry 4.0 [PLAoJ]: a seamless, highly communicative network connecting consumers, producers, and production machines. These rather technical forecasts formed the basis for his work "Power Shift," in which he described in 1991 that the established separation of the aforementioned roles would dissolve due to the close communicative connection between participants in the value chain [TOF90]:

> "Producer and consumer, separated by the industrial revolution, are reunited in the cycle of wealth creation, with the customer contributing not only money but also market and design information that is crucial to the production process.
> Buyer and supplier share data, information, and knowledge.
> One day, customers may also press buttons that activate remote production processes. Consumer and producer merge into a 'prosumer.'"

This last aspect in particular has been confirmed with the spread of Web 2.0 and the new possibilities arising in the context of Industry 4.0. This development began in the automotive industry, where car manufacturers used the web to offer consumers the option to configure their desired model according to their preferences. Initially, consumers had

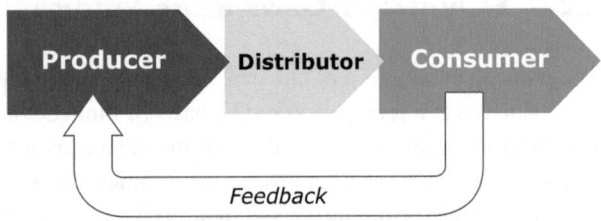

Fig. 4.3 Feedback as an extension of the simplified value chain: Prosumerism. (Original illustration: Peter Hoffmann, Invisible Cow)

only a few configuration options, such as paint color, interior color, or broad choices like engine type. Over time, however, the level of detail in configurators increased steadily. Today, it is not only conceivable but also technically possible for all possible features of a future car to be specified by the customer via a web portal or configurator. This information flows directly into production and to the production machines. The system then predicts when the desired vehicle will be completed and ready for pickup. By pressing the confirmation button, as Toffler predicted, production is initiated.

This is not limited to high-priced, large products like cars. Everyday goods can also be produced and purchased within the framework of prosumerism. An early example is Adidas, which introduced the first web-based sneaker configurator. This allowed prosumers to design their own sneakers, have them manufactured, and then purchase them [VET15].

From an unbiased external perspective, it may indeed appear as if the consumer is taking production into their own hands. Of course, the original separation, as outlined in the previous Sect. 4.1 in connection with the reduced value chain, still remains. The means of production remain in the hands of the producer, and the consumer's influence on the production machines is limited to the extent permitted by the producer. Nevertheless, consumer and producer move so close together that a new, albeit abstract, role emerges within the value chain: the so-called prosumer. Kevin Kelly described this situation very impressively in Wired magazine in 2005 [KEL05]:

> "The producers are the audience, the act of making is the act of watching, and every link is both a point of departure and a destination."

In this scenario, the importance of the distributor may at first glance seem less relevant and insignificant. When focusing solely on the role of infomediary, this may be true. Nevertheless, this situation also opens up new opportunities for the distributor, as it provides the chance to take the first step toward a new role, namely that of a platform economy actor.

To achieve the close communicative link between consumers and producers necessary for realizing the new abstract role of the prosumer, powerful communication channels are required. The effort involved in providing such communication channels should not be underestimated, both in terms of hardware infrastructure and software implementation. This effort is usually not borne by the producers, as they generally lack the necessary expertise to set up and operate such communication channels or platforms. This is where the distributor comes back into play, taking on the role of platform operator and providing the channels and tools for communication between consumer and producer.

For some time now, technical and economic visionaries have recognized, through ongoing technological developments, the possibility of advancing Toffler's idea of uniting consumers and producers in the new role of the prosumer even further. The potential offered by 3D printing, which is now firmly established in industrial manufacturing and is increasingly moving beyond the industrial context to gain a foothold in the consumer market, seems to make this convergence into the prosumer a reality. With the help of 3D printing, the consumer can become the producer of their own physical goods.

4.3 The Fusion in the Web Economy: Produsage

If the reality-virtuality continuum is applied not only to digital artifacts but also to the economic environment, the concept of prosumption examined in the previous Sect. 4.2 as defined by Toffler can be located at the end of complete reality, since the production of physical products is the primary goal. In contrast, at the end of complete virtuality, there would be an economy consisting solely of virtual products and services. In this case, the previously discussed simplified value chain appears entirely different. This can be attributed to the fundamental characteristics of digital objects, which, unlike physical objects, do not need to be individually manufactured using specially designed production machines. Instead, they can simply be copied, with the original and the copy being completely identical. However, this alone does not enable a transformation of the value chain, since even in the digital world, the development or production of digital goods is necessary, although this process naturally differs from the development and production of physical goods.

With the implementation of Web 2.0 technologies and the resulting opportunity for users to contribute their own content to the web in the sense of user-generated content, a new option emerges for transforming roles and their characteristics along the value chain. In 2008, Australian media scholar Axel Bruns outlined the transformative potential of Web 2.0 technologies and their manifestations, for example in blogs, wikis, and the forerunner of the metaverse, Second Life (see Fig. 4.4). Bruns coined the term "produsage" to describe a then-novel form of collaborative creation and use of content on the Internet. Analogous to Toffler, who merged the terms producer and consumer into the new buzzword prosumer, Bruns uses the terms producer and user in English. From these, he creates the "produser" as a new role in which both aspects are fused [BRU07].

Produsage thus refers to a type of value creation that has only become possible through the widespread adoption of the Internet. More precisely, it is not just the advent of the classic Internet, but especially the emergence of Web 2.0 that is relevant here.

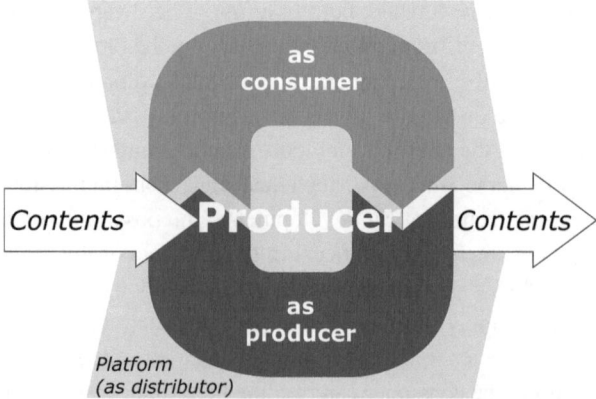

Fig. 4.4 The transformation of the value chain: Produsage. (Own illustration: Peter Hoffmann, Invisible Cow)

4.3 The Fusion in the Web Economy: Produsage

Produsage stands for a form of value creation and collaboration in which users not only consume content but can also actively participate in its creation and optimization. Such participation would not have been feasible with the static content of the original web. By actively involving users, added value is created, which often manifests not only in monetary terms but also in social recognition and individual satisfaction. Bruns's concept of produsage is based on the idea of open access to information on the Internet and collaborative work by users. This mode of content production and use is particularly applicable in the context of Web 2.0 and has contributed to the emergence of numerous successful platforms such as Wikipedia, YouTube, and OpenStreetMap.

The concept of produsage represents a second significant transformation of the value chain, moving in the same direction as prosumption. In contrast to the conventional value chain, as well as the value chain altered by prosumers—both of which were still controlled by a limited number of producers—the idea of produsage enables broader control over production processes, production tools, and the distribution of digital content and products. As a result, these aspects are distributed among a larger number of participants. Consequently, the traditional value chain is permanently dissolved, giving rise to an innovative form of value creation. Here, users do not merely assume a passive role, as in simple consumption, but can actively participate themselves.

There are now numerous examples of both non-commercial and commercial applications within the produsage value chain. The best-known example is probably the online encyclopedia Wikipedia. Here, the active user becomes the so-called produser, who can continue to consume encyclopedia entries as usual without modification. However, the idea behind Wikipedia also allows the produser to create new articles or edit the contributions of other produsers and make them available for further use. Wikipedia demonstrates that non-commercial applications, in particular, can benefit from the idea of produsage. The example also illustrates that produsage can only be successful if a sufficiently large community of active produsers forms around the application's goal. Only then can it be ensured that enough content is created that can be both consumed and "prodused," so that produsers actually become active and enough people are found to participate.

Other frequently cited examples of successful produsage applications include OpenStreetMap and YouTube. However, YouTube does not fully align with Bruns's concept. While content on YouTube and other video platforms is uploaded and provided by users, it is not offered for further processing. A particular challenge of produsage is that the content created, uploaded, and made available by produsers must ultimately be free from commercialization and licensing considerations. This makes produsage, as described by Bruns, especially difficult to implement in commercial contexts. In connection with 3D printing for the consumer market, there have been several attempts to implement produsage. On various web portals dedicated to 3D printing, users could purchase traditional licenses for 3D print models. The idea was that if users modified these models, they would be reimbursed for their costs for using or licensing the models [THIoJ, BAI08]. However, none of these commercial projects were able to establish themselves in the long term. The main reason for their failure is not, as is often claimed, the merely superficial changes made by users. Rather, it became apparent that modeling high-quality 3D models is a complex and demanding task mastered by only a limited number of people. Here, the relatively small size of the active community seems to be an obstacle to success.

The idea of produsage completes Toffler's concept of prosumption by merging the previously separate roles of producer and consumer—or user—into a single new role. Producer and consumer are truly united in this new role, rather than merely being in close communication as in Toffler's model. In this model, there appears to be no longer a role for the distributor, who in the classic value chain played a central intermediary role between producer and consumer, and who also had a smaller role in the prosumption value chain. On closer inspection, however, it becomes clear that the produsage value chain consists of more than just one person with two role components. On the one hand, there is a community that is necessary to generate content and keep the produsage value chain running. On the other hand, a platform is required on which this community can become active and in which the role of the produser can emerge in the first place. Here, the distributor takes the form and function of a platform provider. Without such a provider, there would be no virtual space for the produsage community. Most examples of produsage have a non-commercial background, but operating a platform now offers the opportunity to develop new business models around this type of value chain. Under the term "platform economy," which has been developed in the field of digital business and social science since around 2014, this will play a role in the context of the "Digital 49ers" discussed later.

4.4 The Merged Cross-Economy of the Metaverse: Modusage

To situate the changing value chains in the context of the concepts of prosumption and produsage within the reality-virtuality continuum, they must be positioned at the two extremes of physical reality and complete virtuality. Although, according to Toffler, prosumption only hesitantly departs from the extreme of full reality—since this model integrates only limited aspects of the virtual world—the communication between consumer and producer via the Internet remains a key aspect. This does not change even if the producer, through Industry 4.0 applications, directly forwards information sent by the prosumer to the means of production. Furthermore, the strict separation of roles remains intact in this model.

As discussed in Chap. 2 and especially in Sect. 2.6, it became clear that the metaverse cannot exist at the extreme of physical reality, and is only partially present at the other extreme of complete virtuality. Instead, the metaverse is situated in the flexible space where physical and digital artifacts coexist in varying proportions. Neither the classical value chain nor the models of Bruns or Toffler are applicable to this segment of the reality-virtuality continuum. Therefore, a further modification or extension of the value chain is required for the future metaverse.

To create such a new model of the value chain, as tentatively illustrated in Fig. 4.5, it is necessary to consider various aspects in synchrony. Due to its position between the two extremes, the metaverse typically consists of both real-world and virtual components. This requires that participants within this model must be able to interact with both physical and digital artifacts. It would therefore be sensible to expand the concept of separating the real and virtual worlds and to build a bridge between them. This would enable the emergence of a cross-economy that connects both worlds. The ideas from the two aforementioned models are incorporated into this new model, merging and expanding upon each other.

- In this new model, the original value chain is not considered, as it exists exclusively in the physical world outside the metaverse.
- In the new model, the roles of producer and distributor from the classical models are integrated. The producer continues to provide the means of production, which are used by the new "moduser" to initiate the individualized production of desired artifacts via feedback. The means of production remain the property of the producer. Since the manufactured physical artifacts must be delivered to the moduser, a distributor is required to act as a logistical intermediary between producer and moduser. Whether this role is fulfilled by a separate entity or by the "metaverse" platform itself can be handled flexibly.
- The concept of produsage also integrates seamlessly into this model. Here, the role of the producer is replaced by that of the moduser. In line with Bruns' concept, this person accesses existing digital artifacts, uses and edits them as needed, and then returns them to the virtual world. This editing can take place either within or outside the "metaverse" platform. Naturally, the creation of new artifacts is also considered a form of editing.

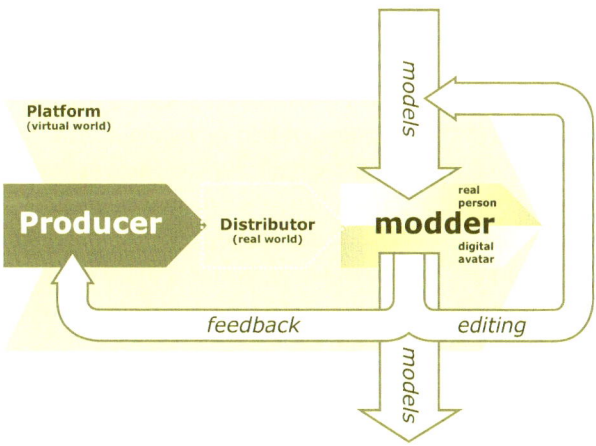

Fig. 4.5 The value chain in the metaverse: Modusage. (Original illustration: Peter Hoffmann, Invisible Cow)

- The new model also includes a platform that represents the virtual world of the metaverse and, on the digital side, assumes the role of distributor, similar to what is depicted in Fig. 4.4 for produsage according to Bruns [BRU07]. The significance of this role is particularly high here, as the platform provides and manages all functionalities of the metaverse. This encompasses not only the usual features of virtual worlds, such as personal interaction and rendering of worlds as 3D models, but also the integration of social interaction capabilities that enable the formation of communities, which Bruns considers fundamental to produsage.
- Similar to the consumer in the traditional value chain, the prosumer in Toffler's model, or the producer in Bruns' model, the so-called moduser occupies the central, active position in the new model. The moduser engages in prosumption through feedback with the producer and, at the same time, "produses" with models contributed by the community as digital artifacts to the platform. In contrast to Bruns' content, which is limited to passive, mostly media-based content, a key difference is that the moduser can also edit complex models and even sophisticated scripts that define the behavior of digital artifacts within the metaverse platform.
- At its core, the moduser consists of two sub-roles. As described from various perspectives above, a fundamental characteristic of the metaverse is the synchronized convergence of digital and physical artifacts. In the physical world, the user is represented by themselves as a person, and in the digital world by their digital twin, the avatar. The person can interact directly with the physical environment and, via the avatar, with the digital environment. At the same time, the avatar can also communicate from the digital world to the physical world, for example, by triggering outputs. For the model to be comprehensive, it is important to note that not only the physical part of the moduser but also the digital avatar can provide feedback to the producer. Furthermore, the editing of digital models can be performed by either the physical or digital sub-role of the moduser. This concept presupposes that the digital twin, which assumes the moduser's role in the virtual world, is capable of acting autonomously.

The new role of the moduser and the connection of its physical and digital components with other actors in the metaverse value chain demonstrate that the modusage model is more than just a combination of Toffler's and Bruns' models. Rather, it becomes clear that, in the metaverse, it will be normal for the value chain to shift back and forth between the physical and virtual worlds. Thus, depending on the degree of digitalization (see also Fig. 4.6), a true "cross economy" emerges between the two worlds, which are economically interdependent. This development offers broad opportunities for the emergence of new, or at least novel, business models, as will be explained in more detail in the following sections.

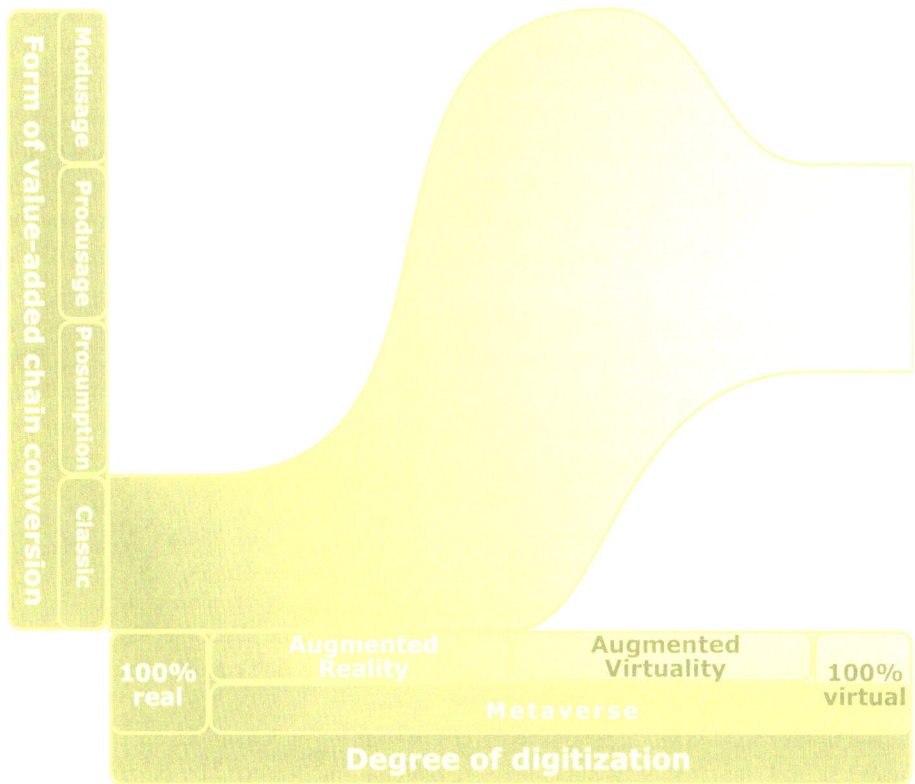

Fig. 4.6 Degree of digitalization vs. value chain model. (Original illustration: Peter Hoffmann, Invisible Cow)

4.5 A Contemporary Form of Modusage: D2A-Commerce

The explanation of personal fusion previously introduced already anticipated a form of modusage that is currently being realized. This refers to so-called Direct-to-Avatar Commerce (D2A).

This new form of commercial strategy was developed specifically for use within the metaverse. It enables brands to sell digital products and services directly to users' avatars, without the need for physical goods or traditional supply chains. This type of commerce is based on the growing importance of digital identities and the personalization of avatars in virtual worlds. The integration of D2A with technologies such as blockchain, non-fungible tokens (NFTs), and virtual marketplaces plays a central role in the economic development of the metaverse, opening up new opportunities for interaction, customization, and brand experiences [KIM23].

D2A is characterized by the direct sale of digital goods such as clothing, accessories, or exclusive virtual experiences to avatars. For example, brands like Gucci, Nike, and

Adidas offer virtual fashion items that can be purchased on platforms such as Roblox or Decentraland. In addition, NFTs play a crucial role by ensuring the uniqueness and ownership of these digital goods, thereby enabling exclusive, cross-platform usage [WIE23].

One of the core components of D2A is its close connection to virtual marketplaces, where users can trade digital assets. Platforms like The Sandbox or Decentraland enable the purchase and sale of virtual real estate, artworks, or in-game items, creating a digital economy that operates exclusively within the metaverse. Blockchain technology secures these transactions and guarantees the authenticity and ownership of the acquired digital products [HUS24].

Beyond the mere sale of digital products, D2A also offers immersive experiences that go beyond traditional e-commerce models. Companies can create exclusive virtual events, concerts, or interactive experiences for avatars, which are unlocked through the purchase of certain digital goods. This strategy enables deeper brand engagement and opens up new revenue streams for companies, as digital goods incur no production or logistics costs and are highly scalable [KAP20].

Despite the numerous advantages of D2A, challenges remain, particularly regarding data privacy, technological dependencies, and interoperability between different metaverses. As digital identities are increasingly monetized, questions arise concerning data security and the protection of users' personal information. Furthermore, the infrastructure of many metaverse platforms is not yet fully mature, which can limit the cross-platform use of digital goods [LAN17].

The future of D2A will depend heavily on both the technological advancement of the metaverse and the increasing integration of artificial intelligence and blockchain technologies, as well as on issues of user acceptance and the actual implementation of platforms. Potential developments include improved interoperability between metaverse platforms, the introduction of hybrid goods that combine both physical and digital components, and personalized recommendations for avatars based on user data. In the long term, D2A could revolutionize digital commerce and set new standards for economic interaction in virtual spaces.

While D2A currently operates mainly in virtual worlds, there are, in line with the modusage concept described above, increasing interfaces with physical production processes. Of particular note here is the 3D printing technology. The combination of these two technologies opens up new possibilities for merging digital and physical goods, expanding commerce between the virtual and real worlds [KIM23].

3D printing technologies make it possible to transform digital designs from the metaverse into physical objects, resulting in a hybrid business model. Digital garments, accessories, or even architectural designs acquired as NFTs in the metaverse can be reproduced in the physical world through additive manufacturing. Such an interface between D2A commerce and 3D printing allows users not only to own virtual objects in digital environments, but also to obtain them as real products if desired. Companies like

Nike and Adidas have already begun offering digital sneaker collections as NFTs, which can be combined with physical counterparts via 3D printing technologies. This creates a new form of product customization, enabling customers to convert their digital designs into tangible goods through manufacturing technologies [WIE23].

From a technological perspective, the connection between D2A commerce and 3D printing is based on advanced CAD designs (Computer Aided Design), which serve as the foundation for both digital and physical products. While these designs are stored and traded as NFTs in the metaverse, the same files can be used for additive manufacturing processes. Blockchain plays an important role here by ensuring the authenticity and uniqueness of digital designs and guaranteeing that only authorized users have access to the print files. This combination could help revolutionize the market for personalized physical products by allowing users to purchase digital goods and then have them reproduced in physical form.

A key and often highlighted advantage of this hybrid usage lies in resource-efficient production. While traditional manufacturing methods are often associated with high material waste and long supply chains, 3D printing can offer a more sustainable alternative. Custom-made objects are produced only as needed, reducing overproduction and minimizing transportation costs. This is particularly attractive for luxury brands that offer exclusive digital fashion and give their customers the opportunity to acquire limited-edition physical versions of these fashion items through 3D printing [KAP20].

In practical application, these technological interfaces are already giving rise to concrete business models. Companies offer digital artists and designers the opportunity to sell their creations as NFTs on virtual marketplaces before using 3D printing for physical production. This development is changing not only e-commerce, but also the way products are designed, acquired, and used. In addition, new potential is emerging for personalized manufacturing and co-creation, as customers are actively involved in the design process and can flexibly move their digital purchases between the physical and virtual worlds [BRY14].

As with any technology, there are obstacles and challenges both in the individual consideration of 3D printing and in its integration with existing business models, which affect the combination of D2A commerce and 3D printing. The necessary interoperability between digital platforms and physical manufacturing processes is not yet fully developed, and there remains a need to establish standards for the protection of intellectual property. Moreover, widespread adoption of these technologies requires increasing acceptance by both companies and consumers. Nevertheless, it is foreseeable that the combination of D2A commerce and 3D printing will set new benchmarks for digital commerce and individualized production in the long term [LAN17].

4.6 The Digital 49ers: New Business Models and Application Areas

Numerous publications on the unexpected and seemingly limitless commercial opportunities emerging in the metaverse suggest that a new digital gold rush may be imminent. Even after discounting predictions from typical marketing sources, there remains a substantial body of serious and independent research that attributes growing significance to the metaverse as an ecosystem. This includes both the roadmap of the German IT industry association Bitkom and internationally renowned think tanks [BIT22, STO22, WEFoJa, PER22]. Almost all such studies and reports divide the economic development of the metaverse into a near-term and a longer-term horizon, indicating that the metaverse is expected to have a more long-term perspective. These publications assume that numerous new and viable business models will emerge in the near future. This near-term horizon typically spans the next 5 to 10 years, while further forecasts are generally avoided, as it is consistently emphasized that it is difficult, if not impossible, to successfully predict business models over a longer period.

However, there appears to be consensus that the metaverse does not merely represent a single business model, but will instead encompass a wide variety of different business models. These models will emerge from the roles of the various actors within the metaverse. Traditional business models, such as advertising-based or subscription-based financing, will continue to exist. At the same time, they will be further developed to enable better integration into the platform economy environment. In particular, newer technological approaches such as NFTs and similar technologies offer significant development potential. One reason for this is the comparison with the economic development of the early World Wide Web. For example, Zühlke comments on this [STO22]:

> "Platform economies in particular are well suited to become the dominant business models in the metaverse. Global or platform-based currency systems, such as those in the crypto and gaming industries, complement today's platform economies."

The broad spectrum of potential future economic actors in the metaverse is particularly interesting:

- First and foremost, the current and future operators of metaverse platforms must of course be mentioned, as well as
- the major technology providers and manufacturers, with Nvidia certainly being the most prominent example [KER21].
- In addition, there are service providers acting as "creators and developers" or offering other professional services for media development.
- The gaming industry should also be included in the "creator and developer" environment, as it can be considered one of the driving forces in the development of the metaverse and will therefore also be economically active.

- Broadly speaking, providers of social media and social media content also fall within the realm of media development, as do
- traditional marketing and advertising agencies.
- It is noteworthy that research institutions such as Fraunhofer, MIT, and others are frequently mentioned in the context of business model development.
- It is also important not to overlook users themselves, who, as participants and developers of new business models, can be economically active in the metaverse as modusers.

It is important that, when examining the economic opportunities that the metaverse offers or could offer, one does not consider only the purely economic fundamentals and mechanisms. Instead, it is essential to embed these within the technical and technological context. While the Internet or World Wide Web may be firmly established as a technology, the metaverse—as the Internet of the future—is still in its developmental phase. Since it is not yet possible to make precise statements about the technical design of the metaverse, future business models will depend heavily on which technologies and implementations can be used for various application areas.

In this context, it is helpful to project current examples of business activities from various industries onto the reality-virtuality continuum. A study by Zühlke, which examines five different industries with regard to their activities in the metaverse, shows that examples of economic activity can be found across nearly all industries and throughout the entire spectrum of the continuum [STO22] (see also Fig. 4.7).

- *Fashion*: A frequently cited example of entrepreneurial activity in the metaverse is the fashion industry. This is evident, for instance, in the fact that, much like in the real world, there are now extensive fashion events in the metaverse. The Decentraland

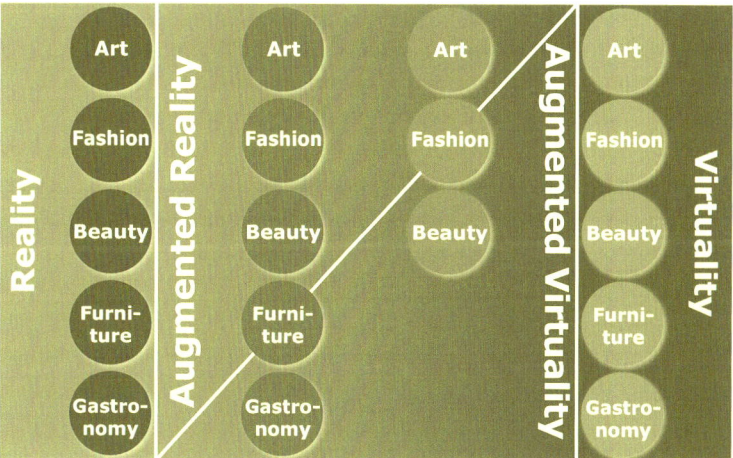

Fig. 4.7 Industry activities in the RVC. (Own illustration: Peter Hoffmann, Invisible Cow)

Fashion Week is probably the best-known event in this regard. The aim here is not, as in the previously mentioned example of the Decentraland Metaverse Music Festival, to take a critical look at this event. Regardless of the size of the participating audience, however, this virtual fashion week illustrates the large number of fashion labels that have already identified the metaverse as a future consumer environment [DEC23, DRA22, METoJa, METoJb]. It is noteworthy that opportunities to connect fashion for the real world with fashion for the virtual world are being explored at an early stage. This is also quite logical, since one of the fundamental ideas behind merging the real and virtual worlds is that users can have an avatar act as their digital twin in the virtual world. Naturally, this digital twin should not look like a simple and cheap "digital mass product," but should reflect the fashion sense of the real person and be dressed accordingly. It is therefore only logical that, for example, Gucci offers a handbag as a fashion accessory for women in the real world and simultaneously makes this bag available for avatars in the virtual world. The price of nearly $4,000 does not appear to be a real obstacle in this context.

- Of course, consumer offerings will continue to be made in the real world in the future, as it is unlikely that traditional department stores or retail shops will disappear entirely, despite the transformation of city centers.
- Nevertheless, some companies are embracing the concept of the digital twin and are offering virtual shopping experiences in VR stores on well-known platforms such as Roblox or Decentraland. This idea is not new, as even in the predecessor of the metaverse, Second Life, not only Adidas but also many other companies from various industries had virtual branches.
- However, numerous applications that connect reality and virtuality can also be found in this area. As described in detail above, augmented reality is one of the oldest application examples for technologies now associated with the metaverse. For example, there are augmented fitting rooms in both large and small formats. The large version may consist of a full-length mirror in a physical store, where digitalized 3D models of clothing items are superimposed onto the user's reflection, following their posture and movements. This allows customers to get an impression of the clothing before purchasing or ordering online, without having to try it on physically. On a smaller scale, this is also available for shoes, for instance. Here, the augmentation is done via a smartphone app that uses the device's display and camera. Augmented virtuality would also be conceivable in this area, although no widely adopted application has yet been demonstrated.

- *Beauty and Cosmetics*: A sector closely linked to the world of fashion is beauty and cosmetics. Although there are currently no large-scale events comparable to the Metaverse Fashion Week, numerous articles in both fashion as well as business and technology magazines already discuss the activities of cosmetics brands aiming to establish themselves in the metaverse. Beauty and cosmetics is an extremely profitable market in the real world, which naturally raises the question of whether the digital

twin can be made even more attractive or digitally enhanced through virtual cosmetics.
- In the real world, cosmetics are typically purchased at brick-and-mortar stores in department stores or specialized retailers, as well as through online commerce. It is expected that this will not change with the establishment of the metaverse.
- The field of augmenting reality and virtuality appears to be an even more promising area for applications and business models in the beauty and cosmetics industry than in the fashion sector, spanning the entire reality-virtuality continuum. For example, augmented reality enables the application of virtual makeup that is visible only in an augmented mirror or on the display of a corresponding smartphone app. In this way, the color of cosmetics or accessories such as contact lenses can be examined and evaluated before purchase or application. Interestingly, the term "augmented virtuality" is also frequently used in this industry example. One concept mentioned in this context is the so-called "face filter," in which the image of the real face is projected onto a made-up avatar in the virtual world. Here, the digital image is superimposed and thus extended with the appearance of the real person.
- However, full virtuality presents itself quite differently for the beauty and cosmetics sector compared to the fashion industry. While entire branches and stores are being relocated to the virtual world in the fashion sector, the beauty sector is, at least for now, still focused on the individual real user. At present, there are no known virtual cosmetics stores for avatars in a virtual world. However, on many platforms and across many cross-platform services, such as ReadyPlayerMe, users can alter not only the fashion but also the cosmetic appearance of their avatars. This goes far beyond traditional cosmetics, as the possibilities for designing avatars are not limited to human, humanoid physiognomy. Instead, any conceivable form can be applied to the avatar, ranging from classic human appearances to cartoon and manga characters, as well as fantasy and furry figures. All of this is conceivable and is indeed being implemented [WEI20, ORT22].

- *Furniture and Interior Design*: The furniture and interior design industry is another sector with numerous activities related to the metaverse. Even before the term "metaverse" became common, the idea existed to view furnishings such as furniture virtually before purchasing, delivery, and installation. This is a logical development, as such applications can make measuring the apartment and the furniture, as well as comparing their dimensions, unnecessary. The virtual piece of furniture is simply projected into the real space to give the customer an impression of how it fits into the living environment. While no one can sit on a virtual chair, it can be moved around the room to check whether it matches the apartment in terms of size and design. Ikea is a particularly active player in this industry, having experimented with a wide range of technologies for several years.

- But not only Ikea, many other furniture retailers also offer a variety of AR applications designed to support customers in selecting furniture and furnishings in various ways [LEWoJ, WEI22]. The underlying idea is the one mentioned above: a digitized 3D model of the furnishing item is integrated into the real living situation to provide a much better impression than a passive image on a screen or the actual piece of furniture still located in the showroom can offer.
- In the furniture and interior design industry, full virtuality is used in various ways. The simplest approach, as in the fashion or other consumer sectors, is to transfer an entire retail store into virtual reality. In this way, the digital twin can view the furnishings in virtual reality just as in a real furniture store. The more technically sophisticated scenario at this end of the reality-virtuality continuum for this industry is to transfer the customer's own apartment into virtual reality and insert the digital equivalent of the desired piece of furniture into the living environment. This requires a complete 3D model of the apartment, which can be created either manually or from a scan using appropriate technical means. However, furnishing the room or apartment becomes challenging if only the architectural dimensions are known. In this case, all furnishings that exist in the real world and decorate the apartment would also have to be modeled or scanned. Earlier examples from before the metaverse should not be forgotten here, such as Second Life or the once highly successful social game "The Sims." In both cases, it was entirely possible to design one's own apartment in the virtual world, which, just like in the real world, could be furnished with pieces of furniture. How closely these matched real furniture depended on the users' willingness and ability to model them.

- *Gaming and Entertainment*: Undeniably, gaming and entertainment are among the most lucrative sectors in computing and the internet. In this area, almost anything is imaginable—and is, in fact, being realized. Although concrete economic objectives are also pursued here, this sector offers a broad experimental field for testing a wide variety of new technologies and creative ideas that span the entire reality-virtuality continuum. Some examples have already been mentioned above. Particularly interesting is the fact that there is a high level of willingness, openness, and enthusiasm for experimentation among both technology and engineering developers and the creators of new business models.
  - Humans as players—Homo ludens—have existed far longer than any ideas for computers, digital, or electronic media. A look at the games sections of bookstores or toy stores reveals an overwhelming number and variety of dice, card, and board games. But games are not the only part of the entertainment industry. For at least as long as games have existed, people have also sought entertainment through, for example, theater or musical performances. Here, too, the range of offerings is extraordinarily broad; in the real world, almost anything is possible, from private campfire concerts to multi-day open-air festivals.

- As already shown above, these activities can easily be implemented in full virtuality. It is now common to find both games and concert events in virtual reality and on metaverse platforms such as Fortnite and Roblox.
- In the field of augmented reality, it is still mainly games that combine and extend both real and virtual elements. Examples include Pokémon Go in the area of augmented reality or the previously mentioned PacManhattan in the area of augmented virtuality. However, augmented reality is also suitable for entertainment events. Here, the examples of Ronnie James Dio, ABBA, and Hatsune Miku should be recalled once again.

- *Art*: The logical continuation of the ideas presented in the entertainment and gaming sectors is to apply and transfer them to the field of art. Ultimately, everything that has been and will be said about the entertainment and gaming sector can be directly applied to art. Art represents an experimental space where anything is possible and, as a look at art history shows, all sorts of things are actually tried out. It is therefore not surprising that there are already examples of art spanning the entire reality-virtuality continuum from times when neither the term "metaverse" nor the terms "virtual" or "augmented reality" were known. Particularly interesting, however, is the fact that in the context of the metaverse and Web3 ideas, the economic aspect of managing art in the virtual world is now gaining importance. The currently probably best-known example of this is Bored Ape, an NFT collection based on the Ethereum blockchain. The prices for such a Bored Ape object seem to be almost unlimited. For example, a rare specimen from this collection is said to have already been sold for about one million US dollars [DRA22].
  - Art in the physical world is ubiquitous and can be found almost everywhere. It does not necessarily have to be in a museum or gallery; art can also exist as part of public space.
  - Even in the realm of complete virtuality, the conventional implementation practices already mentioned are evident. There are real museums that are fully represented in virtuality with all their exhibits and buildings, as well as museums and exhibitions that exist exclusively in virtual reality. However, this is not entirely new, as many museums have already had a presence in Second Life and other early environments. In the area of augmentations, there are also numerous artworks that are older than the term "metaverse" itself. Current examples of augmented reality include guided tours through a city, where digital artworks are added at selected locations using an app on a mobile device. The ARTour in Basel is a frequently cited example in this area [BAS22, WEB22]. A technology that can actually be considered independently of the idea of the metaverse is currently being used in some examples in the field of augmented virtual reality. So-called deep fake art, for example, makes it possible to embed one's own real likeness into well-known works of art. In this way, the Mona Lisa can simply take on your own facial features [SIR22, BBC19].

- *Gastronomy*: In the context of applications and business models in the metaverse, gastronomy is probably not the first thing that comes to mind. The world of IT, computers, and the internet is primarily visual and, in a few cases, auditory. While it is technically possible to integrate all other sensory modalities into this world, the technical effort is often very high and the added value low. Nevertheless, there are numerous ideas for how gastronomy could establish itself in the metaverse or make use of it.
  – There is certainly no need to discuss one hundred percent reality here, since gastronomy takes place in restaurants, hotels, and private settings in the real world.
  – Why should a restaurant be represented entirely virtually? It may make sense for a digital avatar to get a visual impression of a five-star chef's restaurant on a metaverse platform, to get an idea of the menu and the ambiance. However, the question arises as to what the avatar could actually order and enjoy there. In gastronomy and hospitality in the metaverse, the primary focus is not on providing guests with an experience, but rather on using VR applications to support staff training in the real world. Here, spatial arrangements within hotels or workflows can be learned and practiced. The business model of metaverse platforms thus targets professional use rather than the mass or consumer market. Nevertheless, virtual reality will certainly play a role for tourists and guests in the future, for example by allowing them to preview the interior of a cruise ship in virtual reality. In the future, it may even be possible to move entire destinations into virtual reality, enabling people to experience the atmosphere of cities like Venice without actually having to travel there. This idea could be an interesting alternative for heavily frequented tourist destinations like Venice and is currently being discussed [HUG23, SER18]. However, there are currently only a few concepts for how such a scenario could be fully implemented.
  – Although gastronomy enables the development of one hundred percent reality and virtuality as a business environment in the metaverse, this is somewhat more difficult in the area of augmentations. There are indeed some mentions of so-called augmented food experiences, but how these are to be implemented technically and sensorially often remains unclear. Here, too, the question arises as to what added value there would be for the user, which still needs to be determined. In the field of augmented reality, however, there are already examples such as QR codes that supplement menus or beer mats, as demonstrated by Lindenbräu [NET18].

The examples presented illustrate how intensively and comprehensively new business models and options are being explored at the technological level in connection with the metaverse. In contrast to other hyped topics such as 3D printing or artificial intelligence, it is not just a few supposed experts who predict a promising future for the technology and the idea of the metaverse—although it should be noted that this is now also the case for AI. In the metaverse, numerous experts from various fields share a similar opinion. One example is Tim Sweeney, the former game developer and current CEO of Epic Games, who predicted in 2020 [MAR20]:

"Just as every company created a website a few decades ago and then eventually a Facebook page, I believe we are approaching the point where every company will have a real-time live presence in 3D."

An analysis of the numerous publications presenting concepts and models for the future economy in the metaverse reveals an overwhelming number of economic options (see also Fig. 4.8), even when only the most relevant tech and business sources are considered. Fig. 4.8 attempts to present these diverse ideas in a structured way.

4.6.1 Advertising & Marketing

The intensive blending of the real and virtual worlds in the metaverse is amplified by the user's immersion through their avatar or digital twin. This is intended to create a highly individualized experience that appears almost limitless. Although it may sound like typical marketing jargon, it actually reflects the advertising and marketing industry's hope to develop the metaverse into a premier platform for marketing activities. This is achieved by leveraging immersion, interactivity, and personalization with the goal of

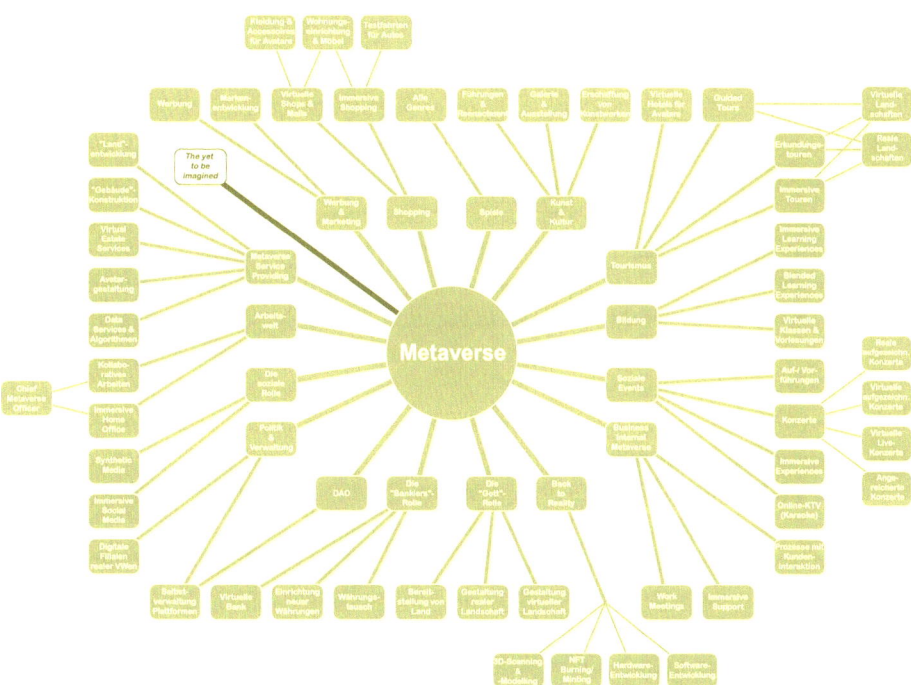

Fig. 4.8 Revised business models around the metaverse. (Own illustration: Peter Hoffmann, Invisible Cow)

increasing marketing efficiency. In fact, the metaverse has already reached the status of a multi-billion-dollar market, attracting investments not only from major brands such as Ralph Lauren, Gucci, and Louis Vuitton. These pioneering brands in the metaverse are already generating impressive returns on their investments and are experimenting with new brand management methods that allow users to try on and purchase clothing, products, and styles, as described in the previous section 4.6 on consumption in the reality-virtuality continuum [BID22, DEW22].

Advertising in the metaverse is particularly aimed at providing an (inter)active experience in which potential customers are actively involved in marketing, rather than being mere passive observers. This presents additional challenges for companies, as they must first overcome the general mistrust of advertising. However, successful campaigns emphasize that the key to success lies in collaborating with existing communities rather than working against them. For example, some brands have successfully established partnerships with the Roblox developer community, which is in some ways comparable to the use of influencers in social media campaigns.

- Within the advertising industry, offering interactive events in the virtual worlds of the metaverse has gained importance as a popular marketing tool. It is now common practice to integrate advertising into such events and to maintain a presence on several of the leading platforms, such as Meta's Horizon Worlds, Decentraland, Sandbox, Fortnite, Roblox, or Minecraft.
- An additional approach is the "try before you buy" strategy, which aims to establish a strong connection between brand and consumer. With this method, customers have the opportunity to actively test and explore the product first, to determine the real added value it offers them. This approach transforms passive marketing into a dynamic experience, placing the focus on the experience itself, which is central to marketing in the metaverse. Such an immersive experience in the metaverse enables customers, for example, to equip their digital twin with new clothing and try it on or out in the virtual world [MIRoJ]. In addition, affordable VR headsets such as the Meta Quest can be used to simulate a realistic driving experience with a new vehicle the customer is interested in.
- Building customer loyalty through collections and collectibles appears to be an effective way to attract interest to a brand. Collecting objects and the fascination it holds for people is a long-established phenomenon in the physical world. More recently, this enthusiasm has extended to digital collections in the metaverse. Promotional campaigns focused on digital collectibles aim to create uniqueness and offer exclusivity through the use of NFT and crypto technologies. Virtual goods have gained considerable significance in the metaverse, with a direct-to-avatar market value of around $30 billion in 2021 and a forecast of well over $50 billion by the end of 2022 [HAC21]. As the presented modusage model shows, a potential metaverse-to-offline consumption is emerging for the future, which will function analogously to the conversion of online-to-offline sales enabled by the internet.

- It is often assumed that using the metaverse necessarily requires expensive hardware components. However, it is frequently overlooked that smartphones can already serve as metaverse-capable devices, suitable for AR applications, for example. There are already numerous companies that have achieved significant success by using smartphone-based AR in metaverse advertising. One example is Home Depot's use of AR to demonstrate to customers how different shades from their range would look in a room [CRE20]. The renowned company Sephora also offers a product range in the cosmetics sector that many consumers are reluctant to purchase online, as these are highly individual products and it is difficult to predict how a particular product will look on one's own skin. As a result, many customers prefer to visit Sephora stores in person. However, by using augmented reality marketing, Sephora has found a way to meet its customers' needs [BAL20c]. For this purpose, a technology called "Modiface" is used, which enables high-quality facial scans. This allows customers to digitally apply Sephora's makeup to their lips and eyes from the comfort of their own home, giving them a realistic impression of how it would look on their face [ABU21, METoJb].

For companies, advertising and marketing in the metaverse means that new approaches and techniques must be developed that have not previously existed in either the real world or the World Wide Web. As a result, many advertising and marketing strategies are currently—and likely will continue to be—discovered through trial and error and experimentation.

Although a smartphone is sufficient for initial entry into the metaverse, the costs for metaverse-compatible devices such as VR headsets and high-performance computers increase for users who wish to enhance the immersion of their (advertising) experiences. This could result in only a limited number of users being able to afford access to such advertising campaigns and events in the metaverse, which is not in the interest of the advertising companies. Furthermore, these companies must also address new cybersecurity concerns if they wish to succeed in the metaverse.

Beyond the marketing of individual products, the metaverse also offers the opportunity to create digital brands. This is becoming an increasingly relevant strategy.

Ongoing digitalization and the development of the metaverse are increasingly influencing how brands are created, presented, and ultimately consumed. Digital brands in the metaverse are no longer merely extensions of physical companies, but can exist as independent, fully virtual identities. They are based on digital business models, typically supported by blockchain technology, non-fungible tokens (NFTs), and immersive user experiences. Such new brands emerge from a combination of innovative design, interactive elements, and cross-platform integration, setting them apart from traditional brands [KAP20].

The creation of a digital brand in the metaverse begins with the development of a unique digital identity, often represented by avatars, virtual spaces, or personalized brand elements. Companies and designers use 3D modeling, virtual reality (VR), and augmented reality (AR) to design entire brand spaces where users can interact with digital products. An example of this is brands like "RTFKT," which offer fully digital sneakers and fashion items as NFTs that can be worn or traded across various metaverse platforms [RTF25]. Through this digital identity, brands create an interactive and immersive environment that enables users to connect with them in new ways [KIM23].

A key component of digital brands in the metaverse is the use of blockchain technology to ensure ownership rights and authenticity. NFTs serve as digital certificates that verify ownership of a virtual product or brand, enabling users to acquire exclusive, limited, or collectible items. This creates new opportunities for brand building and customer loyalty, as users can become not only buyers but also co-creators and investors within the brand ecosystem.

In addition to technological infrastructure, community building is central to the creation of digital brands. Brands in the metaverse often emerge in close collaboration with their user base by introducing participatory elements such as crowdsourced designs, community voting, or exclusive membership models. This interactivity strengthens consumers' emotional attachment to the brand and enables greater brand identification. Digital fashion houses and art collectives are increasingly relying on these mechanisms to create personalized and dynamic brand worlds [WIE23].

A decisive factor for the success of digital brands in the metaverse is cross-platform interoperability. While traditional brands operate in specific markets or geographic regions, digital brands exist in a decentralized, global environment. This enables users to utilize their virtual assets across different platforms and digital spaces. An example of this can be found in the gaming industry, where skins or digital items from games can be used on multiple metaverse platforms. This increases the reach of brands and allows for more sustainable monetization of digital products [LAN17].

Legal frameworks, data protection, and the authenticity of digital identities present significant challenges in this context. As the metaverse is still under development, there are currently no uniform regulations for brand security, which entails risks such as plagiarism or unauthorized use of digital products. Furthermore, the successful establishment of a digital brand requires substantial investments in technology, design, and marketing in order to compete in the growing digital economy [BRY14]. On the one hand, the high level of investment required can be a barrier for smaller companies; on the other hand, however, the technological freedom can also open up entirely new opportunities for such businesses.

4.6.2 Shopping

Both in 2021 and 2022, online retail reached new record sales, and despite inflation and current crises, the outlook remains promising, with the metaverse offering providers in the shopping sector new opportunities for positive development. To keep pace with the growth of the e-commerce sector, companies must adapt their business practices to changing consumer habits and employ multi-channel distribution strategies. The relevance of social media platforms in sales contexts has increased, and numerous companies are planning to create their own virtual universes within the metaverse.

Companies such as Adidas and Netflix have already begun showcasing their products and services in the metaverse. The use of virtual fitting rooms and digital replicas of physical stores is intended to provide consumers with an immersive experience and the opportunity to try out products in a realistic way [FLO22, PAR23].

Other companies and industries are also intensifying their efforts to integrate their businesses and products into the metaverse. In October 2021, Nike filed seven patents with the US Patent Office to sell digital clothing in the metaverse. The company is currently seeking material designers for virtual sports shoes to expand its product development team accordingly [BRA21]. The fashion industry has also recognized the potential of the metaverse and is experimenting with virtual retail concepts. Gucci is perhaps the most prominent example, unveiling the online concept store "Vault" in September 2021 as part of its metaverse strategy. There, customers can "experience" vintage pieces, limited editions, and other items, as well as NFTs selected by the creative director [SCH22]. In June 2022, Gucci Town was launched on the Roblox platform, where users can participate in competitions, create digital artworks, or purchase digital Gucci products. Gucci uses the "Layered Clothing System" to adapt clothing and accessories to the body types of avatars [BED22]. US discount retailer Walmart also plans to enter the metaverse and filed applications with the US Patent Office in December 2021 to enable its own cryptocurrency and the sale of virtual goods. The German supermarket chain Kaufland followed Walmart and other discounters into the metaverse with its "Kaufisland" project, acquiring an island in the Nintendo game Animal Crossing: New Horizon and setting up a virtual supermarket there. The company does not currently pursue primary profit objectives there, but offers users information about food origins and environmentally conscious behavior. In addition, customers or their avatars can relax in a café or cook in an outdoor kitchen on Kaufisland [BUS22a, BUS22b]. It remains to be seen how companies will actually use the metaverse in the future and what impact the digital world will have on consumers.

A key advantage that is repeatedly emphasized in this context is the creation of an entirely new virtual world in which consumers can immerse themselves and interact. This also opens up a range of more or less new possibilities for shopping:

- *Augmented shopping experiences*: Thanks to augmented reality technology, consumers can virtually try on clothing or accessories without having to own the physical product. In addition to the examples mentioned above, the "Sayduck" app allows users to virtually place furniture in their own rooms and assess how it looks [MAR14].
- *Personalization*: Within the metaverse, consumers have the option to create and customize their own avatars. This results in a unique shopping experience, where

products can be tailored specifically to the avatar, as is the case with the "Layered Clothing System" mentioned above.
- *Interactive shopping experiences*: Brands can strengthen their presence and customer loyalty in the metaverse through interactive shopping experiences, including competitions, games, and the collection of digital artworks and artifacts.
- *Virtual payment methods*: Much of the metaverse is designed to use virtual currencies and NFTs for the sale of digital items [HAM22].
- *Global reach*: Similar to the traditional World Wide Web, companies can reach customers worldwide in the metaverse without having to open a physical branch in every country. This makes it easier for small and medium-sized enterprises to offer their products globally.

In recent years, influencer marketing has seen significant growth and will likely be further influenced by the metaverse. Companies benefit from using real or virtual influencers by expanding their reach and targeting specific audiences [METoJb].

Although the metaverse offers many opportunities, challenges such as technical limitations, legal regulatory issues, and uncertainties in an NFT-based economic ecosystem remain. It is important to identify and address these early on in order to fully realize the potential of the metaverse for shopping [BUS22a].

A study by GetApp [PAV23] shows that a considerable number of consumers express interest in the metaverse as a shopping platform (Fig. 4.9). Forty-eight percent of survey participants are interested in the possibility of shopping "virtually in 3D" and trying out items. Clothing is the most appealing category for 75% of respondents, followed by electronics (57%), household items such as furniture (47%), video games (40%), and music (38%). The study also highlights that the metaverse can help bridge the gap between online shopping and the in-store experience. As many as 96% of participants interested in metaverse shopping share this view. Although the metaverse offers companies numerous new opportunities for product presentation and monetization, consumer opinions remain divided as to whether it will fully replace traditional online shopping.

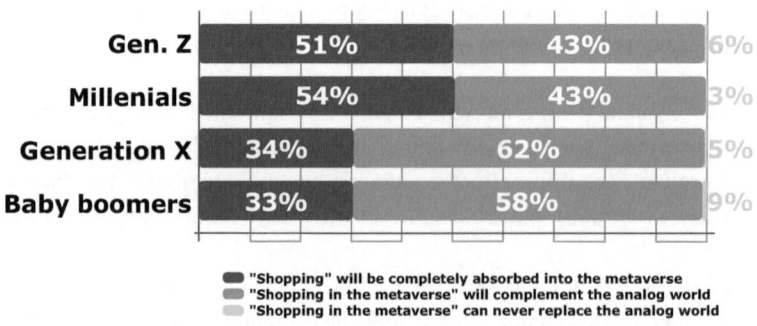

Fig. 4.9 Consumer expectations for the future of shopping. (Based on [PAV23])

However, the study indicates that consumers see convenient shopping, viewing the latest products without tedious waiting, and the option to test items using augmented reality as key advantages of shopping in the metaverse.

4.6.3 Gaming & Games

The continuous technological advancement in the field of video games is leading to increasingly realistic representations of game environments, which in turn heightens players' interest in taking a more active role within the game. The metaverse therefore offers a promising opportunity for players to leverage their agency and creativity to create their own content and interact with other players. The predicted growth in the use of the metaverse—regardless of its eventual form—will have significant impacts on the video game and film/media industries, as users will not only be able to play games and watch VR films themselves, but also immerse themselves in various virtual worlds and participate in social activities within these worlds. Platforms such as "Roblox" already demonstrate that users are capable of creating their own games and content in the metaverse and interacting with one another. Furthermore, ongoing improvements in technologies related to the metaverse are expected to enable the creation of more complex and realistic virtual environments. This development will allow players to immerse themselves in the world of film and experience it directly [JAL22].

The pronounced 3D characteristics attributed to the metaverse constitute a significant factor for all types of products in the gaming sector and represent an important economic factor within the metaverse as a whole. This is largely the result of the close cooperation between the "metaverse" sector and the gaming industry. Users can now immerse themselves in virtual game worlds. This provides them with an immersive experience that goes far beyond what a conventional flat screen can offer, especially when it is also embedded in the player's physical environment. In the future, the metaverse could create worlds in which digital education, networking, work, earning money, and even attending concerts can take place entirely digitally.

Debates about how the development of the metaverse will influence the future of gaming are still in their early stages, but it is foreseeable that ongoing research and development, as well as new projects and platforms such as Decentraland [DEC20] or Axie Infinity [BEL23a] and others, will contribute to making this "the next big thing" in gaming. Competitive games in particular will benefit, as there is now a form of player interaction that was previously impossible and even unimaginable. The combination of all these factors opens up numerous new possibilities for the gaming and entertainment sector:

- The metaverse, with its social character, offers a significant advantage over conventional virtual reality experiences, where users often act alone and in isolation. In the virtual worlds of the metaverse, players have the opportunity to invite multiple

friends from the real world, connect with other users worldwide, build relationships, and participate in additional social activities. While this is possible to some extent in current games, the intensity of social interaction remains very limited.
- The "games-as-a-platform" paradigm enables players to enjoy a more compelling gaming experience characterized by flexibility and expandability. In the virtual world, users have the opportunity to create their own content and even develop smaller games within a game. By participating in supplementary activities, players can use the game environment as a platform-like space [BAT23, KIT16].
- The combination of augmented reality and virtual reality in the metaverse offers players a much more natural experience. The mixed AR/VR activities in the metaverse, for example, allow users to seamlessly transition from an augmented reality group chat to a mixed-reality board game and ultimately into a fully virtual reality world.
- Thanks to the intended interoperability structure of the metaverse, the transferability of virtual assets such as weapons, weapon skins, and other items used by players will be facilitated. Assets acquired in one game could thus be transferred to other game environments, provided that NFTs and any relevant legislation allow for permanent ownership of these objects.
- An additional special aspect that the metaverse is expected to offer in the future is the opportunity to generate income through gaming. Beyond following a linear (game) storyline, gamers can participate in a variety of more or less lucrative activities, such as selling their assets or those obtained in play-to-win games to other users in exchange for cryptocurrencies.
- Individually customizable avatars in the virtual world also represent the players and allow them to gather with friends in a virtual environment and play together. In addition, they can visit virtual worlds created by other gamers, which changes the perception of entire online gaming communities.
- It is predicted that the metaverse will also have a significant impact on the field of e-sports, which is already extremely popular and excites millions of people worldwide. Through the metaverse, e-sports events can become even more immersive and exciting than before, as players can compete in virtual venues while spectators from around the world watch and may even be present in the virtual environment, either passively or actively [ZAV21, SEN22].

4.6.4 Art & Culture

Art has always served as a catalyst for numerous technological and societal developments. It plays a particularly important role in the field of technology. Many artists deliberately experiment with electronic and digital possibilities and can be grouped under the term "post-internet artists." The experimental nature of art enables the exploration of social and technological changes at their fringes. The resulting artworks are already being traded on a virtual market and purchased by collectors [STO22]. Thus, the metaverse is expected to play a significant role for artists and cultural creators in the future. In this world of the metaverse, they can present their works to a global audience and create interactive experiences that would be unthinkable in the physical world. In this context, virtual museums and galleries can emerge, showcasing artworks in digital spaces that do not exist in the physical world. One example is "The VR Museum of Fine Art," where visitors can view art from various eras and by different artists [BEZ19].

The metaverse also opens up opportunities for cultural creators to offer interactive experiences with minimal effort. An example of this is "The Wave XR," a platform that allows users to participate in shared virtual concerts and experience music in an immersive environment [WAVoJ]. In addition, as mentioned several times, entire concerts and theater performances can be held virtually, enabling people from all over the world to participate. In addition to the previously mentioned Ariana Grande, for example, Travis Scott's virtual concert in 2020 also took place on the "Fortnite" platform, reaching over 12 million people [TIP20]. Beyond pure concert events, there are also opportunities for interaction between artists and audiences. Virtual meet-and-greets, where fans can meet their favorite artists, as well as virtual workshops and courses, are examples of this.

Another aspect of the metaverse's relevance to the art world is demonstrated by the "Museum of Other Realities" (MOR), a virtual gallery dedicated to the presentation of immersive art [COA21, MUSoJ, DAM20]. Here, artists can exhibit their works while visitors experience them in an immersive environment independent of the real world. Another example is the "CryptoArt" market, where digital art is traded in the form of NFTs [CRYoJ, LUC22]. Such NFTs can be displayed and exchanged in virtual worlds like Decentraland or Somnium Space. Looking ahead, it is expected that the metaverse will play an even more significant role in the art and culture scene than interactive media and immersive worlds already do today. The focus will be on developing more advanced technologies and tools for modeling and interaction in virtual environments to further expand the possibilities of the metaverse.

With the predicted rise in popularity of the metaverse, it is expected that opportunities for artists will continue to evolve and expand in the future:

- *Second Life*, the oldest virtual world in the context of the metaverse, has existed since 2008 and still has many users. It enables users to create their own virtual spaces such as galleries, theaters, or museums and to exhibit artworks. Well-known museums are also present here with their own virtual exhibition spaces.
- Also based on the Ethereum blockchain, *The Sandbox* is a virtual world in which users can fully create their own virtual worlds. It allows artists to exhibit and sell their artworks by creating their own worlds or integrating their works into existing ones [SPE21].
- *Somnium Space* is an immersive virtual world that specifically offers the opportunity to exhibit and sell artworks in virtual galleries or museums [SOMoJ].
- *SuperRare*, also specializing in digital art and based on Ethereum, enables artists to sell their artworks as digital collectibles represented by unique tokens [SUPoJ].

- *Nifty Gateway* is a platform that allows artists to sell their digital artworks in limited editions. Here too, the Ethereum blockchain is used to ensure the authenticity and uniqueness of the artworks [NIFoJ].
- *Art Planet* (ArtsCloud) is an immersive virtual world where users can create, present, and sell artworks. The platform uses the Unity engine to enable users to easily present their artworks in a 3D environment [ARToJ].

4.6.5 Social Events

Social events are occasions aimed at connecting people to share common interests, maintain relationships, or make new acquaintances. Such events can be held online or offline and encompass a wide range of activities, including concerts, parties, conferences, networking events, and much more. The metaverse offers diverse opportunities for such social events, bringing together people from across the real and virtual world, regardless of their geographic location:

- *Virtual concerts*: Musicians can perform in a virtual environment and invite fans from around the world to participate in the event. There are various ways in which such virtual concerts can be designed in the metaverse.
    - For example, artists can perform on a virtual stage created in a specially developed virtual environment, as described several times above with the example of Ariana Grande. Fans can then control their avatars and gather near the stage to enjoy the concert. The music is either played live by the musicians or broadcast as a recording.
    - An alternative approach to virtual concerts in the metaverse involves using motion-capture technology to transfer the musicians' movements and actions to an avatar in real time. This makes it possible for musicians to perform simultaneously on a real stage and in a virtual environment, offering fans a concert experience in both worlds.
    - Additionally, replaying a once-modeled and programmed concert in the virtual world at different times opens up new avenues for monetization.

    The economic significance of virtual concerts in the metaverse is immense. By leveraging this technology, artists and organizers can also significantly expand their reach by engaging fans worldwide who would not normally be able to attend a physical concert. This means that more tickets can be sold and that fans around the globe gain access to music and artists they would otherwise not be able to experience.

    Moreover, virtual concerts in the metaverse represent a cost-effective alternative to traditional concert events. The expenses for implementing such a virtual concert can be considerably lower than those incurred when planning a real-world concert. This means that more artists and organizers, especially emerging and not yet established artists, can benefit from this technology.

Another advantage of virtual concerts in the metaverse is the creation of new revenue streams. For example, artists and organizers can offer virtual items such as digital tickets, virtual merchandise, and much more as NFTs to generate additional income.
- *Virtual Parties*: In the metaverse, parties represent a form of social interaction where people from around the world come together in a virtual environment to celebrate, dance, and interact collectively. These events can be held in various virtual worlds developed by companies such as Facebook, Roblox, or Fortnite:
  – Virtual parties can take place in a wide range of settings, from virtual clubs and bars to virtual beaches and festivals. The environments are typically designed by the organizers and can be highly detailed to provide a unique and realistic experience. A notable, though sometimes debated, example is the previously mentioned Decentraland Metaverse Music Festival.
  – Virtual parties allow guests to interact with each other by controlling their virtual avatars and sending emotes or text messages. Some platforms also offer voice chat options to make the event even more interactive.
  – Music is an essential component of parties, and this holds true in virtual settings as well. Organizers can often use DJ software or music streaming services to provide music for the event. Participants can create their own playlists or enjoy the music curated by the organizers.
  – Attending virtual parties can often be personalized, with guests designing their own avatars and outfits specifically for a given event. Participants can also create personalized messages and greetings for the occasion.
  – As with all events, security aspects must also be considered for virtual parties to ensure participants feel safe both in the virtual and real world. Organizers may also need to monitor compliance with rules and guidelines to ensure the event remains enjoyable for all guests.

  Virtual parties in the metaverse have the potential to become economically significant. Companies can use such parties to promote their products or services and reach a larger target audience. They can also generate revenue through admission fees or by selling virtual items such as avatars or clothing. DJs and musicians have the opportunity to offer virtual performances, expanding their audience and potentially attracting new fans.

  Moreover, virtual parties provide an opportunity to bring people together during periods of social distancing and travel restrictions, as they are accessible regardless of physical location. Overall, virtual parties in the metaverse have the potential to play a significant role in the future of social interaction and entertainment.
- *Networking Events*: Companies have the opportunity to organize virtual events to bring together experts from around the world and facilitate networking and collaboration. These events can take various forms. For example, companies can hold virtual conferences and networking events entirely within a virtual environment to gather professionals globally. Such events can take place in real time or on demand and offer

a range of tools and features to promote interaction and collaboration among attendees.

An example of this is the virtual platform "VirBELA," which supports companies in planning virtual conferences and networking events. The platform provides a virtual environment where participants can navigate and interact in a 3D space while communicating with each other. Attendees can communicate in both group and one-on-one conversations and navigate through different rooms and thematic areas. They also have the option to share documents and presentations to foster collaboration and knowledge exchange [VIRoJ].

With regard to the economic relevance of networking events in the metaverse, various factors can have an impact. On the one hand, such virtual events can help companies expand their reach and address a broader audience. As a result, they may be able to acquire more customers and grow their business. On the other hand, organizing networking events in the metaverse can lead to cost savings. Compared to physical events, virtual events can often be realized with lower financial expenditure, as there are no costs for participants' travel and accommodation. In the current economic climate, where many companies are striving to reduce expenses and operate more efficiently, this can be particularly advantageous.

Additionally, the metaverse opens up new business opportunities for companies. By creating virtual environments and platforms, firms can offer innovative products and services specifically designed for these settings. For example, they could provide virtual products or services optimized for use across all virtual manifestations of the metaverse.

- *Virtual Trade Shows and Exhibitions* enable providers to showcase their products and services in a digital environment and communicate with customers worldwide. Such events offer companies an innovative opportunity to present their offerings and interact with potential customers globally. Compared to conventional exhibitions, virtual exhibitions offer a range of advantages:
  - A broader reach is achieved through online availability, allowing companies to target potential customers worldwide without incurring travel and accommodation costs.
  - Generally, virtual exhibitions are more cost-effective than traditional ones, as there are no booth rental, travel, or accommodation expenses. However, the management of virtual worlds is also evolving, so it remains uncertain how companies will market virtual exhibitions in the future.
  - Virtual trade shows offer better tracking options, as companies can precisely determine who visited their booths and what interactions took place.
  - Interactive features such as live chats, video presentations, and webinars are usually part of these virtual environments and can be used by companies to present their products and services in an engaging way.

There are various ways to design virtual trade shows in the metaverse. One option is to create a virtual exhibition hall or convention center as a virtual venue for companies. The virtual exhibition hall can have different areas where companies set up their booths and present their products and services interactively to attract visitors and encourage engagement.

Alternatively, virtual booths can be created on platforms such as Roblox, Decentraland, or Second Life. Here, companies have the opportunity to present their products and services at individually designed booths with interactive features such as live chats, webinars, and video presentations.

A clear advantage of virtual trade shows over physical ones is that they can take place year-round, allowing companies to showcase their products and services at any time rather than being limited to an annual event.

- *Virtual Training*: The ability to conduct training sessions and workshops in a virtual environment offers companies and educational providers in the metaverse a relatively new set of options:
  - Training can take place entirely within a virtual environment and include interactive elements such as 3D models, simulations, and animations. In this way, participants can experience and apply what they have learned in a practical manner, even in virtual settings.
  - By additionally leveraging AI and machine learning, virtual training can be personalized to better accommodate the individual learning styles and needs of each participant. For example, specific topics or exercises can be automatically selected based on the individual learning requirements of each participant.
  - The integration of voice and video chat options also enables real-time communication during virtual training sessions. This allows participants to ask questions and receive feedback from trainers and other participants.
  - Virtual training in the metaverse can also promote social learning behavior by dividing participants into interactive groups where they can collaborate and support each other. This fosters teamwork and helps participants better understand and apply what they have learned.

  The significance of virtual training for the economy is expected to be considerable:
  - On the one hand, it is often more cost-effective than traditional training, as there is no need for room rental, travel, or accommodation expenses.
  - On the other hand, it can be easily scaled to reach a large number of participants regardless of their location.
  - In addition, virtual training offers better learning outcomes through interactive elements, personalized experiences, and social learning, and can be designed more flexibly by providing recorded sessions or live streams to meet participants' needs.

  With increasing digitalization, the demand for virtual training in the metaverse is expected to continue to rise, leading to a growing market for companies and providers of virtual training.

4.6.6 Tourism

In the short period of the current hype, the metaverse has also attracted significant attention from the tourism industry. The use of virtual worlds for destination marketing is a relatively new concept, yet it is already having an impact on the tourism sector (see Fig. 4.10).

The metaverse holds great potential for tourism by providing virtual immersive experiences for travelers. Within the virtual world, users can explore destinations and attractions in ways that would not be possible in the real world. For example, virtual exploration of ancient sites allows tourists to visit places like the Colosseum in Rome or the Lighthouse of Alexandria on a virtual level. These virtual tours offer a high degree of flexibility, as they allow visitors to discover sights at their own pace and focus on individual aspects.

In the future, the metaverse is likely to become even more significant for tourism, as it offers travelers the option to participate in virtual experiences and activities. For instance, the metaverse could enable users to take part in virtual activities such as diving, mountain climbing, or skydiving without having to be physically present. It could also give travelers the opportunity to experience different cultures and traditions by virtually attending festivals and celebrations without leaving their own homes. While this may seem unusual at first, there are already some experiences in such rather atypical environments for VR technology. Rulantica, operated by the aforementioned Mack GmbH, where VR is combined with snorkeling and diving, is an example of such approaches [STU19].

Tourism in the metaverse is an industry that is also attracting increasing interest among German users. According to a Bitkom study [BIT22], 21% of Germans can imagine taking their vacation trips with the help of VR headsets from around 2030 onwards, in order to explore the world in a different way and have experiences that would be unattainable in reality and the physical world. Examples of these new possibilities include virtual excursions into the deep sea or into distant historical eras. The potential for virtual travel destinations is clearly great and can help to discover places that are difficult or even impossible to reach, as well as to explore potential vacation destinations virtually in advance. This example was already mentioned in the context of gastronomy in Sect. 4.5, and other destinations such as Machu Picchu in Peru are also considering such solutions.

Fig. 4.10 Travel in the future metaverse. (Adapted from [BIT22b])

4.6 The Digital 49ers: New Business Models ...

Another Bitkom survey [BIT22b] also shows that 87% of respondents believe that traditional travel will continue to be an important change from everyday life in the future. It is assumed that international online portals will continue to dominate travel bookings, while traditional travel agencies are likely to disappear or be displaced. Most vacation experiences are already shared via social media channels and messenger apps, indicating the growing relevance of the digital world in our daily lives. Social media users are also interested in participating in the vacations of their friends and family by viewing holiday photos on social platforms.

Although all this may seem strange, it does not appear far-fetched to take a vacation in the metaverse. In view of technological progress, there is a noteworthy development: "M Social Decentraland," a hotel in the metaverse. This hotel (see also Fig. 4.11) is located near Genesis Plaza, the main entry area of Decentraland, and stands out with its architecture featuring virtual glass walls, neon pink accents, and a large "M" on each side. In the lobby, guests are greeted by an avatar who guides them through the hotel. According to a press release, some lucky virtual guests can even win real hotel surprises [TEO22, MUL23].

> "The goal of M Social is to be unique and different,"

said Kwek Leng Beng, Executive Chairman of Millennium & Copthorne Hotels Limited and also responsible for the virtual project [MIL22]:

> "To look to the future, we must look beyond the traditional model of hospitality and inspire our guests with new immersive experiences. The hotel hopes to redefine hospitality through M Social Decentraland by creating online adventures that integrate into real-life events."

In the future, M Social Decentraland also plans to host special events for holidays and other occasions such as Valentine's Day. In addition, Millennium Hotels and Resorts is

Fig. 4.11 Hotels in the metaverse (here: M Social). ([MUL23, TEO22])

in talks with partners about possible future collaborations on various platforms. Saurabh Prakash, Group Senior Vice President, Commercial, Millennium Hotels and Resorts, told BizBash that the M Social Hotel was launched as a new channel to attract customers and familiarize them with Millennium Hotels and Resorts, especially the M Social brand [TEO22].

Since then, Millennium Hotels and Resorts has been actively advancing the "M Social Decentraland" project. In February 2024, "The Vacay Collection," a virtual extension, was introduced, allowing users to explore digital versions of destinations such as Phuket in the metaverse. This initiative aims to push the boundaries of traditional hospitality and create immersive experiences that connect the physical and virtual worlds [HOS22, HOS24].

The hotel group also plans to enter into partnerships in the future and to hold special events for occasions such as New Year's or Valentine's Day in the virtual hotel. These ongoing efforts underscore Millennium Hotels and Resorts' commitment to exploring innovative approaches and leveraging the potential of the metaverse for the hospitality industry [HOS22] (Fig. 4.12).

4.6.7 Education

As already mentioned in Sect. 4.6.6, the metaverse also presents opportunities for educational purposes by enabling the creation of interactive, immersive, and collaborative learning environments that allow learners to gain a deeper understanding of ideas, concepts, and entire subject areas.

Fig. 4.12 M-Social Vacay Phuket

An example of the application of the metaverse in the school context is the use of virtual worlds such as Second Life or Minecraft. Within such virtual environments, students can carry out both individual and collaborative projects, which help to expand their understanding of concepts such as geometry, architecture, and programming. The design of virtual laboratories is also possible in immersive spaces like the metaverse. In these, students can conduct experiments without relying on physical resources. Furthermore, they can try out inaccessible or hazardous experiments that would be unthinkable or too risky in the real world. This enables them to gain a deeper understanding of scientific ideas and improve their skills in data analysis and problem-solving [RZE20, DAV22, HOW22].

Another example, focusing on social education, involves connecting students from different countries and cultures. Through virtual exchange programs, learners from diverse nations and cultures can collaborate and benefit from one another in a shared virtual environment [RZE20, DAV22, HOW22]. In this way, students are offered a creative, interactive, and more immersive form of learning, which deepens their understanding of ideas and topics.

The metaverse is also gaining increasing acceptance in higher education. It enables students and researchers to present and share their work in innovative ways, fostering collaboration and exchange with peers worldwide. Virtual conferences are one example. They allow participants from around the globe to attend presentations and poster sessions without physical barriers, to exhibit and publish in virtual spaces, and to discuss research findings and ideas in virtual forums.

Furthermore, as already mentioned, virtual laboratories offer researchers numerous possibilities. Experiments that are not feasible in the real world due to resource, safety, or ethical constraints can be conducted here. This enables more effective research and the faster acquisition of new insights [MAC09]. In addition, opportunities arise for collaboration and exchange among researchers worldwide through the use of virtual workspaces. Regardless of location, they can work together on projects and share ideas, which in turn facilitates cooperation between scientists from different countries and promotes international collaboration.

Efforts are also underway to expand learning platforms such as Moodle with the help of the metaverse. Moodle is an open-source platform that allows teachers and instructors to provide and manage learning content online. The metaverse could potentially help make learning platforms like Moodle and similar systems even more efficient and attractive than they already are [SA23, SAAoJ]. One way such platforms can benefit from the metaverse is through integration into existing virtual environments. By linking in this way, teachers and instructors can create an interactive and immersive experience for their students. This can be achieved, for example, by incorporating virtual learning games or simulations that support and enrich the learning process. By integrating access to the metaverse into Moodle, students can also interact and collaborate more intensively to learn together and expand their skills. Furthermore, the metaverse opens up significant opportunities for the personalization of learning content. By strategically using metadata and machine learning, such learning platforms can better capture and adapt to the learning needs and preferences of students. This enables the provision of personalized learning content tailored to the individual needs and interests of students. Overall, the metaverse offers numerous opportunities to optimize teaching and learning platforms like Moodle and others. The integration of virtual worlds, use as a Moodle extension, and adaptation of learning materials all contribute to making these platforms more efficient and engaging [HAN23].

Although some critics view the metaverse as a threat to the traditional education system, it actually represents an enrichment and opens up new ways for students to enhance their skills and expand their knowledge. The conventional education system will continue to play an essential role in the education of students, as they will still need to acquire fundamental skills such as reading, writing, and arithmetic, which are taught there. In addition, the traditional system fosters social skills and the personal development of learners. However, the metaverse can help to extend and optimize the classical education system.

It is, however, essential to consider whether the metaverse is accessible to all students. Especially in Germany, comprehensive high-quality internet access remains a challenge. It would therefore not be surprising if some learners lacked access to the necessary technologies, could not afford the required devices, or had difficulties learning in a virtual environment. For these reasons alone, it is of great importance that the conventional education system is maintained and that students are supported in a variety of ways.

In particular, the integration of AI tools, for example as AI-supported teacher avatars in immersive virtual learning environments, currently appears to offer a new perspective for digital teaching and learning. There is ongoing discussion as to whether such types of avatars can enable an interactive, personalized, and collaborative form of instruction that goes beyond traditional learning methods and even classical e-learning. The goal is to provide students with a more flexible, accessible, and effective educational approach through the use of virtual technologies:

- Such a scenario could begin with entering a virtual classroom designed as a three-dimensional space. Students log in via a learning portal, enter the virtual classroom, and interact with an AI-driven teacher avatar, which can take various forms. This avatar can appear as a "normal" representation of the teacher, but also as a historical figure, scientist, or another famous personality. Based on its integrated AI tools, the avatar analyzes the students' prior knowledge, poses personalized questions and tasks, and provides real-time feedback. Students can communicate with the avatar either verbally or in writing to receive additional explanations. This interactive teaching approach enables dynamic adaptation to individual learning needs [FAD19].
- In addition to the social component arising from the interaction between teacher and student avatars, a key advantage of such virtual learning environments is the ability to enable hands-on learning through simulations and interactive experiments. In science subjects, for example, students could enter a virtual cell to explore the organelles

or conduct experiments on gravitational forces in a digital physics lab. This type of learning not only increases engagement but also improves the understanding of complex concepts through immediate, visual experiences [TOV20].
- To increase student motivation, teacher avatars can incorporate gamified elements into lessons. Puzzles, quizzes, and reward systems such as badges or virtual certificates promote playful learning and allow students to visibly track their progress. In addition, the teacher avatar fosters collaboration among students by moderating group projects and providing targeted individual feedback. Through real-time interaction with students, the avatar can also demonstrate emotional intelligence by recognizing mood changes and adjusting the level of difficulty or teaching method accordingly. For example, the avatar could offer reassuring words if a student appears frustrated or provide additional input if a student seems underchallenged [DME12].

A key strength of using AI-powered teacher avatars lies in the personalization of learning, as instruction can be tailored to the individual needs of students. The virtual environment also eliminates the need for physical presence, increasing accessibility for students from different regions. In addition, such avatars are available around the clock and can support students outside of regular class hours. The immersive nature of the metaverse provides a motivating, interactive learning experience, while the absence of physical resources can reduce costs for schools and institutions [OWO21].

The practical application of such forms of integration already extends to various educational fields. Virtual avatars act as native-speaking teachers and guide students through realistic language exercises in digital environments, such as a café in Paris or a market in Tokyo, during language lessons. In history classes, avatars can take on the roles of historical figures and narrate a past era from a first-person perspective, while students travel through a virtual reconstruction of that time. Similarly, technical training can take place in a virtual workshop, where avatars explain the assembly and operation of machines before students work with them in real-life situations [BAI18].

4.6.8 The Metaverse and the World of Work

The implementation of the metaverse concept will not only create new forms of work on the platforms and within the immersive worlds of the metaverse. New forms of work and new professional roles related to the metaverse will also become established in the physical world. One such previously non-existent role is that of the CMO, the Chief Metaverse Officer. As previously mentioned, Cathy Hackl describes the role of such a CMO in her book "Into the Metaverse" as a strategic leadership position that helps companies unlock the potential of the metaverse. She emphasizes the relevance of this position through its bridging function between technology and business development. Core responsibilities include the development and implementation of strategies for virtual goods, avatars, NFTs, gaming, and technologies such as VR, MR, and AR. In-depth knowledge of cryptocurrencies, blockchain technology, cloud computing, game engines, and digital design is essential [HAC23].

This new role serves as an interface and therefore requires a combination of marketing and communication expertise, strategic business acumen, and technological know-how. The CMO is responsible for shaping and managing the brand's presence in the metaverse, including developing strategies for virtual products and services as well as creating immersive brand experiences. A central part of the CMO's responsibilities is collaboration with various industries that are already making progress in the metaverse, such as fashion and marketing. The CMO should be able to identify and foster partnerships that maximize the metaverse's potential for the company. This also includes monitoring developments in areas such as gaming, synthetic media, spatial computing, and artificial intelligence to identify and leverage new business opportunities.

The Chief Metaverse Officer could play a significant role for companies in the future, enriching the management level as a key leadership position for those organizations that wish to proactively pursue the opportunities of the metaverse. By integrating technological expertise and strategic vision, the CMO can help drive digital transformation and open up new revenue streams in the emerging metaverse.

4.6.9 The Metaverse and Medicine

It is to be expected that the concept of the metaverse will also play a significant role in the medical field. One area where this is already the case is medical education. By creating virtual environments, medical students can simulate scenarios in a realistic setting and thus improve their practical skills. An example of this is virtual emergency medicine simulators, where students are trained to respond and work quickly and effectively in high-stress environments [ZIV03, MEDoJ, VIN15]. The field of telemedicine is also expected to undergo changes due to the metaverse. By using VR, patients and doctors can interact with each other in real time, regardless of their location. This enables patients to receive diagnoses or even treatment from doctors who may be located far away [BAL21b, MAR22]. This, in turn, could help improve healthcare provision, for example in rural areas.

Furthermore, the metaverse will also be used in medical research to accelerate the development of new drugs and therapies. Virtual environments can be used to simulate the effects of drugs on various human organs and systems, or to explore new approaches to medical procedures, potentially saving years of research and development [KAW22].

Clinical treatment and hospitals can also benefit from the metaverse. By integrating virtual reality into hospital operations, they can increase their efficiency and effectiveness, ultimately achieving better patient outcomes. One example is the use of VR for training medical staff. By setting up virtual environments, medical institutions can offer doctors, nurses, and other staff the opportunity to learn and improve practical skills before applying them in the real world. The hope is that this will help reduce training costs and the time required for training, while simultaneously improving the quality of education. In addition, VR technology enables hospitals to offer a broader range of services and, for example, reach patients in remote locations. This can help reduce waiting times for appointments and improve access to high-quality healthcare. Virtual environments also help improve the accuracy of diagnoses and treatment plans. By generating individualized virtual models of patients, doctors and other medical professionals can obtain an accurate representation of the patient's body and make more informed decisions. Moreover, virtual environments can also help improve the planning of surgical procedures and minimize risks [WAN22, WU23].

There are also many opportunities in the field of nursing to benefit from the integration of virtual reality into the metaverse. The technology can help improve the quality of care, increase workflow efficiency, and make life easier for those in need of care. One area where the metaverse can be particularly advantageous in nursing is the training of nursing staff. As in hospitals, virtual environments can be used to train nurses in various situations and improve their skills without putting patients at risk. Ultimately, this also helps to improve the quality of care and patient safety [WAN22].

Another area where the metaverse can be beneficial in nursing is in improving communication between caregivers and patients. Virtual environments can be used to better understand the needs and wishes of those requiring care and to provide them with better support and assistance. In addition, virtual environments have been shown to help reduce social isolation among the elderly by facilitating access to social contacts and activities [WAN22, MOZ23]. Both in nursing and in inpatient hospital care, the metaverse can help increase efficiency. There is potential to improve logistics and workflow planning, for example by using automated systems or virtual assistants that have been optimized on their digital or real twins. This can help save time and resources and improve the quality of care [ADI23, KAL22].

Ultimately, health insurance companies and health insurers also hope to benefit from the metaverse. A prime example is the improvement of patient education. By creating virtual environments, insurers can offer interactive training and information that help patients better understand their health and prepare more effectively for treatment. This, in turn, can improve adherence to treatment plans and ultimately enhance patient health. Business processes such as billing are also expected to benefit from the metaverse by increasing the degree of automation and digitization. Furthermore, insurers could establish and utilize their own virtual environments to accelerate the development of treatment plans and therapies. Conversely, by simulating diseases and treatment plans, insurers can gain a better understanding of which treatments are most effective and what risks are associated with them. This can also help reduce overall healthcare costs by avoiding unnecessary treatments and selecting more effective therapies [SOS22, ADI23, KAL22].

The opportunities that the metaverse opens up in the medical field also present a challenge to the traditional healthcare system. It offers new ways to deliver healthcare services and foster collaboration between patients, providers, and insurers, enabling access to medical services in real time and from anywhere in the world, without requiring patients to physically visit a doctor or medical facility. However, this could lead to traditional "on-site" healthcare systems losing significance. Another challenge is that the metaverse gives patients greater control over their healthcare. Patients can access information and resources to manage their own health, rather than relying on the assistance of doctors or other medical professionals. This, too, could result in a diminished role for doctors and other healthcare professionals in the provision of care [ADI23].

Ultimately, however, the metaverse can help improve access to healthcare services, especially for people living in rural areas or regions with limited access to medical care. By using virtual environments, patients and healthcare professionals can communicate regardless of their location and select any available medical service, making use of them even more extensively than via the WWW.

A particular area of medical applications, which also significantly overlaps with the aforementioned field of care, is so-called Ambient Assisted Living (AAL).

AAL encompasses technologies that enable older or impaired individuals to live independently. This includes smart sensors for health monitoring and emergency prevention, assistive systems such as voice-controlled assistants or automatic reminder functions, as well as communication technologies that facilitate social interaction. These systems are intended to provide users with greater autonomy in daily life while also relieving family members or caregivers.

One of the most important interfaces between AAL and the metaverse lies in the promotion of social interaction. Many older people suffer from social isolation, especially when they have limited mobility. The metaverse, on the other hand, offers virtual spaces where they can meet with family and friends, participate in digital community activities, or build new social networks. Access to virtual worlds could enable older adults to engage more actively in social interactions and discover new forms of participation.

In addition, the metaverse could expand therapeutic applications for AAL environments. Virtual physiotherapy programs guided by AI-powered avatars could enable exercise routines in a motivating environment. Similarly, virtual relaxation or meditation rooms could promote mental health and reduce stress. Especially for people with cognitive impairments, the metaverse could provide a platform for memory training and interactive therapies tailored to the individual needs of users [MAT22b]. The metaverse can also be integrated into AAL environments to offer training for older adults or their caregivers. For example, virtual courses could help users learn to handle new technologies, understand health measures, or manage caregiving tasks. This could improve both the independence of older adults and the efficiency of caregivers [ORT24].

Another potential lies in connecting smart environments with virtual spaces. AAL households already equipped with smart control systems could be extended via the metaverse. For instance, users could enter a virtual representation of their home through a VR headset and control lighting, heating, or security systems there. This could be a significant relief in everyday life, especially for people with mobility limitations [SOU24]. An innovative approach within this connection is the use of digital twins for health monitoring and care. AAL sensors could continuously collect health data, which would be visualized as digital twins in the metaverse. Doctors or caregivers could thus analyze movement profiles or vital signs in real time and take preventive or acute measures. This could enable better medical care and provide early indications of health changes [LU20].

Despite the largely positive potential of connecting AAL and the metaverse, there are two particular challenges that arise from the predominantly demographic characteristics of the "typical" AAL user [SCHwir24, MOR23]:

- Technological barriers represent one of the greatest obstacles, as many older adults may have difficulty using complex devices such as VR headsets or AR systems. The user-friendliness of such technologies must therefore be ensured to enable broad acceptance. In addition, substantial investments are generally required to link AAL systems with metaverse technologies and to ensure that they function reliably and securely.
- User acceptance also plays a crucial role. While some older adults are open to new technologies, others may perceive the metaverse as unnecessary or difficult to understand. The introduction of such systems must therefore be accompanied by comprehensive training offerings and user-friendly interfaces to ensure widespread adoption.

4.6.10 The Business Internal Metaverse

The term "Business Internal Metaverse" or "Intraverse" [MAL22] refers to virtual environments developed specifically for use within a company or organization. As an extension of the intranet, it represents a type of closed virtual ecosystem accessible only to employees, managers, and other authorized individuals within the company. Such a business internal metaverse enables users to meet, communicate, collaborate, and complete tasks in a virtual environment, much like any other "public" metaverse. However, this virtual world integrates applications and tools tailored to the specific needs of the company, such as virtual conference rooms, digital workspaces, training modules, simulation programs, and more.

The concept of the business internal metaverse is still relatively new, but there are already a number of companies utilizing virtual work environments to better connect their employees and more effectively integrate them into internal processes. One example is Spatial, which has developed a virtual work platform that allows users to collaborate in a shared virtual environment, regardless of their physical location [CAR23].

However, the future of this form of the metaverse seems particularly promising in establishing processes that also involve customer interaction. Some examples of such processes include [MAL22, ROE22, CAR23]:

- Companies can set up virtual conference rooms to hold customer meetings. Customers can simply log in via a virtual platform and participate in a virtual meeting without needing to be physically present.

- Companies can also establish customer support services. Customers can use such a virtual customer support platform to ask questions or report issues. The support staff can then respond and provide solutions via the virtual platform. This support representative may be either a real employee or an autonomous support assistant or chatbot.
- Companies can also conduct virtual product presentations. Customers can log in and be guided virtually through the company's products. The advantage here is that customers can view and try out products in an interactive 3D environment without having to be physically present.
- Companies can also offer virtual training sessions for customers within the business internal metaverse. Customers can register for a virtual training and then meet with other participants in a virtual classroom. The training can be conducted either by a real employee or a virtual trainer who guides participants through the session.
- Companies can also host any other type of virtual event in the business internal metaverse. For example, they can set up a virtual, immersive customer forum where customers can discuss ideas and suggestions with each other or with support staff and provide feedback. Virtual product launch events are also conceivable, where customers have the opportunity to try out the company's newly introduced products in an interactive environment.

A particularly significant area for implementing a business internal metaverse is support. "Immersive support" refers to a form of technical support or customer service in which support staff meet customers in an immersive, virtual environment to resolve issues or answer questions. Unlike traditional customer support, which typically takes place via phone or email, immersive support enables more intensive and personalized interaction between customers and support staff. For example, support staff could demonstrate to customers in a virtual, yet realistic environment how to use a product or how to independently resolve a technical issue. This can not only increase customer satisfaction but also improve the efficiency of customer support by resolving issues more quickly and effectively [MON22, MAL22].

In the manufacturing industry, virtual reality (VR) technology is already being used to create simulations of factories and production processes. VR technology can also be used in this context to train employees, preparing them for specific work situations and improving their skills. However, it gains even greater significance through the creation of digital replicas of facilities and entire production and manufacturing units. For example, virtual factories are created in which various production processes can be simulated [GEY23].

The so-called Industry 4.0 is now considered a well-established topic. Its goal is to create an intelligent factory in which production, logistics, technology, and the workforce are interconnected to enable more efficient and flexible production processes. By networking machines, equipment, and systems in real time, autonomous decisions can be made to optimize production processes [PLAoJ]. At first glance, the concepts of Industry

4.0 and the metaverse may not seem to have much in common, but there are some possible connections:

- Both Industry 4.0 and the metaverse are visionary concepts that represent a future of digital optimization and digital coexistence.
- Both concepts leverage technologies such as artificial intelligence, virtual and augmented reality, the Internet of Things, blockchain, and more. Technology is the key to digitizing and optimizing reality.
- Industry 4.0 aims for seamless networking of production facilities, machines, systems, and people to increase efficiency and improve decision-making. The metaverse is an extended form of such networking, enabling people to interact with each other in virtual worlds.
- Both concepts focus on personalization. In Industry 4.0, products and services are tailored to the individual needs of customers. In the metaverse, users can customize their virtual identities, create their own worlds, and in the future, also influence the formation and execution of processes.
- Industry 4.0 collects and analyzes large volumes of data to make better decisions and increase efficiency. Similarly, the metaverse generates vast amounts of data that can be used for personalization and to enhance the user experience.

The integration of Industry 4.0 and the metaverse could thus lead to production processes being simulated in a virtual world to improve the efficiency and flexibility of real-world factories. In such a virtual world, autonomous decisions could be made to optimize production while simultaneously simulating interactions between employees and equipment. By integrating metaverse technologies into Industry 4.0 solutions, new forms of collaboration and employee training could be enabled.

The ideas typically mentioned for the area of maintenance and servicing with the help of the metaverse are not necessarily new:

- By using VR and AR, the metaverse can help train and educate employees. For example, maintenance and service technicians can train in a virtual environment that closely resembles the real-world setting in which they will work.
- In the metaverse, sensors and other devices can be monitored in real time. This enables maintenance technicians to diagnose and resolve issues remotely before downtime occurs.
- The metaverse provides a platform for collaboration between maintenance technicians, engineers, and other professionals. For example, they can work together on a virtual model of a machine to solve problems and implement improvements.
- With the metaverse, maintenance technicians and engineers can visualize and analyze complex information. For instance, they can create 3D models of machines and equipment and access various data in real time to quickly identify and resolve issues.

- By analyzing data in real time, maintenance technicians and engineers can identify patterns and predict when maintenance will be required. This enables preventive maintenance measures to be taken, minimizing downtime and extending the lifespan of machines.

4.6.11 Metaverse Service Providing

Not only the "interior" of the metaverse is suitable for management and operation. The term "Metaverse Service Providing" (MSP) refers to the idea of offering services both within and outside the metaverse. Metaverse platforms are virtual environments where users can interact, create and share content, as well as conduct communicative and business transactions. Individual users in private settings, as well as companies, can use these platforms to communicate and interact, but also to present their own products and services and reach their target audiences. A wide range of services is required for this purpose:

- Development and design of content and applications within and for the platform
- Hosting and management of servers
- Provision of cloud-based storage and processing services
- Security services and identity management within the metaverse and its platforms
- AI and machine learning services to enhance interaction and user experience
- Payment processing and management within the metaverse.

While Sect. 4.6.8 already introduced the CMO as a key role in a metaverse-oriented company, there are, in the context of MSP, a number of additional areas of activity that require appropriate skills.

In the area of customer support, the metaverse enables the creation of virtual helpdesks where customers can interact with digital avatars. Such avatars, much like today's support chatbots, provide personalized real-time assistance. For example, customers can try out products in a virtual environment or resolve issues through interactive demonstrations. Companies like Verizon have already deployed VR technologies to assist customers with troubleshooting in a 3D space, making support more intuitive.

The metaverse also offers opportunities for direct support of software and software systems, allowing complex problems to be addressed through visual and interactive methods. Customers can communicate with support staff via AR-enabled video calls, where agents can use virtual markers or holograms to provide specific instructions. This facilitates troubleshooting and reduces the need for physical intervention. Platforms such as Blitzz already offer AR-supported video calls, where agents use the customer's camera to diagnose and resolve issues through visual cues [BLI21].

With regard to software maintenance, the characteristics of the metaverse enable proactive and predictive approaches. By simulating software environments in virtual spaces, developers can identify potential issues before they arise. In addition, regular maintenance can be performed in a controlled virtual environment, minimizing the risk of downtime. The integration of AI and machine learning into these processes supports continuous monitoring and optimization of software solutions.

Companies specializing in Metaverse Service Providing offer these services and work closely with platform operators and clients to ensure that the needs of both parties are met. Such companies are typically already specialized in the specific requirements of the Internet and therefore possess sufficient experience to provide services for the new environment of the metaverse as well. This area includes services such as "land development" and building construction, which make a significant contribution to the development of virtual worlds in the metaverse by assisting developers and users in designing virtual worlds and buildings:

- Land developers, for example, can design and create virtual landscapes and environments that users can then utilize for their own purposes. They model the topography, vegetation, and other features of virtual worlds and adapt them to optimize immersion and user experience.
- Another important role is played by building construction and modeling. Here, the specific and individual wishes of clients are incorporated so that virtual buildings can be used as virtual offices, shops, apartments, parks, or for other purposes. Companies such as VRJAM [VRJoJ] and Sine Wave Entertainment [SINoJ] offer tools and technologies for creating such virtual buildings and environments, which can then be seamlessly integrated into metaverse platforms.
- Both land development and building construction make a significant contribution to creating the most immersive and engaging virtual environments possible.
- Companies like Decentraland, Somnium Space, and many others offer virtual land for purchase. Decentraland has even advanced this concept further and now offers the possibility to lease or rent acquired virtual land. In addition to the actual development and modeling of virtual "land," there is an opportunity to establish virtual real estate development as a future service offering. Such "Virtual Estate Services" focus on the purchase, sale, and management of virtual land and properties in the metaverse. Examples of this can currently be found primarily among platform providers [STO22]:
    - As mentioned above, Decentraland enables users to buy, sell, and manage virtual land. The company also offers its own tools and services for content and application development on its platform.
    - Somnium Space is another immersive and decentralized virtual world where users can buy, build, and manage land. This platform also offers users a variety of tools and services to design their virtual worlds [SOMoJ, SOM22].
    - The Sandbox offers users the option to create their own virtual worlds and share them with others. Users also have the opportunity to buy, sell, and trade virtual land [THEoJ, THE20].

- Upland takes a different approach to the concept of "land." The virtual land offered here is based on the real world. Users can also buy, sell, and trade virtual properties, but these are digital twins of real-world locations [UPLoJ, CHA22].
- Virtual urban planning pursues broader goals with the concept of Building Information Modeling (BIM). This approach focuses specifically on the construction sector and enables the creation of detailed digital models of individual buildings or entire urban infrastructures. It includes information on geometry, materials, costs, schedules, and other relevant data. BIM is typically used by architects, engineers, construction companies, and other building professionals to manage the entire lifecycle of buildings and urban infrastructures. By linking BIM and the metaverse, virtual environments are created in which buildings and infrastructures can be visualized and manipulated. This opens up new possibilities for collaboration, simulation, and optimization of buildings and infrastructures in the virtual environment [BOR15].
- Companies such as Matterport offer technologies for surveying real-world conditions and creating 3D models of buildings and environments, which can then be integrated into the metaverse, for example, using the aforementioned BIM [JAV21].
- The design of avatars, fashion, and accessories also falls within the scope of "Metaverse Service Providers." Since avatars represent the digital twins of users, the design of avatars and their accessories is an important aspect of metaverse service provision, as it enhances the possibilities for personalizing the user experience and thus increases user acceptance and engagement with the platform. A wide range of companies have already established themselves in this area [STO22]:
  - Daz 3D specializes in creating 3D models, characters, and accessories for various applications, including the metaverse.
  - Morph 3D offers a toolkit for creating and customizing avatars for the metaverse.
  - IMVU is a social media platform specializing in the creation and customization of avatars and offers a wide range of accessories that users can purchase.
  - Second Life is the oldest virtual world and has demonstrated what monetization and management of services in the metaverse can mean. Here, there are examples of tools offered to users for creating their own avatars and accessories, as well as management tools for the real estate market. The power of these tools for trading virtual real estate was demonstrated as early as 2006, when a user became the first millionaire in the metaverse as a real estate agent [RIX22, GOL21].

4.6.12 Back into the Real World

The examples of "Metaverse Service Providing" listed in the previous section primarily refer to services within the "interior" of the metaverse. However, a wide range of services are also necessary for the development and support of individual users as well as entire platforms, which are based in the real world and, so to speak, keep the metaverse "running" from the outside. This includes both software and hardware services in the real world:

- Cloud-based services enable users and platform providers to host and operate their own virtual environments and applications in the metaverse.
- Companies that develop VR headsets and other hardware for immersive applications can easily adapt and offer their products for the metaverse as well.
- 3D modeling software can be provided by companies to facilitate the creation of content and entire environments in the metaverse for users and operators.
- The development of haptic feedback systems enables users to experience the virtual world of the metaverse through tactile sensations and feedback.
- This idea can be further developed by considering additional human sensory modalities to enable barrier-free access to metaverses. In the future, this will gain increased importance, among other things, due to the European Accessibility Act [AMT19] and the German Accessibility Strengthening Act [BMA21].
- Companies can also offer AI-based services that provide users in the metaverse with personalized experiences and recommendations.
- Finally, special devices and apps can be developed for mobile use, enabling users to access the metaverse flexibly while on the go.

4.6.13 The "God Role"

The concept of a "God Role" in the metaverse refers to the idea that users, companies, as well as service providers and platform operators, can possess "god-like" power and control over the design and development of virtual land, environments, and avatars. In many virtual worlds and platforms based on the metaverse concept, it is common for there to be a central authority or a group of individuals responsible for providing virtual land and controlling the design of landscapes and avatars. In a sense, these individuals assume a "God Role," as they have the ability to shape and control the virtual world according to their own vision. They alone can decide which types of buildings and objects are permitted in the virtual world and which are not, and they can also determine who has access to certain areas of the virtual world. From their respective perspectives, they pursue what they see as the best goals for "their" worlds.

The "God Role" is particularly prominent on platforms such as Bit.Country. This metaverse platform enables users to create and manage their own virtual worlds. As a "Metaverse as a Service," it offers an application framework and blockchain infrastructure based on the Metaverse.Network, allowing the creation of custom metaverses and games [BAR23].

A standout feature of Bit.Country is that users can launch "their own metaverse" within just a few seconds, even without technical expertise. (NOTE: This descriptive statement from Coinbureau naturally contradicts the characteristics described by Ball and Parisi!) These "metaverses" (more accurately: these platforms) include a 3D world with a map where virtual land parcels can be owned, traded, and developed. There is also a dedicated NFT marketplace where users can create, display, and trade their NFT collections. The platform also offers "Pulse," a social media feature that allows users to publish content, promote events, and interact with the community.

From a technological perspective, Bit.Country supports both WebAssembly (WASM) and Ethereum-compatible smart contracts, making it easier for developers to create decentralized applications (dApps) and games on the platform. The platform is browser-based, so no additional software downloads are required, and it emphasizes user-friendliness and accessibility [GIToJ].

The platform's native cryptocurrency, $NUUM, serves as a universal means of payment for various activities within the Metaverse.Network protocol. This includes purchasing resources such as land blocks, paying gas fees for transactions, advertising and promotions, as well as trading on the marketplace.

Bit.Country has received significant support from investors and partners, including Animoca Brands, Hypersphere Ventures, and Digital Renaissance. These partnerships underscore the platform's potential to change the way communities and individuals create and experience virtual worlds.

Naturally, the "God Role" described here can also be criticized, as it ultimately creates an imbalance of power and may restrict the freedom of metaverse users—that is, the visitors and participants in these worlds—limiting their ability to freely shape their own experiences and worlds. As a result, some virtual platforms and worlds have begun to give users more control over the design and development of their own virtual environments in order to balance this distribution of power.

The evaluation of this role can therefore be both positive and negative, depending on how it is exercised and also on the values and beliefs of those who assume it. Abuse of centralized control is just as possible in virtuality as it is in reality. Not only can users' freedom and creativity be restricted, but users can also be discriminated against—for example, by being excluded from the virtual world based on their choice of avatar or for no reason at all, or by being denied access to certain parts of the platform and the use of specific services.

Indeed, there have already been reports of abuse in the metaverse [EHL20, LE22]. It is therefore significant that operators of virtual platforms and worlds find ways to ensure, on the one hand, a more equitable distribution of power and, on the other, that the interests and needs of users are placed at the center. This can be achieved, for example, by implementing democratic structures, transparent decision-making processes, and creating an open and inclusive community.

The formation of closed groups, similar to cults and secret societies, could also occur in the context of a "God Role" in the metaverse [END22, MOR22]. If a person or group of people exercising control over part of the virtual land or platform wields their power in an authoritarian or undemocratic manner, this could lead certain users to band together and form a kind of cult or secret society to defend their own interests or to resist the ruling authority. Those who assume the "God Role" can thus play an important part in creating a safe and secure environment, for example by enforcing policies against hate speech or cyberbullying. They can also help prevent fraud or abuse by monitoring users and reporting suspicious activities. Here, too, the analogy to the internet can be useful in highlighting the significance of these developmental potentials. Even if it does not immediately result in a "dark metaverse," platforms such as 4chan or 8chan and others can serve as case studies for countermeasures [DAL15, OHL19].

Of course, not every form of group formation in the metaverse has negative consequences. It is entirely possible for users to come together in positive ways—to collaborate on projects, exchange ideas, or simply form a community of like-minded individuals. The key is to ensure that the role under consideration here is exercised in a way that respects and fosters users' freedom and creativity, and that an open and inclusive community is created, based on mutual respect and cooperation.

Centralized control of a virtual world or platform can also have positive effects, such as helping to maintain a high standard of quality in the virtual world, since operators can set the standards and rules that all users must follow. This can ensure a consistent appearance and user experience, which in turn can increase user engagement and foster community growth. Ultimately, those in the "God Role" can also act as creative catalysts, promoting the development of new ideas and concepts and inspiring the community to contribute their own input. When this role is used positively, it can help maximize the potential of the metaverse as a virtual world that offers new opportunities for interaction, creativity, and collaboration.

4.6.14 DAOs and the Metaverse

DAO stands for Decentralized Autonomous Organization. This refers to organizations that are based on a decentralized network such as blockchain technology, where financial and other transactions as well as the rules of the organization are recorded. In contrast to traditional companies or organizations, which are managed by a central authority, a DAO is a self-organized and autonomous structure that is collectively governed by its members. As a relatively new form of organization, the exact legal status of DAOs remains largely unresolved [CHO17].

In the metaverse, DAOs can be used as tools for community governance and project coordination. They can also be utilized for project funding, decision-making through voting, and resource allocation. DAOs enable users to create a democratic and transparent organization that operates without human intermediaries and is based on consensus. By using smart contracts, a DAO can ensure that decisions and transactions are carried out in a transparent and trustworthy manner, without the need for a central authority or intermediary. This can help foster trust and collaboration within the community, as all members participate on an equal footing and can be involved in decision-making. Furthermore, DAOs can also provide a means to distribute revenues and profits from projects in a fair and transparent way, thereby incentivizing users to contribute to the development and growth of the metaverse [LIU22, MOR20].

An example of a DAO in the metaverse is "The Sandbox." On this platform, players can create their own assets, which can then be sold as NFTs on Ethereum. The governance of the game is managed by a DAO called "The Sandbox DAO," which is controlled by token holders. The DAO decides on the direction of the game, new features and upgrades, and the allocation of resources [SPE21].

In the future, DAOs could play an even more significant role in the metaverse, serving as tools for the creation of decentralized enterprises and autonomous organizations. DAOs could also be used to regulate emerging future markets in the metaverse by making transparent decisions and representing the interests of the community. Conversely, existing DAOs from the metaverse could also derive benefits in the real world by using the metaverse as a tool for creating decentralized organizations and businesses. In the real world, DAOs can be used, for example, to minimize the risk of fraud and corruption by making transparent decisions and reducing the influence of human intermediaries:

- One example is "MolochDAO," which is designed as a decentralized investment platform for funding blockchain startups. This DAO consists of members who deposit ETH tokens into the DAO and collectively decide on investments. MolochDAO is managed by a smart contract and is decentralized, meaning that decisions are made by the community rather than a central authority. It should also be noted that MolochDAO is an evolution of a DAO that was created in response to a hacker attack on its predecessor DAO [DUN19].
- Another example is "MakerDAO," also a decentralized platform, but with the goal of issuing stablecoins on Ethereum. DAO members hold MKR tokens, which grant them voting rights on decisions regarding the management of the platform [SMAoJ].

In the future, DAOs in the metaverse could also be used to connect physical and virtual assets. For example, DAOs could enable the tokenization of real-world real estate, which could then be traded as virtual assets in the metaverse. Additionally, DAOs could be used to decentralize the governance of open-source software projects by allowing decisions to be made by a community rather than a central authority.

DAOs offer a way to create democratic and transparent organizations in both the metaverse and the real world, based on consensus and decentralized governance. However, there are currently only a few political DAOs that explicitly focus on the metaverse. Nevertheless, there are some political organizations that are exploring blockchain technology and the possibilities of DAOs:

- One example of such political initiatives is the party "DEMOKRATIE IN BEWEGUNG" in Germany, which sees itself as a citizens' movement and aims to use blockchain technology to promote direct democracy. The party is working on devel-

oping its own DAO system that will enable members to participate in decision-making and the political agenda of the party [DEMoJ].
- Another example is the "Taipei City Government," which has implemented a blockchain system in Taiwan called "TIPAS" (Taipei Smart City Public Affairs System). TIPAS is intended to improve the transparency and efficiency of government by providing citizens with access to information and government decisions. The platform also uses DAO-like structures to make decisions and perform governance functions [TAIoJ].

Political DAOs and their use in the metaverse still appear to be in a rather early stage of development. It remains to be seen how the underlying technologies and concepts will be adopted by political organizations in the future.

4.6.15 The Banker Role

In the context of the metaverse, the role of the "banker" is of central importance, particularly with regard to the management and creation of digital assets through cryptocurrencies and non-fungible tokens. The banker role in the metaverse acts as a financial service provider, overseeing and supporting the issuance, management, and trading of digital currencies and NFTs.

The creation of new digital assets, known as "minting," is an essential process in the metaverse. During minting, a digital asset—such as an NFT—is created and registered on a blockchain, thereby establishing its uniqueness and ownership. This process requires specialized knowledge of blockchain technology and smart contracts, which is provided by the banker role in the metaverse. Through minting, digital artworks, virtual real estate, or other unique digital goods can be created and traded [KIN22].

In addition, the banker role plays a crucial part in managing the currencies used in the metaverse. Many metaverse platforms have their own cryptocurrencies, which are used for transactions within the virtual world. The banker is responsible for issuing these currencies, setting exchange rates, and ensuring the stability of the virtual financial system. This also includes monitoring cash flows, preventing fraud, and ensuring compliance with regulatory requirements.

A particular aspect of the activities undertaken by the banker role in the metaverse is the provision of financial services such as lending, asset management, and investment advice for virtual assets. Since the value of NFTs and cryptocurrencies can be highly volatile, users require expert advice to make informed financial decisions. The banker provides this expertise and supports users in effectively managing and growing their digital assets.

Finally, ensuring compliance with regulatory requirements must, of course, not be overlooked—this applies both within the metaverse and with respect to real-world laws. As transactions in the metaverse are often cross-border and touch upon different legal jurisdictions, bankers must navigate and implement complex legal frameworks to ensure the legality and security of financial activities [KAR23].

4.6.16 A Social Metaverse?

As digital spaces are both derived from existing social structures and enable new forms of interaction, community, and identity formation, the metaverse and the social development of human society as a whole are in a dynamic relationship. The metaverse, like any other technology, influences social relationships, work processes, access to education, and consumer behavior, while simultaneously reflecting and advancing societal trends.

A key aspect is social interaction and the formation of virtual communities. The metaverse expands traditional social networks by creating immersive environments in which users can interact as avatars. This enables new social activities such as virtual meetings, events, or conferences that transcend geographical boundaries. Such virtual spaces foster the creation of global communities based not on physical proximity, but on shared interests, values, or goals. As a result, new forms of social organization emerge that could complement or even replace traditional structures such as local clubs or neighborhoods. While the metaverse has the potential to overcome isolation, there is also the risk that social bonds may become more superficial [BAI18].

Another central factor is identity formation and self-presentation. Users can freely shape their identity in the metaverse by using avatars that either correspond to their real selves or represent entirely new personalities. This opens up diverse opportunities to explore social roles without being bound by physical limitations. At the same time, the metaverse could contribute to the acceptance of diversity and individuality, as people can construct identities independently of societal norms. However, there is a risk of identity crises or a disconnect between real and virtual existence, especially when virtual identities differ significantly from physical reality [TUR12].

The metaverse also has profound effects on education and social mobility. Virtual learning enables immersive educational experiences in which complex topics are conveyed through interactive simulations and virtual environments. This could particularly benefit people from disadvantaged regions by providing access to high-quality education. Likewise, the metaverse offers new professional opportunities by enabling remote work in virtual offices, digital enterprises, and the trade of virtual goods. While this can promote social mobility by allowing economic participation regardless of geographic and social barriers, existing inequalities could be exacerbated if not everyone has equal access to these digital infrastructures [WIE23].

From a cultural perspective, the metaverse can also bring both positive and challenging developments. On the one hand, it facilitates cultural exchange by enabling people to participate in virtual events, learn about traditions, and make artworks accessible worldwide. On the other hand, the metaverse could contribute to cultural homogenization by amplifying global trends and displacing local traditions. The increasing digitization of cultural content could thus lead to a standardization of social values, challenging existing cultural identities [LAN17].

Another important issue is the influence of the metaverse on personal relationships and social closeness. Virtual relationships can be both platonic and romantic, with new forms of connection created through haptic feedback and immersive experiences. At the same time, there is a risk that users may become increasingly alienated from physical relationships if social interactions are entirely shifted to the virtual world. The challenge lies in finding a balance between virtual and real social interactions to avoid social isolation [BAI18].

The metaverse could also contribute to social justice and inclusion by creating accessible spaces where physical limitations or social stigmas are irrelevant. For example, people with disabilities could participate equally in social life through virtual environments. At the same time, there is a risk that technological access barriers could reinforce existing inequalities. People without internet access or modern devices could be excluded from these developments, leading to new forms of digital exclusion [ORT24].

The virtual world is also not free from conflicts and power structures. Social tensions and discrimination from the real world could be transferred into the metaverse. Cyberbullying, the formation of virtual echo chambers, or algorithmic bias could intensify social inequalities in digital spaces. Furthermore, the distribution of power within the metaverse is problematic, as large technology companies often control virtual platforms and could thus monitor or influence social interactions. The associated surveillance could endanger user autonomy and establish new forms of digital power [ZUB19].

Despite these challenges, the metaverse also holds potential for social change and movements. It can serve as a platform for political activism by bringing people together worldwide to support common causes. Virtual protests, fundraising events, and digital campaigns could help promote social justice. At the same time, however, there is a risk that disinformation and manipulation through targeted influence in the metaverse will pose new challenges for public opinion formation [MOR11].

How the metaverse is designed and used will be crucial in determining whether it enriches or challenges existing social structures.

4.6.17 Politics and Administration

A likely age-old insight of every politician is: "You have to meet people where they are." Following this maxim, it follows that the metaverse is also a political space, or will develop into one. Thus, the political development of human society and the metaverse are in an exciting and potentially transformative relationship, as the metaverse is not only a technological space but also a platform that enables new political structures, power relations, and social dynamics—and may even create them itself. This development touches on fundamental aspects of politics, including governance, civic participation, the distribution of power, freedom, and regulation.

The metaverse is not just a technological development, but also a space shaped by political and social dynamics. It therefore requires its own governance structures to ensure order, fairness, and security. These structures can be managed either centrally by companies such as Meta or in a decentralized manner through so-called Decentralized Autonomous Organizations (see also Sect. 4.6.14). This raises the fundamental question of who sets the rules in the metaverse and how democratic participation can be ensured. The historical development of political systems, from monarchies to modern democracies, could be mirrored in the metaverse if users demand greater say and the transparency of governance models is increased [DEF18].

The question of power and control is central to the political organization of the metaverse. While centralized platforms grant large technology companies significant control over data, access, and economic activities, decentralized, blockchain-based approaches offer the possibility of a more democratic structure. Users could thus gain greater autonomy over their digital identities, data, and resources. These power struggles in the metaverse reflect historical conflicts between centralized and decentralized power structures, such as between absolutism and democracy. At the same time, monopolies or abuse by powerful actors in virtual spaces could give rise to new forms of digital resistance or virtual activism [ZUB19].

As the metaverse grows in importance, questions of civil rights and digital freedoms also come to the fore:

- Who owns users' digital identities?
- What rights do avatars have as virtual representations of individuals?
- How is privacy protection ensured?

Such questions become especially relevant when surveillance mechanisms, censorship, or algorithmic discrimination in the metaverse restrict digital freedom. In addition, the ownership of virtual assets, particularly in the form of non-fungible tokens (NFTs), raises new challenges regarding property rights and their enforceability. As in the real world, movements for digital rights could also emerge in the metaverse, similar to historical struggles for human rights that have sought to secure fundamental freedoms in the past [FLO20, FLO21].

The metaverse could also enable new forms of political participation and democracy. Virtual elections, voting, or digital parliaments could provide platforms where citizens can participate in political processes regardless of their geographic location. Blockchain technologies could enable transparent and tamper-proof voting mechanisms, while virtual spaces could serve as venues for direct political participation. On the one hand, these developments could strengthen democratic processes; on the other, they could also foster new forms of digital nationalism or ideologically driven virtual communities. Whether the metaverse will complement or challenge existing democratic systems remains one of the central political debates in this field [BRY14].

Economic power relations in the metaverse are also subject to political dynamics. Virtual economies are developing with their own currencies, markets, and business models in which digital goods and services are traded. As in the real world, social inequalities could manifest in the metaverse if access to economic resources remains unevenly distributed. Issues of taxation, regulation, and fair distribution of wealth must therefore also be considered in virtual spaces. This could lead to the emergence of new political movements advocating for digital justice and the equitable distribution of virtual wealth [LAN17].

Unfortunately, conflicts and power struggles are also likely to play a role in the metaverse. Cybercrime, geopolitical tensions, and digital protest movements could establish virtual spaces as new arenas for political confrontation. While the metaverse can be a place for global dialogue and cooperation, it also carries the risk of exacerbating social tensions, especially if users are pushed into ideologically isolated digital communities or echo chambers. New forms of political activism, such as virtual demonstrations or campaigns against digital surveillance, could emerge in response to such developments [MOR11].

Of particular importance is the ethical regulation and the need for global standards for the metaverse. International politics faces the challenge of defining data protection, rights, and security in virtual spaces. Without clear rules, imbalances of power could arise between states and large technology companies, influencing the balance of the digital world. The need for global agreements to regulate the metaverse is reminiscent of earlier international cooperation, such as the United Nations or the Paris Climate Agreement, which serve as examples of multilateral approaches to solving global problems [SCHwa17].

Education and political education could acquire a new dimension in the metaverse. Virtual educational platforms enable interactive learning experiences, such as simulations of historical events or virtual parliaments that convey political knowledge in innovative ways. Through these new learning methods, citizens could become better informed and develop a broader understanding of political processes. Historically, education has been a key factor in the democratization of societies, and in the metaverse it could play a similar role in promoting political participation and critical thinking [MAS22].

Even today, it is clear that the metaverse has not only technological but also profound political implications. Governance structures, civil rights, economic power relations, and new forms of political participation are at the center of this development. The metaverse could accelerate or transform historical processes such as democratization, civil rights, and social justice by opening up new spaces for political organization and decision-making. The long-term political shaping of the metaverse will influence not only the virtual but also the physical world, and may give rise to new political models that transcend national borders.

4.6.18 The yet to be Imagined

Technical and technological development, not only in the metaverse but especially there, is diverse and progressing at high speed. "The yet to be imagined" in the context of the metaverse refers to future experiences and technologies that are currently neither conceivable nor possible. It embodies the idea that the metaverse can and will be a space where new types of experiences become possible and emerge—experiences that are not yet truly imaginable. While this may sound like science fiction, a look at the history of almost any technology shows that there have always been developments and application ideas that were not addressed or even conceivable at the outset. Human creativity has always been a fundamental driver of development and the discovery of new fields of application.

It is foreseeable that the integration of additional human sensory and action modalities—beyond those currently standard—in the interaction between human users and IT systems and the Internet will receive a significant boost through the metaverse:

For example, gustatory experiences could be developed in the metaverse for virtual restaurants or shops, making the enjoyment and thus the sale of food and beverages possible even in virtual environments. Scents and tastes could be virtually reproduced to provide a more immersive experience. This could even go so far that, with the help of 3D printers, food is produced and consumed directly on site in the metaverse [BLU23, SNI23].

Olfactory experiences can also be simulated in the metaverse. For instance, perfumes and fragrances can be generated in the virtual world using special devices. These devices can release specific scent molecules to simulate a particular smell. In the real world, there are already a few, albeit rare, devices for this purpose [SCH23a, LIU23].

Brain interfaces (BCI, Brain-Computer Interface), which are being researched and developed in numerous institutions, could also contribute in the future to making the metaverse even more immersive. Such a brain interface enables users to interact with the metaverse by using their brainwaves directly, without the need for other interaction devices such as keyboards, mice, or even voice input. By wearing a special headset, the user's brain activity can be recorded and analyzed to control actions in the metaverse. This technology could also be used to create "new senses," allowing users to gather additional information and experience the world in new ways [RAB15, BON21].

Not only sensory channels but also actuator modalities can be incorporated into the development of the metaverse. The use of prostheses and implants is also being discussed in the context of the metaverse [BON22]. People with physical disabilities can use prostheses and implants to enhance their abilities in the metaverse and gain new experiences. For example, a person with a prosthetic arm could use a BCI system to grasp and move objects.

The examples mentioned illustrate the merging of technical devices with the human body. The metaverse and transhumanism are therefore closely connected, as both concepts are based on this fusion of human and technology. At its core, transhumanism is a philosophical movement that advocates the use of technology to enhance human abilities and experiences [BOS14, HUB20]. It is based on the idea that humans, through the use of technology and scientific progress, will be able to improve their physical and cognitive abilities. The metaverse, on the other hand, offers a virtual environment in which technology and reality can merge to create an immersive experience, enabling users to move within an alternate reality. The metaverse can thus certainly be seen as part of this movement, as it allows users to expand their experiences and redefine their identities. In this metaverse, users can, for example, enhance their cognitive abilities by interacting with intelligent virtual assistants or by learning new skills in the virtual world. At the same time, users can also improve their physical abilities by moving through virtual worlds or by interacting with and within the virtual world using robots and artificial limbs. All these are aspects associated with transhumanism, where technological enhancements are used to expand and improve human capabilities.

A number of technologies already exist that are associated with both the metaverse and transhumanism, such as the aforementioned examples of brain-computer interfaces, prostheses and implants, and new artificial senses. A good example of this connection between the metaverse and transhumanism is Neil Harbisson, who was already introduced in Sect. 3.1. He is an artist and activist who was born with the rare condition of monochromacy, which causes impaired color vision. However, Harbisson initiated the development of an implant called the "Eyeborg," which enables him to "hear" colors and thus perceive an extended color spectrum [BAN12, THO13, DON17]. He can also use this ability in the metaverse to experience the world in a new way.

Harbisson has been a strong advocate for the use of such technologies in the context of the metaverse. He believes that the metaverse offers an opportunity to redefine and expand human identities and experiences. By sharing his experiences and technologies with others, he hopes to expand people's imagination and create new possibilities for the further development of the human species [MAA22]. However, what the metaverse and transhumanism will ultimately look like as a vision of the future cannot—and should not—be predicted at this point.

4.7 And how is that Supposed to Work?

Another strand in the further development of the Internet is the already mentioned Web3. In contrast to Web 2.0, where centralized platforms such as Google, Facebook, or Amazon control the majority of user activities, Web3 is designed for the use of decentralized protocols and technologies. In this Web3, data, applications, and assets are no longer stored on centralized servers, but on distributed networks of computers, known as distributed ledger technology. The idea of this distribution is largely based on blockchain technology, but also on other technologies and protocols such as the Inter-Planetary File System (IPFS) [SCH19a, IPFoJ, LUN16].

Unlike Web 2.0, Web3 is designed for the use of decentralized protocols and technologies. This results in differences between Web 2.0 and Web3 in various aspects:

- *Control*: Web 2.0 platforms control the data and activities of users on their platforms. In contrast, since Web3 is designed to be decentralized, users are intended to retain control over their data and their interactions on the web.
- *Security*: In Web 2.0, data and applications are stored on centralized servers, which creates a large attack surface for hackers and data loss. Since Web3 is intended to be decentralized, other protocols and technologies such as blockchain are used, which are expected to increase the security and integrity of data and applications.
- *Transparency*: In Web 2.0, the business models of platforms are often opaque, which can come at the expense of user privacy. In contrast, Web3 business models are intended to be more transparent and traceable, offering users more opportunities to protect their privacy.
- *Innovation*: In Web 2.0, innovation is often controlled by the major "GAFA" players. This leads to little room for new ideas and developments. In contrast, Web3 is intended to provide more freedom for developers and users, creating more space for innovation.

Such and other frequently cited differences demonstrate that the idea of Web3 represents a fundamental shift in how the Internet is intended and can be used. In particular, the decentralized and more transparent infrastructure is expected to contribute to this transformation by returning control over data and interactions to users. The use of new decentralized technologies enables Web3 to bypass many of the centralized control mechanisms of Web 2.0 [NAB23]. This decentralization is expected to yield a number of advantages in Web3 in the future:

- *Security*: By storing data and applications on many different computers within the network, it becomes more difficult to attack, hack, or manipulate them. The use of cryptographic methods and algorithms further ensures the integrity of data and applications.
- *Transparency*: The decentralized approach also offers greater transparency, as every participant has access to the same information. This also means that it is more difficult to spread false or misleading information.
- *Independence*: Furthermore, this enables users and developers to act independently, without being dependent on centralized platforms. This opens up greater freedom and flexibility in the development and use of applications and services in Web3.
- *Interoperability*: By using open standards and protocols, the decentralized infrastructure of Web3 can enable better interoperability between different applications and services. This, in turn, can lead to improved user-friendliness and smoother information exchange.

4.7 And how is that supposed to work?

The overarching goal of Web3 is based on the hope of building a truly open and democratic Internet that can be used by everyone. This was a goal envisioned for both the original Web and Web 2.0, but neither ever achieved—or could achieve—it. It is therefore remarkable that, despite this highly idealistic aim, many economic and commercial aspects are also being discussed in the context of Web3. These include the currently much-debated non-fungible tokens, smart contracts, and, of course, cryptocurrencies.

Cryptocurrencies are digital currencies that are secured and managed using cryptographic methods. In the metaverse, these currencies can play an important role by providing a secure and transparent way to transfer and store financial value within the virtual ecosystem. In addition to well-known cryptocurrencies outside the metaverse, such as Bitcoin and ETHER, numerous platforms also operate their own currencies. One example is ROBUX, the currency within Roblox. Like other currencies such as SAND on the Sandbox platform or MANA in Decentraland, ROBUX is used to buy and sell digital goods and services within the game. As with their "big brothers" Bitcoin and ETHER, cryptographic methods are also used here to ensure the security and integrity of the currency. In addition to commercial and financial objectives, these proprietary platform currencies are certainly also intended to bind users to the platform, since virtual assets such as land or digital artworks are tied to the respective platform. Switching to another platform is associated with significant effort. Nevertheless, many platforms are increasingly relying on the well-known Bitcoin and, even more so, on ETHER, which could at least simplify switching from one platform to another.

Another way cryptocurrencies are used in the metaverse is through the integration of decentralized financial services, known as DeFi. Such applications allow users to access a wide range of financial services, such as borrowing or lending money, trading assets, or earning interest on deposits. By using cryptocurrencies, these services can be offered in a decentralized and transparent manner, providing users with greater freedom and autonomy. It is likely that in the future, more and more virtual currencies and financial services will emerge in the metaverse, based on the principles of cryptocurrencies and decentralization [ZET20].

Decentralization also benefits marketplaces in Web3 and the metaverse, as peer-to-peer platforms enable users to trade directly with each other without the need for a central intermediary. Traditional marketplaces such as eBay or Amazon rely on centralized systems, where the marketplace operator controls pricing, payment processing, and fraud protection. In contrast, decentralized marketplaces allow users to trade directly with one another by leveraging smart contracts, NFTs, and thus blockchain technology to facilitate and secure transactions. A well-known example of such a decentralized marketplace is OpenSea, which claims to be the largest marketplace for NFTs [OPEoJ]. OpenSea enables users to trade NFTs directly with each other, without the involvement of an intermediary such as a gallery or auction platform. Transactions are processed via smart contracts, which ensure that the seller transfers the NFT upon receipt of payment and that the buyer actually receives the NFT.

Through such decentralized marketplaces in the metaverse, users gain greater control over the trading of virtual goods and services that they have modeled and now wish to manage themselves, as described above, leading to increased transparency and efficiency in trading transactions. Buyers also benefit from such marketplaces, as they can help reduce buyer and seller fees due to the absence of a central intermediary.

Beyond commercial aspects, it is also important from the user's perspective to have control not only over the artifacts "modused" and acquired in the metaverse, but even more so to be certain of one's own identity. This refers not only to protection against the "loss" of one's own avatar, but also to the management and control of personal data. Protecting one's privacy and knowing that personal data is secure are intended to contribute to a safer and more trustworthy virtual experience in the metaverse. In Web3, identity management is therefore regarded as an important tool. Two decentralized approaches are commonly cited in Web3, and another in the metaverse, for the purpose of identity management [ALZ20, SED21]:

- *Decentralized Identifiers* (DIDs) are a concept that enables users to manage their identity across different services and platforms. A DID consists of a unique identifier stored on a blockchain and controlled by the user. This allows users to manage their identity without relying on a central authority that stores and manages personal data.
- *Verifiable Credentials* (VCs) are digital certificates that allow users to prove their identity and the accuracy of their personal data. VCs can be issued by various services and platforms and contain encrypted information controlled by the user. Users can use these certificates to verify their identity and/or to gain access to certain services or platforms.
- In addition, identity management in the metaverse is also achieved through the use of *avatars*. These can be linked to various identity solutions to ensure that the user's identity is protected and verified.

These characteristics of Web3 are also crucial for the implementation of the metaverse. The metaverse requires a decentralized infrastructure, as it is a digital ecosystem composed of numerous diverse applications and content used simultaneously by many users. The metaverse therefore cannot be controlled by a single centralized platform, as this would restrict freedom, security, and innovation. For realizing the idea of the metaverse, Web3 is thus an essential foundation, as it provides the decentralized infrastructure needed to build an open and free digital ecosystem. By using decentralized technologies, developers and users of the metaverse can act independently while ensuring the security and integrity of the platform.

The metaverse and its underlying technologies, together with Web3, represent promising innovations that appear ready for adoption. The components mentioned so far, as well as others, have already demonstrated their functionality to a certain extent. However, these demonstrations have mostly been isolated and, in most cases, limited in scale. As a result, there remain a considerable number of limitations and challenges that must be addressed, the most important of which are as follows:

- *Scalability*: The metaverse requires an enormous amount of computing power and storage capacity to process the virtual world and user interactions. The exact scale of these requirements is unpredictable. However, the mere prospect that the metaverse could one day attract as many or more users than currently use the internet stretches the imagination regarding the necessary computing resources and storage needs. The current Web3 infrastructure is insufficient to meet these demands. While some scaling solutions currently available appear promising, they still require further development to fulfill the requirements of the metaverse.
- *Interoperability*: The various platforms and services within the metaverse must be able to communicate with each other in order to provide users with a seamless and comprehensive experience. This necessitates a higher degree of interoperability between the different technologies and platforms in Web3.
- *Data privacy and security*: Since user identity and personal data play a crucial role in the metaverse, appropriate data protection and security measures must be implemented to ensure that this information remains safe and secure. Whether the approaches mentioned above are sufficient in this regard still needs to be examined in detail.
- *Accessibility*: To fully realize the potential of the metaverse, users must have access to suitable hardware and infrastructure. Currently, access to this technology is limited, and it remains unclear how quickly the affordability and availability of hardware and infrastructure can be improved.

4.8 A Success Story?

According to many forecasts, the metaverse is expected to achieve greater economic and societal relevance in the foreseeable future than any previous technology. By 2028, the metaverse is projected to reach a market size of over 800 billion US dollars, while some analysts, such as Morgan Stanley, even estimate a market volume of more than eight trillion US dollars [KAN21, CHI22]. Tim Sweeney, founder of the video game company Epic Games and developer of Fortnite, describes the metaverse as a "multi-trillion-dollar opportunity." As early as 2016, he stated [TAK16]:

> "This Metaverse is going to be far more pervasive and powerful than anything else. If one central company gains control of this, they will become more powerful than any government and be a god on Earth."

However, there are also some more cautious voices. For example, Evelyn R. Miralles, Chief Principal Engineer at NASA's Lyndon B. Johnson Space Center, says [BAL22]:

> "At the moment metaverse is in the path to the 'peak of inflated expectations' phase."

In doing so, she indirectly refers to the annually presented Gartner Hype Cycle, which illustrates which technologies could be disruptive in the short and long term and which technologies large companies should work with to open up new markets and opportunities. The Hype Cycle depicts the typical reception of a disruptive technology in the form of a curve:

- After a technology is discovered (Innovation Trigger), interest rises and …
- … expectations become inflated (Peak of Inflated Expectations).
- This is followed by a phase of disappointment, as the technology fails to meet expectations (Trough of Disillusionment).
- Subsequently, the technology develops further and finds its real use cases (Slope of Enlightenment), …
- … until it finally becomes useful and widely adopted (Plateau of Productivity).

Gartner also examined the context of the metaverse and presented a corresponding Hype Cycle in 2022. In this, several technologies relevant to immersive realities were analyzed in more detail. To this end, Gartner examined more than 2,000 technologies and selected 25 of them, which are defined as "must-know innovations to drive competitive differentiation and efficiency." These 25 technologies were incorporated into the Hype Cycle. Among these technologies are Web3, NFT, and "digital humans." According to Gartner, these technologies will be of great interest over the next 5 to 10 years. In addition, Gartner identifies three so-called "macro themes" in this study:

- The expansion of immersive experiences,
- The acceleration of automation through artificial intelligence (AI), and
- The optimization of technology delivery to the market.

Some of the technologies listed in this Hype Cycle had already been considered by Gartner in their analyses since at least 2017, thereby acknowledging the technological potential they are likely to have in the future, as shown in Fig. 4.13 [PER22].

Tech companies, especially Facebook, also see the potential that is presumably inherent in the metaverse and view a strategic future in this virtual world. Despite the positive perception by business consultants and analysts, however, the other possibility remains [MAT22]:

> "The hype surrounding the metaverse will lead to billions of euros being spent on nonsense. A lot of dumb money will flow into virtual real estate and digital trinkets."

On the positive side, a considerable number of companies are already working on "serious" applications in and around the metaverse:

- Digital twins of cities and factories are being developed to enable remote management and maintenance using VR technologies.

4.8 A Success Story?

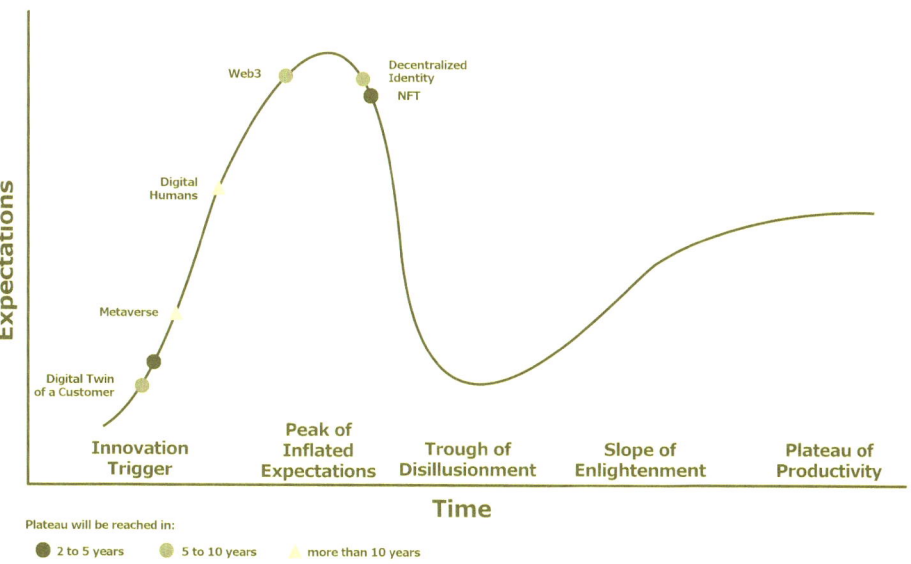

Fig. 4.13 The metaverse and relevant technologies. (Based on the Gartner Hype Cycle [PER22])

- Digital twins of humans help doctors prepare for surgeries by allowing the patient's virtual body to be rotated and enlarged before an operation, making it easier to determine where the scalpel should be applied.
- Similarly, digital twins of human organs can help the pharmaceutical industry develop better drugs and test them more extensively in virtual environments than would be possible in reality.

In addition, investments are being made in powerful infrastructures that can also benefit other application areas in the future. However, the wide range of possible use cases also shows that it is unlikely a single, complete, and unified virtual world called the "metaverse" will emerge. Rather, it is expected that many independent small platforms will be created, which, in the best case, will allow for easy switching between them.

Not least due to the impressive speed of development and adoption of VR and AR in recent years, the concept of the metaverse has increasingly come into focus. As mentioned several times above, this has gone so far that the metaverse is seen as the next major evolutionary stage of the Internet. However, one aspect should be considered here that is easily overlooked.

During the development of the WWW, a particular user mentality has emerged, which is likely to change only slowly and could therefore stand in the way of the (rapid) success of the metaverse [BAL21]:

> "Metaverse Users don't spend money."

Most Internet users expect that access to the services and information they use online will be available free of charge. In fact, many social media platforms, search engines, and other online services are initially accessible at no cost. Their funding is provided indirectly through advertising.

However, this expectation can be an obstacle to the success of the metaverse. Operating the metaverse requires a large amount of resources, including advanced technology and human labor to keep it running. The costs for developing and operating such a platform are immense and cannot be fully covered by advertising. This, in turn, means that alternative funding models must be found. One such model is that users have to pay for access to the metaverse.

However, many users who are accustomed to free services lack the understanding or willingness to do so. This already makes life difficult for high-quality journalistic content or media content such as music and film in today's WWW. This could therefore lead to insufficient revenue being generated on and through the platforms and services in the metaverse to finance and maintain their operation.

To solve this problem, users need to develop a new understanding of the value of the metaverse and the resources required for its development and operation. Incentives must be created for users who are willing to pay for access to the metaverse and for virtual goods or experiences. Companies should also work on creative ways to generate revenue that do not rely solely on advertising.

4.9 (Not Only) Economic Concerns: Metaverse-Hopping!

Metaverse-hopping refers to users switching from one metaverse platform to another in order to explore different virtual worlds and gain new experiences. From a technical perspective, this could mean that users need to access various tools, technologies, and application programming interfaces provided by the respective platforms. To facilitate such transitions, the platforms would need to be interoperable, as Ball [BAL22] and Parisi [PAR21] also consider necessary. Such interoperability means that platforms must offer the ability for data and applications to be exchanged seamlessly. In addition to established data exchange formats such as XML, JSON, or IFC, more advanced standards like OpenXR and WebXR could also be used, which aim to provide a unified interface for the development of XR applications [W3CoJc, BUIoJ, JSOoJ, KHR19, W3CoJd].

Furthermore, a corresponding platform could support the integration of applications and content from other metaverse platforms in order to create a truly seamless experience for users, without anything akin to a media discontinuity. However, such integration would foreseeably entail a variety of technical challenges, such as handling a wide range of data formats for diverse application areas and ensuring the security and integrity of data exchanged between different platforms and applications.

As already mentioned in the previous Chap. 3, it is still unclear how the metaverse will ultimately be structured. On the one hand, there is the possibility of a unified metaverse, in which there is a single central platform used by all users and in which all digital worlds are integrated. Such a metaverse would have the advantage that each user would only have one single, unified digital identity to maintain and manage. This would certainly also benefit users' social interaction, since "people know and recognize each other," regardless of which platform they meet on.

On the other hand, it is more likely that the metaverse will consist of many parallel platforms that differ in structure, functionality, and application focus. Each platform could specialize in certain application areas or target groups, thus offering a greater variety of specialized use cases. Moreover, it is conceivable that competition between different platforms could lead to more innovation and higher quality offerings.

Which of these possibilities will become reality depends on many factors, such as fundamental technological developments on the one hand, and on the other hand, user acceptance and usage, as well as the decisions of the companies operating in the industry. It is therefore likely that in the future there will be a mix of different platforms tailored to the diverse needs and interests of users, some of which—just as in today's WWW—will become so large that they can be regarded as the de facto standard of the metaverse.

Currently, the risk of this "metaverse-hopping" is still largely hypothetical. While most platforms that offer modeling and integration options generally allow objects to be used as starting points for hyperlinks, much like in the classic WWW, when such an object is activated by the user or their avatar, the platform "teleports" the user to the referenced hyperlink destination. However, what sounds so simple in theory presents several technical hurdles in practice. For example, there is no universally defined coordinate model that applies to all metaverse platforms. In addition, the integration of such hyperlinks is usually a special feature that is not readily accessible. Rather, the development tools provided by the platforms often require users to have considerable programming expertise for such use cases.

4.9.1 A Unified Metaverse?

A unified metaverse offers a range of advantages not only for users but also for businesses, with some benefits overlapping and others differing. The main advantages for users include the following aspects:

- *Interoperability*: A unified metaverse would allow users to navigate between different virtual worlds without losing their identity or virtual possessions. Users could seamlessly switch between various metaverse platforms and take their virtual assets and identities with them.
- *Shared Experience*: A unified metaverse would enable users to easily connect with people from around the world and participate together in activities such as gaming,

sports, education, or culture. A larger user base would also allow for a broader variety of activities and experiences.
- *Efficiency*: A unified metaverse would allow users to handle tasks such as shopping, communication, and education on a single platform. This would save time and increase efficiency.

The main advantages for businesses, on the other hand, are:

- *Larger Target Audience*: A single metaverse platform would enable businesses to present their products and services to a larger audience without the need for porting. A greater number of users would also mean a larger pool of potential customers.
- *Efficiency*: A unified metaverse would allow businesses to manage and offer their products and services more efficiently. Companies would not need a separate metaverse platform, thus saving time and money.
- *Collaboration*: A unified metaverse would make it easier for businesses to collaborate and form economic partnerships. A single metaverse platform would allow companies to integrate their products and services, creating a more cohesive experience for users.

Although the number of advantages of a unified metaverse is not insignificant, there are also a number of disadvantages that apply to both users and businesses and must be considered in detail. The main disadvantages for users include the following aspects:

- *Monopoly Position*: A largely unified metaverse platform could potentially occupy a monopolistic position in the market, leading to a lack of competition. As in the real world or in certain areas of the Internet, particularly the WWW, this could result in users facing higher prices and fewer choices.
- *Reduced Innovation*: The lack of competition with only a single metaverse platform could lead to fewer innovations and new ideas, or even worse, to design and technology decisions that ultimately result in a developmental dead end.
- *Centralized Control*: A unified metaverse could also mean a simple, centralized means of control, raising concerns about privacy and surveillance practices.

	Advantages	Disadvantages
Users	1. Easy navigation and interoperability 2. Ability to combine different metaverse experiences 3. Better integration of content and data across different services and applications 4. Easier access to social interactions and communities	1. Limited choice and experiences restricted to a single platform 2. Possible lack of competition and innovation 3. Potentially higher prices and fees 4. Potentially greater dependence on a single platform

	Advantages	Disadvantages
Businesses	1. Larger user base and market opportunities 2. Better integration of services and applications 3. Opportunity to build and promote brand identity 4. Easier development and publication of content	1. Possible restrictions and regulations imposed by a single platform 2. Potentially higher fees and greater dependence on a single platform 3. Possible lack of competition and innovation 4. Potentially higher risks if the platform fails or is hacked

The main disadvantages for businesses, on the other hand, are:

- *Loss of Autonomy*: A single unified metaverse platform could result in businesses losing autonomy and control over their products and services, and could also force them to comply with certain rules and regulations that may conflict with their corporate or organizational culture.
- *Limited Access to User Data*: A single metaverse platform could make it more difficult for businesses to access user data, as all data would be stored in a central database.
- *Risk of Market Disruption*: A unified metaverse could potentially lead to market disruptions, as changes to the platform or unforeseen problems could have a greater impact on the businesses operating on the platform and their business models.

4.9.2 Diverse Metaverses?

Diversity in the form of multiple platforms could therefore prove to be advantageous. From the user's perspective, the benefits differ from those for businesses. Looking at the potential advantages for users, we find:

- *More Choices*: With many parallel metaverse platforms, users would have more options and could choose the platform that best suits their needs and preferences.
- *Competition Drives* **Innovation**: The existence of many parallel metaverses fosters competition between platforms, which could lead to more innovation and new ideas. This would ultimately provide users with greater freedom of choice and better experiences.
- *Privacy Protection*: Multiple parallel metaverses could help better protect users' privacy, as there would be less centralized control and fewer central databases.

The main advantages for businesses, on the other hand, are:

- *More Opportunities for Market Participation*: The existence of many parallel platforms offers businesses more opportunities to enter the market, thereby increasing competition among providers.

- *Better Control over Products and Services*: Businesses have greater control over their products and services when multiple parallel platforms exist. They can specifically choose the platform that best fits their products and services.
- *Better Analytics and Marketing Opportunities*: Businesses can access more user data by engaging on multiple parallel platforms. This provides them with better analytics and marketing opportunities to improve their products and services.

However, there are also some clear disadvantages for users:

- *Fragmentation*: The existence of many parallel platforms could mean that the user base is split across different platforms. This fragmentation of the user base could further lead to fewer interactions and experiences within each individual platform.
- *Compatibility issues*: The existence of many parallel platforms can result in compatibility problems, as certain content and applications may not be available or functional on all platforms.
- *Difficulties with interoperability*: Users may find it challenging to switch between different parallel metaverses, interact across them, or transfer content from one platform to another. This is especially the case when development strategies, such as differing interaction paradigms or forms, are in competition.

In addition to disadvantages for users, disadvantages for companies must also be considered:

- *Challenges in target group analysis*: With the existence of many parallel platforms, it can become more difficult for companies to conduct target group analysis, which means that more resources must be allocated to marketing and advertising.
- *Difficulties in application development*: The existence of many parallel platforms poses a challenge for companies in application development, as applications may need to be developed and maintained across multiple platforms.
- *Higher costs*: Companies may face higher costs for developing applications and content on many parallel platforms, as they require more resources and experts to manage and maintain their products across multiple platforms.

It is difficult to say whether the advantages of a single metaverse will ultimately outweigh those of many parallel metaverse platforms. The outcome will depend on which factors become economically significant in the future and what kind of experience users and companies are seeking. It does not seem unlikely that a hybrid solution will emerge in the future, in which different metaverse platforms can interact with each other while still retaining their individual identities and controls.

	Advantages	Disadvantages
Users	1. Greater variety of metaverse experiences 2. Competition can lead to better prices and services 3. Avoidance of monopolies and privacy concerns 4. Opportunity to participate in specialized metaverses	1. More difficult navigation and interoperability between different platforms 2. Managing multiple accounts across different platforms can be challenging 3. Possible restrictions on exchanging content and data between different platforms 4. Potential lack of critical mass in specialized metaverses
Companies	1. Opportunity to operate in specialized metaverses 2. Competition can drive innovation and improved products 3. Possible avoidance of monopolies and privacy concerns 4. Opportunity to participate in different metaverse ecosystems	1. Potential lack of critical mass in specialized metaverses 2. Higher development costs due to the need to develop for multiple platforms 3. Possible restrictions on exchanging content and data between platforms 4. Challenges in building a brand identity when companies must present themselves on multiple platforms

The development of a unified metaverse appears to be a greater technical challenge, raising many complex questions compared to the development of multiple individual solutions:

- *Scalability*: A unified metaverse must be able to manage a very large number of users as well as a very large number of active applications and dynamic content simultaneously. High scalability is required to maintain performance and user experience.
- *Interoperability*: A unified metaverse must also be able to integrate and connect different types of applications and content from various providers. This requires the development of standardized interfaces and protocols that can be used by all developers.
- *Security*: A unified metaverse must be secure in order to ensure user privacy and safety. This requires the development of robust security protocols and protection mechanisms to prevent unauthorized access to sensitive data and applications.
- *Scripting capability*: A unified metaverse must also be able to support a wide range of scripting languages and environments to enable a broad spectrum of applications and content.
- *Infrastructure*: Furthermore, a unified metaverse requires a solid infrastructure to efficiently manage and deliver all applications and content. This necessitates the development of powerful cloud computing systems, networks, and storage solutions.
- *Virtual economy*: A unified metaverse must be able to support a virtual economy in which users can buy and sell applications, services, and digital currencies. This requires the development of secure payment and trading mechanisms.

- *Immersive technology*: Finally, a unified metaverse must also be able to support immersive technologies such as AR and VR in order to achieve broad user acceptance in the first place.

In the development of many parallel platforms, these challenges are met by other challenges:

- *Interoperability*: With the existence of many parallel platforms, it becomes increasingly difficult to exchange applications and content between them. Developers must design interfaces and protocols that enable the integration and connection of applications and content across different platforms.
- *Scalability*: Each parallel platform must be capable of managing a large number of users and applications to ensure good usability and user experience. Scalability is therefore one of the, if not the most, critical technical challenges when multiple parallel platforms exist.
- *Standardization*: The standardization of interfaces and protocols, as touched upon in the context of interoperability, requires a high degree of coordination among platform developers and operators.
- *Compatibility*: Each parallel platform may be based on a different technological foundation, further complicating compatibility. Developers must therefore ensure that their applications and content run on as many platforms as possible and are compatible across them. The immense scale of this problem is already evident when considering the few operating systems available for mobile computing and smartphones.
- *Security*: Each parallel platform must be secure enough to guarantee user privacy and safety. This requires the development of robust security protocols and protection mechanisms to prevent unauthorized access to sensitive data and applications.
- *Competition*: The existence of many parallel platforms can lead to intense competition among them. Developers must ensure that their metaverses are attractive to both users and businesses in order to successfully compete with other metaverses.

It is interesting to consider that the development of many parallel platforms may also foster the emergence of new business models, for example, those based on the integration of multiple platforms, such as for the migration of content and applications between different platforms.

4.10 The Extended Economic Environment

With Computer Aided Manufacturing (CAM), software and computer systems were introduced into industrial manufacturing processes with the aim of controlling, automating, and optimizing them. The origins of CAM date back to the 1940s and 1950s, when the first attempts were made to develop numerical control (NC) systems for machine tools. The first commercially successful NC systems were introduced in the 1960s. However, the true revolution in computer-aided manufacturing began in the 1970s, when the first CAM systems entered the market. These systems leveraged advances in computer technology to automate and optimize manufacturing processes. Since then, CAM systems have continuously evolved and have become an integral part of modern production facilities. CAM systems enable engineers and technicians to transfer design data directly from Computer Aided Design (CAD) software to machine controls and production equipment. This process improves the efficiency, accuracy, and speed of production. CAM systems are used in a wide range of industries, including automotive, aerospace, electronics, and medical technology [SCH03, LAN94].

The development of Computer-Aided Manufacturing (CAM) has contributed in recent years to the optimization and increased efficiency of production processes. By linking Industry 4.0 and cyber-physical systems, efforts have been made to further improve such processes by making them more networked and automated. The concept of the metaverse now opens up the possibility for the next, even more advanced step: the creation of virtual worlds in which the physical and digital realms merge. This combination of CAM, Industry 4.0, and the metaverse is intended to further optimize production processes, reduce costs, and at the same time open up new business opportunities [GLU23, BMBoJ]:

- The integration of computer-aided manufacturing in the form of CAM and the metaverse enables the development of virtual production lines, which help companies optimize and simulate their production processes before implementing them in the real world. Using AR or VR, employees can interactively examine these virtual production lines and optimize the processes.
- By linking Industry 4.0 and the metaverse, digital twins of machines and equipment can be generated from the aforementioned simulations. This will enable companies to monitor the condition of their equipment in real time during operation, plan maintenance more efficiently, and detect potential disruptions at an early stage.
- Furthermore, the combination of CAM and the metaverse offers interesting opportunities for training and education, allowing employees to be trained in virtual environments to better understand and learn processes and workflows. With the use of AR or VR, employees can even be trained for hazardous situations without being exposed to actual risk.
- The combination of cyber-physical systems and the metaverse also allows for the enhancement of monitoring and control of production facilities in the real world through real-time visualizations in virtual environments.

The advantages of this combination of CAM, Industry 4.0, and the metaverse are manifold:

- Companies can optimize and increase the efficiency of their production processes through the use of virtual production lines and digital twins. Early detection and resolution of disruptions lead to increased productivity and reduced downtime.
- Employees benefit from realistic virtual environments for training and education enabled by AR or VR. Better training increases employee qualifications and generally contributes to improved product quality.
- By combining cyber-physical systems and the metaverse, companies can respond more quickly to changes and adapt their production processes more rapidly. Digital twins of real production lines are easier to modify than physical equipment, making it simpler and more cost-effective to test the impact of changed production processes in simulations before adapting the real facility after a successful simulation.
- Early detection of disruptions and optimal maintenance planning enable cost savings in maintenance. This helps to reduce overall production costs, prevent potential equipment damage, and thus consume less material and energy while reducing waste.

However, the integration of CAM, Industry 4.0, and the metaverse not only impacts industrial production processes but also fundamentally transforms the world of work. As automation and digitalization advance, existing professions are evolving and entirely new occupational profiles are emerging. In this context, it is also necessary to consider changes to both existing and new professions that arise from the convergence of the traditional physical world and the metaverse. This will undoubtedly bring about significant changes in the workplace. Some of the most affected professions are those directly involved with technology and virtual environments. Yet, even occupations previously considered far removed from technology may be impacted by these developments:

- *Virtual environment designers* will be in high demand in the future, as they play a crucial role in designing user interfaces, models, and avatars used in the metaverse. They must possess a deep understanding of the metaverse's capabilities to ensure an optimal user experience.
- *Software developers* will continue to play a key role in the metaverse, as they are responsible for creating the programs and applications used within it. They must be able to develop robust applications that are fast, reliable, and meet security standards, while taking into account requirements from both the real and virtual worlds.
- Similarly, the field of *social work* may be affected by the concept and implementation of the metaverse. Increasingly, people will meet and interact in virtual environments. It is not far-fetched to assume that social workers will be needed to understand the potential psychological effects of the metaverse on society and to provide comprehensive support and counseling for individual users or user groups within the metaverse.

4.10 The Extended Economic Environment

- As mentioned several times above, the *business world* will also not be spared from the effects of the metaverse. There is great hope that commerce and the management of virtual goods—such as clothing and accessories for avatars, gadgets for games, or even entire apartments and furnishings—will be possible in the virtual worlds of the metaverse. Sales and marketing professionals will need to learn how to advertise effectively in virtual, immersive environments to attract customers and increase revenue.

The examples presented here will, in all likelihood, represent only the tip of the iceberg when it comes to professions affected by changes brought about by the metaverse. It is still unclear what additional professions will emerge or be influenced by the metaverse. The dynamic that is already becoming apparent will be further intensified by the increasing use of AI-based services in the metaverse, a trend that is becoming ever more pronounced. AI can help make virtual environments more realistic and interactive, while also enabling new forms of assistance and interaction. Even the professions mentioned above could undergo far-reaching changes as a result of AI:

- AI-powered tools can be used to automate or optimize design processes. Designers can leverage these tools to work more efficiently and potentially enhance their creativity.
- AI can be utilized in software and (data) model development to shorten development times and reduce errors. This allows developers to focus on more complex tasks and achieve higher productivity.
- The assessment and evaluation of the psychological effects of the metaverse on society, as well as the development of interventions and prevention systems, can be supported by social work. However, social workers must be able to understand the limitations of AI and recognize that human interaction remains indispensable in certain cases.
- AI-based marketing tools can create personalized advertising campaigns and optimize the analysis of customer behavior. In sales and marketing, these tools can be useful for developing more effective campaigns and ultimately increasing sales.

In addition to the examples already mentioned regarding the impact on the world of work, numerous other examples can easily be found that address and cover specific tasks in immersive environments within the metaverse:

- Architects who design and "construct" virtual buildings and spaces in the virtual world.
- Event organizers who plan and manage virtual events on metaverse platforms.
- Virtual personal coaches who offer fitness classes and training in virtual worlds.
- Lawyers who provide legal advice on virtual matters, such as disputes over intellectual property or data protection.

- Sales representatives who market and sell virtual products or services in the virtual world.
- Real estate agents who buy, sell, or rent virtual properties in the virtual world.
- Social media managers who specifically manage the social media presence of individuals or companies on virtual world platforms.
- Psychologists or therapists who offer psychological counseling or therapy in the virtual world under its unique conditions.
- Content creators and modelers who produce digital content such as videos, photos, or music in the virtual world.
- Teachers or tutors who provide instruction or tutoring in the virtual world.

The requirements and skills for such professions with the specific context of the "metaverse" naturally vary widely. However, some key competencies do overlap.

When considering the world of work in the metaverse, it becomes clear that an understanding of the underlying technologies is crucial in nearly all professions. This includes knowledge in areas such as 3D modeling, programming, and a fundamental grasp of the technical nature of virtual reality. Moreover, many metaverse professions are characterized by the need for creative thinking, with the ability to develop and implement original ideas potentially being even more important than in the physical world. In this context, it is important to emphasize that communication skills are essential in a virtual world, where interactions with others increasingly occur not just through text or speech, but also through visual communication such as the form and behavior of avatars. In addition, many metaverse professions require a high degree of collaboration with others and within virtual teams. The dynamic nature of the metaverse, which is not only currently but will also in the future be in constant flux due to rapid technological progress, demands that professionals quickly adapt to new technologies and trends. In some professions, such as virtual sales representatives or content creators, the ability to analyze data to identify trends and make informed decisions is of great importance. Furthermore, certain professions, such as virtual personal trainers or virtual teachers, require a strong customer orientation and the comprehensive ability to understand and respond to customer needs.

The transformation of occupational profiles and the emergence of entirely new professions have a direct impact on the world of work. On the one hand, there will be effects on the traditional relationship between employee and employer, as not only the professions themselves are changing, but also the ways of working within these professions will differ from those in traditional occupations rooted in the physical world. In addition, these new professions will bring new requirements for vocational education and training, which must also be adapted to the new circumstances.

The metaverse will undoubtedly have a significant impact on the world of work, affecting both employees and employers. Among the advantages for employees is the ability to easily access jobs and employment opportunities from around the globe. This offers them greater flexibility and freedom in choosing their workplace. Additionally, the metaverse will promote the creation of new professions and career opportunities, particularly in the field of virtual world and game development. As it is a new technology, there will also be an increased demand for training and continuing education, enabling employees to enhance their skills. However, challenges for employees are also to be expected. They will need to acquire new skills and, above all, be willing to do so, such as knowledge in virtual world and game development, proficiency with virtual tools and platforms, and the ability to interact with virtual clients and colleagues. Furthermore, employees who work primarily in the metaverse may feel isolated and find it difficult to build relationships and networks. Since the metaverse is a new technology, there are currently no regulations or laws in place to protect employees from abuse or violations of their labor rights.

There are also advantages for employers, such as access to a larger pool of talent worldwide, increasing the likelihood of finding and attracting the best candidates for their company. The use of virtual tools and platforms can also enhance the efficiency of business processes and thus increase productivity. Moreover, by utilizing virtual workplaces and tools, employers can save costs, such as office rent and travel expenses. These advantages are accompanied by challenges for employers as well. They must invest in the necessary technology and infrastructure to support virtual workplaces and tools. In addition, they need to invest in the training and development of their workforce to ensure that employees possess the skills and competencies required to work effectively in the metaverse. Finally, employers must ensure that virtual workplaces and tools are secure and comply with data protection regulations to safeguard the security of both employees and the company.

However, the emergence of new professions and roles in the metaverse also requires an adaptation of vocational education and training, as well as the entire education system. To meet the specific requirements and competencies of professions in the metaverse, specialized training and qualification programs may be necessary. This may imply that existing training programs or education systems need to be modified to address these new demands.

One example of this is the teaching of technical skills and knowledge that are essential for many professions in the metaverse. Educational institutions such as schools, universities, and other organizations could adapt their curricula and training programs to prepare learners for the requirements of these professions. Furthermore, the creation of new professions and roles could lead to the development of new training and qualification programs tailored to these specific requirements. This may require collaboration between educational institutions and companies or organizations to align training with the needs of the industry.

Overall, it is likely that the emergence of new professions in the metaverse will also necessitate adjustments to the education system itself to ensure that people are prepared for the demands of these roles. To achieve this, certain skills and competencies must be fostered. Some of the most important competencies that may be particularly relevant in the metaverse include technical proficiency, creativity, adaptability, and communication skills. In addition, other competencies related to the virtual environment of the metaverse may also become increasingly important, such as proficiency with digital tools, virtual communication and collaboration, data protection and security, organization and time management, as well as intercultural understanding.

Schools, universities, and other educational institutions can foster these competencies to prepare people for the requirements of professions in the metaverse. Likewise, companies can contribute by providing training and professional development to ensure that their employees acquire and further develop the necessary skills.

References

[ABU21]   Abukhadra, Salwa (05.12.2021). Sephora Leading The Way With Augmented Reality. In: Medium, Marketing in the Age of Digital. Online: https://medium.com/marketing-in-the-age-of-digital/sephora-leading-the-way-with-augmented-reality-c117eed0faa0 (Retrieved: 28.05.2023).

[ADI23]   Adigozel, Ozgur; Mérey, Tibor; Mathews, Madeline (19.01.2023). The Health Care Metaverse Is More Than a Virtual Reality. In: Boston Consulting Group: Health Care Payers, Providers, Systems & Services/Article. Online: https://www.bcg.com/publications/2023/reaping-the-benefits-of-the-healthcare-metaverse (Retrieved: 28.05.2023).

[ALZ20]   Alzahrani, Bander (2020). An Information-Centric Networking Based Registry for Decentralized Identifiers and Verifiable Credentials. In: IEEE Access, vol. 8, pp. 137198–137208, 2020, https://doi.org/10.1109/ACCESS.2020.3011656.

[AMT19]   Amtsblatt der Europäischen Union: RICHTLINIE (EU) 2019/882 DES EUROPÄISCHEN PARLAMENTS UND DES RATES vom 17. April 2019 über die Barrierefreiheitsanforderungen für Produkte und Dienstleistungen. Online: https://eur-lex.europa.eu/legal-content/DE/TXT/HTML/?uri=CELEX:32019L0882 (Retrieved: 17.05.2023).

[ARToJ]   Artscloud (o.J.). Art Planet—Oasis of Inspiration. In: Artscloud. Online: https://artscloud.net/artplanet (Retrieved: 28.05.2023).

[BAI08]   Baichtal, John (20.11.2008). Thingiverse.com Launches A Library of Printable Objects. In: Wired. Online: https://www.wired.com/2008/11/thingiversecom/ (Retrieved: 23.05.2023).

[BAI18]   Jeremy Bailenson (2018). Experience on Demand: What Virtual Reality Is, How It Works, and What It Can Do. W. W. Norton & Company, New York. ISBN-13: 978-0393253696.

[BAL20]   Ball, Matthew (13.01.2020). What It Is, Where to Find it, and Who Will Build It. Online: https://www.matthewball.vc/all/themetaverse (Retrieved: 17.05.2023).

[BAL20c] Balcazar, Cristina (29.11.2020). How Augmented Reality lets Sephora "try on" something different. In: Medium, Marketing in the Age of Digital. Online: https://medium.com/marketing-in-the-age-of-digital/how-augmented-reality-lets-sephora-try-on-something-different-23b4446fd5c1 (Retrieved: 28.05.2023).

[BAL21]   Ball, Matthew (29.06.2021). Virtual Platforms and the Metaverse. In: matthewball.vc. Online: https://www.matthewball.vc/all/virtualplatformsmetaverse (Retrieved: 17.05.2023).

References

[BAL21b] Ball, Matthew (28.06.2021). Evolving User + Business Behaviors and the Metaverse. In: The Metaverse Primer. Online: https://www.matthewball.vc/all/userbehaviorsmetaverse (Retrieved: 17.05.2023).

[BAL22] Ball, Matthew; Furness, Thomas; Inbar, Ori; Kalinowski, Caitlin; Lange, Danny; Lebaredian, Rev; Mann, Steve; Miralles, Evelyn; Rosedale, Philip; Trevett, Neil; Yuan, Yu (14.06.2022): Metaverse decoded by top experts. In: Versemaker: Metaverse Lands-cape & Outlook Series. Online: https://versemaker.org/download (Retrieved: 10.05.2023).

[BAN12] Bannister, Matthew (23.01.2012). Outlook. In: bbc.co.uk. BBC World Service. p. 16m41s. (Retrieved: 17.05.2023).

[BAR23] Jan Barley (Last updated: May 23, 2023). Bit.Country Review: A Game-Changing, Groundbreaking Metaverse? coinbureau.com. Online: https://coinbureau.com/review/bit-country-review/. (Retrieved: 14.02.2025).

[BAS22] BaselLive (16.05.2022) ARTour—Digitale Kunst in einer neuen Dimension. Online: https://basellive.ch/blog/artour-digitale-kunst-in-einer-neuen-dimension-entdecken/wf6w (Retrieved: 10.05.2023).

[BAT23] Batchelor, James (10.05.2023). EA investing in building "games as a platform". In: Gamesindustry.biz. Online: https://www.gamesindustry.biz/ea-investing-in-building-games-as-a-platform (Retrieved: 28.05.2023).

[BBC19] BBC (24.05.2019). Mona Lisa 'brought to life' with deepfake AI. In: BBC Tech. Online: https://www.bbc.com/news/technology-48395521 (Retrieved: 10.05.2023).

[BED22] Bedingfield, Will (04.04.2022). Roblox's 'Layered Clothing' Is Here—but Don't Call It an NFT. In: Wired Culture. Online: https://www.wired.co.uk/article/roblox-layered-clothing (Retrieved: 28.05.2023).

[BEL23a] Belocerkov, Andreas (10.02.2023). Blockchain-Gaming—Mehr als nur der Traum vom Spielen um Geld. In: Wirtschaftsinformatik & Management. https://doi.org/10.1365/s35764-023-00451-9.

[BER89] Berners-Lee, Tim (1989). Information Management: A Proposal. In: CERN, W2C. Online: https://www.w3.org/History/1989/proposal.html (Retrieved: 23.05.2023).

[BEZ19] Bezmalinovic, Tomislav (29.09.2019). Virtual Reality und Kunst: Die besten Apps und Erfahrungen für Kunstliebhaber. In: Mixed VR und Kunst. Online: https://mixed.de/virtual-reality-und-kunst-die-zehn-besten-apps-und-erfahrungen-fuer-kunstliebhaber/ (Retrieved: 28.05.2023).

[BID22] Business Insider Deutschland (03.01.2022). Ralph Lauren verkauft digitale Kleidung im Metaverse—Analysten glauben, es ist der Beginn eines Milliardengeschäfts. In: Business Insider Deutschland. Online: https://www.businessinsider.de/wirtschaft/ralph-lauren-verkauft-digitale-kleidung-im-metaverse/ (Retrieved: 17.05.2023).

[BIT22] bitkom (2022). Wegweiser in das Metaversum—Technologische und rechtliche Grundlagen, geschäftliche Potenziale, gesellschaftliche Bedeutung. In: Bitkom e. V., AG Metaverse Forum, Projektleitung: Dr. Sebastian Klöß. Online: https://www.bitkom.org/Bitkom/Publikationen/Wegweiser-Metaverse (Retrieved: 10.05.2023).

[BIT22] bitkom (2022). Wegweiser in das Metaversum—Technologische und rechtliche Grundlagen, geschäftliche Potenziale, gesellschaftliche Bedeutung. In: Bitkom e. V., AG Metaverse Forum, Projektleitung: Dr. Sebastian Klöß. Online: https://www.bitkom.org/Bitkom/Publikationen/Wegweiser-Metaverse (Retrieved: 10.05.2023).

[BIT22b] Bitkom Presseinformation (05.06.2022). Ein Fünftel der Deutschen möchte im Metaverse Urlaub machen https://www.bitkom.org/Presse/Presseinformation/Digitaler-Tourismus-2022 (Retrieved: 10.05.2023).

[BLI21]   Blitzz (2025). Customer Support in the Metaverse? It's Closer than You Might Think. Blitzz Blog. Online: https://blitzz.co/blog/customer-support-in-the-metaverse. (Retrieved: 14.02.2025).

[BLU23]   Blutinger, Jonathan; Cooper, Christen; Karthik, Shravan; Tsai, Alissa; Samarelli, Noa; Storvick, Erika; Seymour, Gabriel; Liu, Elise; Meijers, Yorán; Lipson, Hod. (2023). The future of software-controlled cooking. npj Science of Food. 7. https://doi.org/10.1038/s41538-023-00182-6.

[BMA21]   BMAS (22.07.2021): Barrierefreiheitsstärkungsgesetz. Gesetz zur Umsetzung der Richtlinie (EU) 2019/882 des Europäischen Parlaments und des Rates über die Barrierefreiheitsanforderungen für Produkte und Dienstleistungen (BFSG). https://www.bmas.de/DE/Service/Gesetze-und-Gesetzesvorhaben/barrierefreiheitsstaerkungsgesetz.html (Retrieved: 17.05.2023).

[BMBoJ]   BMBf (o.J.). Was ist Industrie 4.0? In: Bundesministerium für Bildung und Forschung. Online: https://www.plattform-i40.de/IP/Navigation/DE/Industrie40/WasIndustrie40/was-ist-industrie-40.html (Retrieved: 22.5.2023).

[BON21]   Bonci, Andrea; Fiori, Simone; Higashi, Hiroshi; Tanaka, Toshihisa; Verdini, Federica (2021). An introductory tutorial on brain—computer interfaces and their applications. In: Electronics, 10(5), 560.

[BON22]   Bonifacic, Igor (23.05.2022). Meta's 'MyoSuite' AI platform could help doctors develop better prosthetics. In: engadget.com. https://www.engadget.com/meta-myosuite-annoucemed-183850677.html (Retrieved: 17.05.2023).

[BOR15]   Borrmann, André; König, Markus; Koch, Christian; Beet, Jakob (2015). Building Information Modeling. Technologische Grundlagen und industrielle Praxis. Springer Vieweg, Wiesbaden 2015, ISBN 978-3-658-05605-6.

[BOS14]   Bostrom, Nick (2014). Introduction—The Transhumanist FAQ: A General Introduction. In: Mercer, C., Maher, D.F. (eds) Transhumanism and the Body. In: Palgrave Studies in the Future of Humanity and Its Successors. Palgrave Macmillan, New York. https://doi.org/10.1057/9781137342768_1

[BRA21]   Braun, Jennifer (03.11.2021). Nike meldet Marken für virtuelle Nutzung an. Fashion Network. Online: https://de.fashionnetwork.com/news/Nike-meldet-marken-fur-virtuellenutzung-an,1349436.html (Retrieved: 20.05.2025).

[BRU07]   Bruns, Axel (2007): Produsage: Towards a Broader Framework for User-Led Content Creation. In Proceedings Creativity & Cognition. Washington, DC. 6.

[BRY14]   Erik Brynjolfsson; Andrew McAfee (2014). The Second Machine Age: Work, Progress, and Prosperity in a Time of Brilliant Technologies. W. W. Norton & Company, New York. ISBN: 978-0-393-35064-7.

[BUIoJ]   Building Smart (o.J.). IFC Specifications Database. In: Building Smart International. Online: https://technical.buildingsmart.org/standards/ifc/ifc-schema-specifications/ (Retrieved: 22.5.2023).

[BUS22a] Business Insider Deutschland (22.02.2022). „Kauf Island" und „Phil Leita": Wie Kaufland mit einer eigenen Insel ins Metaverse startet. In: Business Insider. Online: https://www.businessinsider.de/wirtschaft/kauf-island-und-phil-leitawie-kaufland-mit-einer-eigenen-insel-ins-metaverse-startet-a/ (Retrieved: 10.05.2023).

[BUS22b] Business Punk Redaktion (21.01.2022). Kaufland eröffnet eigenen Store im Animal-Crossing-Universum. In: Business Punk. Online: https://www.business-punk.com/2022/01/kaufland-eroeffnet-eigenen-store-im-animal-crossing-universum/ (Retrieved: 10.05.2023).

[BUS45]   Bush, Vannevar (1945). As We May Think. Atlantic Monthly 176 (July 1945) pp. 101–108.

References

[CAR23]	Carter, Rebekah (27.03.2023). Introducing Spatial AR Collaboration—Turn any room into an augmented workspace. In: UCToday Collaboration. Online: https://www.uctoday.com/collaboration/introducing-spatial-ar-collaboration/ (Retrieved: 28.05.2023).
[CHA22]	Chang, Olivia (18.03.2022). Ein Stück Metaverse. In: Forbes. Online: https://www.forbes.at/artikel/ein-stueck-metaverse.html (Retrieved: 17.05.2023).
[CHI22]	Chittum, Morgan (01.02.2022): Morgan Stanley Sees $8 Trillion Metaverse Market—In China Alone. In: Blockworks. Online: https://blockworks.co/news/morgan-stanley-sees-8-trillion-metaverse-market-eventually (Retrieved: 17.05.2023).
[CHO17]	Chohan, Usman. (2017). The Decentralized Autonomous Organization and Governance Issues. SSRN Electronic Journal. https://doi.org/10.2139/ssrn.3082055.
[COA21]	Coates, Charlotte (31.07.2021). Virtual Reality is a big trend in museums, but what are the best examples of museums using VR? In: MuseumNext. Online: https://www.museumnext.com/article/how-museums-are-using-virtual-reality/ (Retrieved: 17.05.2023).
[CRE20]	Crets, Stephanie (22.10.2020). Augmented reality boosts conversion for Home Depot. In: Digital Commerce 360. Online: https://www.digitalcommerce360.com/2020/10/22/augmented-reality-boosts-conversion-for-home-depot/ (Retrieved: 28.05.2023).
[CRO22]	Crowther, Samuel; Ford, Henry (1922). My Life and Work. Garden City, N.Y., Doubleday, Page & company, 1922.
[CRYoJ]	CryptoArt (o.J.). Online: https://cryptoart.io (Retrieved: 17.05.2023).
[DAL15]	Dale, Brady (14.08.2015). 8Chan Kicked Out of Google Search Results. In: Observer Business. Online: https://observer.com/2015/08/google-blocks-8chan-from-search/ (Retrieved: 20.05.2023).
[DAM20]	Damiani, Jesse (26.02.2020): The Museum Of Other Realities Officially Opens Its Virtual Doors To The Public. In: Forbes. Online: https://www.forbes.com/sites/jessedamiani/2020/02/26/the-museum-of-other-realities-officially-opens-its-virtual-doors-to-the-public/ (Retrieved: 17.05.2023).
[DAV22]	Davis, Lakisha (11.01.2022). How the Metaverse Is Shaping the Future of Education. In: metapress. Online: https://metapress.com/how-the-metaverse-isshaping-the-future-of-education/ (Retrieved: 23. 07. 2022).
[DEC20]	Decentraland (20.02.2020). The gates to Decentraland have opened!. In: Decentraland Blog. Online: https://decentraland.org/blog/announcements/decentraland-launch/ (Retrieved: 17.05.2023).
[DEC23]	Decentraland (27.02.203). Tradition and Innovation Collide: Decentraland Metaverse Fashion Week 2023. In: Announcements. Online: https://decentraland.org/blog/announcements/tradition-and-innovation-collide-decentraland-metaverse-fashion-week-2023 (Retrieved: 17.05.2023).
[DEMoJ]	Demokratie in Bewegung (o.J.). Demokratie in Bewegung. Online: https://dib.de/ (Retrieved: 17.05.2023).
[DEC23]	Decentraland (27.02.203). Tradition and Innovation Collide: Decentraland Metaverse Fashion Week 2023. In: Announcements. Online: https://decentraland.org/blog/announcements/tradition-and-innovation-collide-decentraland-metaverse-fashion-week-2023 (Retrieved: 17.05.2023).
[DEF18]	Primavera De Filip; Aaron Wright (2018). Blockchain and the Law: The Rule of Code. Harvard University Press. ISBN-13: 978-0674976429.

[DEW22]   Dewerne, Yvonne (24.01.2022). Gucci, Louis Vuitton, Balenciaga: Diese Luxusunternehmen sind schon längst im Metaverse. In: Esquire. Online: https://www.esquire.de/style/smart-fashion/nft-metaverse-modebrands-louis-vuitton-gucci-nike-balenciaga (Retrieved: 17.05.2023).

[DME12]   Sidney D'Mello; Art Graesser (2012). Dynamics of affective states during complex learning. In: Learning and Instruction—LEARN INSTR. 22. https://doi.org/10.1016/j.learninstruc.2011.10.001.

[DON17]   Donahue, Michelle Z. (09.11.2017). Ein farbenblinder Künstler wurde zum ersten Cyborg der Welt. In: National Geographic. Online: https://www.nationalgeographic.de/wissenschaft/2017/04/ein-farbenblinder-kuenstler-wurde-zum-ersten-cyborg-der-welt (Retrieved: 21.05.2023).

[DRA22]   Draht, Moritz (24.11.2022). „Danke für den guten Deal" Bored Ape für fast eine Million US-Dollar verkauft. In: BTC-Echo. Online: https://www.btc-echo.de/schlagzeilen/nft-dauerbrenner-bored-ape-fuer-fast-eine-million-dollar-verkauft-155084/ (Retrieved: 17.05.2023).

[DUN19]   Duncan, James (12.05.2019). MolochDAO: a primitive solution. In: Medium, MetaCartel DAO. Online: https://medium.com/metacartel/molochdao-a-primitive-solution-d11cc522b18e (Retrieved: 20.05.2023).

[EHL20]   Ehlert, Cindy; Rüdiger, Thomas-Gabriel (2020). Defensible Digital Space: Die Übertragbarkeit der Defensible Space Theory auf den digitalen Raum. In: Cyberkriminologie: Kriminologie für das digitale Zeitalter (2020): 151–171.

[END22]   Enderle, Rob (08.08.2022). The Metaverse Future: Are You Ready To Become a God? In: TechNewsWorld. Online: https://www.technewsworld.com/story/the-metaverse-future-are-you-ready-to-become-a-god-176974.html (Retrieved: 17.05.2023).

[FAD19]   Charles Fadel; Wayne Holmes; Maya Bialik (2019). Artificial Intelligence In Education: Promises and Implications for Teaching and Learning. Independently published. ISBN-13: 978-1794293700.

[FLO20]   Luciano Floridi (2020). The Ethics of Artificial Intelligence and Robotics: Principles, Challenges, and Opportunities. https://doi.org/10.1093/oso/9780198883098.001.0001.

[FLO21]   Luciano Floridi (2021). Ethics, Governance, and Policies in Artificial Intelligence (Philosophical Studies Series Book 144). Springer. ASIN: B09KWY93J2.

[FLO22]   Flohr, Nicholas (29.08.2022). Für „The Gray Man" kooperiert Netflix mit dem Metaverse Decentraland. In: Finanzen.net. Online: https://www.finanzen.net/nachricht/devisen/metaverse-erlebnis-fuer-34-the-gray-man-34-kooperiert-netflix-mit-dem-metaverse-decentraland-11655915 (Retrieved: 28.05.2023).

[GEY23]   Geyer, Mike (21.03.2023). BMW Group Starts Global Rollout of NVIDIA Omniverse. In: Nvidia Blog. Online: https://blogs.nvidia.com/blog/2023/03/21/bmw-group-nvidia-omniverse/ (Retrieved: 20.05.2023).

[GIToJ]   Github (o.J.). bit-country/Metaverse-Network. Online: https://github.com/bit-country/Metaverse-Network. (Retrieved: 14.02.2025).

[GLU23]   Glushkova, Todorka (2023). Modeling in Cyber-Physical Systems. In: Povdiv University Press, ISBN 978-619-7663-49-5.

[GOL21]   Golden, Jessica (02.11.2021). Nike is quietly preparing for the meta-verse. In: CNBC. Online: https://www.cnbc.com/2021/11/02/nike-is-quietly-preparing-for-themetaverse-.html (Retrieved: 17.05.2023).

[HAC23]	Cathy Hackl (2023). Into the Metaverse: The Essential Guide to the Business Opportunities of the Web3 Era. Bloomsbury Business, Dublin. ISBN-13: 978-1399401807.
[HAM22]	Hammer, Peter (19.04.2022). Walmart: an der Schwelle des Metaversums. In: W&V. Online: https://www.wuv.de/Themen/Markenstrategie/Walmart-an-der-Schwelle-des-Metaversums (Retrieved: 10.05.2023).
[HAN23]	Han, Jining; Geping Liu; Yuxin Gao (2023). Learners in the Metaverse: A Systematic Review on the Use of Roblox in Learning. In: Education Sciences 13, no. 3: 296. https://doi.org/10.3390/educsci13030296.
[HOS22]	HospitalityNet (2022). Millennium Hotels and Resorts Launches M Social Decentraland. hospitalitynet. Online: https://www.hospitalitynet.org/news/4110172.html. (Retrieved: 14.02.2025).
[HOS24]	HospitalityNet (2024). M Social Phuket Launches „The Vacay Collection" In Decentraland. hospitalitynet. Online: https://www.hospitalitynet.org/news/4120222.html. (Retrieved: 14.02.2025).
[HOW22]	Howell, Jame (10.02.2022). Metaverse For Education—How Will The Metaverse Change Education?. In: 101 Blockchain. Online: https://101blockchains.com/metaverse-for-education/ (Retrieved: 23. 07. 2022).
[HRZoJ]	HRZ Justus Liebig Universität Giessen (o.J.). Historie. Online: https://www.uni-giessen.de/de/fbz/svc/hrz/org/mitarb/abt/3/zms/schulung/webtechniken/internet/historie (Retrieved: 17.05.2023).
[HUB20]	Huberman, Jenny (2020). Introduction: Thinking through Transhumanism. In Transhumanism: From Ancestors to Avatars. In: New Departures in Anthropology, pp. 1–20. Cambridge: Cambridge University Press. https://doi.org/10.1017/9781108869577.001
[HUG23]	Hughes, Rebecca Ann (15.02.2023). Do You Have To Pay To Visit Venice? Here's What To Know About The Entry Fee. In: Forbes. Online: https://www.forbes.com/sites/rebeccahughes/2023/02/15/do-you-have-to-pay-to-visit-venice-heres-what-to-know-about-the-entry-fee/ (Retrieved: 10.05.2023).
[HUS24]	Muhammad Hussain; Shahid Khalil; Raza Hasan; Muhammad Khuram Khalil (2024). The Metaverse Marketing Revolution: How Virtual Worlds Are Redefining Digital Advertising and Paving the Way for Corporate Success. In: AI-Driven Marketing Research and Data Analytics (pp. 360–377), IGI Global. https://doi.org/10.4018/979-8-3693-2165-2.ch020
[IPFoJ]	IPFS (o.J.). IPFS powers the Distributed Web. Online: https://ipfs.tech/ (Retrieved: 28.05.2023).
[JAL22]	Jalalow, Damir (11.11.2022). Wie treibt Metaverse den Gaming-Sektor voran? In: Metaverse Post. Online: https://mpost.io/de/how-does-metaverse-drive-the-gaming-sector/ (Retrieved: 17.05.2023).
[JAV21]	Javaid, Mohd; Haleem, Abid; Singh, Ravi Pratap; Suman, Rajiv (2021). Industrial perspectives of 3D scanning: Features, roles and it's analytical applications. In: Sensors International, Volume 2, 2021, 100114, ISSN 2666-3511, https://doi.org/10.1016/j.sintl.2021.100114.
[JSOoJ]	JSON Schema (o.J.). JSON Schema. In: JSON Schema. Online: https://json-schema.org/ (Retrieved: 22.5.2023).
[KAL22]	Kalis, Brian; McHugh, Jenica; Safavi, Kaveh T.; Truscott, Andrew (05.09.2022). Accenture Digital Health Technology Vision 2022. In: Accenture: Digital Health. Online: https://www.accenture.com/de-de/insights/health/digital-health-technology-vision (Retrieved: 28.05.2023).

[KAN21] Kanterman, Matthew; Naidu, Nathan (01.12.2021). Metaverse may be $800 billion market, next tech platform. In: Bloomberg Intelligence. Online: https://www.bloomberg.com/professional/blog/metaverse-may-be-800-billion-market-next-tech-platform/ (Retrieved: 17.05.2023).

[KAP20] Jean-Noël Kapferer; Vincent Bastien (2020). The Luxury Strategy: Break the Rules of Marketing to Build Luxury Brands. Kogan Page, London. ISBN-13: 978-0749464912.

[KAR23] David Karp (2023). The role of legal and compliance in the metaverse. McKinsey. Online: https://www.mckinsey.com/featured-insights/in-the-balance/the-role-of-legal-and-compliance-in-the-metaverse. (Retrieved: 14.02.2025).

[KAW22] Kawarase, Mrudul A; Anjankar, Anish (08.11.2022). Dynamics of Metaverse and Medicine: A Review Article. In: Cureus 14(11): e31232. https://doi.org/10.7759/cureus.31232.

[KEL05] Kelly, Kevin (01.08.2005). We Are the Web. In: Wired. Online: https://www.wired.com/2005/08/tech/ (Retrieved: 17.05.2023).

[KER21] Kerris, Richard (Juni 2021). The Metaverse Begins: NVIDIA Omniverse and a Future of Shared Worlds. Von: Nvidia. Online: https://www.nvidia.com/en-us/on-demand/session/computex2021-com2104/ (Retrieved: 17.05.2023).

[KHR19] Khronos (18.03.2019). Khronos Releases OpenXR 0.90 Provisional Specification for High-performance Access to AR and VR Platforms and Devices. In: Khronos Press Release. Online: https://www.khronos.org/news/press/khronos-releases-openxr-0.90-provisional-specification-for-high-performance-access-ar-vr-platforms-and-devices (Retrieved: 22.5.2023).

[KIM23] Kim, Se (2023). Virtual fashion experiences in virtual reality fashion show spaces. Frontiers in Psychology. 14. https://doi.org/10.3389/fpsyg.2023.1276856.

[KIN22] Sonja Kind (2022). Non-fungible Tokens (NFTs). Themenkurzprofil Nr. 54, Büro für Technikfolgen-Abschätzung beim Deutschen Bundestag (TAB). Online: https://publikationen.bibliothek.kit.edu/1000143464. (Retrieved: 14.02.2025).

[KIT16] Kitatus (1507.2016). Games-As-A-Platform—The Future of Games or an Inconvenience?. In: Medium. Online: https://medium.com/@Kitatus/games-as-a-platform-the-future-of-games-or-an-inconvenience-505e719a2cdf (Retrieved: 28.05.2023).

[LAN94] Lange, Rüdiger und Günter Watzlawik (1994). Lexikon der CA-Anwendungen: CAD. CAM/CAE/CAI/CIM. In: VDE-Verlag, 1994. ISBN 10: 3800719207 ISBN 13: 9783800719204.

[LAN17] Jaron Lanier (2017). Dawn of the New Everything: Encounters with Reality and Virtual Reality. Henry Holt and Company, New York. ISBN-13: 978-1627794091.

[LAY07] Layton, Julia (26.01.2007): Can I make my living in Second Life? In: howstuffworks. https://computer.howstuffworks.com/internet/social-networking/networks/second-life.htm (Retrieved: 10.05.2023).

[LE22] Le, Trang (22.07.2022). Sexual assault in the metaverse is part of a bigger problem that technology alone won't solve. Von: (Monash University). Online: https://lens.monash.edu/@politics-society/2022/07/22/1384871/sexual-assault-in-the-metaverse-theres-nothing-virtual-about-it (Retrieved: 17.05.2023).

[LEWoJ] Lewis, Irene (o.J.). Augmented Reality in the Furniture Industry: 5 Benefits of Using AR for Shopping Apps. In: CGIFURNITURE. Online: https://cgifurniture.com/augmented-reality-in-furniture-industry/ (Retrieved: 10.05.2023).

[LIU22]	Liu, Lu; Zhou, Sicong; Huang, Huawei; Zheng, Zibin (2021). From Technology to Society: An Overview of Blockchain-Based DAO. In: IEEE Open Journal of the Computer Society, vol. 2, pp. 204–215, 2021, https://doi.org/10.1109/OJCS.2021.3072661.
[LIU23]	Liu, Yiming; Yiu, Chun, Zhao, Zhao; Park, Wooyoung; Shi, Rui; Huang, Xingcan; Zeng, Yuyang; Wang, Kuan; Wong, Tsz; Jia, Shengxin; Zhou, Jingkun; Gao, Zhan; Zhao, Ling; Yao, Kuanming; Li, Jian; Sha, Chuanlu; Gao, Yuyu; Zhao, Guangyao; Huang, Ya; Yu, Xinge (2023). Soft, miniaturized, wireless olfactory interface for virtual reality. Nature Communications. 14. https://doi.org/10.1038/s41467-023-37678-4.
[LU20]	Yuqian Lu; Chao Liu; Kevin Wang; Huiyue Huang; Xun Xu (2019). Digital Twin-driven smart manufacturing: Connotation, reference model, applications and research issues. In: Robotics and Computer-Integrated Manufacturing. 61. https://doi.org/10.1016/j.rcim.2019.101837.
[LUC22]	Luck-Hille, Esmay (02.11.2022). NFTs and CryptoArt: a revolution. In: University of Oxford: Oxford Talks. https://talks.ox.ac.uk/talks/id/d8dff615-efa4-4008-bd83-fadfe9d9fc8f/ (Retrieved: 17.05.2023).
[LUN16]	Lundkvist, Christian; Lilic, John (17.02.2016). An Introduction to IPFS. In: Medium, ConsenSys. Online: https://medium.com/@ConsenSys/an-introduction-to-ipfs-9bba4860abd0 (Retrieved: 28.05.2023).
[MAA22]	Maas, Hartwin (2022). Der Cyborg in der Industrie 5.0. In: Wissensmanagement Wissenplus. Online: https://www.wissensmanagement.net/themen/artikel/artikel/der_cyborg_in_der_industrie_50.html?no_cache=1&cHash=ccceebb6c6361250801a6ea32472b88f (Retrieved: 17.05.2023).
[MAC09]	Maciuszek, Dennis; Martens, Alke. (2009). Virtuelle Labore als Simulationsspiele. INFORMATIK 2009—Im Focus das Leben, Beitrage der 39. Jahrestagung der Gesellschaft fur Informatik e.V. (GI). 1965–1979.
[MAL22]	Mallis, Athina (14.09.2022). Meet the intraverse, the metaverse's office-based cousin. In: Digital Nation News Web3. Online: https://www.digitalnationaus.com.au/news/meet-the-intraverse-the-metaverses-office-based-cousin-585182 (Retrieved: 28.05.2023).
[MAR14]	Martikainen, Mikko (07.04.2014). Mikko Martikainen, CEO, Sayduck, Finland. In: The Sin Off Stories. Online: https://www.the-spin-off.com/news/stories/Mikko-Martikainen-CEO-Sayduck-Finland-8141 (Retrieved: 28.05.2023).
[MAR22]	Marr, Bernhard (23.02.2022). The Amazing Possibilities Of Healthcare In The Metaverse. In: Forbes. Online: https://www.forbes.com/sites/bernardmarr/2022/02/23/the-amazing-possibilities-of-healthcare-in-the-metaverse/?sh=59f2f2109e5c (Retrieved: 23. 07. 2022).
[MAS22]	Paul Mason (2022). How to Stop Fascism: History, Ideology, Resistance. Allen Lane. ISBN-13: 978-0141996394.
[MAT22]	Matthes, Sebastian (14.02.2022). Der Hype um das Metaverse wird dazu führen, dass Milliarden Euro für Unsinn ausgegeben werden. In: Handelsblatt. Online: https://www.handelsblatt.com/meinung/editorial-der-hype-um-das-metaverse-wird-dazu-fuehren-dass-milliarden-euro-fuer-unsinn-ausgegeben-werden/28058770.html (Retrieved: 17.05.2023).
[MAT22b]	Maja J. Matarić (2022). Socially Assistive Robotics: Methods and Implications for the Future of Work and Care. In: Robophilosophy (2022). Online: http://www.us-robotics.us/med-proposals/ccc-ws.pdf. (Retrieved: 14.02.2025).

[MEDoJ] Medinstrukt (o.J.). Simulation in der Notfallmedizin. Online: https://www.medinstrukt.de/notfallschulungen/simulation-in-der-notfallmedizin/ (Retrieved: 17.05.2023).

[METoJa] Metamandrill (o.J.). Metaverse Werbung; Arten von Metaverse Marketing & Beispiele. In: metamandrill metaverse information. Online: https://metamandrill.com/de/metaverse-werbung-2/ (Retrieved: 17.05.2023).

[METoJb] Metamandrill (o.J.). AR-Marketing; Top-Beispiele für Augmented-Reality-Marketing. In: metamandrill information. Online: https://metamandrill.com/de/ar-marketing/#great-examples-of-ar-marketing (Retrieved: 17.05.2023).

[MIL22] Millennium (27.04.2022): Millennium Hotels and Resorts Launches M Social Decentraland. In: jospitalitynet. https://www.hospitalitynet.org/news/4110172.html (Retrieved: 10.05.2023).

[MIRoJ] Mirrorworld (o.J.). Try Before You Buy with AR. In: Mirrorworld. Online: https://www.mirrorworld.media/try-before-you-buy/ (Retrieved: 28.05.2023).

[HAC21] Hackl, Cathy (29.01.2021). How Brands Can Thrive In The Direct To Avatar Economy. In: Forbes. Online: https://www.forbes.com/sites/cathyhackl/2021/01/29/how-brands-can-thrive-in-the-direct-to-avatar-economy/ (Retrieved: 28.05.2023).

[MON22] Monsanto, Charlton; Embry, Alexandre; Shankavaram, Darshan; Smith-Bingham, Alex; Zhang, Jiani; Rolley, Carina; Huestegge, Nica; Denaro, Andrea; Buvat, Jerome (2022). Total Immersion: How Immersive Experiences And The Metaverse Benefit Customer Experience And Operations. In: Capgemini Insights. Online: https://www.capgemini.com/us-en/insights/research-library/total-immersion-how-immersive-experiences-and-the-metaverse-benefit-customer-experience-and-operations/ (Retrieved: 28.05.2023).

[MOR11] Evgeny Morozov (2011). The Net Delusion: The Dark Side of Internet Freedom. PublicAffairs, New York. ISBN-13: 978-1586488741.

[MOR20] Morrison, Robbie; Mazey, Natasha C. H. L.; Wingreen, Stephen C. (27.05.2020). The DAO Controversy: The Case for a New Species of Corporate Governance? In: Frontiers in Blockchain, Vol. 3, 2020. https://doi.org/10.3389/fbloc.2020.00025 ISSN=2624-7852. Online: https://www.frontiersin.org/articles/10.3389/fbloc.2020.00025 (Retrieved: 20.05.2023).

[MOR22] Morrison, Ryan (24.02.2022). Metaverse users will be granted god-like powers to create their own virtual world just by speaking things into existence, Zuckerberg reveals. In: Dailymail.Com. Online: https://www.dailymail.co.uk/sciencetech/article-10547361/Metaverse-users-granted-god-like-powers-create-virtual-world.html (Retrieved: 17.05.2023).

[MOR23] Alexis Morris, Jie Guan, Amna Azhar (01.06.2023). An XRI Mixed-Reality Internet-of-Things Architectural Framework Toward Immersive and Adaptive Smart Environments. In: IEEE International Symposium on Mixed and Augmented Reality Adjunct (ISMAR-Adjunct). https://doi.org/10.1109/ISMAR-Adjunct54149.2021.00024.

[MOZ23] Mozumder, Md Ariful Islam; Armand, Tagne Poupi Theodore; Uddin, Shah Muhammad Imtiyaj; Athar, Ali; Sumon, Rashedul Islam; Hussain, Ali; Cheol Kim, Hee (2023). Metaverse for Digital Anti-Aging Healthcare: An Overview of Potential Use Cases Based on Artificial Intelligence, Blockchain, IoT Technologies, Its Challenges, and Future Directions. In: Applied Sciences 13, no. 8: 5127. https://doi.org/10.3390/app13085127.

[MUL23] Mullenlowe Group (22.02.2023). Metaverse Builders. In: Web In Travel. Online: https://www.mullenlowegroup.com/news/metaverse-builders/ (Retrieved: 10.05.2023).

References

[MUSoJ]   Museum of Other Realities (o.J.). https://www.museumor.com/ (Retrieved: 17.05.2023).

[NAB23]   Nabben, Kelsia (2023). Web3 as 'self-infrastructuring': The challenge is how. In: Big Data & Society, 10(1). https://doi.org/10.1177/20539517231159002.

[NET18]   netzreich GmbH (16.04.2018): Augmented Bier—Die neue Version ist online. Online: https://www.youtube.com/watch?v=EpPaQ9Qfci4. (Retrieved: 10.05.2023).

[NIFoJ]   Nifty (o.J.). Nifty Gateway. In: Nifty. Online: https://niftygateway.com (Retrieved: 28.05.2023).

[MAR20]   Martens, Todd (13.05.2020). Epic's Tim Sweeney reveals a more connected, 'Fortnite'-driven, game-unified world. In: Los Angeles Times, Entertainment & Arts. Online: https://www.latimes.com/entertainment-arts/story/2020-05-13/epic-games-outlines-a-fortnite-driven-more-connected-future (Retrieved: 10.05.2023).

[OHL19]   Ohlheiser, Abby (05.08.2019). Will taking down 8chan stop the worst people on the Internet? In: The Washington Post, Technology, Internet Culture. Online: https://www.washingtonpost.com/technology/2019/08/05/will-taking-down-chan-stop-worst-people-internet/ (Retrieved: 20.05.2023).

[OPEoJ]   OpenSea (o.J.). OpenSea. Online: https://opensea.io/about (Retrieved: 28.05.2023).

[ORT22]   Ortiz, Laura (2022). Risks of the Metaverse: A VRChat Study Case. In: The Journal of Intelligence, Conflict, and Warfare. 5. 53–128. https://doi.org/10.21810/jicw.v5i2.5041.

[ORT24]   Íñigo Morete Ortiz (2024). How can the Metaverse help to bridge the digital divide? Telefonica Blog. Online: https://www.telefonica.com/en/communication-room/blog/metaverse-bridge-digital-divide/. (Retrieved: 14.02.2025).

[OWO21]   Mieczyslaw Owoc; Agnieszka Sawicka; Paweł Weichbroth (2021). Artificial Intelligence Technologies in Education: Benefits, Challenges and Strategies of Implementation. In: Artificial Intelligence for Knowledge Management (pp. 37–58). https://doi.org/10.1007/978-3-030-85001-2_4.

[PAR21]   Parisi, Tony (22.10.2021). The Seven Rules oft he Metaverse—A framework for the coming immersive reality. In: Medium. Online: https://medium.com/meta-verses/the-seven-rules-of-the-metaverse-7d4e06fa864c (Retrieved: 22.5.2023).

[PAR23]   Parashar, Radhika (13.04.2023). Adidas Expands 'Into The Metaverse' Web3 Initiative with Chapter 1 of ALTS Dynamic NFTs. In: Gadgets360. Online: https://www.gadgets360.com/cryptocurrency/news/adidas-metaverse-web3-initiative-chapter-1-alts-dynamic-nft-series-3945006 (Retrieved: 28.05.2023).

[PAV23]   Pavlakoudis, Rosalia (31.01.2023). Wird das Metaverse Shopping grundlegend verändern? Verbrauchermeinungen sind gemischt. In: GetApp. Online: https://www.getapp.de/blog/3415/wird-das-metaverse-shopping-entscheidend-veraendern#Jeder-Zweite-ist-am-Metaverse-Shopping-interessiert (Retrieved: 17.05.2023).

[PER22]   Perri, Lori (10.08.2022). What's New in the 2022 Gartner Hype Cycle for Emerging Technologies. In: Gartner Insights. https://www.gartner.com/en/articles/what-s-new-in-the-2022-gartner-hype-cycle-for-emerging-technologies (Retrieved: 17.05.2023).

[PLAoJ]   Plattform Industrie 4.0 (o.J.). Was ist Industrie 4.0? Von: BMBF, BMWK. Online: https://www.plattform-i40.de/IP/Navigation/DE/Industrie40/WasIndustrie40/was-ist-industrie-40.html (Retrieved: 17.05.2023).

[RAB15]   Rabie,Ramadan; Samah, Refat; Marwa, Elshahed; Rasha, Ali (2015). Basics of Brain Computer Interface. In: Intelligent Systems Reference Library. 74. 31–50. https://doi.org/10.1007/978-3-319-10978-7_2.

[REDoJ]   Redaktion ComputerWeekly.de, TechTarget (2015). Definition ARPANET/DARPANET. Online: https://www.computerweekly.com/de/definition/ARPANET-DARPANET (Retrieved: 17.05.2023).

[RIX22]   Rixecker, Kim (23.02.2022): Metaverse-Selbstversuch: Wir waren da—und schwer gelangweilt. In: t3n. Online: https://t3n.de/news/metaverse-selbstversuch-decentraland-1451407/ (Retrieved: 17.05.2023).

[ROE22]   Roe, David (20.01.2022). Where the Metaverse and Digital Workplace Meet. In: Reworked. Online: https://www.reworked.co/digital-workplace/where-the-metaverse-and-digital-workplace-meet/ (Retrieved: 28.05.2023).

[RTF25]   RTFKT (2025). Brand. Online: https://rtfkt.com/. (Retrieved: 14.02.2025).

[RZE20]   Rzeszewski, Michał; Evans, Leighton (2020). Virtual Place During Quarantine—a Curious Case of VRChat. In: Rozwój Regionalny I Polityka Regio-nalna, no. 51 (November), 57–75

[SA23]   Sá Maria José; Serpa Sandro (2023). Metaverse as a Learning Environment: Some Considerations. In: Sustainability. 2023; 15(3):2186. https://doi.org/10.3390/su15032186.

[SAAoJ]   SaaSHub (o.J.). Moodle VS Metaverse—Compare Moodle VS Metaverse and see what are their differences. In: SaaSHub. Online. https://www.saashub.com/compare-moodle-vs-metaverse (Retrieved: 28.05.2023).

[SCH03]   Schoonmaker, Stephen J. (2003). The CAD guidebook: a basic manual for understanding and improving computer-aided design. In: Marcel Dekker, New York. ISBN 0-8247-0871-7. OCLC 50868192

[SCH19a]   Schüffel, Patrick; Groeneweg, Nikolaj; Baldegger, Rico (2019). The Crypto Encyclopedia: Coins, Tokens and Digital Assets from A to Z. In: Hochschule für Wirtschaft Fribourg/Growth Publisher, Bern. Bern/Fribourg August 2019.

[SCH22]   Schulz, Madelein (27.10.2022). Gucci Vault opens metaverse world in The Sandbox with games and vintage fashion. In: Vogue Business. Online: https://www.voguebusiness.com/technology/gucci-vault-opens-metaverse-world-in-the-sandbox-with-games-and-vintage-fashion (Retrieved: 28.05.2023).

[SCH23a].   Schlott, Karin (10.05.2023). Wenn die Computerblume duftet. In: Spektrum.de. Online: https://www.spektrum.de/news/virtuelle-realitaet-wenn-die-computerblume-duftet/2137641 (Retrieved: 17.05.2023).

[SCHm21a]   Schmidt, Cord (2021): Wie das Internet zum Metaverse wird. In: hy—the Axel Springer Consulting Group. Online: https://hy.co/2021/12/01/into-the-metaverse-oder-die-naechste-aera-des-internets/#1 (Retrieved: 10.05.2023).

[SCHwa17]   Klaus Schwab, (2017). The Fourth Industrial Revolution. Crown Business. ISBN-13: 978-1524758868.

[SCHwir24] Martin Schwirn (2024). The future of collaboration in virtuality. In: Computer Weekly. Online: https://www.computerweekly.com/feature/The-future-of-collaboration-in-virtuality. (Retrieved: 14.02.2025).

[SEC19]   Second Life (2019). Guide to Jobs in Second Life (Version 27.07.2019). In: Second Life Wiki. Online: https://wiki.secondlife.com/wiki/Guide_to_Jobs_in_Second_Life (Retrieved: 10.05.2023).

[SED21]   Sedlmeir, Johannes; Smethurst, Reilly; Rieger, Alexander; Fridgen, Gilbert (2021). Digital Identities and Verifiable Credentials. In: Business & Information Systems Engineering 63, 603–613 (2021). https://doi.org/10.1007/s12599-021-00722-y.

[SEN22]   Sensorium (16.11.2022). Esports And The Metaverse. In: Sensorium Blog Gaming. Online: https://sensoriumxr.com/articles/esports-and-the-metaverse (Retrieved: 28.05.2023).

[SER18]	Seraphin, Hugues; Sheeran, Paul; Pilato, Manuela. (2018). Over-tourism and the fall of Venice as a destination. Journal of Destination Marketing & Management. 9. https://doi.org/10.1016/j.jdmm.2018.01.011 (Retrieved: 10.05.2023).
[SINoJ]	Sine Wave Entertainment (o.J.): https://sinewaveentertainment.com (Retrieved: 17.05.2023).
[SIR22]	Sirisha (29.07.2022). You Can Be Monalisa in Seconds, Thanks to this Deepfake Tech. In: Analytics Insight. Online: https://www.analyticsinsight.net/you-can-be-monalisa-in-seconds-thanks-to-this-deepfake-tech/ (Retrieved: 10.05.2023).
[SMAoJ]	Smart Valor (o.J.). Maker (MKR). In: Smart Valor Digitale Asset Börse. Online: https://smartvalor.com/de/maker (Retrieved: 20.05.2023).
[SNI23]	Snider, Mike (21.03.2023). Is 3D printing the future of food? Well, if you like cheesecake things are already cooking. In: USA Today. Online: https://eu.usatoday.com/story/news/nation/2023/03/21/food-future-3-d-printed-cheesecake-dessert/11514028002/ (Retrieved: 17.05.2023).
[SOM22]	Somnium Space (on Medium.com) (Sep 12, 2022): Somnium Space partners with Prusa Research and Vrgineers to further develop its open source "Somnium VR ONE" headset. Online: https://somniumspace.medium.com/somnium-space-partners-with-prusa-research-and-vrgineers-to-further-develop-its-open-source-8d1dca-74dae2 (Retrieved: 17.05.2023).
[SOMoJ]	Somnium Space (o.J.). Somnium Space. Online: https://somniumspace.com (Retrieved: 17.05.2023).
[SOS22]	Sosa [2022]. Metaverse, insurance, and mental health. The new new thing. In: SOSY Blog. Online: https://www.sosa.co/blog/metaverse-insurance-mental-health (Retrieved: 28.05.2023).
[SOU24]	Phonesouda Souphamith; Phouthone, Vongpasith; Khamkone Sengaphay; Ngaviseth Phomvongsa; Tiengthong Phengphachanh (2024). Integration of Virtual Reality and Smart Home System: Current Trends, Challenges, and Innovations. In: IJSDR—International Journal of Scientific Development and Research (www.IJSDR.org), ISSN:2455-2631, Vol.9, Issue 9, page no.65–72. Online: https://ijsdr.org/papers/IJSDR2409009.pdf. (Retrieved: 14.02.2025).
[SPE21]	Speakman, Jay (22.11.2021). Was ist The Sandbox?—Das Metaversum. In: Blockzeit.com. Online: https://blockzeit.com/de/was-ist-sandbox-das-metaversum/ (Retrieved: 17.05.2023).
[STO22]	Stoyanov, Nadine; Moser, Christian; Kwiatkowski, Marta (2022). Extended Retail—Die Zukunft des Handels ist grenzenlos. Zühlke und GDI/Studie zu „Extended Retail". Von:—Zühlke Engineering AG. Online: https://www.zuehlke.com/de/extended-retail-die-zukunft-des-handels-ist-grenzenlos (Retrieved: 17.05.2023).
[STU19]	Stuttgarter Nachrichten (28.11.2019). Europa-Park Rust: Rulantica jetzt für alle offen. In: stuttgarter-nachrichten.de. In: Stuttgarter Nachrichten. Online: https://www.stuttgarter-nachrichten.de/inhalt.europa-park-rust-es-ist-angebadet.9b719233-02e7-4628-bee7-32e18fa91acd.html (Retrieved: 28.05.2023).
[SUPoJ]	SuperRare (o.J.). SuperRare. In: SuperRare. Online: https://niftygateway.com (Retrieved: 28.05.2023).
[TAIoJ]	Taipei City Government (o.J.). Taipei City Government. Online: https://www.gov.taipei/ (Retrieved: 17.05.2023).
[TAK16]	Takahashi, Dean (09.12.2016). The DeanBeat: Epic graphics guru Tim Sweeney foretells how we can create the open Metaverse. In: Venture Beat. Online: https://venturebeat.com/games/the-deanbeat-epic-boss-tim-sweeney-makes-the-case-for-the-open-metaverse/ (Retrieved: 17.05.2023).

[TEO22]	Teo, Cheryl (09.05.2022). M Social stamps its 'M' in the metaverse. In: Travel Weekly Asia. Online: https://www.travelweekly-asia.com/Travel-News/Travel-Technology/Millennium-Hotels-and-Resorts-launches-world-s-first-hotel-in-the-metaverse (Retrieved: 10.05.2023).
[THE20]	The Sandbox (30.06.2020): What Is The Sandbox? In: Medium.com. Online: https://medium.com/sandbox-game/what-is-the-sandbox-850de68d893e (Retrieved: 17.05.2023).
[THEoJ]	The Sandbox (o.J.). The Sandbox. Online: https://www.sandbox.game (Retrieved: 17.05.2023).
[THIoJ]	Thingiverse (o.J.). About. In: Thingiverse. Online: https://www.thingiverse.com/about (Retrieved: 23.05.2023).
[THO13]	Thoma, Jörg (08.05.2013). Wie klingt ein Sonnenuntergang? In: golem.de. Online: https://www.golem.de/news/eyeborg-wie-klingt-ein-sonnenuntergang-1305-99161.html (Retrieved: 17.05.2023).
[TIP20]	Tip (24.04.2020). Rapper Travis Scott sorgt für „Fortnite"-Rekord. In: Soiegel.de Netzwelt. Online: https://www.spiegel.de/netzwelt/web/fortnite-konzert-von-rapper-travis-scott-sorgt-fuer-nutzerrekord-a-b377df69-74d2-4103-bbaa-98b40392afaf (Retrieved: 28.05.2023).
[TOF80]	Toffler, Alvin (1980). The Third Wave. Bantam Books, London.
[TOF90]	Toffler, Alvin (1990). Powershift: Knowledge, Wealth and Violence at the Edge of the 21st Century (1990) Bantam Books, London.
[TOV20]	Dina Fajardo Tovar; Vincent Jonker; Wolfgang Hürst (2020). Virtual Reality and Augmented Reality in Education: A review. Universiteit Utrecht. Online: https://www.uu.nl/sites/default/files/20200204_rapportage-literatuurstudie-AR-VR.pdf. (Retrieved: 14.02.2025).
[TUR12]	Sherry Turkle (2012). Alone Together: Why We Expect More from Technology and Less from Each Other. Basic Books, New York. ISBN-13: 978–0465031467.
[VET15]	Vetter, Philipp (18.08.2015). Das Adidas-Experiment mit dem personalisierten Schuh. In: Welt. Online: https://www.welt.de/wirtschaft/article145329973/Das-Adidas-Experiment-mit-dem-personalisierten-Schuh.html (Retrieved: 17.05.2023).
[VIN15]	Vincent, M. A.; Sheriff, S.; Mellott, S. (2015). The efficacy of high-fidelity simulation on psychomotor clinical performance improvement of undergraduate nursing students. In: Computers, Informatics, Nursing: CIN. 2015 Feb;33(2):78–84. https://doi.org/10.1097/cin.0000000000000136. PMID: 25636043.
[VIRoJ]	Virbela (o.J.). Virbela: A Virtual World for Work, Education & Events. In: Virbela. Online: https://www.google.com/url?sa=t&rct=j&q=&esrc=s&source=web&cd=&ved=2ahUKEwjW2dfogYz_AhUJh_0HHYAZBEUQFnoECAwQAQ&url=https%3A%2F%2Fwww.virbela.com%2F&usg=AOvVaw0hgmxWhCRbGh99HKe6cJzG (Retrieved: 28.05.2023).
[VRJoJ]	VRJAM The Multiverse Plattform (o.J.). Revolutionising Live Events fort he WEB3 World. Online: https://vrjam.com/ (Retrieved: 17.05.2023).
[UPLoJ]	Upland (o.J.). Upland. Online: https://www.upland.me/ (Retrieved: 17.05.2023).
[WAN22]	Wang, Ge; Badal, Andreu; Jia, Xun; Maltz, Jonathan; Mueller, Klaus; Myers, Kyle; Niu, Chuang; Vannier. Michael; Yan, Pingkun; Yu, Zhou; Zeng, Rongping (2022). Development of metaverse for intelligent healthcare. In: Nature Machine Intelligence. 4. 1–8. https://doi.org/10.1038/s42256-022-00549-6.
[WAVoJ]	Wave (o.J.). The Show Must Go Beyond. In: Wave XR. Online: https://wavexr.com/about/ (Retrieved: 28.05.2023).

[WEB22]	Weber, Urs (11.10.2022). ARTour—Kunstspaziergang durch Basel mit Augmented Reality. In: Tourismuspresse, Schweiz Tourismus. https://www.tourismuspresse.at/presseaussendung/TPT_20221011_TPT0004/artour-kunstspaziergang-durch-basel-mit-augmented-reality-bild (Retrieved: 10.05.2023).
[WEFoJa]	World Economic Forum (o.J.). Defining and Building the Metaverse. In: World Economic Forum. https://initiatives.weforum.org/defining-and-building-the-metaverse/home (Retrieved: 21.05.2023).
[WEI20]	Weiss, Christoph (22.05.2020). Kreatives Chaos in VRChat. In: ORF Radio FM4. Online: https://fm4.orf.at/stories/3002767/ (Retrieved: 10.05.2023).
[WEI22]	Wei, Hongtao; Tang, Lei; Wang, Wenshuo; Zhang, Jiaming (26.05.2022). Home Environment Augmented Reality System Based on 3D Reconstruction of a Single Furniture Picture. In: Sensors 2022, 22(11), 4020; https://doi.org/10.3390/s22114020.
[WIE23]	Brenda, Wiederhold, Brenda (2023). (Mental) Healthcare Consumerism in the Metaverse: Is There a Benefit? In: Cyberpsychology, behavior and social networking. 26. 145–146. https://doi.org/10.1089/cyber.2023.29269.editorial.
[WU23]	Wu, Tzu-Chi; Ta, Chien; Ho, Bruce (2023). A scoping review of metaverse in emergency medicine. In: Australasian Emergency Care, Volume 26, Issue 1, 2023, Pages 75–83, ISSN 2588-994X, https://doi.org/10.1016/j.auec.2022.08.002. Online: https://www.sciencedirect.com/science/article/pii/S2588994X22000525 (Retrieved: 28.05.2023).
[W3CoJc]	W3C (o.J.). Extensible Markup Language (XML). In: W3C. Online: https://www.w3.org/XML/ (Retrieved: 22.5.2023).
[W3CoJd]	W3C (o.J.). WebXR Device API. In: W3C. Online: https://www.w3.org/TR/webxr/ (Retrieved: 22.5.2023).
[ZAV21]	Zavian, Ellen M. (07.12.2021). Esports And The Metaverse—Predictions For 2022. In: Forbes Business, Sports Money. Online: https://www.forbes.com/sites/ellenzavian/2021/12/07/esports-and-the-metaversepredictions-for-2022/ (Retrieved: 28.05.2023).
[ZET20]	Zetzsche, Dirk Andreas; Arner, Douglas W.; Buckley, Ross P. (30.09.2020). Decentralized Finance (DeFi). In: Journal of Financial Regulation, 2020, 6, 172–203. https://doi.org/10.2139/ssrn.3539194. Online: https://ssrn.com/abstract=3539194 (Retrieved: 28.05.2023)
[ZIV03]	Ziv, Amitai;Wolpe, Paul; Small, Stephen; Glick, Shimon (2003). Simulation-Based Medical Education: An Ethical Imperative. Academic medicine: journal of the Association of American Medical Colleges. 78. 783–8. https://doi.org/10.1097/01.SIH.0000242724.08501.63.
[ZUB19]	Shoshana Zuboff (2019). The Age of Surveillance Capitalism: The Fight for a Human Future at the New Frontier of Power. PublicAffairs, New York. ISBN-13: 978-1610395694.

The Metaverse vs. Current Trends 5

The concept of the metaverse has evolved rapidly in recent years and can now be considered established, even though the term "metaverse" is arguably overused (see also Chap. 10—The Current Addendum 1—Still Relevant: Is the Hype Already Over?). This establishment encompasses both its acceptance as a field of technological research and development, as well as its acceptance in business and society. Both technological advances and economic investments have now ushered the concept into a new phase of relevance.

In 2025, various development trends are evident, each pursuing different priorities: from social interaction spaces and digital economic environments to educational and work settings. Companies such as Meta, Microsoft, and Apple are investing heavily in the development of immersive technologies, while blockchain technologies and NFTs are contributing to the monetization of digital assets. At the same time, issues of regulation, data security, and ethical use are at the center of the debate surrounding the metaverse [DWI22, FLO20, FLO21].

The idea of the metaverse is closely linked to other technological trends such as the Internet of Things (IoT), which is also increasingly connecting physical and digital worlds, as well as the ongoing development of Web3 as a decentralized, user-centric internet structure. In addition, advances in artificial intelligence—especially in the field of generative AI—are driving the interactivity and adaptability of virtual worlds. In the long term, quantum computing could also play a role by revolutionizing the processing of large volumes of data and enabling complex simulations, although this remains highly speculative at present.

To simplify the confusing landscape of terminology, "the metaverse" will be discussed below in relation to other current trends and, where necessary, distinguished from them.

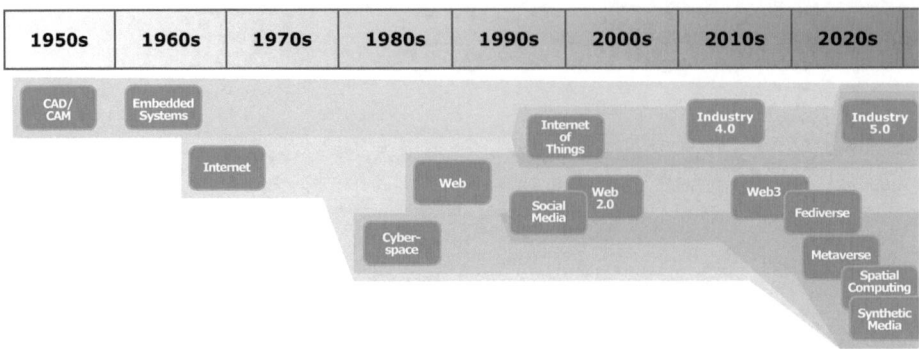

Fig. 5.1 Chronology of related terms. (Own illustration: Peter Hoffmann, Invisible Cow)

5.1 The Metaverse—Another Attempt at a Definition

Based on the considerations outlined above, the metaverse can be understood as a virtual, immersive space in which physical and digital worlds merge, allowing people to interact—often via avatars—in social, economic, and cultural activities. It is frequently described as the next iteration of the internet and is built on technologies such as virtual reality and augmented reality, which is why "innovative" marketing strategists sometimes refer to it as "Web 3D." The set of relevant technologies also includes blockchain, the Internet of Things, and artificial intelligence. This creates a seamless connection between physical and digital reality and enables immersive experiences that prioritize interactivity and personalization. Users can move freely within virtual environments, create digital identities, and own virtual assets such as NFTs or real estate. The metaverse thus provides a space for a wide range of applications, including virtual meetings, gaming, education, and commerce. It combines social interaction, economic activity, and creative freedom in a new digital dimension. Visionaries such as Matthew Ball, Tony Parisi, and Cathy Hackl define the metaverse as an interoperable, persistent platform that prioritizes openness, decentralized control, and the convergence of 2D and 3D worlds [BAL22, HAC21, PAR21]. It represents a transformative change that will have a lasting impact on how we communicate, work, spend our leisure time, and learn (Fig. 5.1).

5.2 The Metaverse vs. Web3

"Web3" is often used to describe the next stage in the evolution of the internet, characterized by decentralization, blockchain technology, and greater user sovereignty. In contrast to previous generations of the internet, which were based on centralized platforms and intermediary actors, Web3 pursues an approach in which data and applications are no longer controlled exclusively by large technology companies, but are organized across a network of distributed computers. This structure is made possible in particular by blockchain technology, which ensures transparent, secure, and immutable data storage [BUT21]. This development has already been briefly described in Chap. 4—Another Dimension: Economic Convergence (see also Fig. 4.1 Web 1–2–3).

A key feature of Web3 is decentralization, which prevents individual institutions or companies from exercising excessive control over online infrastructures. While today's Web 2.0 is dominated by centralized servers, Web3 applications use decentralized networks that are automated by smart contracts. This creates a system in which users are not only consumers but also active participants in the digital infrastructure. This decentralization reduces dependence on platforms such as Google, Facebook, or Amazon and enables greater transparency and resilience against censorship and data monopolies [WOO14].

The driving idea behind Web3 is also the concept of digital ownership. Users own their data and digital assets, secured by technologies such as non-fungible tokens (NFTs) and crypto wallets. While in Web 2.0 personal data is often monetized by companies, in Web3 users have the ability to directly control their digital identities and content. This fosters new economic models, such as play-to-earn games or creator economies, in which artists, developers, and content producers can monetize their work without intermediaries [ABD24].

Interoperability is also crucial for the development of Web3. Unlike the closed ecosystems of centralized platforms, Web3 enables seamless communication and exchange of data and digital assets between different applications and networks. Open protocols and smart contracts allow different blockchain systems to interact, creating an open and interconnected digital ecosystem. This interoperability fosters innovation and gives users greater freedom in choosing platforms and services without being tied to specific providers [BEL20].

In its final implementation, Web3 represents a fundamental change in internet architecture by placing decentralization, user sovereignty, and interoperability at its core.

Web3 and the metaverse are two concepts that are expected to jointly shape the future development of the internet, while focusing on different priorities. Web3 refers to a decentralized version of the World Wide Web, whereas the metaverse, by contrast, describes virtual worlds that enable immersive online interactions. While both developments are interconnected, they emphasize different aspects. Web3 aims to transform the internet's infrastructure through decentralization and increased user control. It is based on blockchain technology and promotes peer-to-peer interactions without the need for central authorities. In contrast, the metaverse focuses on creating immersive digital experiences in which users can interact, work, play, and socialize in real time.

The integration of decentralized and peer-to-peer (P2P) technologies into immersive virtual worlds offers promising new possibilities on the one hand, but also presents specific challenges. Traditionally, many virtual environments are based on centralized architectures, where a main server manages data, interactions, and resources. However, this approach can lead to scalability issues, single points of failure, and potential privacy concerns. Decentralized and P2P approaches aim to overcome these limitations by distributing control and data exchange among the participants in the network.

- An example of the application of decentralized techniques in virtual worlds is the concept of the "Virtual Net," a decentralized architecture for mobile virtual worlds. This architecture addresses the challenges of object state updates and consistency in mobile environments by implementing fault-tolerant management of user content and object states. By distributing responsibilities among network participants, greater scalability and robustness are achieved [SHE18].
- Another example is the implementation of decentralized virtual time in P2P collaboration environments. By introducing a shared time base, participants in distributed virtual environments can act in sync without relying on a central time authority. This promotes coherence and consistency of interactions in a decentralized environment [IEE21].

The application of P2P techniques in immersive environments enables direct connections between users, thereby reducing latency and minimizing dependence on central servers. A practical example is the development of P2P video calls in virtual reality environments, where technologies such as BabylonJS are used to create detailed and interactive 3D environments. Although these implementations are still in the development phase, they demonstrate the potential for decentralized communication in immersive contexts [POS24].

Despite these advantages, decentralized and P2P approaches are challenging to implement in immersive worlds. Ensuring data and state consistency, managing network stability and reliability, as well as addressing security concerns, are complex tasks that require careful planning and implementation. In addition, the resource constraints of mobile devices and the variability of network conditions can impact performance and user experience.

Another difference between the two concepts lies in their respective focus. As previously described, Web3 aims to democratize the internet by introducing decentralized protocols and blockchain technology, thereby shifting control over data and content from centralized platforms back to users. This enables users to manage their digital identities and assets independently, often using cryptocurrencies and non-fungible tokens. The metaverse, on the other hand, seeks to create virtual environments that offer immersive and interactive experiences. In these digital worlds, users can interact with each other through avatars, participate in events, or purchase virtual goods [PAT24].

Despite these different emphases, there are overlaps between Web3 and the metaverse. Both concepts aim to change the way people interact digitally. Technologies attributed to Web3, such as blockchain and NFTs, are being used in the metaverse to secure ownership of digital assets and enable decentralized economic systems within virtual worlds. This integration could lead to a new era of the internet, in which users have control over their data and digital identities while being able to interact seamlessly in virtual worlds.

One hope for the integration of Web3 into the metaverse is that it will democratize virtual worlds by giving users control over their data and digital assets. By leveraging blockchain technology and decentralized networks, users can manage their digital identities and assets independently, without relying on central authorities. This not only promotes user autonomy but also builds trust in digital interactions. At the same time, the use of NFTs, the development of proprietary cryptocurrencies, and virtual goods open up new business models for companies. Businesses can sell and monetize digital products and services—such as virtual real estate, digital artworks, or exclusive virtual experiences—directly to users.

A technical advantage of this integration is the possibility of "borderless" interoperability. Through standardized protocols and decentralized networks, different metaverse platforms can be more easily interconnected, enabling the creation of a unified digital space. This would allow users to move seamlessly between different virtual worlds and use their digital assets across platforms.

As always, these potential benefits are accompanied by significant challenges. The three most important are as follows: [ARB22, GUR22, RUT22]

- The integration of both technologies requires significant innovation, particularly with regard to scalability, security, and user-friendliness. Current technical infrastructures must be further developed to meet the demands of a global user base.
- Regulatory issues present another challenge. Topics such as data protection, copyright, and the taxation of digital assets have not yet been fully resolved. Clear legal frameworks are needed to protect the rights of both users and companies, while not hindering innovation.
- There is also a risk that, without appropriate infrastructure and measures to promote digital inclusion, these technologies will remain exclusive and thus exacerbate digital inequality. It is crucial to ensure access to the necessary technologies and educational resources for all segments of society in order to enable broad participation.

5.3 The Metaverse vs. Fediverse

The term Fediverse refers to the federation of various decentralized, interoperable platforms for social media, blogging, video sharing, and other online services. The word is a portmanteau of "federation" and "universe" and describes a network of independent servers that can communicate with each other via common protocols. A central feature of the Fediverse is decentralization: there is no central authority controlling the entire network. Instead, each server—often referred to as an "instance"—operates its own community with individual rules and moderation policies. This structure enables users to retain control over their data and content and fosters the creation of user-centric digital spaces.

Communication between the various platforms in the Fediverse is based on open standards such as ActivityPub, a protocol that enables the exchange of messages and content between different services. This allows users of different platforms to interact with each other, similar to how email communication works between different providers. Examples of platforms in the Fediverse include Mastodon (a decentralized alternative to Twitter), Pixelfed (an alternative to Instagram), and PeerTube (a decentralized video platform similar to YouTube) [LUT23]. The Fediverse thus offers an alternative approach to the (further) development of the Internet, which, like Web3, is based on decentralization and interoperability. It enables the creation of digital spaces controlled by users and thus represents an alternative to centralized platforms.

Both the Fediverse and the Metaverse can be seen as alternative approaches to the future development of the Internet, aiming for decentralization and the creation of user-centric digital spaces, but with different emphases and technologies. The Fediverse consists of decentralized, interoperable platforms for social media, blogging, video sharing, and more, and is based on open standards such as ActivityPub, which enable communication between different platforms. The main feature of the Fediverse is decentralization. There is no central operator controlling the platforms, and users retain control over their data and content. While the Fediverse focuses on the decentralization of social networks, the Metaverse aims to create comprehensive virtual worlds in which physical and digital realities merge.

Integrating the Fediverse into immersive worlds such as the Metaverse offers several potential advantages. Through the decentralization of the Fediverse, users in virtual environments could retain greater control over their data and content, leading to increased data sovereignty. In addition, the interoperability of the Fediverse enables seamless communication between different platforms, which could enrich social interaction in immersive worlds. For example, users from different Fediverse platforms could interact in a shared virtual environment without being tied to a central platform.

However, connecting various decentralized platforms with different immersive platforms foreseeably results in high technical complexity. Not only must direct techniques and interfaces be developed, but communication between technical modules must also be ensured through standardized protocols.

5.4 The Metaverse vs. IoT & Embedded Systems

Embedded systems and the Internet of Things (IoT) are closely related concepts that shape the modern technological landscape. An embedded system is a specialized computer system that is integrated as an essential component within a larger mechanical or electronic system, performing specific functions within that system. Typically, such systems consist of a microcontroller or microprocessor, memory, and peripheral devices, and are designed to efficiently execute particular tasks, often in real time. Applications can be found in a wide range of fields, including consumer electronics, the automotive industry, medical technology, and telecommunications [GIL23].

5.4 The Metaverse vs. IoT & Embedded Systems

The Internet of Things, on the other hand, refers to a network of physical devices equipped with sensors, software, and other technologies to collect, exchange, and analyze data. These devices are interconnected via the Internet or other communication networks and can automatically respond to environmental conditions as well as provide real-time information to support decision-making processes. Examples include smart home appliances such as intelligent thermostats and lighting systems, wearable devices like fitness trackers, and industrial IoT systems in manufacturing.

The connection between embedded systems and IoT is fundamental: embedded systems provide the hardware and software foundation for IoT devices, enabling them to perform their specific functions and communicate with other devices. While an embedded system traditionally operates as a standalone unit, integration into the IoT extends its capabilities through connectivity and interoperability. This symbiosis makes it possible to collect and analyze large volumes of data, resulting in smarter and more adaptive systems that can efficiently respond to dynamic environments.

Both concepts are of interest to the metaverse, as they represent established and effective approaches to merging digital and physical devices.

IoT, embedded systems, and the metaverse are three interconnected concepts, each playing specific roles in modern technology. Embedded systems are specialized computer systems integrated into larger devices or machines to perform dedicated tasks. They consist of hardware and software optimized for particular functions and often operate in real time. Such systems are found in a variety of applications, from household appliances and medical devices to automotive control systems [ASI23].

The Internet of Things describes a network of physical devices equipped with sensors, software, and other technologies to collect and exchange data. These devices are connected via the Internet and enable remote monitoring, control, and automation. Examples include smart thermostats, networked lighting systems, and wearable fitness trackers.

The metaverse, by contrast, represents an immersive virtual environment in which users can interact through digital avatars. It combines various realities with other digital technologies to create a seamless fusion of the physical and digital worlds.

Both IoT and the metaverse are based on the integration of hardware and software to enable interactive and connected experiences. Embedded systems often form the basis for IoT devices by providing the necessary hardware and firmware that allow these devices to perform their specific functions and communicate with other systems. In the context of the metaverse, IoT devices and embedded systems can help connect physical environments with virtual worlds, for example through sensors that provide real-time data to control virtual simulations.

The main difference between embedded systems and IoT lies in connectivity. While embedded systems are designed for specific tasks within a device or machine and often operate in isolation, IoT devices are intended to communicate with other devices and systems over networks. The metaverse differs from both in that it is a virtual environment aimed at creating immersive experiences, drawing on both IoT technologies and embedded systems to achieve seamless integration of physical and digital worlds.

Real-time interaction is a central feature of both IoT and the metaverse. In IoT, embedded systems enable the immediate capture and processing of data, allowing timely responses to environmental changes or user commands. In the metaverse, real-time interaction is crucial for an immersive experience, as users act through their avatars in virtual spaces and interact with other users or digital objects. Controlling avatars in the metaverse requires precise, low-latency data transmission to ensure natural and responsive movements. The same applies to the control of robots in the IoT context, where embedded systems are responsible for real-time processing of sensor data and execution of control commands. The integration of IoT and the metaverse can lead to innovative applications, such as physical robots being controlled in real time by virtual avatars or virtual simulations being based on real-world sensor data (Fig. 5.2).

IoT and embedded systems can play a crucial role in shaping immersive worlds by seamlessly connecting the physical and digital spheres. As specialized computer systems integrated into devices to perform specific tasks, embedded systems enable the capture, processing, and transmission of data from the physical world in the context of IoT, thereby providing a foundation for immersive applications.

By integrating IoT and embedded systems into immersive environments, real-time sensor data can be used to dynamically and interactively shape virtual worlds. For example, temperature, light, or motion data from the real world can be incorporated into virtual simulations to create a more authentic experience. This fusion of physical and digital information allows users to immerse themselves deeply in virtual scenarios based on real-world data [MICoJ].

Another example of the meaningful application of IoT and embedded systems in immersive worlds is the development of mixed reality architectures that create adaptive and intelligent environments. Such architectures use IoT devices and embedded systems to collect context-sensitive data and adapt the virtual environment in real time based on this information. This leads to an enhanced user experience and opens up new possibilities in areas such as education, entertainment, and industrial simulation [MOR23].

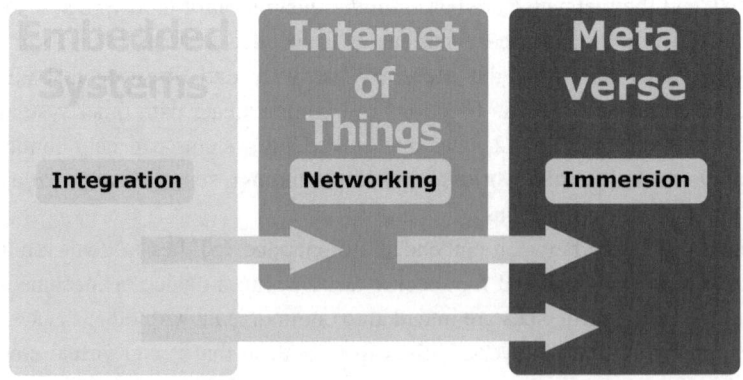

Fig. 5.2 Embedded Systems–IoT–Metaverse

5.5 The Metaverse vs. Spatial Computing

Spatial Computing refers to a technological approach in which digital information and content are seamlessly integrated into the physical space to create immersive and interactive environments. This concept bridges the physical and digital worlds, enabling the boundaries between them to become increasingly blurred [GIL24].

The key technologies often associated with Spatial Computing include:

- **Augmented Reality**: The projection of digital objects into the physical world, allowing users to perceive enhanced information within their real environment.
- **Virtual Reality**: The complete immersion of users in a digital environment that is isolated from the physical world.
- **Mixed Reality**: A combination of AR and VR, in which physical and digital objects interact and merge in real time.
- **Sensing and Tracking**: The use of devices to capture the user's position, movement, and environment, enabling precise interaction with digital content.
- **3D Mapping**: The digital modeling of the physical world to facilitate interactions between users and their environment.

The goal of Spatial Computing is to merge the physical world with digital elements in such a way that a seamless and intuitive user experience is created. By integrating these technologies, applications can be developed that operate in both the real and virtual worlds, enabling new forms of interaction and experience.

The close connection between Spatial Computing and the Metaverse is evident, as both concepts aim to create immersive and interactive environments that link the physical and digital worlds. Spatial Computing serves as one of the key technologies that enable the realization of the Metaverse by supporting the integration and interaction of physical and digital elements in real time.

Spatial Computing and the Metaverse are closely related concepts, both aiming to merge the physical and digital worlds and create immersive, interactive environments. Spatial Computing refers to the technological approaches and interfaces that make it possible to seamlessly integrate digital information and content into physical space. The Metaverse, on the other hand, is understood as a collective virtual space that emerges from the convergence of physically persistent virtual reality and digitally augmented physical spaces. It represents a comprehensive digital environment in which users interact through avatars, economic systems exist, and digital ecosystems are developed. While Spatial Computing provides the technological foundations and interfaces, the Metaverse constitutes the resulting virtual world in which these technologies are applied [WOL24].

A key difference between the two concepts lies in their focus. Spatial Computing centers on the integration and interaction of digital content within the physical space through technological means. It provides the tools and methods to connect digital and physical worlds. The Metaverse, in contrast, focuses on the creation and experience of comprehensive virtual worlds in which users can interact and engage in a wide range of activities. It is the result of the large-scale application of Spatial Computing technologies [SCHmi23b].

In immersive worlds, Spatial Computing plays a crucial role by enabling the fusion of physical and digital reality. Through the integration of AR and VR, users can immerse themselves in virtual environments that interact with the real world. For example, in training or production, virtual training environments can be created in which employees experience realistic scenarios without being exposed to physical hazards. This not only promotes learning but also increases efficiency and safety [MHP24].

In addition, Spatial Computing enables location-independent collaboration, allowing teams to interact in shared digital spaces. This increases efficiency and productivity, as employees can work together regardless of their physical location. The immersion and interactivity enabled by Spatial Computing enhance employee engagement and motivation, which also contributes to increased productivity [FEL23].

Another application example is the merging of digital and real worlds in industrial settings. Spatial Computing optimizes workflows in various sectors such as design, industry, and medicine by enabling collaboration and communication independent of physical location. It also opens up the potential to create productive work environments in smart offices and comfortable living spaces in smart homes by using contextual data for automatic adjustments.

5.6 The Metaverse vs. Synthetic Media & Social Media

Two initially independent concepts that at first seem unrelated to the context of the Metaverse are Synthetic Media and Social Media. They fundamentally influence the way content is created, shared, and consumed.

Synthetic Media refers to the artificial production, manipulation, and modification of data and media through automated means, particularly using artificial intelligence and machine learning. This includes the generation of videos, images, texts, and audio files that are created wholly or partially by AI. Examples include deepfakes, where AI-generated videos realistically depict people, text-to-image generators such as DALL·E that create images based on text input, as well as AI-generated avatars and speech synthesis systems.

Social Media, on the other hand, refers to internet-based platforms and applications that enable users to create, share, and interact with information, ideas, personal messages, and other content such as videos within virtual communities and networks. Typical features of social media include the ability to connect, exchange user-generated content, and participate in online communities. Platforms such as Facebook, Instagram, Twitter, and TikTok are prominent examples of social media.

5.6 The Metaverse vs. Synthetic Media & Social Media

The connection between Synthetic Media and Social Media becomes particularly apparent in the context of the Metaverse, where an immersive virtual environment enables social, economic, and cultural interactions. Synthetic Media provides new tools for generating and personalizing content that are crucial for immersive and interactive experiences in the Metaverse. For example, AI can be used to create realistic avatars or virtual worlds that enrich the user experience in the Metaverse.

While Social Media aims to promote the exchange and networking of content, particularly in two-dimensional digital spaces, Synthetic Media enables the automated creation and customization of content regardless of dimensionality. The Metaverse, in turn, primarily offers three-dimensional, immersive spaces in which users can interact and gain a wide range of experiences. The integration of Synthetic Media into the Metaverse can lead to even more realistic and personalized virtual experiences, while Social Media serves as a platform for the dissemination and discussion of this content.

Synthetic Media and Social Media can contribute both to the creation and, in particular, to the (further) development of immersive worlds by enabling the creation, distribution, and interaction with content.

Synthetic Media generated or modified by artificial intelligence and machine learning in the form of media content such as videos, images, texts, and audio files enables the creation of realistic simulations and virtual characters that can be used in immersive environments. For example, AI-generated avatars can be used in virtual training environments to simulate realistic interactions, which is particularly beneficial in the education and corporate sectors. Medical students, for instance, can practice with synthetic patients, or professionals can be trained in risk-free, simulated scenarios [PAT23].

Social Media, on the other hand, encompasses internet-based platforms and applications that enable users to create, share, and interact with content in virtual communities. In immersive worlds, social media platforms can serve as interfaces through which users share their experiences, collaboratively create content, and maintain social interactions in virtual spaces. The integration of social media into immersive environments fosters the formation of communities and the exchange of user-generated content, which increases user immersion and engagement.

The combination of Synthetic Media and Social Media in immersive worlds thus offers significant potential, as the use of AI-generated content can create more personalized and realistic experiences, while social media platforms support the dissemination and exchange of these experiences. This leads to deeper immersion and increased user engagement in virtual environments.

The ethical background and questions regarding the acceptance of such automatically generated content will not be addressed here.

5.7 Overview of Differences and Similarities

5.7.1 Metaverse, Web3, Fediverse

Characterization

Feature	Metaverse	Web3	Fediverse
Definition	Virtual, immersive 3D worlds where users interact via avatars.	Decentralized internet based on blockchain technology.	Network of federated, decentralized platforms for social networking and communication.
Technological Focus	VR, AR, 3D rendering, AI, IoT	Blockchain, cryptocurrencies, NFTs, smart contracts	Federated servers, open protocols (e.g., ActivityPub)
Decentralization	Can be centralized (Meta, Microsoft) or decentralized (Decentraland).	Decentralized through blockchain protocols and peer-to-peer networks.	Decentralized through distributed servers and community-driven platforms.
Interaction	Real-time interaction in 3D spaces via avatars, voice, and gestures.	Transactions, ownership of digital assets, governance via DAOs.	Text, image, and video sharing; social interaction through posts and comments.
Immersion	Highly immersive through VR/AR and multisensory experiences.	Less immersive, with a stronger focus on infrastructure and digital property rights.	Not immersive, based on traditional social interaction formats.
User Control	Varies by platform: centralized or decentralized with asset ownership.	Strong user control over digital identities, data, and assets.	High degree of control through server choice and self-management of content.
Economic Models	Trade in virtual goods, NFTs, event tickets, advertising.	Cryptocurrencies, token-based economy, DAOs for organization.	Less economically oriented, often donation-based or ad-free.
Open Standards	Partially closed (centralized providers), partially open (decentralized).	Open blockchain protocols enable interoperability.	Open protocols such as ActivityPub promote interoperability between platforms.
Application Areas	Social interaction, virtual events, education, gaming, virtual economy.	Decentralized finance (DeFi), digital property rights, NFTs, DAOs, tokenization.	Social networking, communication, media sharing, community management.
Examples	Decentraland, The Sandbox, Meta Horizon	Ethereum, Solana, Polkadot, OpenSea	Mastodon, PeerTube, Pixelfed, Friendica

5.7 Overview of Differences and Similarities

Characterization			
Feature	Metaverse	Web3	Fediverse
Ethical Challenges	Data privacy, concentration of power by central providers.	Energy consumption (proof-of-work systems), speculation, regulatory uncertainty.	Moderation, responsibility of server administrators, fragmentation of communities.
Target Audience	Users seeking immersive social and economic experiences.	Technologically savvy users and developers who promote decentralization and ownership.	Users who prioritize privacy, independence, and social networking.
Main Users	End users, developers, companies	Consumers, industry, public infrastructure	Manufacturers and operators of devices, machines, and systems.
Application Areas	Social interaction, education, gaming, virtual economy.	Smart homes, industrial automation, smart cities.	Control and monitoring in machinery, medical technology, consumer electronics.
Collaboration	Users interact directly with the virtual environment.	Devices interact with each other autonomously or semi-autonomously.	Embedded systems support IoT devices through data processing and control.
Economic Models	Trade in virtual goods, NFTs, advertising.	Sale of connected devices, data services, and maintenance.	Sale of devices and systems, licensing of embedded technologies.
Challenges	Data privacy, energy consumption, centralization of power.	Security, data privacy, interoperability.	Limited computing power, security, cost optimization.

Differences			
Feature	Metaverse	IoT	Embedded Systems
Primary Focus	Virtual experiences and social interaction.	Automation and connectivity.	Control and operation of individual devices.
Levels of Interaction	Directly between user and virtual world.	Between devices or between devices and the cloud.	Within a device or system.
Technological Objective	Immersion and interactivity.	Efficiency and automation.	Reliability and accuracy.

5.7.2 Metaverse, IoT, Embedded Systems

Characterization			
Feature	Metaverse	IoT	Embedded Systems
Definition	Virtual, immersive 3D worlds where users interact as avatars and experience content.	Network of physical devices connected via the Internet to collect and communicate data.	Specialized computer systems integrated into physical devices to control specific functions.
Technological Focus	VR, AR, 3D rendering, blockchain, AI	Sensors, actuators, networks, cloud services	Microcontrollers, processors, firmware
Decentralization	Can be centralized (e.g., Meta) or decentralized (e.g., Decentraland).	Often centralized, but increasingly decentralized (edge computing, local networks).	Localized, but often part of a network or larger system.
Interaction	Real-time interaction via avatars, voice, and gestures in virtual worlds.	Automatic data collection and control of devices or processes.	Direct control and optimization of specific device functions.
Immersion	Highly immersive through VR/AR and multisensory experiences.	Not immersive, focus on automation and connectivity.	No immersion, purely functional implementation.
Connection to Reality	Simulates real or fictional environments.	Connects real devices and systems to digital networks.	Embedded in physical devices, without direct connection to the virtual world.
Examples	Decentraland, The Sandbox, Meta Horizon Worlds	Smart homes, connected vehicles, wearables	Controllers in household appliances, medical technology, industrial plants
Data Processing	Large volumes of real-time data, often on centralized or decentralized servers.	Data is collected locally and processed either centrally or decentrally.	Processing is local, often with limited computing power.
Energy Consumption	High energy demand for VR, servers, and graphics.	Varies greatly, from battery-powered sensors to energy-intensive devices.	Generally energy-efficient, optimized for specific tasks.
User Focus	End users, businesses, developers	Consumers, industry, infrastructure	Device and system developers, manufacturers

5.7 Overview of Differences and Similarities

Characterization			
Feature	Metaverse	IoT	Embedded Systems
Main User Groups	People seeking immersive social or business experiences.	Users and companies aiming for automation and increased efficiency.	Manufacturers and operators of specific devices and systems.
Application Areas	Social interaction, education, gaming, virtual economy.	Smart homes, industrial automation, smart cities.	Control and monitoring in machines, cars, medical technology.
Collaboration	Users interact directly with the virtual environment.	Devices communicate autonomously or semi-autonomously with each other.	Embedded systems support IoT devices through data processing and control.
Economic Models	Trade in virtual goods, NFTs, advertising.	Sales of connected devices, cloud services, data analytics.	Sales of hardware and software licenses.
Challenges	Data privacy, energy consumption, concentration of central power.	Security, data privacy, interoperability.	Limited computing power, security, cost optimization.

Differences			
Feature	Metaverse	IoT	Embedded Systems
Primary Focus	Virtual experiences and social interaction.	Connectivity and automation.	Control of specific device functions.
Immersiveness	Highly immersive, multisensory.	Functional and utilitarian.	Purely functional, no immersion.
Level of Abstraction	User-centered virtual worlds.	Device- and network-centered systems.	Device-centered processes and tasks.

5.7.3 Metaverse, Spatial Computing

Characterization		
Feature	Metaverse	Spatial Computing
Definition	Virtual, immersive 3D worlds where users interact as avatars and experience content.	Technology that connects the physical and digital worlds through 3D data and sensors to make physical spaces interactive.
Focus	Social interaction, virtual environments, and immersive experiences.	Linking physical space and digital information for functional applications.
Technology	VR, AR, 3D rendering, blockchain, AI	AR, VR, AI, sensors, IoT, edge computing, spatial mapping

Characterization

Feature	Metaverse	Spatial Computing
Interaction	Users interact with virtual worlds and avatars.	Users interact with digital information projected onto physical spaces.
Immersion	Highly immersive, often in fully virtual environments.	Functionally immersive, through the overlay of digital content onto real spaces.
Relation to Reality	Can be completely independent of the physical world.	Direct connection to the physical world through data overlays.
Application Areas	Virtual events, social interaction, gaming, education, commerce.	Navigation, architecture, maintenance, healthcare, smart cities.
Technological Basis	Primarily software and 3D rendering, optionally with hardware (VR/AR).	Hardware such as cameras, sensors, and AR glasses, complemented by software for spatial mapping.
User-Centricity	Focuses on virtual experiences for social and economic interaction.	Focuses on integrating digital information into physical spaces.
Examples	Decentraland, The Sandbox, Meta Horizon Worlds	Microsoft HoloLens, Magic Leap, Google Maps AR
Data Processing	Processing large volumes of data for 3D models and interactions.	Real-time data processing for spatial recognition and information projection.
Economic Models	Trade in virtual goods, NFTs, advertising.	Licensing of software and hardware, optimization of processes in the physical world.
Challenges	Data privacy, high energy requirements, accessibility.	High technical requirements (hardware and sensors), data privacy, interoperability.

Differences

Feature	Metaverse	Spatial Computing
Spatial Reference	Can exist independently of the real world.	Is always linked to the physical world.
Primary Focus	Virtual experiences and social interaction.	Functional integration of digital content into physical spaces.
Immersiveness	High immersion in virtual spaces.	Immersion is purpose-driven and contextual.
Hardware Dependency	Can often be purely software-based (e.g., desktop).	Usually requires specialized hardware such as AR glasses or sensors.

5.7.4 Metaverse, Synthetic Media, Social Media

Characterization			
Feature	Metaverse	Synthetic Media	Social Media
Definition	Virtual, immersive 3D worlds where users interact as avatars.	AI-generated content such as videos, images, text, or speech.	Platforms that enable social interaction and content sharing.
Technological Focus	VR, AR, blockchain, 3D rendering, AI	AI, deep learning, text-to-image/-video, speech synthesis	Algorithms for feed curation, livestreaming, image/video uploads
Immersion	Highly immersive through VR/AR and multisensory experiences.	Can generate immersive content for VR/AR and other formats.	Low immersion, focus on consumable content (text, images, videos).
Interaction	Real-time interaction in 3D environments.	Content responds to user requirements through AI personalization.	Asynchronous or synchronous communication, e.g., comments, likes, livestreams.
User Control	Control over avatars, virtual assets, and interactions.	Personalized content can be created or customized.	Limited control due to algorithm-driven feeds.
Content Creation	Users create virtual worlds, avatars, and content.	AI automatically generates content based on user input.	Users create and share content such as text, images, and videos.
Application Areas	Virtual events, education, gaming, social interaction, commerce.	Personalized advertising, media production, avatars, automated content.	Communication, brand advertising, news sharing, community building.
Economic Models	Trading NFTs, virtual goods, events.	Sale of AI-generated content, licensing of tools.	Advertising-based, influencer marketing, content monetization.
Interactivity	High interactivity through avatars, gestures, speech, and social spaces.	Users interact via input to receive personalized content.	Moderate, e.g., through comments, likes, sharing, or messaging.
Data Processing	Large volumes of data for 3D rendering and real-time social interaction.	AI processes large amounts of data for content creation.	Data analysis for personalized feeds and ad placement.
Ethical Challenges	Data privacy, identity theft, centralization.	Deepfakes, misuse of AI-generated content, copyright issues.	Data misuse, algorithmic manipulation, fake news.

Characterization

Feature	Metaverse	Synthetic Media	Social Media
Examples	Decentraland, The Sandbox, Meta Horizon Worlds	DALL·E, deepfake tools, ChatGPT, Synthesia	Instagram, TikTok, Twitter, Facebook
Target Audience	Users seeking immersive social and economic experiences.	Creatives, businesses, marketing professionals, content producers.	Users who use social networks and content sharing for communication and entertainment.

Differences

Feature	Metaverse	Synthetic Media	Social Media
Immersiveness	Highly immersive, multisensory.	Can generate immersive content, but is not immersive itself.	Low-immersion 2D experience.
Content Creation	User-generated 3D content in real time.	AI generates content based on input.	Users manually create and share content.
Primary Focus	Virtual worlds and social interaction.	Automated and personalized media production.	Communication and content sharing.
Technological Requirements	VR/AR hardware, blockchain for decentralized platforms.	AI models, computing power, training data.	Algorithms and platform integration.

References

[ABD24] Zain Ul Abdeen (2024). A Beginner's Guide to NFTs: The Future of Digital Ownership. Medium. Online:https://medium.com/@zain_ul_abdeen/a-beginners-guide-to-nfts-the-future-of-digital-ownership-bf2ece282f3e. (Retrieved: 14.02.2025).

[ARB22] Jana Arbanas; Allan V. Cook; Chris Arkenberg (2022). The metaverse and Web3: The next internet platform. Deloitte Insights. Online: https://www2.deloitte.com/us/en/insights/industry/technology/web3-and-metaverse-the-future-of-the-internet.html. (Retrieved: 14.02.2025).

[ASI23] Rameez Asif; Syed Raheel Hassan (2023). Exploring the Confluence of IoT and Metaverse: Future Opportunities and Challenges. IoT, 4(3), 412–429. https://doi.org/10.3390/iot4030018.

[BAL22] Ball, Matthew; Furness, Thomas; Inbar, Ori; Kalinowski, Caitlin; Lange, Dan-ny; Lebaredian, Rev; Mann, Steve; Miralles, Evelyn; Rosedale, Philip; Trevett, Neil; Yuan, Yu (14.06.2022): Metaverse decoded by top experts. In: Verse-maker: Metaverse Lands-cape & Outlook Series. Online: https://versemaker.org/download (Retrieved: 10.05.2023).

References

[BEL20]	Rafael Belchior; André Vasconcelos; Sérgio Guerreiro; Miguel Correia (2020). A Survey on Blockchain Interoperability: Past, Present, and Future Trends. https://doi.org/10.48550/arXiv.2005.14282.
[BUT21]	Vitalik Buterin (2021). The Meaning of Decentralization. Medium. Online: https://medium.com/@VitalikButerin/the-meaning-of-decentralization-a0c92b76a274. (Retrieved: 14.02.2025).
[DWI22]	Yogesh K. Dwivedi; Laurie Hughes; Abdullah M. Baabdullah; et.al. (2022). Metaverse beyond the hype: Multidisciplinary perspectives on emerging challenges, opportunities, and agenda for research, practice and policy. In: International Journal of Information Management, Volume 66, 2022, 102542, ISSN 0268-4012. https://doi.org/10.1016/j.ijinfomgt.2022.102542.
[FEL23]	Torsten Fell. Intuitive Interaktion, gemeinsames Arbeiten und Lernen in einer hypriden Realität. Institute for Immersive Learning. Online: https://www.immersivelearning.institute/spatial-computing-raeumlicher-computer-consulting. (Retrieved: 14.02.2025).
[FLO20]	Luciano Floridi (2020). The Ethics of Artificial Intelligence and Robotics: Principles, Challenges, and Opportunities. https://doi.org/10.1093/oso/9780198883098.001.0001.
[FLO21]	Luciano Floridi (2021). Ethics, Governance, and Policies in Artificial Intelligence (Philosophical Studies Series Book 144). Springer. ASIN: B09KWY93J2.
[GIL23]	Alexander S. Gillis; Ben Lutkevich (2023). What is an embedded system? TechTarget. Online: https://www.techtarget.com/iotagenda/definition/embedded-system. (Retrieved: 14.02.2025).
[GIL24]	Alexander S. Gillis; George Lawton (12.02.2024). Spatial computing. TechtTarget. Online: https://www.techtarget.com/searchcio/definition/spatial-computing. (Retrieved: 14.02.2025).
[GUR22]	Michael Gurock; Larissa de Lima; Jason Ekberg (2022). The Economic Potential of Web3 Metaverses. Oliver Wyman Forum. Online: https://www.oliverwymanforum.com/future-of-money/2022/july/the-economic-potential-of-web3-metaverses.html. (Retrieved: 14.02.2025).
[HAC21]	Hackl, Cathy (27.10.2021). The metaverse is coming. Cathy Hackl explains why we should care. In: Freethink. Online: https://www.freethink.com/hard-tech/building-the-metaverse-cathy-hackl-gives-us-a-glimpse-of-the-future (Retrieved: 21.05.2023).
[IEE21]	IEEE Xplore. (2021). Implementing Decentralized Virtual Time in P2P Collaborative Environments. Retrieved von https://ieeexplore.ieee.org/document/9459326/. (Retrieved: 14.02.2025).
[LUT23]	Ben Lutkevich (25.07.2023). Fediverse. TechTarget. Online: https://www.techtarget.com/whatis/definition/fediverse (Retrieved: 14.02.2025).
[MHP24]	MHP (11.07.2024). Spatial Computing: Die Revolution für Produktion und Schulung. MHP Blog. Online: https://www.mhp.com/de/insights/blog/post/spatial-computing. (Retrieved: 14.02.2025).
[MICoJ]	MICL (oJ9. Embedded Systems and the Internet-of-Things. Michigan Integrated Circuits Laboratory. Online: https://micl.engin.umich.edu/sensing-systems. (Retrieved: 14.02.2025).
[MOR23]	Alexis Morris, Jie Guan, Amna Azhar (01.06.2023). An XRI Mixed-Reality Internet-of-Things Architectural Framework Toward Immersive and Adaptive Smart Environments. In: IEEE International Symposium on Mixed and Augmented Reality Adjunct (ISMAR-Adjunct). https://doi.org/10.1109/ISMAR-Adjunct54149.2021.00024.

[PAR21]   Parisi, Tony (22.10.2021). The Seven Rules oft he Metaverse—A framework for the coming immersive reality. In: Medium. Online: https://medium.com/meta-verses/the-seven-rules-of-the-metaverse-7d4e06fa864c (Retrieved: 22.5.2023).

[PAT23]   Dan Patterson (2023). Deepfakes for good? How synthetic media is transforming business. TechInformed. Online: https://techinformed.com/deepfakes-for-good-how-synthetic-media-is-transforming-business. (Retrieved: 14.02.2025).

[PAT24]   Andy Patrizio (2024). Web3 vs. metaverse: What's the difference? TechTarget. Online: https://www.techtarget.com/whatis/feature/Web3-vs-metaverse-Whats-the-difference. (Retrieved: 14.02.2025).

[POS24]   Positive Intentions. (2024). P2P Video Calls in Virtual Reality: A New Frontier for Decentralized Communication. Online: https://positive-intentions.com/blog/p2p-video-calls-in-virtual-reality/. (Retrieved: 14.02.2025).

[RUT22]   Rutgers Business Insights. (2022). Challenges facing the adoption of Web3 and the metaverse. O https://www.business.rutgers.edu/business-insights/challenges-facing-adoption-web3-and-metaverse. (Retrieved: 14.02.2025).

[SCHmi23b] Dirk Schmidt (17.08.2023). The Metaverse vs. Spatial Computing. bizztech.io. Online: https://bizztech.io/metaverse-versus-spatial-computing. (Retrieved: 14.02.2025).

[SHE18]   Shen, B., & Guo, J. (2018). Virtual Net: a Decentralized Architecture for Interaction in Mobile Virtual Worlds. Retrieved von https://arxiv.org/abs/1811.05941. (Retrieved: 14.02.2025).

[WOL24]   Konrad Wolfenstein (24. April 2024). Spatial Computing im Industrial Metaverse—Die Extended Reality im industriellen Sektor, Fertigungsindustrie, Logistik und Supply Chain. Online: https://xpert.digital/spatial-computing. (Retrieved: 14.02.2025).

[WOO14]   Gavin Wood (2014). Ethereum: A Secure Decentralised Generalised Transaction Ledger. Ethereum Whitepaper/Final Draft. Etherplan. Online: https://etherplan.com/ethereum-yellow-paper.pdf. (Retrieved: 14.02.2025).

More Relevant than ever: Artificial Intelligence in the Metaverse?

6

This chapter constitutes Addendum 1 in the first edition of this work. To illustrate the rapid pace of development, this section will initially remain unchanged and will later be compared with the most recent developments at the end.

Preparations and fundamental research for this book date back to spring 2022. At that time, there were three technological domains whose development progressed largely independently of one another. The first was the Web3 domain, in which blockchain technology, cryptocurrencies, and non-fungible tokens played a central role in the implementation of new services. Second was the metaverse, which also partially relied on blockchain and NFTs, resulting in some overlap with Web3. Finally, there was the field of artificial intelligence, whose development appeared to be driven primarily by marketing factors. While these domains advanced in peaceful coexistence, sometimes with greater, sometimes with lesser overlap, and at seemingly steady speeds, this changed abruptly in October/November 2022. The trigger was the release of the AI-powered service ChatGPT by OpenAI, which impressively demonstrated the capabilities and potential of AI-based applications [DOU23]. As a result, new use cases were presented and discussed almost daily, with applications for other media forms such as images and video quickly emerging. This led to discussions about the development of autonomous chatbots based on such services, which in turn raised the next logical question: to what extent can autonomous chatbots be coupled with digital twins, i.e., avatars in the metaverse [ISL23]? This established the connection between AI and the metaverse complex. Since this connection has the potential to significantly influence the future development of the metaverse, this topic will be briefly discussed in this work.

First, a general overview of the intersection between AI and the metaverse will be provided, followed by an analysis and presentation of the current state of development as of May 2023.

Virtual assistants and chatbots are two commonly used AI technologies in the metaverse [AHU23, THA23, ZHO23]. These refer to "intelligent" programs that help users retrieve information, complete tasks, and manage their interactions within the metaverse [PER22]. They typically possess natural language processing capabilities, machine learning, and connections to knowledge databases to efficiently and accurately respond to user queries [CHE17]. Chatbots, by contrast, are AI-driven text or voice dialog systems capable of communicating with users in the metaverse in natural language and engaging in social interaction [JAI18]. They are frequently deployed in virtual environments to provide customer service, technical support, or entertainment [LUG16]. By leveraging techniques such as deep learning and neural networks, chatbots are increasingly able to conduct complex and human-like conversations [VIN15].

Although the concept of the metaverse is still relatively new, significant progress has been made in recent years in integrating virtual assistants and chatbots into the metaverse. Examples include the integration of Apple's Siri and Amazon's Alexa into virtual reality platforms, as well as the development of AI-powered chatbots for virtual games and social platforms such as Fortnite and VRChat [MAL23].

The integration of AI into virtual worlds and games plays a significant role in the development of avatars and non-player characters (NPCs) [YAN18]. The application of AI technologies such as machine learning and natural language processing (NLP) has enabled the creation of AI-driven avatars and NPCs that can simulate human-like behaviors and interactions in real time [RIE14].

- One example is the use of deep learning techniques to transfer users' facial expressions and gestures to their avatars in real time, thereby enhancing nonverbal communication in virtual environments [THI16]. Similarly, AI algorithms based on reinforcement learning enable NPCs to learn autonomously and adapt to users' actions and decisions, providing a more realistic and immersive gaming experience [VIN19].
- Another example of AI application in this area is procedural content generation, where AI algorithms are used to automatically create not only new environments or objects, but also new characters in the metaverse [SHA16]. This technique can help reduce development time and costs while promoting greater diversity and dynamism in virtual worlds [HEN13].

However, the growing prevalence of AI-driven avatars and NPCs in the metaverse also raises ethical questions, particularly regarding the boundaries between real and artificial identities, the potential dehumanization of social interaction, and the responsibility of developers for the actions of their AI-controlled characters [MOU15].

Certainly, advances in computer graphics and simulation in recent years have also contributed significantly to the development and improvement of the metaverse [THA21]. In particular, the integration of AI into these areas has enabled users to experience increasingly realistic and immersive environments. One example of AI use in computer graphics is the application of generative adversarial networks (GANs) to create realistic and high-resolution textures and 3D models [KAR17]. This technique makes it possible to generate detailed and diverse objects and environments in the metaverse, enhancing users' immersion in the virtual world [GOO14].

With regard to simulation, the application of AI technologies such as machine learning and deep learning has enabled the development of advanced physics, particle, and fluid simulations that run in real time. These improvements help users experience more realistic interactions with objects and environments in virtual worlds [KAJ86].

Furthermore, AI-based techniques have also enabled improvements in real-time rendering and optimized calculation of lighting scenarios, resulting in more realistic light and shadow effects in virtual environments [RIT12]. These developments are crucial for achieving higher visual quality and aesthetics in the metaverse.

The rapid advances in computer graphics and simulation made possible by AI highlight the enormous potential of these technologies to further transform and enhance the metaverse. Future developments are expected to blur the boundaries between the real and virtual worlds even further and intensify users' immersion in the metaverse [ISO17].

The integration of AI into the metaverse has the potential to significantly enhance the user experience by enabling more realistic, personalized, and thus more immersive experiences [MIK11]. Advances in AI technologies such as machine learning (ML), natural language processing, and computer vision are helping to make user interactions in virtual environments more human-like and seamless. One aspect in which AI improves the user experience in the metaverse is the adaptability of the environment, the objects it contains, and both autonomous and externally controlled avatars. By leveraging ML, virtual worlds and systems can recognize and analyze users' preferences and behavioral patterns to provide individually tailored content and recommendations [FOR17]. These personalized experiences foster a stronger user attachment to the metaverse and increase user satisfaction [OST01].

Another important factor contributing to the improvement of user experience is the ability of AI systems to support natural language and multimodal communication [CAS00]. By leveraging NLP and deep learning, AI-driven avatars and NPCs can engage in fluent, human-like conversations in real time, thereby enhancing social interaction and collaboration within the metaverse. Furthermore, advances in AI-based computer graphics and simulation enable users to experience more realistic and visually appealing environments and objects in the metaverse [THA21]. These improvements help increase users' immersion in the virtual world and create a stronger sense of presence.

The ongoing development of AI makes it possible to create dynamic and adaptive content in the metaverse that is tailored to the individual needs, preferences, and interactions of users [YAN18]. This leads to increased immersion and user engagement, as virtual worlds can respond much more flexibly than before to users' actions and decisions [DOR10]. One approach to creating dynamic content is procedural generation, in which AI algorithms are used to automatically generate new game and environment elements [SHA16]. This method allows for an almost unlimited variety of content and enables virtual worlds to be changed and adapted in real time based on user interactions.

Another aspect of AI-driven adaptability lies in the use of machine learning and reinforcement learning to optimize the behavior of avatars and NPCs [VIN19]. By learning from and adapting to user actions, AI-driven characters can provide more realistic and human-like interactions tailored to the individual needs of users [RIE14]. In addition, the application of technologies such as NLP and sentiment analysis enables the detection and interpretation of user emotions and moods in real time [CAM13]. As a result, virtual environments and characters can respond to users' emotional states and offer appropriately adapted interactions and experiences.

The creation of dynamic and adaptive content and interactions through the use of AI technologies has the potential to fundamentally change our understanding of what the metaverse is or should be, by providing individually tailored experiences that increase user engagement and satisfaction. Further research and integration of AI into the metaverse is expected to lead to more innovative and highly personalized virtual environments and experiences [BAI07].

The integration of Generative Pre-trained Transformer (GPT) models into the metaverse represents a novel approach to developing interfaces between artificial intelligence and virtual worlds. In light of rapid technological advances, it is becoming increasingly clear that the metaverse is not merely an abstract concept, but rather a real manifestation in the physical world. With the emergence of more complex structures within the metaverse, the question now arises as to how other novel technologies, such as GPT, can be leveraged to accelerate and optimize the creation and design of these virtual environments. GPT is capable of generating natural-sounding text and can be applied in numerous use cases.

In the context of the metaverse, GPT offers a wide range of potential benefits and applications. One such application is the creation of virtual assistants and chatbots that can help users navigate the metaverse and accomplish various tasks. This may include, for example, finding specific locations or connecting with other participants. In addition, GPT can be used to generate content for the metaverse, such as guides, descriptions of virtual locations, or even dialogues between different characters or avatars.

An additional application of GPT in the metaverse is enabling interactive experiences in virtual reality. In this context, GPT can be used to capture and generate responses based on user input. This allows for the development of virtual games, events, or films in which GPT can generate responses and storylines individually for each participant.

Beyond the direct applications of GPT technology in the virtual context of the metaverse, there are several advantages that could help promote the idea of the metaverse. One of the key benefits is that GPT can help make this virtual environment more accessible and user-friendly for a global audience.

By using GPT to generate text and content in a wide variety of languages, users from different linguistic backgrounds can gain easier access to the metaverse and enjoy it more fully. Communication between users from different cultural and linguistic backgrounds could thus be facilitated by AI-powered tools through automated real-time translation [MET22]. Furthermore, the use of GPT functionalities enables the creation of realistic, believable virtual characters or avatars and immersive experiences, making it possible to develop a lifelike and advanced representation of the metaverse. GPT is also capable of generating content tailored to the individual interests and priorities of users. This can be used for personalized metaverse experiences, which may be particularly attractive to consumers seeking an optimal experience. The use of GPT also leads to improved accessibility, enabling users to accomplish tasks more effectively. Finally, GPT makes it possible to create virtual assistants and other interactive characters that make the metaverse more accessible and understandable for users who may not have the necessary prior knowledge or skills, such as inexperienced consumers.

AI, especially driven by the rapid development of various GPT approaches and models, will foreseeably play a major role in shaping the future direction and evolution of the metaverse. Here, too, it seems that only the creativity of developers will define the limits of what is possible.

This reflects the state of the interplay between AI and the metaverse as of about two years ago. Even though this may not sound like a long period, a great deal of innovation can occur in technology in just two years. This is even more true in the field of computer science and IT. While Mark Zuckerberg's announcement in 2021 of a focus on the metaverse sent shockwaves through the tech industry, the launch of ChatGPT on November 30, 2022, must be described as the starting point of a tsunami. Rarely before has a technology so forcefully transformed (and driven) both technical/technological research and development, as well as found its way into both private and professional application domains.

This is equally true for the integration of artificial intelligence into the metaverse, as has already been indicated in various places here (e.g., in Sects. 2.7—The Metaverse as an Information-Centric Web, 3.6.2—Physical Merging, 4.5—A Contemporary Form of Modusage: D2A-Commerce, and 5.6—The Metaverse vs. Synthetic Media & Social Media). AI technologies make it possible to design virtual environments in a more dynamic and realistic way, for example by creating the intelligent avatars discussed above, which can respond to human interactions. Both as NPCs and, in the future, as autonomous user representatives, these are based on AI models to understand and generate natural language in real time, resulting in more authentic and personalized user experiences.

Another area of AI influence in the metaverse is the automated generation of content. The term "synthetic media" has now become established for this. (see also Sect. 5.6—The Metaverse vs. Synthetic Media & Social Media) By using generative AI models, not only objects and scenarios but also entire virtual worlds can be efficiently created and adapted. This greatly reduces development costs and further fosters user creativity. For example, AI systems can generate individual 3D models or entire landscapes based on user input, tailored to the individual preferences of users [CHA23].

AI also contributes to the personalization of the metaverse by helping to analyze user behavior and preferences, thereby providing tailored content and recommendations. This makes it possible to optimize the user experience and strengthen user engagement with the virtual environment. In the e-commerce sector of the metaverse, for example, AI can offer personalized product recommendations and provide virtual shopping assistants that address the individual needs of customers. This is already influencing the development of new business models, such as the D2A model described above. (See Sect. 4.5—A current form of mod usage: D2A commerce) [ROO23].

However, in addition to the impact on user opportunities, it must not be overlooked that the implementation of such AI-powered applications—such as the automated generation of entire immersive virtual environments and, perhaps even more so, real-time interaction with intelligent avatars—requires immense computing power. To meet these demands, platform operators must invest in highly powerful hardware solutions. This includes the much-discussed specialized processors and memory technologies that are specifically optimized for AI workloads. For example, advanced graphics processing units (GPUs) and tensor processing units (TPUs) are used to enable the parallel processing of large volumes of data and thus enhance the performance of AI models [RUT24].

Since AI applications (not only) in the metaverse continuously process extremely large amounts of data, energy consumption is a critical factor. Research is therefore focusing on the integration of non-volatile memory technologies, such as magnetoresistive random access memory (MRAM), which can both reduce energy requirements and increase data processing speed. Such memory solutions make it possible to minimize latency while maximizing the efficiency of AI operations [PAR22].

Ultimately, the seamless integration of AI into metaverse platforms also requires close coordination between hardware and software. This includes the development of specialized hardware accelerators optimized for specific AI algorithms, as well as the adaptation of software architecture to make optimal use of hardware resources. Through this cooperative development, platform operators can ensure that their systems meet the high demands for performance and scalability required for immersive AI experiences in the metaverse.

It can certainly be said without exaggeration that AI and the metaverse are in a symbiotic relationship:

- AI drives the development of the metaverse by enabling scalability, personalization, and interactivity.
- At the same time, the metaverse provides a space in which AI systems can find new application opportunities.

This interplay will play a key role in the further development of the digital society, but, as with any (new) technology, it also presents challenges that must be addressed with care. These ethical and societal, as well as technical and technological, questions will not be pursued further here, as there are no simple or short-term answers. Ultimately, there is only the hope that it will be ensured that the technology is used for the benefit of users.

References

[AHU23] Ahuja, Abhimanyu S.; Polascik, Bryce W.; Doddapaneni, Divyesh; Byrnes, Eamonn S.; Sridhar, Jayanth (2023). The digital metaverse: Applications in artificial intelligence, medical education, and integrative health. In: Integrative Medicine Research, Volume 12, Issue 1, 2023, 100917, ISSN 2213-4220, https://doi.org/10.1016/j.imr.2022.100917.

[BAI07] Bainbridge, William. (2007). The Scientific Research Potential of Virtual Worlds. Science (New York, N.Y.). 317. 472–6. https://doi.org/10.1126/science.1146930.

[CAM13] Cambria, Erik; Schuller, Björn; Xia, Yunqing; Havasi, Catherine (2013). New Avenues in Opinion Mining and Sentiment Analysis. Intelligent Systems, IEEE. 28. 15–21. https://doi.org/10.1109/MIS.2013.30.

[CAS00] Cassell, Justina; Sullivan, Joseph; Prevost, Scott; Churchill, Elizabeth F. (Eds.). (2000). Embodied conversational agents. In: MIT press.

[CHA23] Vinay Chamola; Gaurang Bansal; Tridib Kumar Das; Vikas Hassija; Naga Siva Sai Reddy; Jiacheng Wang; Sherali Zeadally; Amir Hussain; F. Richard Yu; Mohsen Guizani; Dusit Niyato (28 Jul 2023). Beyond Reality: The Pivotal Role of Generative AI in the Metaverse. https://doi.org/10.48550/arXiv.2308.06272.

[CHE17] Chen, Hongshen; Liu, Xiaorui; Yin, Dawei; Tang, Jiliang (21.11.2017). A Survey on Dialogue Systems: Recent Advances and New Frontiers. In: ACM SIGKDD Explorations Newsletter, Volume 19, Issue 221, November 2017, pp 25–35. https://doi.org/10.1145/3166054.3166058.

[DOR10] Dormans, Joris. (2010). Adventures in level design: Generating missions and spaces for action adventure games. https://doi.org/10.1145/1814256.1814257.

[DOU23] Douglas, Will (03.03.2023). The inside story of how ChatGPT was built from the people who made it. In: MIT Technology Review Artificial intelligence. Online: https://www.technologyreview.com/2023/03/03/1069311/inside-story-oral-history-how-chatgpt-built-openai/ (Retrieved: 29.05.2023).

[FOR17] Forsyth, Carol; Graesser, Arthur; Foltz, Peter (2017). Assessing conversation quality, reasoning, and problem solving with computer agents. https://doi.org/10.1787/9789264273955-17-en.

[GOO14] Goodfellow, Ian; Pouget-Abadie, Jean; Mirza, Mehdi; Xu, Bing; Warde-Farley, David; Ozair, Sherjil; Courville, Aaron; Bengio, Y. (2014). Generative Adversarial Networks. Advances in Neural Information Processing Systems. 3. https://doi.org/10.1145/3422622.

[HEN13] Hendrikx, Mark; Meijer, Sebastiaan; Velden, Joeri; Iosup, Alexandru. (2013). Procedural Content Generation for Games: A Survey. ACM Transactions on Multimedia Computing, Communications, and Applications (TOMCCAP). 9. https://doi.org/10.1145/2422956.2422957.

[ISL23] Islam, Arham (21.03.2023). A History of Generative AI: From GAN to GPT-4. In: Marktechpost. Online: https://www.marktechpost.com/2023/03/21/a-history-of-generative-ai-from-gan-to-gpt-4/ (Retrieved: 29.05.2023).

[ISO17] Isola, Phillip; Zhu, Jun-Yan; Zhou, Tinghui; Efros, Alexei (2017). Image-to-Image Translation with Conditional Adversarial Networks. 5967–5976. https://doi.org/10.1109/CVPR.2017.632.

[JAI18] Jain, Mohit; Kumar, Pratyush; Kota, Ramachandra; Patel, Shwetak (2018). Evaluating and Informing the Design of Chatbots. 895–906. https://doi.org/10.1145/3196709.3196735.

[KAR17]   Karras, Tero; Aila, Timo; Laine, Samuli; Lehtinen, Jaakko (2017). Progressive Growing of GANs for Improved Quality, Stability, and Variation.

[KAJ86]   Kajiya, J. T. (1986). The rendering equation. In: ACM SIGGRAPH Computer Graphics, 20(4), 143–150.

[LUG16]   Luger, Ewa; Sellen, Abigail (2016). "Like having a really bad PA": The Gulf between User Expectation and Experience of Conversational Agents. In Proceedings of the 2016 CHI Conference on Human Factors in Computing Systems (pp. 5286–5297). ACM.

[MAL23]   Malik, Aisha (27.02.2023). Snapchat launches an AI chatbot powered by OpenAI's GPT technology. In: TechCrunch. Online: https://techcrunch.com/2023/02/27/snapchat-launches-an-ai-chatbot-powered-by-openais-gpt-technology/ (Retrieved: 21.05.2023).

[MET22]   Meta (19.10.2022). Using AI to Translate Speech For a Primarily Oral Language. In: Meta Newsroom. Online: https://about.fb.com/news/2022/10/hokkien-ai-speech-translation/ (Retrieved: 29.05.2023).

[MIK11]   Mikropoulos, Tassos; Natsis, Antonis (2011). Educational virtual en-vironments: A ten-year review of empirical research (1999–2009). In: Computers & Education. 56. 769–780. https://doi.org/10.1016/j.compedu.2010.10.020.

[MOU15]   Mouton, Francois; Malan, Mercia M.; Kimppa, Kai K.; Venter, H.s. (2015): Necessity for ethics in social engineering research. https://doi.org/10.1016/j.cose.2015.09.001.

[OST01]   Osterloh, Margit; Frey, Bruno; Frost, Jetta (2001). Managing Motivation, Organization and Governance. In: Journal of Management and Governance. 5. 231–239. https://doi.org/10.1023/A:1014084019816.

[PAR22]   Vivek Parmar, Syed Shakib Sarwar, Ziyun Li, Hsien-Hsin S. Lee, Barbara De Salvo, Manan Suri (2022). Memory-Oriented Design-Space Exploration of Edge-AI Hardware for XR Applications. In: TinyML Research Symposium 2023. https://doi.org/10.48550/arXiv.2206.06780.

[PER22]   Perri, Lori (10.08.2022). What's New in the 2022 Gartner Hype Cycle for Emerging Technologies. In: Gartner Insights. https://www.gartner.com/en/articles/what-s-new-in-the-2022-gartner-hype-cycle-for-emerging-technologies (Retrieved: 17.05.2023).

[RIE14]   Riedl, Mark; Young, Robert (2014). Narrative Planning: Balancing Plot and Character. J. Artif. Intell. Res. (JAIR). 39. https://doi.org/10.1613/jair.2989.

[RIT12]   Ritschel, Tobias; Dachsbacher, Carsten; Grosch, Thorsten; Kautz, Jan (2012). The State of the Art in Interactive Global Illumination. In: Computer Graphics Forum. 31. 160–188. https://doi.org/10.1111/j.1467-8659.2012.02093.x.

[ROO23]   Room (03.03.2023). Wie KI das Metaverse beleben wird. Rooom Blog. Online: https://www.rooom.com/de/blog/wie-ki-das-metaverse-beleben-wird. (Retrieved: 14.02.2025).

[RUT24]   Rutronik (24.04.2024). Metaverse—Hardware für eine Welt aus Daten. Rutronik Blog. Online: https://www.rutronik.com/de/article/metaverse-hardware-fuer-eine-welt-aus-daten. (Retrieved: 14.02.2025).

[SHA16]   Shaker, Noor; Togelius, Julian; Nelson, Mark J. (2016). Procedural content generation in games (Computational Synthesis and Creative Systems). In: Computational Synthesis and Creative Systems, Springer International.

[THA21]	Thalmann, Nadia; Interrante, Victoria; Thalmann, Daniel; Papagiannakis, George; Sheng, Bin; Kim, Jinman; Gavrilova, Marina (2021). Advances in Computer Graphics 38th Computer Graphics International Conference, CGI 2021, Virtual Event, September 6–10, 2021, Proceedings: 38th Computer Graphics International Conference, CGI 2021, Virtual Event, September 6–10, 2021, Proceedings. https://doi.org/10.1007/978-3-030-89029-2.
[THA23]	Thakur, S.S., Bandyopadhyay, S., Datta, D. (2023). Artificial Intelligence and the Metaverse: Present and Future Aspects. In: Hassanien, A.E., Darwish, A., Torky, M. (eds) The Future of Metaverse in the Virtual Era and Physical World. Studies in Big Data, vol 123. Springer, Cham. https://doi.org/10.1007/978-3-031-29132-6_10.
[THI16]	Thies, Justus; Zollhöfer, Michael; Stamminger, Marc; Theobalt, Christian; Nießner, Matthias (2016). Face2face: Real-time Face Capture and Reenactment of RGB Videos. In: Proc. Computer Vision and Pattern Recognition (CVPR), 2016, IEEE.
[VIN15]	Vinyals, Oriol; Le, Quoc (2015). A Neural Conversational Model. ICML Deep Learning Workshop, 2015.
[VIN19]	Vinyals, Oriol; Babuschkin, Igor; Czarnecki, Wojciech; Mathieu, Michaël; Dudzik, Andrew; Chung, Junyoung; Choi, David; Powell, Richard; Ewalds, Timo; Georgiev, Petko; Oh, Junhyuk; Horgan, Dan; Kroiss, Manuel; Danihelka, Ivo; Huang, Aja; Sifre, Laurent; Cai, Trevor; Agapiou, John; Jaderberg, Max; Silver, David (2019). Grandmaster level in StarCraft II using multi-agent reinforcement learning. Nature. 575. https://doi.org/10.1038/s41586-019-1724-z.
[YAN18]	Yannakakis, Georgios N.; Togelius, Julian (2018): Artificial Intelligence and Games. In: Springer Link. Online: https://link.springer.com/book/10.1007/978-3-319-63519-4 (Retrieved: 21.05.2023).
[ZHO23]	Zhou, Pengyuan (12.04.2023). Unleashing ChatGPT on the Metaverse: Savior or Destroyer? In: University of Science and Technology of China. Online: https://www.researchgate.net/publication/369387206_Unleashing_ChatGPT_on_the_Metaverse_Savior_or_Destroyer (Retrieved: 21.05.2023).

7 What must not be Missing: Criticism

As a virtual world primarily based on advances in VR, AR, and blockchain technologies, the metaverse presents both opportunities and risks with respect to the physical world. One possible consequence of the increasing prevalence of the metaverse is a decline in real-world social interactions, as people may spend a significant portion of their time in this virtual environment. This could have negative effects on social relationships and mental health, including the neglect of physical health due to lack of exercise [ZUC13].

Furthermore, the metaverse enables the creation of a parallel world characterized by norms and values that differ from those of physical reality. This carries the risk that cultural identities and value systems may be transformed and, as a result, influence the real world. Increased dependence on technology could also lead to difficulties in making independent decisions and solving problems. This may be particularly true if the metaverse becomes the primary medium for communication and interaction, potentially limiting the ability to interact effectively in the physical world [LES06].

In addition, privacy concerns related to the metaverse must be taken into account, as comprehensive monitoring of the virtual world could compromise users' privacy. Moreover, cyberbullying and cybercrime may become more prevalent, with potential impacts on the physical world.

The future challenge, therefore, lies in understanding the metaverse as a potential parallel world that can influence physical reality. It thus appears essential that the development of the metaverse is aligned with the physical world and that possible mutual effects are considered. Among other things, regulatory authorities should ensure that the development of the metaverse proceeds responsibly and that privacy and security concerns are adequately addressed, in order to promote the positive aspects of the metaverse without negative consequences.

The future development of the metaverse and its impact on the real world are currently uncertain. On the one hand, there is the possibility that social parallel societies may emerge if certain groups of people withdraw from the real world and prefer to live in the virtual world. This could lead to further fragmentation of society as a whole, with different identities and communities forming in the virtual and real worlds. On the other hand, the metaverse can also play a positive role in fostering global collaboration and a sense of belonging, depending on how it is developed and used [RHE00].

There are various risks that must be considered in the discussion about the metaverse. A central concern is the danger of addictive behaviors, which can lead to the neglect of real-world responsibilities and have negative effects on mental health. Such behaviors and the resulting potential for addiction are already known from MMORPGs and are likely to become even more pronounced in the more immersive worlds of the metaverse. In addition, the metaverse could deepen social divides by granting privileged groups access to technology while others remain excluded.

User interaction within a virtual world also entails significant security and privacy risks, such as hacking, data breaches, fraud, identity theft, and cyberbullying. Furthermore, there is concern that dependence on technology could increase through the metaverse, leading to a loss of autonomy, independence, and social skills. Finally, there is a risk that governments and corporations could use the metaverse to manipulate opinions and behaviors by sending targeted messages to specific user groups [LAN14, MAY11, NIS09].

7.1 The General Themes of Criticism

The metaverse is a virtual world that is highly dependent on technology. However, this dependence on technology also gives rise to increasing privacy concerns that can affect users of the metaverse.

First of all, the metaverse and the applications on its platforms can collect an enormous amount of data about their users. Every action a user performs within the virtual world can be recorded and stored. These data can be used to analyze and monetize user behavior within the virtual world. There is also the possibility that these data could be used by third parties such as advertisers or governments [LANoJ, LAN14, ZUB19].

Another issue is the potential risk of identity theft. Since the metaverse allows for virtual identities, it can be difficult to ensure that users are who they claim to be. This is already evident to some extent on the current Internet and the World Wide Web. This risk can lead to fraud and other illegal activities. Moreover, the metaverse can be a prime target for hackers and cybercriminals. As the metaverse manages a significant volume of financial transactions and sensitive information, a security breach could have serious consequences [GIE23].

As is already the case on the current Internet and the World Wide Web, it is even more important in the technologically much more complex environment to consider that users may not fully understand what data are being collected about them and how these data are used. This can lead to a lack of transparency and result in users being unable to make informed decisions about which data they wish to disclose and which they do not [LAN14, SAL23].

To address these privacy concerns, regulatory authorities must ensure that the metaverse is subject to strict data protection policies. Developers of individual platforms within the metaverse should also ensure transparency regarding the data they collect and how they are used. Users must be able to control their data at all times and decide which data they wish to disclose and which they do not. It is also important that security measures are implemented to protect user data from potential security breaches.

A central aspect of the idea of the metaverse is the possibility of connecting people from different parts of the world. However, since the virtual world of the metaverse has no geographical boundaries, it can be difficult to determine which law applies in this virtual world or in parts of it. In principle, the applicable law initially depends on where the operator of the respective platform on which users interact is located and which laws apply in that country. For example, if the operator of the metaverse is based in the USA, it is initially subject to the laws of the USA and the respective states. However, users of the metaverse may come from different parts of the world and be subject to different laws and legal systems. It is possible that the metaverse is operated in a country whose laws are contrary to those of another country. In this case, users may have different legal claims depending on their nationality and place of residence.

However, it is possible that some aspects of the metaverse may not be covered by existing laws and regulations. Since the metaverse is a relatively new technology, there are still no specific laws or regulations for many situations that address the particularities of virtual worlds. In this case, it seems highly relevant for governments and international organizations to work together to create appropriate legal frameworks for the metaverse [DEA21, DEF18, DEF19].

As a vision, it is also conceivable that the metaverse could develop its own legal system in the future. Users of the metaverse could, given sufficient transparency and agreement, agree on a common code of conduct that regulates certain behaviors within the virtual world. Such self-regulation could help resolve conflicts and protect users of the metaverse. In any case, it will be a major legal challenge to determine which law applies in an internationally networked virtual world such as the metaverse. It may be that a combination of national and international laws, regulations, and self-regulatory measures is the most sensible way to govern the metaverse.

In such an internationally networked, virtual world as the metaverse, there are a multitude of data protection concerns. Users constantly leave digital traces as they interact within the metaverse, which may result in their personal data being shared with operators, developers, or other users. It is therefore essential that data protection law in the metaverse is comprehensive and appropriate to safeguard users' privacy and rights. However, data protection laws can vary from country to country, making it challenging to establish a unified data protection framework for the metaverse. The EU General

Data Protection Regulation (GDPR), for example, applies to all companies processing personal data of EU citizens, regardless of where the company is located. This means that metaverse operators processing data of EU citizens must comply with the GDPR.

Another issue in the metaverse is that it can be equally difficult to determine jurisdiction for data protection violations. For example, if a company is based in the USA and processes personal data of users from Europe, it must first be clarified which data protection authority is responsible for monitoring and enforcing data protection laws [EURoJ].

To address these challenges, internationally valid standards for data protection and data security in the metaverse should be established as soon as possible. It is also important that metaverse operators have clear privacy policies that all users of the metaverse must adhere to. Furthermore, users of the metaverse should have the right to control and delete their personal data.

Another, more technically oriented, way to ensure data protection in the metaverse is the introduction and use of blockchain technologies. This can help guarantee the integrity and security of personal data by storing it in a decentralized network that only authorized individuals can access.

In addition to the data protection aspects considered so far, another major area of concern emerges, as the metaverse introduces a new dimension of tax issues. A central activity for users in the metaverse will foreseeably be, much like in the days of Second Life, the ability to buy, own, and trade real estate. In this context, there are a number of questions regarding the taxation of real estate and real estate transactions that remain largely unresolved [DEF18, DEF19].

Extending this line of thought, questions regarding the taxation of income from the ownership of virtual real estate should not be overlooked. If a user purchases a plot of land in the metaverse and rents it out or otherwise generates profits from it, the question arises as to whether taxes must be paid on these earnings and which tax laws and regulations apply. The situation becomes even more complex when users come from different countries with varying tax laws and regulations that need to be reconciled. This issue is further exacerbated when it comes to the taxation of cryptocurrencies, which are already frequently used in the metaverse. Due to their decentralized nature and the difficulty of tracing their origin, cryptocurrencies present a challenging tax issue. When users use cryptocurrencies to buy or sell virtual real estate in the metaverse, it is unclear how the profits from these transactions should be taxed [FAI17, MOR16].

In some countries, governments and authorities have begun to address these questions and are developing guidelines for the taxation of virtual real estate in the metaverse. However, most countries have not yet issued specific guidelines, further complicating the international legal situation. To resolve such issues, governments and international organizations must work together to develop clear guidelines and regulations for tax-relevant transactions. It is important that these regulations are fair and consistent and apply equally to users from different countries.

The metaverse is being discussed as a potential vision of the future in which people can interact, conduct business, learn, and play. These activities require a sophisticated technical infrastructure, which has ecological impacts. Criticism of the ecological impact of the metaverse focuses mainly on energy consumption and the associated greenhouse gas emissions. Creating and maintaining the infrastructure for such a virtual world requires an enormous amount of energy. The computing power needed for generating 3D graphics, simulations, and AI-based interactions consumes a great deal of electricity. It is foreseeable that energy consumption will further increase as the number of users of the metaverse grows.

Another issue is that many of the companies building and operating the metaverse run their servers in regions with cheap electricity, which are often still powered by coal plants. However, the use of fossil fuels for electricity generation has been proven to increase greenhouse gas emissions and thus contributes to global warming. There are, however, companies that are trying to minimize these and other environmental impacts. Some are turning to renewable energy and using technologies such as AI to optimize energy consumption. It remains to be seen, however, whether these efforts will be sufficient to reduce the environmental impact of the growing metaverse [ARA21, BLU19, MON11].

Overall, the criticism of the ecological impact of the metaverse appears justified. As the metaverse continues to grow, the companies operating the platforms and infrastructures must manage their resources more responsibly. Regulatory authorities must also ensure that environmental considerations are taken into account in the design and use of the metaverse, even in virtual environments. Only in this way can the metaverse realize its benefits without having negative effects on the real environment.

7.2 The merging of the political world?

The metaverse is increasingly being viewed as a phenomenon with the potential to bring about significant changes in society. These changes affect social, economic, and political aspects and are not limited to individual states, but impact both the developed and developing world.

From a social perspective, the metaverse has the potential to enable an expanded form of social interaction and to change the way people communicate and interact with one another. It can serve as a platform in both the developed and developing world, where people can express their creativity, create art, and shape virtual identities. It also enables the overcoming of physical barriers such as distance or language and promotes global collaboration. However, there is a risk that the metaverse could contribute to increased social isolation and undermine traditional social relationships.

Economically, the metaverse offers numerous opportunities, particularly in the area of virtual real estate and virtual commerce. In the developed world, companies can offer virtual products and services, while users can use digital currencies to shop in the virtual world. This, in turn, can create jobs and foster innovation. In the developing world, the metaverse can contribute to economic development and poverty reduction by providing access to new markets and opportunities. However, there is a risk that the metaverse could exacerbate existing economic inequalities by offering more opportunities to those with access to the necessary resources and skills.

Politically, the metaverse can enable new forms of civic participation and serve as a platform for the discussion and dissemination of political ideas. This applies to both the developed and developing world, where the metaverse can help amplify the voices of marginalized groups and provide a platform for political change. Nevertheless, there is a risk that the metaverse could be dominated by authoritarian regimes or corporations, leading to further global divisions. As a result, the need for regulation and ethical guidelines is increasingly being discussed to ensure that the metaverse does not lead to further social, economic, and political inequalities, especially between the developed and developing world.

7.3 Or Rather the Division of the Political World?

In the previous section 7.2, the merging of the political world was examined as a potential consequence of implementing the idea of the metaverse. In contrast, it is also important to consider the possibility that the realization of the metaverse could instead lead to a division of society or the international community. Such a division could have far-reaching consequences on social, economic, and political levels.

The effects of a division caused by the metaverse could include increased fragmentation and isolation, exacerbating inequality in the creation of wealth and political power, as well as undermining political stability and cooperation. It is therefore crucial to carefully analyze the societal impacts of the metaverse in order to promote a more just and integrated world. In particular, a split between the developed and developing worlds brought about by the metaverse could further deepen existing inequalities on social, economic, and political levels.

Social consequences of this division could include increased isolation and fragmentation within society. Individuals with access to the metaverse might distance themselves from the physical world and weaken their social ties, while those without access could feel isolated and cut off. This divide could lead to strong polarization and radicalization, as groups with differing access to the metaverse increasingly focus on their virtual identities and social circles.

From an economic perspective, such a division could contribute to further inequality by excluding certain regions or population groups from the economic opportunities of the metaverse. Businesses and individuals with access to the metaverse could gain competitive advantages over those without, leading to an imbalance in job creation and economic development. This gap could exacerbate income inequality between countries and place additional strain on the already fragile economies of the developing world.

The potential division of the world through the metaverse could also deepen political differences between various regions and countries. This is because some countries or governments might attempt to control or restrict their citizens' access to the metaverse, which in turn could further limit freedom of expression and political participation. In this context, people with access to the metaverse could form virtual political groups and potentially become alienated from the physical world. This phenomenon could create an imbalance in political power and influence, further widening the gap between the developed and developing worlds [MOZ11, PIL11, SHI09].

At the political level, the metaverse could cause a split between the developed and developing worlds, which in turn could intensify political differences and tensions. Governments in the developed world might also seek to control or regulate access to the metaverse in order to protect their own interests. At the same time, governments in the developing world could view access to the metaverse as a threat to their sovereignty and accordingly control or limit access. Such a division has the potential to create further imbalances in political power and influence, which could negatively affect political stability and cooperation between the countries involved.

Undoubtedly, the metaverse has the potential to deepen the digital divide between the developed and developing worlds and to reinforce already existing social, economic, and political disparities. To prevent such a split, various measures should be taken. First and foremost, it is essential to provide people in the developing world with access to the metaverse by establishing the necessary infrastructure to deliver fast and reliable internet. Governments, international organizations, and the private sector should cooperate to facilitate access to the metaverse. Furthermore, emphasis should be placed on education and training so that people in the developing world can use the metaverse effectively. This helps to improve their skills and enables them to make the most of the opportunities offered by the metaverse. Additionally, it is important to promote cultural sensitivity and ensure that the metaverse is accessible and relevant to all cultures. Developers must take care to respect cultural differences and avoid reinforcing cultural stereotypes and prejudices [SUD22, WEF22].

Careful regulation of the metaverse can help ensure fairness and security for all. Regulatory authorities should ensure that the metaverse does not contribute to deepening existing social, economic, and political disparities. Finally, cooperation between governments, international organizations, and the private sector should be promoted to achieve common goals and ensure that the metaverse is accessible and beneficial to everyone.

Governments and international institutions such as the United Nations play a crucial role in shaping the metaverse to avoid discrepancies between the developed and developing worlds. Through various measures, including regulation, infrastructure development, education and training, international cooperation, and consumer protection, governments can help make the metaverse fair and accessible to all, without exacerbating existing regional disparities.

On the one hand, governments can play a significant role in regulating the metaverse by, for example, establishing dedicated regulatory authorities to ensure fairness and security for all users and to prevent the deepening of social, economic, and political inequalities. On the other hand, they can promote investment in the necessary infrastructure, such as broadband internet and mobile networks, to provide people in the developing world with access to the metaverse and its benefits. In addition, governments can develop training and education programs to ensure that people in the developing world have the skills and knowledge required to use the metaverse effectively. This may also include the development of appropriate curricula in schools and universities to prepare young people for the use of the metaverse.

Furthermore, international cooperation is essential to develop common standards and regulations that ensure the metaverse does not deepen existing differences between the developed and developing worlds. Finally, governments can protect consumers from fraud and abuse in the metaverse by enacting laws and regulations aimed at safeguarding consumers and preventing fraudulent practices.

The implementation of regulations and ethical guidelines at the political level is a necessary measure to ensure that the use of technologies such as the metaverse is safe and beneficial to society, without causing negative consequences. One of the possible challenges is the emergence of a further digital divide between those who have access to the metaverse and those who do not. Regulations and ethical guidelines can address this issue to ensure accessibility and fairness for all [LANoJ].

Moreover, abuse and violations of privacy and personal rights can occur in the metaverse. The introduction of regulations and ethical guidelines helps to minimize such risks by setting standards for privacy protection and the prevention of abuse. At the political level, such regulations and guidelines can also ensure that companies operating in the metaverse act responsibly and align their business practices with social and environmental interests. This also ensures fair treatment of users, who must not be disadvantaged by fraudulent practices or discrimination.

Since the metaverse is still a relatively new phenomenon and its effects on society have not yet been fully explored, this requires the development of regulations and ethical guidelines that are flexible enough to accommodate changes and new developments related to the metaverse. In summary, it is therefore of utmost importance to develop and enforce regulations and ethical guidelines at the political level to shape the use of the metaverse in a way that benefits society as a whole and does not result in negative consequences.

7.4 But: A View from a Different Perspective

In contrast to industrialized nations, so-called developing countries exhibit a significantly higher conviction that the metaverse will impact daily life, compared to wealthier countries. A survey commissioned by the World Economic Forum (WEF), with results published in 2022 by the market research firm Ipsos, revealed a markedly greater enthusiasm for the metaverse and for virtual and augmented reality in developing countries as opposed to high-income countries [WEF22, IPS22a, IPS22b].

The survey, which included more than 21,000 adult participants from 29 countries, found that 52% had heard of the metaverse and 50% had a positive attitude toward its use in everyday life. In countries such as China, India, Peru, Saudi Arabia, and Colombia, two-thirds or more of respondents reported positive feelings. In particular, 78% of respondents in China expressed positive attitudes, followed by 75% in India.

By contrast, the countries with the highest incomes showed the lowest levels of enthusiasm and awareness regarding the metaverse, such as Japan (22%), the United Kingdom (26%), Belgium (30%), Canada (30%), France (31%), and Germany (31%).

The survey results also indicate that developing countries such as South Africa, China, and India believe that metaverse applications—such as virtual learning, entertainment, digital social interaction, and remote surgery—will have a significant impact on people's lives. In high-income countries like Japan, Belgium, and France, there was less conviction about such changes.

Additionally, developing countries overall appear to be more enthusiastic about cryptocurrencies and blockchain, as analyses by organizations such as CB Insights, Deloitte, and the cryptocurrency exchange Gemini from 2021 and 2022 illustrate [CBI21, DEL21, GEM22]. These reports show that in 2021, half of respondents in India, Brazil, and the Asia-Pacific region acquired their first cryptocurrency. Inflation and currency devaluation were identified as the main drivers for cryptocurrency adoption in these regions. In countries experiencing currency devaluation of 50% or more, the likelihood of planning to purchase cryptocurrency is five times higher than in countries with lower inflation.

The discrepancy in acceptance and enthusiasm for emerging technologies such as the metaverse, VR/AR, and cryptocurrencies between developing and high-income countries may be attributable to various factors. One possible explanation is the differing willingness to adopt technology:

- Developing countries may view innovative technologies as an opportunity to bridge economic and social development gaps and to make their economies more competitive.
- Furthermore, limited access to traditional financial services in developing countries may increase the appeal of cryptocurrencies by providing an inclusive alternative that is accessible regardless of geographic location or socioeconomic status. In countries with high inflation rates and currency devaluation, cryptocurrencies may serve as a hedge against such risks and offer a more stable store of value than the local currency.

The willingness to adopt new technologies may also be related to educational and infrastructural factors. Developing countries with a younger population and better digital infrastructure may be more inclined to embrace technologies such as the metaverse and cryptocurrencies. Younger individuals are generally more tech-savvy and adaptable to change. Cultural differences and attitudes may also play a role in the perception and acceptance of new technologies. In some cultures, there may be a greater willingness to try and adapt to new technologies, while in others, skepticism or reluctance toward change may prevail. To gain a comprehensive understanding of the underlying causes of these disparities, a detailed analysis of the survey results as well as additional research would be necessary.

References

[ARA21] Aratani, Lauren (27.02.2021). Electricity Needed to Mine Bitcoin Is More Than Used by 'Entire Countries.' In: The Guardian. Online: https://www.theguardian.com/technology/2021/feb/27/bitcoin-mining-electricity-use-environmental-impact (Retrieved: 20.05.2023).

[BLU19] Blum, Andrew (2012). Tubes: A Journey to the Center of the Internet. Ecco (2012).

[CBI21] CB Insights (01.02.2022). State Of Blockchain 2021 Report. In: CB Insights Research Report. Online: https://www.cbinsights.com/research/report/blockchain-trends-2021/ (Retrieved: 28.05.2023).

[DEA21] Deakin, Simon; Markou, Christopher (29.06.2021). Is Law Computable: Critical Perspectives on Law and Artificial Intelligence. Oxford: Hart Publishing.

[DEF18] De Filippi, Primavera; Wright, Aaron (2018). Blockchain and the Law: The Rule of Code. Harvard University Press.

[DEF19] De Filippi, Primavera; Wright, Aaron (04.10.2019). The Rule of Code vs. The Rule of Law. In: Medium: Harvard University Press. Online: https://hup.medium.com/the-rule-of-code-vs-the-rule-of-law-8dfe75631fee (Retrieved: 20.05.2023).

[DEL21] Deloitte (2021). Deloitte's 2021 Global Blockchain Survey – A new age of digital assets. In: Deloitte Insights. Online: https://www2.deloitte.com/us/en/insights/topics/understanding-blockchain-potential/global-blockchain-survey.html (Retrieved: 28.05.2023).

[EURoJ] Europäische Kommission (o.J.). Für wen gilt die Datenschutz-Grundverordnung? In: Europäische Kommission. Online: https://commission.europa.eu/law/law-topic/data-protection/reform/rules-business-and-organisations/application-regulation/who-does-data-protection-law-apply_de (Retrieved: 20.05.2023).

[FAI17] Fairfield, Joshua. (2017). Owned: Property, Privacy, and the New Digital Serfdom. Cambridge University Press. https://doi.org/10.1017/9781316671467.

[GEM22] Gemini (2022). 2022 Global State of Crypto. In: Gemini. Online: https://www.gemini.com/state-of-crypto (Retrieved: 28.05.2023).

[GIE23] Giese, Sascha (27.02.2023). Metaversum 2023 – Neues Terrain, alte Gefahren. In: IT-Daily. Online: https://www.it-daily.net/it-sicherheit/cloud-security/metaversum-2023-neues-terrain-alte-gefahren (Retrieved: 20.05.2023).

[IPS22a] Ipsos (25.05.2022). Enthusiasm for the metaverse and extended reality is highest in emerging countries. In: Ipsos. Online: https://www.ipsos.com/en-ch/global-advisor-metaverse-extended-reality-may-2022 (Retrieved: 20.05.2023).

[IPS22b] Ipsos (2022). How the world seas the metaverse and extended reality – A 29-country Global Advisor survey. In: Ipsos. Online: https://www.ipsos.com/sites/default/files/ct/news/documents/2022-05/Global%20Advisor%20-%20WEF%20-%20Metaverse%20-%20May%202022%20-%20Graphic%20Report.pdf (Retrieved: 20.05.2023).

[LAN14] Lanier, Jaron (2014). Who Owns the Future? Simon & Schuster.

[LANoJ]	Lanier, Jaroin (o.J.). Who Owns the Future. In: Web Ressources tot he book Who Owns the Future by Jaron Lanier. Online: http://www.jaronlanier.com/futurewebresources.html (Retrieved: 20.05.2023).
[LES06]	Lessig, Lawrence. (2006). Code Version 2.0. Basic Books.
[MAY11]	Mayer-Schönberger, Viktor (2011). Delete: The Virtue of Forgetting in the Digital Age. Princeton University Press.
[MON11]	Monserrat, Steven Gonzaleze (27.01.2022). The Cloud Is Material: On the Environmental Impacts of Computation and Data Storage. In: MIT Shcwarzman College of Computing. Online: https://mit-serc.pubpub.org/pub/the-cloud-is-material/release/1 (Retrieved: 20.05.2023).
[MOR16]	Morse, Edward A. (2016). Regulation of Online Gambling. In: Research Handbook on Electronic Commerce Law 449 (John A. Rothchild ed).
[MOZ11]	Morozov, Evgeny (2011). The Net Delusion: The Dark Side of Internet Freedom. Perseus Book Group, Philadelphia 2011, ISBN 978-1-58648-874-1.
[NIS09]	Nissenbaum, Hellen (2009). Privacy in Context: Technology, Policy, and the Integrity of Social. Life. Stanford University Press.
[PIL11]	Pilkington, Ed (13.01.2011). Evgeny Morozov: How democracy slipped through the net. In: The Guardian. Online: https://www.theguardian.com/technology/2011/jan/13/evgeny-morozov-the-net-delusion (Retrieved: 20.05.2023).
[RHE00]	Rheingold, Howard (2000).The Virtual Community: Homesteading on the Electronic Frontier. The MIT Press.
[SAL23]	Salvi, Vishal (13.04.2023). Neue Technologien, alte Herausforderungen: Die dunkle Seite der Metaverse Security. In: Security Insider. Online: https://www.security-insider.de/die-dunkle-seite-der-metaverse-security-a-0de3030b47342c6af81dff-534f1e848e/ (Retrieved: 20.05.2023).
[SHI09]	Shirky, Clay (2009).Here Comes Everybody: The Power of Organizing Without Organizations. Penguin Books.
[SUD22]	Sudan, Randeep; Petrov, Oleg; Gupta, Garima (09.03.2022). Can the metaverse offer benefits for developing countries? In: World Bank Blogs. Online: https://blogs.worldbank.org/digital-development/can-metaverse-offer-benefits-developing-countries (Retrieved: 20.05.2023).
[TUR11]	Turkle, Sherry (2011). Alone together: Why we expect more from technology and less from each other. Basic Books.
[WEF22]	World Economic Forum (25.05.2022). How enthusiastic is your country about the rise of the metaverse? In: WeFOrum. Online: https://www.weforum.org/agenda/2022/05/countries-attitudes-metaverse-augmented-virtual-reality-davos22/ (Retrieved: 20.05.2023).
[ZUB19]	Zuboff, Shoshana (2019). The Age of Surveillance Capitalism: The Fight for a Human Future at the New Frontier of Power. PublicAffairs.
[ZUC13]	Zuckerman; Ethan (17. Juni 2013). Rewire: Digital Cosmopolitans in the Age of Connection. Norton & Company; 1. Edition.

The Real Vision

All discussions that engage with the metaverse, whether positively or critically, ultimately share a fundamental weakness that manifests in two distinct forms:

- On the one hand, these discussions remain superficial and fundamentally vague, as the metaverse is viewed as an all-encompassing and thus overwhelmingly large future construct.
- On the other hand, many discussions are based on isolated examinations of small and highly specific niches and use cases, which are not placed in any overarching context.

Both perspectives share the same weakness: it is ultimately never precisely known what the metaverse will be, or more specifically, how the metaverse will be structured both technically and functionally. Nevertheless, both established national and international organizations as well as renowned experts from a wide range of disciplines are attempting to identify potential applications and use cases.

8.1 The Institutional Perspective on the Metaverse

In recent years, the metaverse has attracted significant attention from various national and international organizations interested in the social, economic, technological, and political aspects of this vision:

- The *International Telecommunication Union* (ITU), a United Nations agency, is committed to promoting information and communication technologies worldwide. It is interested in the metaverse because it advocates for the creation of an inclusive, open, and secure digital space.

- The *Institute of Electrical and Electronics Engineers* (IEEE) is an international organization dedicated to research, development, and the promotion of technological innovation. It is interested in the metaverse because, like the IEEE, it is seen as a technology with the potential to fundamentally change the way people live and work.
- The *World Wide Web Consortium* (W3C) is the international community responsible for standardizing the Internet. The W3C is interested in the metaverse because it views it as the next stage in the evolution of the WWW and aims to create or at least enable an open and accessible digital space.
- The *World Economic Forum* (WEF) is interested in the metaverse because it sees the potential to revolutionize the way people work, learn, and interact. The WEF aims to explore the opportunities and challenges of the metaverse and to develop recommendations for its sustainable design.
- In addition, various organizations such as the *Electronic Frontier Foundation* (EFF) and *Privacy International* are interested in the metaverse to ensure that it respects users' privacy and civil rights.
- Numerous *governments* and national organizations are also showing interest in the metaverse, recognizing both its potential and its impact on the economy, education, healthcare, and culture. They seek to ensure that their countries and citizens benefit from the opportunities the metaverse offers.
- Finally, many *technology companies* as well as industry associations such as the VR/AR Association (VRARA) and the Augmented Reality for Enterprise Alliance (AREA) are participating in the discussion and development of the metaverse, recognizing its potential to create new business models and revolutionize existing industries.

The following sections will take a closer look at the ITU and IEEE, the W3C, the WEF, as well as the Metaverse Standards Forum and their respective perspectives on the metaverse.

8.1.1 ITU and IEEE

The International Telecommunication Union (ITU) and the Institute of Electrical and Electronics Engineers (IEEE) are two leading international organizations involved with technologies and standards related to the metaverse. Both organizations have different areas of focus and objectives, but both are working to advance the development of the metaverse and to ensure that it is open, accessible, and secure.

The ITU is a specialized agency of the United Nations focused on the standardization and development of information and communication technologies (ICT). It is deeply engaged in the research and development of the metaverse, concentrating on three main aspects: standardization, digital access, and security and privacy. In terms of standardization, the ITU is continuously developing international standards aimed at ensuring interoperability, compatibility, and accessibility within the metaverse. This process ensures that different metaverse platforms can communicate effectively with each other and that users can move seamlessly between these platforms, resulting in a unified user experience [ITUoJa, ITUoJb].

Furthermore, the ITU is committed to making the metaverse accessible to everyone, regardless of factors such as geographic location, income level, or educational background. The organization supports a variety of initiatives aimed at bridging the digital divide and facilitating access to the metaverse for disadvantaged communities. These efforts help ensure that the metaverse becomes an inclusive and accessible space for all, maximizing its potential benefits and impact on society.

Finally, the ITU places great emphasis on security and privacy in the metaverse. To achieve this goal, the organization develops guidelines and best practices aimed at minimizing cybersecurity risks and ensuring the protection of users' privacy in the metaverse. By establishing such frameworks, the ITU helps create a safe and trustworthy environment for users, allowing them to engage in interactions and activities without concerns about the security of their personal data. Overall, the ITU's commitment to standardization, digital access, and security and privacy in the metaverse demonstrates its dedication to creating an open, inclusive, and secure digital space for all.

The IEEE, as a globally active technological and scientific organization, focuses primarily on technological innovation, standardization, and knowledge transfer in various fields of electrical engineering, electronics, and computer science. The IEEE's relationship to the metaverse is shaped by its interest in the technological, ethical, and social aspects of metaverse development. Like the ITU and others, the IEEE aims to develop the metaverse into an open, inclusive, and ethically responsible digital space that takes human needs into account and has the potential to fundamentally change the way we live, work, and interact [IEEoJa, IEEoJb].

The IEEE is dedicated to developing technology standards and best practices to ensure seamless interoperability and integration of various systems within the metaverse. In this context, the organization participates in working groups and committees focused on creating such standards. Ethical and social issues arising from technological innovations like the metaverse are of great importance to the IEEE. This is reflected in initiatives such as "Ethically Aligned Design," which has established ethical principles and recommendations for the development and implementation of AI and autonomous systems. In the context of the metaverse, the IEEE is committed to ensuring that the underlying technologies and systems adhere to ethical principles such as fairness, transparency, and privacy.

As a central institution for promoting research and knowledge transfer in the field of the metaverse, the IEEE publishes scientific journals and organizes conferences and workshops. In addition, it supports research projects and provides educational materials and resources to enable its members to stay informed about the latest developments and trends in the metaverse and to participate actively.

Finally, the IEEE strives to connect various stakeholders from industry, academia, and government to work together on shaping the metaverse. Through its global reach, it fosters collaboration and knowledge exchange to drive innovation and ensure that the metaverse becomes an open, inclusive, and sustainable ecosystem.

In cooperation with the Council of Europe, the IEEE Standards Association published a report in January 2024 entitled "The Metaverse and its Impact on Human Rights, the Rule of Law and Democracy." This report examines the potential impact of the metaverse on human rights, the rule of law, and democracy, and emphasizes the need for a human-centered approach in the development of these technologies [IEE23].

8.1.2 World Wide Web Consortium W3C

The World Wide Web Consortium (W3C) is the international organization dedicated to the development of web standards to ensure the interoperability and user-friendliness of the Internet [W3CoJa]. With regard to the metaverse, the W3C's role is primarily defined by its function as a standards organization and its vision of an open, accessible, and secure digital environment.

The development of standards is a central aspect of the W3C's work in relation to the metaverse. Since the metaverse is viewed as an extension of the Internet, the W3C sees it as its mission to develop standards and guidelines that ensure the interoperability, usability, and accessibility of the metaverse [W3CoJb]. This is achieved through the development of standards for interfaces, protocols, and data formats that enable different metaverse platforms and applications to communicate and collaborate seamlessly. By providing such standards, the W3C can ensure that the metaverse functions as a coherent digital environment in which users can move effortlessly between different platforms and applications without encountering compatibility issues [BER19]. In addition, W3C standards help promote security and privacy in the metaverse by providing clear guidelines for handling sensitive user information [W3CoJc].

Like others, the W3C views the metaverse as an advanced extension and further development of the Internet, in which technologies such as VR, AR, and WebXR will be interconnected to enable an immersive, interactive, and seamless digital experience. The integration of the metaverse with these technologies is seen as a crucial factor in creating an open, accessible, and interoperable digital space.

WebXR is a collection of standards and application programming interfaces (APIs) developed by the W3C to deliver VR, AR, and mixed reality content in virtually all types of web browsers [W3CoJe]. This technology facilitates the development and deployment of immersive content across various platforms and devices by enabling developers to create unified applications that work on different hardware. The W3C regards WebXR as a key building block for the metaverse, as it enables the interoperability and general accessibility of VR and AR content on the web. By developing web standards and APIs that support VR and AR content, the W3C enables developers to create and deliver immersive

3D content over the Internet [W3C23a]. The integration of VR and AR into the metaverse contributes to the creation of an immersive, interactive, and continuous user experience that spans multiple platforms and devices.

The W3C is actively committed to realizing a metaverse that is accessible to all users, regardless of their technical skills, cultural background, or physical limitations [W3CoJf]. To achieve this goal, the W3C develops guidelines and best practices that promote the accessibility of the metaverse. This includes, for example, considering accessibility in the design of user interfaces or developing technologies that enable people with disabilities to have full access to the metaverse [W3CoJg]. The W3C emphasizes the importance of accessibility and inclusion for the metaverse and supports the development of technologies and standards that enable all users to utilize virtual reality, augmented reality, and WebXR content regardless of their abilities or device limitations [W3CoJe]. This can be achieved by considering accessibility in the design of user interfaces and developing technologies that allow people with limitations or disabilities to fully experience the metaverse. Furthermore, the W3C places great importance on ensuring that the metaverse is a safe and secure space for its users. To this end, the organization develops standards and guidelines that ensure privacy protection, data security, and the confidentiality of communications. The W3C also provides best practices for metaverse development aimed at protecting user security and privacy and reducing vulnerability to cyberattacks or data breaches [W3CoJh].

The W3C advocates for an open and interoperable metaverse based on open standards and technologies [W3CoJf]. This is intended to enable the connection of different platforms and applications and to give users the ability to move seamlessly between various metaverse environments. Openness and interoperability also foster innovation and competition, as they make it possible to develop new applications and services that build on existing platforms and standards.

Through the development of standards and guidelines, as well as collaboration with other organizations, companies, and developers, the W3C aims to help make this vision of the metaverse a reality and to develop the metaverse into a positive and inclusive environment for the future version of the Internet.

8.1.3 World Economic Forum

The World Economic Forum (WEF), which positions itself as an international organization with the goal of fostering collaboration among businesses, governments, and other stakeholders to address global challenges and promote progress and prosperity, views the "Metaverse as the next major computing platform" [DAS23, WEFoJa, WEFoJb].

The WEF is of particular interest regarding the metaverse, as it has launched a number of initiatives and projects to explore and promote the potential of the metaverse. The metaverse is seen as a forward-looking technology that could have far-reaching effects on how we work, play, communicate, and connect.

The WEF aims to create a platform for the exchange of knowledge, ideas, and best practices in the field of the metaverse. It has already organized a series of events and workshops where experts from various fields come together to discuss the impact of the metaverse on society. In this way, the World Economic Forum plays a significant role in exploring and promoting the potential of the metaverse. It provides a platform for sharing ideas and best practices and helps raise awareness of the metaverse's societal implications.

In addition, the WEF has established a working group focused on the metaverse, which concentrates on exploring the potential of the metaverse and addresses topics such as data protection, security, and regulation. According to the WEF's vision, this working group is intended to enable experts and interested parties from various fields to exchange information on the latest developments, challenges, and opportunities of the metaverse. Among other things, the working group is to serve as a communication platform. An online community is to be formed, allowing members to contribute, engage in discussions, share resources, and participate in virtual events. The community is expected to comprise a broad range of stakeholders, including academics, technology experts, representatives from governments and businesses, as well as other interest groups.

Furthermore, a series of events and workshops are being organized that focus on the metaverse and bring together experts from various related fields to discuss the impact of the metaverse on the economy and society. These events are intended to help raise awareness of the metaverse's potential and provide a platform for the exchange of knowledge and ideas.

Another goal is to identify and share best practices for addressing the challenges of the metaverse. This includes, for example, discussions on data protection, security, and regulation to ensure that the metaverse is developed in a way that aligns with the interests of the global society. The World Economic Forum has already identified and discussed a number of economic applications of the metaverse that could be implemented in the foreseeable future. One such application is that the metaverse could enable companies to sell their products and services within a virtual environment. This could simplify commercial processes and increase their efficiency.

The WEF also sees the possibility that the metaverse could enable the creation of virtual currencies to be used within the virtual world. This could reduce transaction costs and facilitate business operations. In addition, virtual real estate could be bought, sold, and rented within the metaverse, leading to new business models and expanding the real estate market.

The metaverse's potential ability to allow companies to hire virtual employees who can perform tasks within the virtual world could increase workforce flexibility and efficiency. There is also the possibility that the metaverse will enable companies to advertise their products and services within the virtual world, creating new advertising opportunities and expanding the advertising market.

Finally, the WEF sees the metaverse as a potential foundation for the establishment of virtual financial services, such as virtual banks and insurance companies. This could expand access to financial services and enlarge the financial services market. Overall, the metaverse offers a variety of economic applications that could be realized in the future, thus contributing to a transformation of the economic landscape.

These potential applications formulated by the WEF should not be seen as final or exhaustive. Rather, the WEF considers it more than likely that further applications and fields of application will emerge in the future. This is also underscored by the WEF's activities and publications.

For example, in March 2024, the WEF published the report "Navigating the Industrial Metaverse: A Blueprint for Future Innovations" in collaboration with Accenture, which describes the industrial metaverse as a catalyst for the next phase of the industrial revolution. The report forecasts that the metaverse will grow into a global market worth 100 billion US dollars by 2030 and highlights the transformative impact of integrating digital and physical realities [WEF24a].

Also in March 2024, the report "Metaverse Identity: Defining the Self in a Blended Reality" was published, in which the WEF examines the importance of identity in the metaverse. In this report, the WEF emphasizes the need for a secure, inclusive, and privacy-oriented approach to designing identities in immersive digital environments [WEF24b].

In addition, the WEF has launched the initiative "Defining and Building the Metaverse" to promote the development of a secure, interoperable, and economically viable metaverse. This initiative brings together various stakeholders to develop guidelines and frameworks for the metaverse.

8.1.4 Metaverse Standards Forum

The development of an open and inclusive metaverse presents a significant challenge, particularly with regard to the need to develop and adopt standards for interoperability. This requirement has been defined as a central objective by the Metaverse Standards Forum (MSF). Kevin Collins, Managing Director at Accenture, emphasizes the importance of interoperability: "Regardless of whether you subscribe to a single metaverse or a multiverse model, users need interoperability to realize the value of the metaverse" [SCH23].

Collins further explains that interoperability is necessary for different platforms to interact with each other and for users to seamlessly switch between these platforms while retaining their identity, assets, and communications. He believes that the efforts of the MSF will help promote and coordinate the development and adoption of the required standards to ensure the creation of a connected and consistent metaverse.

To promote the development of open standards for the metaverse and support collaboration across the industry, leading industry organizations and companies have established the Metaverse Standards Forum. So far, 1800 members have joined the MSF, including the usual and expected companies such as Google, Meta, Microsoft, and Nvidia. In addition, institutions like the Khronos Group and the W3C, as well as many other hardware and software companies, have announced their participation in the MSF [MSFoJ, RAV22].

The MSF was founded with the goal of fostering consensus-based collaboration between various standards organizations and companies. Specifically, this means defining and aligning requirements and priorities for metaverse standards, accelerating the availability of such standards, and reducing duplication of effort within the industry. Neil Trevett, current chair of the MSF, Vice President of Ecosystem Development at Nvidia, and President of the Khronos Group, described the forum as "a unique venue for coordination between standards organizations and industry."

To take a pragmatic approach, the forum supports projects such as the development of prototypes, hackathons, plugfests, and open-source tools to accelerate the testing and adoption of metaverse standards. At the same time, it is developing a unified terminology and deployment guidelines. Given the numerous standards organizations in this field, it may initially seem confusing to establish yet another group. However, IT leaders hope that these new efforts will consolidate existing work and identify areas for further harmonization.

The MSF emphasizes that it intends to coordinate the requirements and resources of other standards organizations rather than create new standards. To this end, it collaborates with various standards organizations in related fields, including the Khronos Group, the World Wide Web Consortium (W3C), the Open Geospatial Consortium, Open AR Cloud, the Spatial Web Foundation, and many others. Frank Palermo, Executive Vice President and Head of Technology, Media and Telecommunications (TMT) at Virtusa, a digital engineering consulting firm, stresses that this coordination will help participants consider the types of standards needed for both consumer and enterprise use cases. "It is important to have some cooperating bodies that think through standards. Otherwise, different companies will build their own variations of the metaverse across a variety of technologies, which may not easily work together," said Palermo, who therefore believes that data exchange is one of the most important technical areas that must be considered for standardization. Virtual worlds may have different ways of representing the size, shape, behavior, sounds, and animations of objects. Standards such as Khronos Group's glTF help ensure the efficient transmission and loading of 3D objects. Other standards are emerging to describe the physical properties of objects, how objects are assembled, and how they are animated. For example, 3D Tiles streams massive 3D datasets in real time, while Universal Scene Description organizes collections of objects in such 3D scenes, PhysX brings in the physical and behavioral properties of objects, and MaterialX describes the texture and appearance of objects.

8.2 The Perspective of Professionals and Users

In addition to governmental and economic organizations, the topic of the "metaverse" has also attracted the interest of many individuals and professionals from a wide range of industries, including technology entrepreneurs, game developers, investors, artists, and academics. Some relevant names have already been mentioned at various points so far, but there is also a growing circle of interested parties:

- *Mark Zuckerberg*, CEO of Meta, formerly Facebook, is strongly committed to the idea of the metaverse and believes it will be the next major technological revolution. Meta has heavily invested in projects such as Oculus Rift to further develop and make the metaverse accessible [HOL21].
- *Tim Sweeney*, CEO of Epic Games, the company behind Fortnite, has also shown great interest in the metaverse. Sweeney sees the metaverse as an opportunity to create a shared digital world where people can come together, play, and interact [WEB23].
- *Philip Rosedale* is a pioneer in the field of virtual worlds and has founded both Second Life and High Fidelity. He is fascinated by the vision of the metaverse and is working to develop technologies and platforms that make it possible [HAT22].
- *Matthew Ball* is an investor and currently one of the most well-known experts in the metaverse space. He publishes extensively on the metaverse and shares his ideas about how it might develop and change the world in numerous articles and essays [BALLoJ].
- As already illustrated by earlier examples, *Cathy Hackl* is a futurist and expert in augmented and virtual reality. She is enthusiastic about the vision of the metaverse and often speaks about how it could transform the future of work, education, entertainment, and social interaction. Hackl is also involved in developing applications and strategies for the metaverse and is an important voice in the discussion of its potential and challenges [HACoJ].
- *Amy Webb* is a futurist, author, and founder of the Future Today Institute. In her publications on the future of technology and the internet, she has addressed the metaverse and emphasized the importance of ethics and responsibility in shaping it. She particularly warns that without careful planning and regulation, it could lead to a dystopian future.
- *Steve Mann* is the pioneer in wearable computing and augmented reality par excellence. Although he is not explicitly known as a proponent of the metaverse vision, his work has had a significant impact on the development of technologies that could enable the metaverse. Mann has focused on creating interfaces and devices that extend human perception and enable interaction with digital worlds. These technologies are now considered crucial for the realization of the metaverse [MAN13].

The following section will take a closer look at Matthew Ball, Cathy Hackl, Amy Webb, and Steve Mann, and their respective perspectives on the metaverse.

8.2.1 Matthew Ball

With a professional background in the media and technology industries, Matthew Ball has established himself as one of the leading voices on the topic of the metaverse. He sees the metaverse as a new form of virtual reality that goes far beyond the current internet as well as today's VR and AR applications, creating an open, persistently connected world in which people, businesses, and machines can interact. He was among the first to describe the metaverse as a continuation of the development of the internet and predicts that it will become a central platform for a wide range of applications and business models. In his contributions, he emphasizes that the metaverse brings with it significant challenges and opportunities, including issues of privacy, security, and regulation.

However, he considers it important that the metaverse must not be controlled by a single company, but should be supported by an open infrastructure that enables everyone to create and share content and applications. He sees the metaverse as an opportunity for a new wave of innovation and possibilities in the virtual world, which will be significant for both businesses and end users [BAL20].

Tony Parisi, who, among other achievements, played a significant role in integrating VR into the WWW through his work on the Virtual Reality Markup Language (VRML), formulated seven rules for the metaverse based on Ball's statements, which have served as the foundation for the work of many others [PAR21] (Fig. 8.1).

1. *The metaverse is not a new product, but a new platform*
   Ball emphasizes that the metaverse is not simply a new application or technology, but rather a platform where various applications and technologies converge and which continuously evolves and grows by integrating different applications and technologies and creating new opportunities for users. Therefore, the metaverse should not be viewed as a single product or service, but as an open, scalable, persistent, and boundless virtual (application) environment that is utilized by many different applications

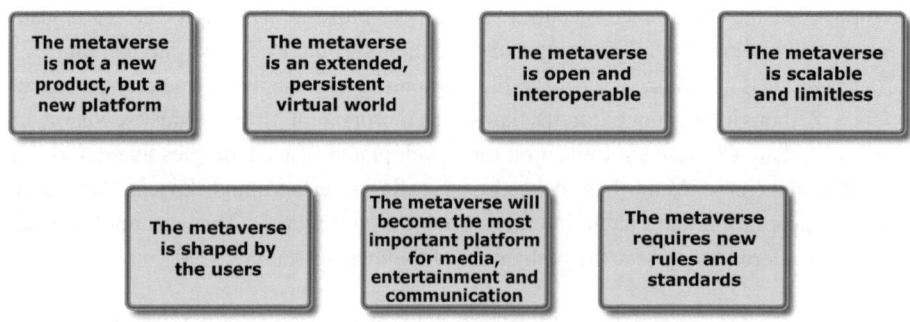

Fig. 8.1 Seven rules for the metaverse. (Adapted from: Tony Parisi [PAR21])

and is only made possible through a variety of technologies. This platform enables users to interact across a wide range of diverse yet interconnected environments, including games, social networks, e-commerce, education, and other applications.

By creating such a platform, the metaverse becomes an ecosystem in which the applications and services within it can interact with each other and provide users with a seamless experience. This means that the metaverse can be used not only for the creation of new applications and content, but also for the integration and interaction with existing technologies.

2. *The metaverse is an extended, persistent virtual world*

   In contrast to conventional VR applications, which are limited to individual sessions, the metaverse will be a persistently connected world accessible around the clock. This means that users can access and immerse themselves in the metaverse at any time, and that their interactions and their consequences within the virtual world are maintained even when they leave the platform or a particular application. This persistence enables users to build lasting relationships with other users, acquire and manage resources and property within the virtual world, and engage in a wide variety of activities within the virtual environment.

   This rule also demonstrates that, as a persistent virtual world, the metaverse offers a completely new experience that goes beyond traditional VR applications. It allows users to deepen their experiences within the virtual world and to engage in various activities while remaining in a consistent environment.

3. *The metaverse is open and interoperable*

   According to Ball, the metaverse must be open so that anyone can create and share their own content and applications. It must also be interoperable, allowing different applications and platforms to communicate with each other. This, in turn, almost inevitably means that the metaverse is not simply an extension of today's Internet, but a completely new type of platform that enables new forms of interaction and experience.

   Whereas today's Internet mainly consists of individual websites and applications displayed in a two-dimensional browser window, the metaverse will essentially be a three-dimensional world in which users can immerse themselves and interact and communicate in real time, including gaming, social networking, e-commerce, and education. This also implies that it will be a new kind of platform, enabling entirely new applications and business models that go beyond traditional online interactions and transactions.

4. *The metaverse is scalable and boundless*

   The metaverse must be scalable to meet the demands of millions of users and countless applications and content. It must also be boundless to enable seamless integration and interaction between different users and applications. Ball formulates this rule by stating that the metaverse must be a platform on which other platforms and applications can be built. Developers and companies create their own applications and content that function within the virtual world. These applications and content can then be used by other developers and companies in the spirit of produsage and modusage to enhance and expand their own applications and services. Only in this way can the metaverse become an open ecosystem in which different applications and services work together seamlessly.

5. *The metaverse is shaped by its users*

   The metaverse is intended to be shaped and developed by its users, rather than by a few large companies or institutions, as is generally the case with today's Internet. This would mean that users have control and can influence the development of the platform. It also follows that the metaverse must be decentralized, as this is the only way to ensure that control over the virtual world does not rest with a single company or organization, but with a collaborative community of users and developers. Ideally, decentralization should help ensure that the metaverse is transparent and fair.

6. *The metaverse will become the most important platform for media, entertainment, and communication*

   Not only according to Ball, but also according to other experts, the metaverse will become the most important platform for media, entertainment, and communication in the future, as it enables entirely new forms of experiences and interactions. This also includes the significance of user-generated content in the metaverse, which can encompass artworks, music, videos, games, virtual objects, and much more.

   The importance of user-generated content in the metaverse lies in its ability to continuously expand and improve the virtual world. It allows users to express their creativity and integrate their own ideas and visions into the virtual environment. Furthermore, user-generated content can help make the metaverse an open, diverse, and accessible ecosystem. However, this requires that the various applications and services within the metaverse can work together seamlessly, regardless of who created them.

7. *The metaverse requires new rules and standards*

   New rules and standards are of particular importance to ensure the privacy, security, and quality of users and their user experience. These rules and standards should be developed collaboratively by the entire industry. This also includes social interaction as an important part of the human experience, which the metaverse ultimately aims to replicate in the virtual world. This means that the metaverse must be a place where people can meet, communicate, collaborate, play, and much more. To make this possible, social interaction features must be provided, such as chat rooms, forums, groups, games, and events. These interaction options should include both formal and informal opportunities to meet the needs of different user groups.

   The importance of social interactions in the metaverse lies in their ability to foster human connections and relationships in the virtual world, enabling users to share common interests, form friendships, and even find a kind of virtual home.

8.2 The Perspective of Professionals and Users

These seven rules reflect Ball's vision of what the metaverse will look like as an open, scalable, boundless, and user-shaped platform, as well as the challenges and opportunities it presents. They form a framework that developers and companies should take into account when designing and implementing the metaverse. By following these rules, they can ensure that the metaverse is developed in a way that meets the interests and needs of users while also adhering to general ethical and moral standards [CNB21].

When users feel that the metaverse is open, transparent, and fair, and is designed to meet their needs, they are more likely to engage with and actively participate in the virtual world. These rules help foster user trust and acceptance. They also provide guidance for designing a virtual world that is based on the needs and interests of users while fulfilling ethical and moral standards.

However, like many others, the rules established by Matthew Ball are open to criticism from various perspectives and depending on the critics' backgrounds. Some critics argue that Ball's principles are too idealistic and impractical. They contend that implementing these principles could be extremely complicated or even unattainable given the numerous challenges involved in constructing a virtual world.

Other critics believe that the rules proposed by Ball could stifle innovation by imposing excessive restrictions on developers and companies. These critics advocate for allowing innovation and creative ideas in order to fully realize the potential of the metaverse. Conversely, another perspective criticizes Ball's rules for possibly not sufficiently considering the business interests of companies and developers. Here, the argument is that the rules are too focused on user interests, thereby neglecting the commercial dimension of the metaverse.

Finally, there is also the view that the rules proposed by Ball are simply not relevant for all user groups in the metaverse. These critics argue that certain user groups have different needs and interests that are inadequately addressed by Ball's rules.

8.2.2 Cathy Hackl

Cathy Hackl is an internationally recognized author on augmented and virtual reality and the metaverse. She is a speaker, consultant, author, and founder of a VR/AR think tank [HAC0].

With regard to the metaverse, she is a highly influential voice in the discussion about the future of this virtual world. She believes that the metaverse will soon play an important role in our society, as it provides a space where people from all over the world can come together and interact. She has also helped raise awareness of the metaverse by speaking about its potential and challenges at conferences and in the media. Through her expertise in AR and VR, Cathy Hackl has emphasized the particular importance of these technologies for the metaverse. She believes that AR and VR will enhance the user experience in the metaverse and enable people to immerse themselves even more deeply in the virtual world. In addition, she also stresses the importance of data protection and ethical standards, not only in general but especially for the metaverse, and calls for an open and transparent discussion about how this virtual world should be shaped. She maintains that it is important to establish these standards as early as possible to ensure that the metaverse becomes and remains a positive and safe environment.

Hackl sees the metaverse as a virtual world seamlessly integrated with the real world, where people, companies, and even governments will interact. She believes that the metaverse will play a major role in the future, as it offers a central space where people from around the globe can come together and interact without being physically present. In her view, the metaverse should provide an immersive, interactive, and personalized experience that enables users to interact with other people, virtual objects, and digital information. She therefore envisions its implementation as a combination of various technologies such as AR, VR, AI, blockchain, and others.

In various previous sections, examples have been provided illustrating how Cathy Hackl envisions the future metaverse and the applications it will enable. In her contributions to the discussion on the use of the metaverse, she presents an even broader range of applications, in which the metaverse serves as a …

- … platform for virtual conferences and events.
- … means for retailers to open virtual stores where customers can select and purchase products without leaving their homes.
- … platform for virtual education, where pupils and students can attend virtual classrooms and interact with teachers and other students from around the world.
- … platform for virtual collaboration, where employees work together on projects in virtual spaces.
- … opportunity to take virtual journeys to visit historical sites or fantastic worlds.

Hackl's views point in a direction quite similar to that described by Matthew Ball. She also predicts that the digital economy of the metaverse will be several times larger than today's digital economy and emphasizes the enormous economic opportunities the metaverse can offer. However, she places even greater emphasis than Ball on the relevance of ethical standards and data protection regulations and their early definition to ensure that the metaverse remains a positive and safe environment.

Another topic on which Cathy Hackl has commented is Ball's predictions regarding the speed at which the metaverse will grow. Matthew Ball believes that the metaverse will grow faster than the internet and that it will become an important part of our society within 10 to 20 years. Cathy Hackl fundamentally agrees, but also emphasizes that the development of the metaverse is still in its early stages and that there are still many challenges and obstacles to overcome, thus putting Ball's statements into perspective.

In January 2023, she published "Into the Metaverse: The Essential Guide to the Business Opportunities of the Web3 Era." In this book, Hackl offers insights from her perspective into how the metaverse works and its significance for businesses. She discusses how brands can leverage the metaverse to unlock new business opportunities and highlights the relevance of technologies such as gaming, synthetic media, spatial computing, and artificial intelligence [HAC23].

Hackl advocates the vision of merging digital and physical reality. She emphasizes the importance of spatial computing and predicted in a January 2024 interview that AI-powered wearables will come to the forefront this year. Hackl stated: "We will move away from smartphone screens. Many of these devices will become spatial computers. A new era of AI-driven spatial computer hardware is just beginning" [MOR23b].

8.2.3 Amy Webb

Amy Webb is a futurist, entrepreneur, and author specializing in the study of technology trends. She is renowned for her work in the field of futures research and has written several books on technology and innovation [WEBoJb]. Amy Webb is considered one of the leading experts on technology trends, and her work influences many industries and companies. Her assessments and predictions regarding the metaverse are therefore taken seriously by many experts and decision-makers in the tech industry.

With regard to the metaverse, Amy Webb has frequently written about and given talks on how the metaverse will shape the future of life and work. She also views the metaverse as a technological evolution of the internet and believes that it will play an increasingly important role in the coming years [KER23].

Despite her recognized expertise, Webb does not provide a definitive description of how the metaverse will ultimately develop, as she acknowledges that it is still in its early stages and many questions remain unanswered. Nevertheless, Webb attempts to describe possible scenarios for the metaverse. She generally envisions the metaverse as a future space where people come together virtually to work, play, and interact in a variety of environments. She particularly emphasizes the entirely new form of collaboration that emerges when physical boundaries and distances no longer matter. Uniquely, Webb's scenarios include the possibility of an evolving cross-economy, in which people own digital identities and assets that they can also use in the real world. She describes the metaverse as a kind of parallel world, where people can shape their lives in new and creative ways, yet one that is closely intertwined with the real world. Webb also predicts that the metaverse will enable a wide range of applications, from entertainment and education to healthcare and beyond.

From these general scenarios, Webb develops a series of concrete use cases.

- Virtual workplaces where people from all over the world collaborate by meeting in shared virtual work environments. In the future, metaverse platforms will enable a significantly higher level of immersion in virtual meetings and collaborative work on documents and projects.
- Virtual conferences and events that take place in virtual environments, eliminating the need for travel and event costs.

- Entertainment, where people immerse themselves in virtual worlds and have interactive experiences that would not be possible in the real world, such as historical events and worlds or virtual experiences like movies.
- Digital identities and virtual assets that people can own and use in the metaverse, but also utilize in the real world. For example, people could earn a type of cryptocurrency in a virtual environment and then spend it in the real world.
- In healthcare, Webb sees the potential to offer virtual treatments and consultations in the metaverse, allowing doctors and patients to meet in a virtual environment to prepare for or even conduct treatments.

8.2.4 Steve Mann

The Canadian researcher and developer Steve Mann is a pioneer in the field of wearable computing and augmented reality. Since the 1980s, he has been working and conducting research on the paradigm of wearable computing, which he has since further developed into what is now known as Humanistic Intelligence [MAN02]. He has also made a number of significant contributions to the development of AR glasses and systems. Since 1998, he has shaped the concept of "Sousveillance" (undersight, or surveillance from below), in which wearable cameras are used to monitor the activities of those in power [HOF23, MAN12].

Mann has also made important contributions with regard to the metaverse. He developed the concept of "Mediated Reality," in which AR technology is used to overlay the physical world with virtual information, thereby creating an enhanced reality. This concept forms the basis for many of the AR applications used in the metaverse today and represents an evolution of the originally more technology-focused AR paradigm. In the future, this could play an important role in the metaverse, as it enables users to immerse themselves in an augmented reality while continuing to interact with the physical world.

In the context of his own work, Steve Mann has also commented on his vision of the metaverse and believes that such an evolution of the Internet will play an important role in the future. He sees the metaverse as a place where people can experience an augmented reality and interact with one another in ways that go beyond the physical world. In addition to being a virtual space with many different applications such as gaming, social interaction, education, and work, he also sees it as a place where people can express and share their creativity and ideas, and where the boundaries between the physical and virtual worlds become blurred.

Mann does not, however, commit to a specific vision of what the metaverse will look like. Rather, he argues that the appearance of the metaverse will depend greatly on who uses it and for what purposes it is implemented. He expects that there will be a wide variety of different metaverses, each tailored to specific target groups and fulfilling a diverse range of functions. Some could be highly realistic and represent an exact copy of the physical world, while others might be more surreal and fantastical. Nevertheless,

Mann also identifies the typical use cases of virtual conferences and workplaces, social interaction, education, gaming, as well as art and creativity.

The wearable computing defined by Steve Mann refers to computer-based systems that are worn directly on the human body to enable seamless integration and constant interaction with the digital world. Sensors, actuators, and processing units are used to collect and analyze data about the environment, the movements, and the physiological states of the wearer. The metaverse, by contrast, is a collective virtual space composed of a multitude of digital environments and simulations, shared by many users.

The connection between wearable computing and the metaverse lies in the way these technologies interact and complement each other. Wearable computing devices, such as smart glasses or haptic suits, can make the experience of the metaverse more immersive and interactive. They allow users to transfer their physical presence into the virtual world and make their interactions with digital objects or other users more realistic. At the same time, the metaverse can serve as a platform for the development and deployment of wearable computing applications. For example, users could use specialized wearables to monitor their health data in the metaverse or track their fitness goals. Companies could offer virtual work environments in which employees are equipped with wearable computing devices to enhance productivity and collaboration.

Combining the wearable computing paradigm with the idea of the metaverse can create a deeper and more immersive experience that enriches both individuals and society as a whole. The focus here is on the respective flow of information. In wearable computing, the flow of information concerns the exchange of data between the sensors, actuators, and processing units integrated into the body-worn devices. These devices continuously collect data about the environment, the physiological states, and the activities of the wearer. They then process this information to generate useful insights and provide them to the user in real time. These insights can be used to trigger notifications, make adjustments to the user interface, or even perform physical actions via actuators. For this context, Steve Mann has created a diagram of information flows (see Fig. 8.2). In the metaverse, by contrast, the flow of information consists of communication and interaction between users, digital objects, and environments within the virtual space. Information is exchanged in the form of text, audio, video, and other media, which users can share and use together in real time. The platforms on which the metaverse is built collect and process this data to offer users personalized and context-aware experiences. A comparison of the information flows between wearable computing and the metaverse reveals both differences and similarities.

- *Type of data*: Wearable computing focuses primarily on capturing personal and environmental data from the user, while the metaverse emphasizes interactions and the exchange of information between users and virtual environments.
- *Contextualization*: Wearable computing devices process the collected data to place it in a useful and personal context for the user. In the metaverse, contextualization

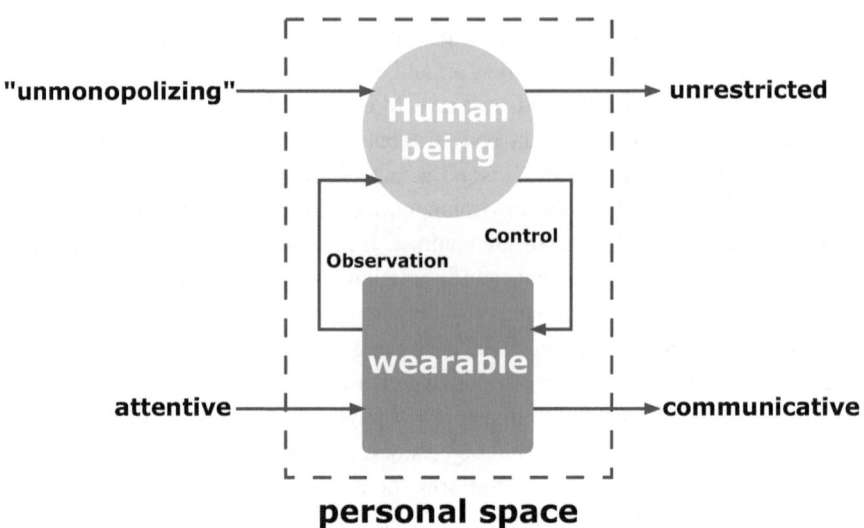

Fig. 8.2 The flow of information in the wearable computing paradigm. (Adapted from [MAN98])

occurs through the adaptation of environments, objects, and interactions based on the needs and preferences of users.
- *Real-time interaction*: Both wearable computing and the metaverse rely on real-time interaction and communication to enable a seamless and engaging user experience.
- *Data processing*: Wearable computing devices process data internally and can even make decisions and perform actions without relying on external systems. In the metaverse, by contrast, data processing usually takes place on central servers or in the cloud.

In combination, wearable computing and the metaverse can expand the flow of information and create an even more immersive and personalized experience. Wearables can serve as an interface between the physical and virtual worlds, enabling users to bring information from their environment into the metaverse or vice versa. This creates a deeper connection between the real world and the virtual world of the metaverse, resulting in a unique and fascinating user experience.

8.3 The Metaverse – the Operating System of the Future?

Based on the previous considerations, an architecture of the metaverse and its anticipated infrastructure can be developed, which is layered and embedded in the real world. This architecture and a computer operating system share parallels, particularly with regard to the organization and management of resources as well as the interaction between different layers and components. Both systems make it possible to organize and control complex structures and processes at a higher level of abstraction, in order to improve the user experience and increase efficiency.

A computer operating system is responsible for managing a computer's hardware resources and running software applications. Similar to the architecture of the metaverse, an operating system is divided into multiple layers, each covering different functions and aspects of the system. The lowest layer is the hardware on which the operating system runs. Above this lies the system layer, which provides fundamental operating system functions such as file systems, memory management, and process management. The next layer consists of system applications and services that offer additional features and tools for the user. Finally, the top layer comprises user applications that are used directly by end users.

The relationship between a possible architecture of the metaverse, as proposed in Fig. 8.3, and an operating system can be seen in the way both systems are based on layers to enable efficient interaction and management. In both cases, the various layers are used to abstract complex processes and structures, thereby providing a better user experience. In the metaverse architecture, the focus is on integrating digital and physical worlds, whereas an operating system is designed to manage computer resources and execute software applications. Despite these differences, both systems can be viewed as platforms that provide an interface between users and the underlying technology. They enable interaction and collaboration in a structured and abstracted environment, making complex processes more efficient and user-friendly. In this context, the metaverse can be seen as an extended, immersive, and interconnected environment that goes beyond the capabilities of a traditional operating system. While an operating system provides the foundation for interacting with computers and running applications, the metaverse opens up new possibilities for communication, collaboration, and interaction between people, machines, and the physical world.

At their core, the metaverse and traditional operating systems pursue different objectives and therefore have different priorities. While traditional operating systems are designed to maximize user efficiency and productivity, the metaverse focuses on creating shared experiences and fostering social interactions. Nevertheless, as mentioned above, Matthew Ball often directly compares the metaverse to a computer's operating system. Just as an operating system is the fundamental software that enables a computer to run applications and manage various hardware components, Ball sees the metaverse as the foundational platform that allows users to engage in a wide range of applications and activities. The metaverse is essentially a virtual world where users can interact, trade, and play. However, much like an operating system supports various applications and programs, the metaverse can also support different types of activities at a higher level, from virtual meetings to gaming and shopping experiences.

Just as an operating system requires various technologies and functions to operate properly, the metaverse relies on technologies such as VR, AR, AI, and blockchain to create, operate, and secure the virtual world. For example, VR technology is used to

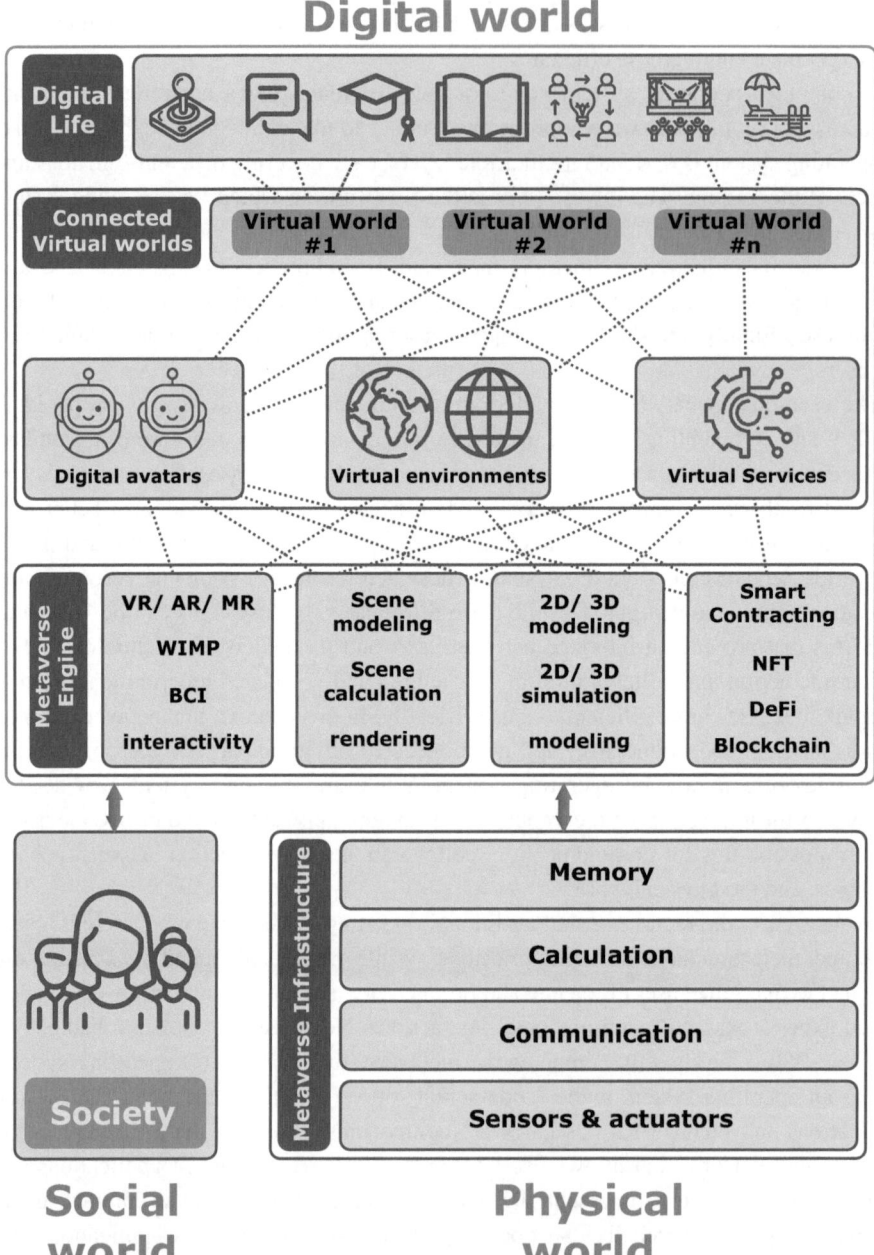

Fig. 8.3 An architectural diagram for the metaverse. (Adapted from [JAB22, DED09])

create a more immersive and realistic virtual environment, while AI systems can help develop intelligent NPCs and virtual assistants. Similar to how an operating system requires regular updates for drivers and security features, the metaverse must also be regularly "updated" to ensure it functions properly and remains secure. One way to achieve this is through the use of blockchain technologies, which enable a transparent and secure transaction history. Finally, as with an operating system, interoperability and compatibility are crucial factors in the metaverse. Seamless integration of different applications and systems allows users to access and utilize a wide range of services and activities without interruption. Therefore, the metaverse must be capable of supporting a variety of devices, platforms, and applications to provide users with an optimal experience.

The question of whether the metaverse could be considered the operating system of the future is highly significant, as the metaverse as a concept has the potential to transform and, ideally, improve human life in many areas.

A key difference between the two systems lies in the metaverse's focus on social interactions and shared experiences, whereas traditional operating systems primarily focus on running applications and services. The metaverse enables users to communicate, collaborate, and play together in real time, while traditional operating systems are mainly designed to optimize user productivity and efficiency. Another important distinction is that the metaverse is built on cloud computing technology, whereas traditional operating systems typically run on a single computer or server. As a result, the metaverse offers superior scalability and flexibility, allowing multiple users to interact within the same virtual world simultaneously.

The convergence of the metaverse and traditional operating systems is an important step toward realizing the metaverse's potential as the operating system of the future. Traditional operating systems such as Windows, macOS, and Linux are designed to control and manage the core functionality of devices like computers and smartphones. They provide users with an interface to run applications and programs, store and organize files, access the internet, and much more.

In contrast, the metaverse offers a fully immersive experience, enabling users to live, work, and play in a virtual environment. It provides opportunities for immersive learning and training experiences, virtual collaboration, e-commerce, and more. When these two concepts are brought together, they can create a powerful operating system at a higher level that leverages the best of both worlds.

One way to achieve the convergence of the metaverse and traditional operating systems is to integrate metaverse platforms as applications or programs within traditional operating systems. For example, a user could launch a metaverse platform by opening the corresponding application on their computer or smartphone, just as they would with any other program or app. The metaverse platform would be seamlessly integrated into the traditional operating system, allowing users to switch between different application modes. Switching between "classic" office applications, which run and are operated outside the metaverse, and immersive experiences within the metaverse would thus be easily possible.

Another possibility is for traditional operating systems to natively integrate metaverse features. For instance, operating systems could offer an integrated virtual interface in the form of a VR view, giving users direct access to the metaverse from their operating system. This would allow users to transition seamlessly from the traditional operating system to the metaverse without significant media or interaction disruptions.

Such convergence between the metaverse and traditional operating systems will be an important step in developing the metaverse as a "true" operating system of the future. This will enhance integration and interoperability between traditional and virtual environments, making it possible to unlock the metaverse for broader application and use.

Contrary to the particularly optimistic forecasts, the metaverse has continued to develop over the past two years, but not to the extent that it can currently be regarded as the operating system of the future. Instead, significant progress has been made in individual, related technologies:

- New operating systems for XR devices: Google, in collaboration with Samsung and Qualcomm, introduced "Android XR," an operating system specifically designed for extended reality devices. This system aims to provide an open platform for future XR applications.
- Market launch of mixed reality headsets: Apple released the "Apple Vision Pro," a mixed reality headset that seamlessly integrates digital content with the physical world. Although it offers innovative features, adoption has remained limited due to its high price.
- Integration of artificial intelligence: The convergence of AI and metaverse technologies has led to new forms of interaction. AI is increasingly being used to design virtual worlds and enhance the user experience.

Even though the metaverse has made significant technological advances, it has still not achieved the status of a universal operating system. However, this does not mean that this technological vision is dead. Developments in XR operating systems, mixed reality devices, and AI integration are laying the foundation for future innovations in this field.

References

[BAL20]   Ball, Matthew (13.01.2020). What It Is, Where to Find it, and Who Will Build It. Online: https://www.matthewball.vc/all/themetaverse (Retrieved: 17.05.2023).
[BALLoJ] Ball, Matthew (o.J.). The Metaverse Primer. In: Mathhewball.vc. Online: https://www.matthewball.vc/the-metaverse-primer (Retrieved: 21.05.2023).
[BER19]   Berners-Lee, Tim (12.03.2019). 30 years on, what's next #ForTheWeb? In: World Wide Web Foundation. Online: https://webfoundation.org/2019/03/web-birthday-30/ (Retrieved: 21.05.2023).

References

[CNB21] CNBC (15.11.2021). Metaverse similar to rise of internet, Matthew Ball says. In: CNBC, Closing Bell. Online: https://www.cnbc.com/video/2021/11/15/metaverse-similar-to-rise-of-internet-matthew-ball-says.html (Retrieved: 28.05.2023).

[DAS23] Das, Basudha (17.01.2023). Davos 2023: WEF launches metaverse platform to tackle crises, challenges; Check details here. In: Business Today. Online: https://www.businesstoday.in/wef-2023/story/davos-2023-wef-launches-metaverse-platform-to-tackle-crises-challenges-check-details-here-360692-2023-01-17 (Retrieved: 21.05.2023).

[DED09] Dede, Chris. (2009). Immersive Interfaces for Engagement and Learning. Science (New York, N.Y.). 323. 66-9. 10.1126/science.1167311.

[HAC23] Cathy Hackl (2023). Into the Metaverse: The Essential Guide to the Business Opportunities of the Web3 Era. Bloomsbury Business, Dublin. ISBN-13: 978-1399401807.

[HACoJ] Hackl, Cathy (o.J.). Cathy Hackl. In: Forbes. Online: https://www.forbes.com/sites/cathyhackl/ (Retrieved: 21.05.2023).

[HAT22] Hatmaker, Taylor (13.01.2022). Second Life's creator is returning to advise the original metaverse company. In: TechCrunsch. Online: https://techcrunch.com/2022/01/13/second-life-philip-rosedale-returns-linden-lab-high-fidelity/ (Retrieved: 21.05.2023).

[HOF23] Hoffman, Jascha (10.12.2003). Sousveillance. In: The New York Times Magazine. Online: https://www.nytimes.com/2006/12/10/magazine/10section3b.t-3.html?_r=0 (Retrieved: 21.05.2023).

[HOL21] Hollister, Sean (22.07.2021). California sues Activision Blizzard over a culture of 'constant sexual harassment'. In: The Verge. Online: https://www.theverge.com/2021/7/22/22588215/facebook-mark-zuckerberg-metaverse-interview (Retrieved: 21.05.2023).

[IEE23] IEEE (2024). The metaverse and its impact on human rights, the rule of law and democracy. Online: https://rm.coe.int/the-metaverse-impact-on-and-its-impact-on-human-rights-the-rule-of-law/1680ae6bce. (Retrieved: 14.02.2025).

[IEEoJa] IEEE Metaverse Standards Committee (CTS/ MSC) (o.J.). Demystifying, Defining, Developing, and Deploying the Metaverse. In: IEEE. Online: https://sagroups.ieee.org/metaverse-sc/ (Retrieved: 28.05.2023).

[IEEoJb] IEEE Metaverse Working Group (CTS/ MSC/ MWG) (o.J.). IEEE P2048: Standard for Metaverse: Terminology, Definitions, and Taxonomy. In: IEEE. Online: https://sagroups.ieee.org/2048/ (Retrieved: 28.05.2023).

[ITUoJa] ITU (o.J.). About International Telecommunication Union (ITU). In: ITU About. Online: https://www.itu.int/en/about/Pages/default.aspx (Retrieved: 28.05.2023).

[ITUoJb] ITU FG-MV (o.J.). ITU-T Focus Group on metaverse (FG-MV). In: ITU Focisgroups. Online: https://www.itu.int/en/ITU-T/focusgroups/mv/Pages/default.aspx (Retrieved: 28.05.2023).

[JAB22] Jaber, Tanya Abdulsattar (2022). Security risks of the metaverse world. In: International Journal of Interactive Mobile Technologies, Vol. 16 No. 13, 2022. Online: https://online-journals.org/index.php/ijim/article/view/33187 (Retrieved: 28.05.2023).

[KER23] Kerler, Wolfgang (11.03.2023). Die Futuristin Amy Webb fürchtet, dass Künstliche Intelligenz zu einem schlechteren Internet führen könnte In: 1e9. Online: https://1e9.community/t/die-futuristin-amy-webb-fuerchtet-dass-kuenstliche-intelligenz-zu-einem-schlechteren-internet-fuehren-koennte/18894 (Retrieved: 21.05.2023).

[MAN02] Mann, Steve. (2002). Humanistic Intelligence as a Basis for Intelligent Image Processing. https://doi.org/10.1002/0471221635.ch1. (Retrieved: 21.05.2023).

[MAN12]   Mann, Steve (02.11.2012). Eye Am a Camera: Surveillance and Sousveillance in the Glassage. In: Time. Online: https://techland.time.com/2012/11/02/eye-am-a-camera-surveillance-and-sousveillance-in-the-glassage/ (Retrieved: 21.05.2023).

[MAN13]   Mann, Steve (01.03.2013). My „Augmediated": Life What I've learned from 35 years of wearing computerized eyewear. In: IEEE Spectrum. Online: https://spectrum.ieee.org/view-from-the-valley/consumer-electronics/portable-devices/steve-mann-the-man-who-invented-wearable-computing (Retrieved: 21.05.2023).

[MAN98]   Mann, Steve (Mai 1998). Definition of Wearable Computer. Wearcomp.org. Online: https://www.wearcomp.org/wearcompdef.htm l (Retrieved: 20.05.2025).

[MOR23b] Caroline Morris (2024). Seeing the future: Cathy Hackl's vision for how digital-physical reality will take shape. Mastercard Innovation Newsroom. Online: https://www.mastercard.com/news/perspectives/2024/seeing-the-future-cathy-hackl-s-vision-for-how-digital-physical-reality-will-take-shape. (Retrieved: 14.02.2025).

[MSFoJ]   MSF (o.J.). The Metaverse Standards Forum. In: MSF. Online: https://metaverse-standards.org/# (Retrieved: 28.05.2023).

[PAR21]   Parisi, Tony (22.10.2021). The Seven Rules oft he Metaverse – A framework for the coming immersive reality. In: Medium. Online: https://medium.com/meta-verses/the-seven-rules-of-the-metaverse-7d4e06fa864c (Retrieved: 22.5.2023).

[RAV22]   Ravenscraft, Eric (03.07.2022). What, Exactly, Is the Metaverse Standards Forum Creating? In: Wired Story. Online: https://www.wired.com/story/metaverse-standards-forum-explained/ (Retrieved: 28.05.2023).

[SCH23]   Schukz, Yogi (04.01.2023). Where's the beef in the Metaverse? In: IT Worls Canada. Online: https://www.itworldcanada.com/blog/wheres-the-beef-in-the-metaverse/519980 (Retrieved: 28.05.2023).

[WEB23]   Webster, Andrew (23.03.2023). Tim Sweeney explains how the metaverse might actually work. Online: https://www.theverge.com/2023/3/23/23652928/tim-sweeney-interview-epic-games-fortnite-metaverse (Retrieved: 21.05.2023).

[WEBoJb] Webb, Amy (o.J.). Biography. In: NYU Stern. Online: https://www.stern.nyu.edu/faculty/bio/amy-webb (Retrieved: 21.05.2023).

[WEF24a] WEF (12 March 2024). Navigating the Industrial Metaverse: A Blueprint for Future Innovations. WEF. Online: https://www.weforum.org/publications/navigating-the-industrial-metaverse-a-blueprint-for-future-innovations. (Retrieved: 14.02.2025).

[WEF24b] WEF (12.03.2024). Metaverse Identity: Defining the Self in a Blended Reality. WEF. Online: https://www.weforum.org/publications/metaverse-identity-defining-the-self-in-a-blended-reality/?utm_source=chatgpt.com. (Retrieved: 14.02.2025).

[WEFoJa] World Economic Forum (o.J.). Defining and Building the Metaverse. In: World Economic Forum. https://initiatives.weforum.org/defining-and-building-the-metaverse/home (Retrieved: 21.05.2023).

[WEFoJb] World Economic Forum (o.J.). Agenda Articles, filtered by "The Metaverse". In: World Economic Forum. https://www.weforum.org/agenda/the-metaverse/ (Retrieved: 21.05.2023).

[W3CoJa] W3C. (o.J.). About W3C. In: W3C. Online: https://www.w3.org/Consortium/ (Retrieved: 21.05.2023).

[W3CoJb] W3C. (o.J.). Web Standards. In: W3C. Online: https://www.w3.org/standards/ (Retrieved: 21.05.2023).

[W3CoJc] W3C. (o.J.). Privacy and Security. In: W3C. Online: https://www.w3.org/Privacy/ (Retrieved: 21.05.2023).

[W3CoJe] W3C. (2020). Immersive Web Working Group Charter. In: W3C. Online: https://www.w3.org/2020/05/immersive-web-wg-charter.html (Retrieved: 21.05.2023).

[W3CoJf]	W3C (2021). W3C Mission. In: W3C. Online: https://www.w3.org/Consortium/mission (Retrieved: 21.05.2023).
[W3CoJg]	W3C Web Accessibility Initiative (2021). Introduction to Web Accessibility. In: W3C. Online: https://www.w3.org/WAI/fundamentals/accessibility-intro/ (Retrieved: 21.05.2023).
[W3CoJh]	W3C Privacy Interest Group (2021). Privacy Interest Group (PING) Charter. In: W3C. Online: https://www.w3.org/2019/09/privacy-ig-charter.html (Retrieved: 21.05.2023).
[W3C23a]	W3C. (03.03.2023). WebXR Device API. In: W3C. Online: https://www.w3.org/TR/webxr/ (Retrieved: 21.05.2023).

Now is the time to Build! 9

"I'm not saying that we will eliminate physical labor, because we are still physical beings in a physical world, but I do think that the concept of work is expanding, and gaming is part of that future." (Cathy Hackl)

In light of rapid technological advancements and the growing significance of the metaverse, it is crucial to recognize and leverage the opportunities these virtual worlds offer at an early stage [KAU22, LAW22]. Even though technical standards are still lacking, what Cathy Hackl said remains true and important: "Now is the time to build!" The metaverse still holds enormous potential for creative collaboration, education, and social interaction, just waiting to be unlocked [DED09].

Only through active participation in shaping the metaverse and focusing on its sustainable and inclusive development can each individual user contribute to creating a positive and future-proof environment. Supporting community projects that address issues such as environmental protection, social justice, or education can help ensure that the metaverse becomes a place that not only serves entertainment but also provides real societal value [BAI10].

Scientists, technology developers, artists, and educators are called upon to explore the diverse possibilities of the metaverse and to actively work on shaping and improving these virtual worlds. In this way, a future in the metaverse can emerge that fosters creativity, enriches social interactions, and expands the boundaries of what is possible.

In this vision, creative freedom and collaboration are harnessed to develop innovative solutions to pressing global challenges such as environmental protection, social justice, and education [DED09]. The metaverse can serve as a testing ground where new ideas and approaches are trialed before being implemented in the real world [KAU22, LAW22].

To ensure a sustainable future in the metaverse, it is important that ethical and ecological considerations are taken into account from the outset. This includes the responsible use of resources and data, as well as the promotion of inclusion and accessibility to ensure that everyone has the opportunity to participate in and benefit from the metaverse. Creating a shared, creative, and sustainable future in the metaverse requires collaboration among scientists, technology developers, artists, educators, and users from around the world. Through joint commitment and the willingness to transcend existing boundaries, we can unlock the potential of the metaverse and create a better future for all.

In the metaverse, creativity plays a central role by enabling users to design their own environments and avatars [WILoJ, WAL21]. This individual freedom of design fosters artistic expression and allows users to create virtual galleries in which their artworks can be displayed. The possibilities are virtually limitless in terms of the type and scope of artistic creations that can emerge in the metaverse.

In addition to individual design, the metaverse also offers opportunities for collaborative creation. Community projects and shared worlds allow users to work together and pool their creative energies to create unique and extensive virtual experiences [BAI10]. In this context, open-source platforms and shared resources are becoming increasingly important, as they enable users to access, further develop, or modify existing content. This not only fosters creativity but also encourages the exchange of ideas and collaboration among users.

The creative freedom and individual design possibilities in the metaverse make a significant contribution to the appeal and diversity of these virtual environments. By promoting artistic expression and collaboration, the metaverse offers countless opportunities for users to express themselves, experiment, and learn new skills.

"I always say: in the metaverse, we are all world builders—and now is the time to build!"
(Cathy Hackl)

References

[BAI10]   Bainbridge, William Sims (2010). Online Worlds: Convergence of the Real and the Virtual. Human-Computer Interaction Series, Springer 2010, ISBN 978-1-84882-824-7.

[DED09]   Dede, Chris. (2009). Immersive Interfaces for Engagement and Learning. Science (New York, N.Y.). 323. 66–9. https://doi.org/10.1126/science.1167311.

[KAU22]   Kauffeld, Simone; Tartler, Darien; Gräfe, Hendrik; Ann-Kathrin, Windmann; Sauer, Nils (2022). What will mobile and virtual work look like in the future? – Results of a Delphi-based studyWie sieht die mobile und virtuelle Arbeit der Zukunft aus? – Ergebnisse einer Delphi-basierten Studie. Gruppe. Interaktion. Organisation. Zeitschrift für Angewandte Organisationspsychologie (GIO). 53. https://doi.org/10.1007/s11612-022-00627-8.

[LAW22]	Lawton, Geroge (18.11.2022). How will the metaverse affect the future of work? In: TechTarget. Online: https://www.techtarget.com/searchcio/tip/How-will-the-metaverse-affect-the-future-of-work (Retrieved: 21.05.2023).
[WAL21]	Walden, Stephanie (06.05.2021). Guide to Virtual Reality Art: What It Is and How to Make VR Art Yourself. In: Skillshare Blog. Online: https://www.skillshare.com/en/blog/guide-to-virtual-reality-art-what-it-is-and-how-to-make-vr-art-yourself/art (Retrieved: 21.05.2023).
[WILoJ]	Wilk, Elvia (o:j.). Will virtual reality conquer the artworld?. In: ArtBasel. Online: https://www.artbasel.com/stories/virtual-reality-technology-and-art (Retrieved: 21.05.2023).

10 The Current Addendum 1—Still Relevant: Is the Hype Already over?

The mere use of the term "metaverse" has recently attracted significant attention in both industry and research. At the beginning of this year, it seemed unthinkable that the virtual space could exist without a metaverse. Numerous companies invested heavily in establishing a presence in the metaverse, while countless start-ups emerged and the shares of companies such as Roblox and Matterport, which were already active in the metaverse, saw substantial increases in value. Recently, however (as of early May 2023), a certain sense of disillusionment appears to be setting in.

Rising interest rates as a result of the current higher inflation have led many companies to reconsider their visionary ambitions in the metaverse due to financial constraints. A prominent example is Facebook, which was penalized for its costly plans in and with the metaverse by a nearly 70% drop in its share price. The company only began to recover when CEO Mark Zuckerberg scaled back these plans and focused on cost efficiency and revenue in the current business. This was immediately followed by the question of whether the metaverse was already passé [LIN23].

Interest in the metaverse has noticeably declined compared to the peak of the discussion about a year ago, as can be seen, for example, in the global online search queries for the term "metaverse." In addition, the value of virtual real estate has also dropped significantly compared to physical real estate over the same period. Some decentralized virtual worlds have also experienced a decline in daily user numbers, falling short of expectations. Critics argue that the metaverse was merely a bubble driven by hype and marketing that has now burst [KEM23, PAL22].

Despite the apparently burst hype surrounding the metaverse, the concept should not be prematurely dismissed as a failure. The potential of the metaverse as a new way to host virtual events and create unique, immersive experiences for participants remains, even if the anticipated breakthrough has yet to occur [ZIE22].

The numerous metaverse concepts have been—and continue to be—hotly debated. However, the actual results have so far proven to be significantly less impressive than predicted. One example is the Decentraland Metaverse Fashion Week 2023, where visitor numbers dropped considerably compared to the previous year [DRE23, SAN23]. As a result, interest is increasingly shifting toward artificial intelligence, with Chat-GPT currently serving as the most prominent example.

Despite the disappointing results regarding the metaverse, hybrid and online events continue to enjoy great popularity. However, the general public does not appreciate navigating virtual worlds to the extent originally anticipated. According to James Au, an analyst and journalist specializing in the metaverse, metaverse platforms are growing slowly but steadily and are adapting to the circumstances. In the first quarter of 2023, such platforms recorded an increase of 15 million users, reaching a total of 520 million monthly active users, according to a report by the analyst firm Metaversed. The analysis covers 149 platforms that are either already live or in development, with the majority being browser-based and some relying on the use of VR headsets. Au emphasizes that the study primarily focuses on prominent platforms with strong usage in the USA and Europe. Free Fire (formerly Garena Free Fire) [OBE21], a game primarily known and widespread in Southeast Asia and South America that reaches about 10 percent of the world's population, is, for example, not included in this analysis. Despite layoffs in the technology sector overall, metaverse platforms continue to hire staff. According to Au, more than 800 job postings were recorded, despite the current trend of IT technology companies laying off large numbers of employees [AU23, METoJa, METoJb, METoJc].

Furthermore, a report by S&P Global Market Intelligence shows that around 120 companies are working on metaverse technologies, including data integration for digital twins and also in the context of the Internet of Things, avatars, and secure identity management. Not only the software sector, but also hardware development remains an actively pursued area, such as the (further) development of input/output technologies like haptics, holography, spatial audio, and, of course, augmented reality. Investments in technologies and applications related to the metaverse exceeded 24 billion US dollars last year, with the largest investments, according to S&P Capital IQ Pro, coming from Meta Platforms, Epic Games, Infinite Reality, and Roblox Corp. [HUG23, JOH23].

Despite the apparent collapse of the bubble, several hundred million people are currently using or visiting "the metaverse," although the majority of users rely on regular screens and only a minority use VR headsets. According to a report by 451 Research, a subsidiary of S&P Global Market Intelligence, the metaverse is conceived as a "long-term vision for the next phase of the internet," which "encompasses a unified, shared, immersive, and persistent virtual 3D space where people interact with each other and with data, complementing rather than replacing the physical world." Ian Hughes, an analyst at 451 Research, predicts that the metaverse will eventually become as popular as social media. Nevertheless, this transformation will occur gradually, with Hughes comparing the adoption of the metaverse to the mainstream implementation of videoconferencing over the past three years [HUG23, JOH23].

Interestingly, the use of the metaverse spans a wide age range, including teenagers and young adults as well as middle-aged individuals and seniors. According to Au, seniors in particular are increasingly using Second Life, despite the technical challenges and requirements of the platform. The various age groups use the metaverse to explore different worlds with a variety of goals, often adopting different identities [AU23].

Another issue raised by Au concerns Meta's strategy. Meta is not only investing heavily in niche products such as headsets, but is also tying its metaverse to Facebook profiles, which are in turn linked to users' real identities. However, this does not align with the primary interests of the majority of users. Rather, most people visit the metaverse to form communities, including anime fans, gamers, and furries. The popular platform VRChat, for example, hosts an extensive nightclub rave scene and numerous social games.

Recently, even Mark Zuckerberg has tempered the enthusiasm surrounding the metaverse, stating that it will no longer be the main focus of his company's activities in the near future, as was originally planned. The company is now prioritizing efficiency and cutting 11,000 jobs, with the possibility of several thousand more to follow. The Reality Labs division, responsible for producing the Meta Quest VR headsets, reported a loss of $13.7 billion last year. In contrast, Apple has been announcing the launch of its own augmented reality headset since 2015. However, its market release has been postponed several times, most recently to fall 2023. Once this product is released, it is expected to be a major success for Apple and to drive the metaverse sector forward in much the same way Apple revolutionized the smartphone. Despite the significant investments in headsets, Au notes that they are unlikely to become the primary mainstream technology for the metaverse in the foreseeable future. Even today, successful metaverse platforms such as Roblox, Fortnite, and VRChat are mainly accessed via smartphones, tablets, gaming consoles, and PCs. According to Au, screen-based platforms are therefore expected to remain the dominant future of the metaverse. On a smartphone or other display-based device, users can quickly switch their attention between the metaverse environment and the real world. In contrast, virtual reality requires users' full attention. Au emphasizes that VR headsets are at a disadvantage in terms of usability and rapid environmental awareness, simply because wearing them separates users from the real world. Moreover, these devices are not only partly insecure with regard to user data and carry a social stigma, but are also expensive. For example, Meta's latest Oculus headset currently costs around $1,500 and also has a short battery life [AU23, BER23].

> "Ninety-five percent of global executives we surveyed last year said they believe the metaverse will have a positive impact on their industry within five to ten years," says McKinsey [MCK22a, MCK22b].

The current focus on the metaverse and its commercial and industrial applications appears to lie mainly with large corporations and industrial enterprises. For example, Microsoft is integrating metaverse features into its collaboration tool Teams by deploying its proprietary Mesh platform on Azure. This technology was presented at the World

Economic Forum in Davos in January 2023, allowing many participants to gain their first hands-on experience with the metaverse, as Hughes notes. Siemens and Nvidia are collaborating on the development of Nvidia's metaverse platform Omniverse to build a virtual factory where autonomous robots can be trained. In addition, people can work in this virtual reality to study the ergonomics and efficiency of a factory hall prototype. Companies will be able to combine these technologies with the Internet of Things and digital twins to track assets throughout their entire lifecycle. Accenture has also made significant consulting investments in the metaverse, including the purchase of thousands of headsets, as Hughes reports [NVIoJ, DUS23].

Another example of the emerging "industrial metaverses" is the collaboration between the BMW Group and NVIDIA, who aim to move the planning of highly complex manufacturing systems into the metaverse using the aforementioned Omniverse platform. The virtual factory planning tool integrates various planning data and applications, enabling real-time collaboration without compatibility barriers. The platform brings together data from different design and planning tools and creates photorealistic real-time simulations in a collaborative environment. Employees at different locations and in different time zones can access the simulations and jointly plan or optimize processes or production facilities. Previous virtual factory planning tools struggled with data compatibility and up-to-date information. The Omniverse platform solves these problems by merging live data from relevant databases into a shared simulation, eliminating the need to re-import data. This enables planners and production specialists to plan more accurately and quickly, without interface losses or compatibility issues [GEY23, BMW21].

It appears that the peak of the initial hype cycle has passed and a gap has emerged between reality and expectations. Nevertheless, the aforementioned 95% of surveyed global executives are unusually united in their belief that the metaverse will have a positive impact on their respective industries within the next five to ten years. In fact, implemented use cases are continuously increasing, raising hopes that a well-established enterprise metaverse will reach the consumer and end-user market in the not-too-distant future.

References

[AU23]   Au, Wagner James (27. Juni 2023). Making a Metaverse That Matters: From Snow Crash & Second Life to A Virtual World Worth Fighting For. Wiley.

[BER23]   Berger, Dennis (14.01.2023). VR-Brillen-Verkäufe: Zahlen und Hintergründe. In: Mixed. Online: https://mixed.de/vr-brillen-verkaeufe-uebersicht/ (Retrieved: 20.05.2023).

[BMW21]   BMW Broup (13.04.2021). BMW Group und NVIDIA heben virtuelle Fabrikplanung auf die nächste Ebene. In: Pressemeldung. Online: https://www.press.bmwgroup.com/deutschland/article/detail/T0329569DE/bmw-group-und-nvidia-heben-virtuelle-fabrikplanung-auf-die-naechste-ebene?language=de (Retrieved: 20.05.2023).

[DRE23]	Dredge, Stuart (06.04.2023). Only 26,000 people attended Decentraland's Metaverse Fashion Week. In: Music:ally. Online: https://musically.com/2023/04/06/only-26000-people-attended-decentralands-metaverse-fashion-week/ (Retrieved: 21.05.2023).
[DUS23]	Dusold, Julia (04.06.2022). Nächste Ebene der Digitalisierung: Metaverse für die Industrie: Siemens und Nvidia gehen es an. In: Produktion. Online: https://www.produktion.de/technik/zukunftstechnologien/metaverse-fuer-die-industrie-siemens-und-nvidia-gehen-es-an-308.html (Retrieved: 20.05.2023).
[GEY23]	Geyer, Mike (21.03.2023). BMW Group Starts Global Rollout of NVIDIA Omniverse. In: Nvidia Blog. Online: https://blogs.nvidia.com/blog/2023/03/21/bmw-group-nvidia-omniverse/ (Retrieved: 20.05.2023).
[HUG23]	Hughes, Ian; Barbour, Neil; Partridge, Brian; Paxton, Michael (24.01.2023). Metaverse primer: Examining the future of all digital interaction. In: S&P Global Market Intelligence. Online: https://www.spglobal.com/marketintelligence/en/news-insights/research/metaverse-primer-examining-the-future-of-all-digital-interaction (Retrieved: 20.05.2023).
[JOH23]	Johnston, Alex (01.03.2023). Blockchain and the metaverse, part 1: Opportunities In: S&P Global Market Intelligence. Online: https://www.spglobal.com/marketintelligence/en/news-insights/research/blockchain-and-the-metaverse-part-1-opportunities (Retrieved: 20.05.2023).
[KEM23]	Kemp, Simon (28.01.2023). Digital 2023 Deep-Dive: Is the Metaverse going in reverse? In: Datareportal. Online: https://datareportal.com/reports/digital-2023-deep-dive-metaverse-in-reverse (Retrieved: 20.05.2023).
[LIN23]	Lindner, Roland (27.04.2023). Meta wächst wieder. In: Frankfurter Allgemeine. Online: https://www.faz.net/aktuell/wirtschaft/unternehmen/meta-ist-wieder-auf-wachstumskurs-18851388.html (Retrieved: 20.05.2023).
[MCK22a]	McKinsey & Company (21.06.2022). Studie: Das Metaverse kann bis 2030 einen Wert von bis zu 5 Billionen Dollar erreichen. In: McKinsey Press Release. Online: https://www.mckinsey.com/de/news/presse/2022-06-21-metaverse (Retrieved: 20.05.2023).
[MCK22b]	McKinsey & Company (2022). Value creation in the metaverse. In: McKinsey Growth, Marketing & Sales. Online: https://www.mckinsey.com/capabilities/growth-marketing-and-sales/our-insights/value-creation-in-the-metaverse (Retrieved: 20.05.2023).
[METoJa]	Metaversed (o.J.). The Metaverse Reaches 400m Monthly Active Users. In: Metaversed. Online: https://www.metaversed.consulting/blog/the-metaverse-reaches-400m-active-users (Retrieved: 20.05.2023).
[METoJb]	Metaversed (o.J.). Introducing the Web3 Metaverse Index. In: Metaversed. Online: https://www.metaversed.consulting/blog/introducing-the-web3-metaverse-index (Retrieved: 20.05.2023).
[METoJc]	Metaversed (o.J.). The Web3 Metaverse Index: February 2023 update. Online: https://www.metaversed.consulting/blog/the-web3-metaverse-index-february-2023-update (Retrieved: 20.05.2023).
[NVIoJ]	Nvidia (o.J.) Siemens und Nvidia – Aufbau des industriellen Metaverse. In: Nvidia Omniverse. Online: https://www.nvidia.com/de-de/omniverse/digital-twins/siemens/ (Retrieved: 20.05.2023).
[OBE21]	Obedkov, Evgeny (17.08.2021). Mobile battle royale Free Fire surpasses 150 million peak daily active players. Game World Observer. Online: https://gameworldobserver.com/2021/08/17/garena-free-fire-surpasses-150-million-peak-daily-activeplayers. (Retrieved: 20.05.2025).

[PAL22] Paleja, Ameya (06.04.2022). Could the metaverse become a big flop? Here's what Google Trends says. In: Interesting Engineering. Online: https://interestingengineering.com/culture/metaverse-flop-google-trends (Retrieved: 20.05.2023).

[SAN23] Sander Lutz (08.04.2023). And the Winner of Metaverse Fashion Week 2023 Is… In: Decrypt. Online: https://decrypt.co/125737/winner-decentraland-metaverse-fashion-week-2023 (Retrieved: 21.05.2023).

[ZIE22] Ziegener, Daniel (17. October 2022). Niedrige Nutzerzahlen: Kaum jemand interessiert sich für Metas Metaversum. In: Golem. Online: https://www.golem.de/news/niedrige-nutzerzahlen-kaum-jemand-interessiert-sich-fuer-metas-metaversum-2210-168982.html (Retrieved: 20.05.2023).

Glossary

Augmented Reality (AR) Augmented Reality (AR) means "enhanced reality." In this context, human perception of the real (physical) environment is enriched with digital information.

Initially, the concept of AR was based on enhancing perception by inserting location-specific and precisely aligned 3D objects. To reduce technical complexity, AR has since been downgraded in development to the extent that the insertion of 2D objects and/or text is now also referred to as AR.

Augmented Virtuality (AV) Like AR, Augmented Virtuality also involves a blending or "augmentation" of human perception. While AR assumes that real-world elements predominate in perception, in Augmented Virtuality, perception is dominated by digital or virtual objects. This occurs, for example, when a user is immersed in a virtual or VR world and a video chat with a real person is displayed in a window within that environment.

Blockchain Blockchain is a decentralized digital database technology that stores information in chronologically ordered, cryptographically secured blocks and distributes them across a network of computers. This architecture ensures transparency, tamper-resistance, and traceability of transactions, making it particularly relevant for cryptocurrencies, smart contracts, non-fungible tokens (NFTs), and applications in the metaverse. Due to its decentralized nature, blockchain reduces reliance on central authorities, but at the same time presents challenges regarding scalability, energy consumption, and regulatory frameworks.

Brain Computing Interface (BCI) A Brain Computing Interface (BCI) is an interface between a user's brain and a computer system. It enables direct communication and interaction by capturing and interpreting brain signals. These signals can be used to perform actions and control devices. The transmission of information to the user is also a key focus of research. The goal of BCI is, among other things, to assist people with physical disabilities, enabling them to interact with computers and applications as easily and seamlessly as possible.

CAVE CAVE stands for "Cave Automatic Virtual Environment" and refers to an immersive VR environment. Projections are displayed on multiple sides of a room. The user stands inside this room, effectively within the projected VR world, and can move through this world using tracking technology integrated into the space.

CAVEs are used, among other fields, in medicine, architecture, and design for the visualization of complex scenarios, for example in the form of realistic simulations.

Digital Twin The term "digital twin" refers to a virtual representation of a physical object, system, or process. It is created and maintained through continuous real-time data collection and analysis. The digital twin enables precise modeling and simulation of the state, behavior, and performance of the real-world object. This allows for predictions to be made, problems to be identified, and solutions to be developed. Digital twins are used in various fields such as industry, medicine, and urban planning. In the context of the metaverse, user avatars are intended to become digital twins that can also act autonomously within the virtual environment.

Direct Interaction By using hand controllers, gesture recognition, or other input methods, users can grasp, manipulate, and interact with objects as if they were physically present. This type of interaction enables a more immersive and realistic VR experience, allowing users to actively engage with the virtual world.

Emotes Emotes are short animated or static images that represent emotions or gestures and are used in online chats and social media. Unlike emojis, which are predefined symbols, emotes are often created by users or selected from a library. They are a popular means of communication for expressing emotions or adding humor. While emojis are universally understood, emotes often have a specific meaning within certain online communities and their unique cultures.

Extended Reality (XR) The debate over whether the two extremes—"100% Reality" and "100% Virtuality"—of the reality-virtuality continuum should also be considered part of Extended Reality is resolved by Bellalouna et al., who define Extended Reality as the sum of AR, AV, and VR.

Graphical User Interface (GUI) A "Graphical User Interface" (GUI) is a visual interface that enables users to interact with a computer or application. Instead of text-based commands, GUIs use icons, menus, and graphical elements such as buttons and windows to make operation more user-friendly. The GUI allows users to perform actions simply by clicking, dragging, and dropping, which simplifies operation and reduces the learning curve.

Head-Mounted Display (HMD) A "Head-Mounted Display" (HMD) refers to a wearable device that is worn on the user's head and is designed to provide immersive access to applications or information. It consists of a pair of glasses or a helmet in which one or more displays are integrated. By wearing the HMD, virtual content is presented directly in front of the user's eyes, allowing them to immerse themselves in virtual reality (VR) or augmented reality (AR).

Immersion/Immersivity Immersion refers to the state of being deeply engaged or absorbed, while immersivity describes the quality or degree to which this immersion is strong and convincing. Both concepts play an important role in the design of entertainment and educational/learning systems, as well as in medical and therapeutic applications.

Immersive Environment/Immersive World By combining realistic graphics, interactive elements, and immersive sound, users' senses are engaged to enable an experience that is nearly lifelike. Immersive worlds open up new possibilities for entertainment, learning, and exploration.

Interaction Paradigm An interaction paradigm describes the fundamental way in which people interact with technology. It encompasses the design of user interfaces, interaction patterns, and conventions.

The chosen interaction paradigm influences how users perceive information, perform actions, and communicate with systems. Examples of interaction paradigms include the graphical user interface, voice control, and gesture control. An effective interaction paradigm enables intuitive and efficient interaction between humans and technology.

Internet The Internet is a global network of computers that enables the exchange of information and resources worldwide. It connects millions of devices and is based on the TCP/IP protocol. It encompasses various services such as email, file sharing, video streaming, and much more.

The Internet forms the foundation for the World Wide Web (WWW).

Internet of Things (IoT) The term "Internet of Things" (IoT) refers to the interconnection of physical devices that communicate with each other via sensors and Internet network connections. This enables them to collect and exchange data, as well as perform actions to enhance the efficiency and functionality of everyday life. Ranging from smart homes to industrial automation, the IoT aims to enable seamless integration of technology into the environment and to facilitate and optimize the automation of processes.

Lost in Hyperspace "Lost in Hyperspace" is a term from information design that refers to the feeling of being lost in an overwhelming information space. It describes the state in which users are unable to find their way due to poor navigation or unclear content structure. This can lead to frustration and disorientation. To avoid this problem, it is important to design clearly defined navigation paths and an intuitive user interface to help users avoid getting lost in the vastness of the information space.

Location Awareness Location awareness refers to the ability of a device or application to detect a user's location and make it available for further use. By utilizing GPS, Wi-Fi, or other technologies, location awareness can be used to provide personalized information, services, or recommendations based on the current location. This enables functionalities such as navigation, finding nearby stores, or adjusting settings according to the surrounding environment.

Media Discontinuity The term "media discontinuity" refers to the transition between different communication or information carriers, such as paper and digital media. This transition can result in interruptions, loss of information, or frictional losses. A media discontinuity occurs when data or content must be transferred from one medium to another. This can lead to misunderstandings or inefficient processes. The goal is to minimize media discontinuities in order to enable seamless interaction between different media.

Mixed Reality (MR) Mixed Reality refers to the extension of AR and, in part, AV by enabling direct interaction with virtual objects. Such interaction is not provided for in the classic AR paradigm.

Debate arises from the question of whether the two extremes—"100% reality" and "100% virtuality"—of the reality-virtuality continuum should also be considered part of Mixed Reality.

Mixed Reality is also frequently referred to synonymously as "Extended Reality."

Modusage The term "Modusage" combines Toffler's concept of prosumption and Bruns' concept of produsage to describe the characteristics of the cross-economy of the metaverse, which will create a new form of value creation that transcends the boundary between the virtual and real worlds. Products and services from one world can be utilized not only within their own domain but also in the other.

The merging of the physical and digital worlds enables both the interpretation and integration of the traditional value chain as well as the community-oriented value chain of the digital world.

Motion Capturing Motion Capturing (MoCap) is a technique for recording human movement. Sensors are attached to a person's body to capture their movements. The recorded data is then transferred to digital characters or models to create realistic animations. Motion Capturing was originally developed for the film industry and video games. Today, MoCap is also used in sports analysis and medicine to represent movements precisely and realistically.

In the context of the metaverse or virtual worlds, more realistic avatar movements are intended to achieve a higher level of immersion.

Multimedia In the context of (media) informatics applications, multimedia refers to the individual or combined presentation of different media, which may be either time-dependent or time-independent.

This presentation can involve a single medium or any possible combination thereof at a specific point in time, or a temporal sequence of such combinations within a contextual framework.

Multimedia may include the possibility for a user to directly or indirectly influence the combination or the temporal sequence of the individual media.

Multimodality Multimodality refers to a system's ability to perceive and exchange information through multiple senses. It enables interaction by combining various modalities such as speech, gesture, gaze, and touch. Utilizing multiple channels allows for more diverse and effective communication. Multimodality is applied in human-computer interaction, for example in voice assistants, virtual reality, and user interfaces, to create more natural and intuitive interactions.

Natural User Interface (NUI) Natural User Interfaces (NUI) are user interfaces designed to enable natural forms of interaction between humans and computers. Instead of conventional input devices such as keyboard and mouse, NUIs use human actions like gestures, speech, or touch to capture commands. This aims to enhance the user experience and lower the barriers to technology interaction, enabling seamless and user-friendly communication between humans and computers.

NFT (Non-Fungible Token) An NFT (Non-Fungible Token) is a unique digital asset stored on a blockchain that verifies the ownership and authenticity of a digital object, such as artwork, music, collectibles, or virtual real estate. Unlike fungible cryptocurrencies like Bitcoin or Ethereum, NFTs are not interchangeable, as each token possesses individual characteristics. This technology enables new forms of digital ownership, particularly in the art market, gaming industry, and the metaverse, but also raises questions regarding sustainability, copyright, and market stability.

Proactivity Proactivity, both in general and in computer science, refers to anticipatory action and the ability to identify potential problems or needs at an early stage and take appropriate measures. Rather than waiting for reactive solutions, proactivity aims to implement preventive actions to enhance the efficiency, reliability, and security of IT systems.

Through proactive approaches, potential issues can be avoided or at least minimized, leading to smoother and more effective use of technology.

Produsage Produsage is a term coined by Axel Bruns that describes the merging of production and usage in collaborative online communities. In this context, users are not merely passive consumers but active co-creators of content. They produce, edit, and share information in an open, participatory manner.

Produsage enables the community to collectively generate knowledge and drive innovation. It is about cooperative creativity and collective engagement, fostering a dynamic and open form of collaboration.

Prosumption The term prosumption was coined by Alvin Toffler and describes the concept that individuals are not only consumers of products, but also simultaneously producers. With ongoing digitalization and technological advancements, people today can create, edit, and share content themselves in many areas. Prosumption unites the roles of producing and consuming within a single person and represents a merging of traditional consumer and producer activities. This trend has an impact on the economy, culture, and society, as it changes the balance of power between companies and consumers.

Rendering Rendering refers to the process of generating images, animations, or videos from a 2D or 3D scene. In this process, two- and three-dimensional models, textures, and lighting information are converted into a displayable format. Calculations are used to add shadows, reflections, and other visual effects in order to achieve realistic or stylized results.

Reality-Virtuality Continuum (RVC) The reality-virtuality continuum is a concept in computer science that describes the transition between real and virtual environments. It represents a spectrum on which various technologies and applications are positioned, ranging from the real world on one end to the fully virtual world on the other. The continuum includes, for example, augmented reality, mixed reality, and virtual reality, and offers increasing immersion and interaction for the user.

Smart Contract A smart contract refers to a self-executing digital contract protocol that is stored on a blockchain and automatically verifies and enforces predefined conditions without the need for a central authority or intermediary. These programmable contracts enable transparent, secure, and immutable transactions in areas such as finance, supply chains, real estate, or the metaverse. Through automation, smart contracts reduce costs and sources of error, but they also present challenges regarding legal recognition, security vulnerabilities, and susceptibility to coding errors.

Spatial Computing Spatial computing refers to the integration of digital information into the physical environment through technologies such as augmented reality (AR), virtual reality (VR), mixed reality (MR), as well as sensors and artificial intelligence (AI). By capturing the environment, movement, and user interactions, spatial computing enables a seamless connection between the real and virtual worlds. It is applied in areas such as Industry 4.0, healthcare, education, and the metaverse, creating immersive and interactive experiences that go beyond traditional screen-based interfaces.

Synthetic Media Synthetic media refers to digital content generated or manipulated by artificial intelligence (AI) and machine learning (ML), including images, videos, audio files, and text. This technology enables the automated creation of realistic media, for example through deepfake videos, text-to-image generators, or AI-powered speech synthesis. Synthetic media is used in fields such as entertainment, advertising, education, and the metaverse, but also raises ethical concerns regarding copyright, disinformation, and identity misuse.

Treadmill/VR-Treadmill A VR treadmill is a VR input/output technology that enables users to move within virtual environments by physically walking or running on a treadmill or similar device.

By integrating sensors and motion capture technologies, VR treadmills can track the user's movements and transfer them into the virtual world, creating a more immersive VR experience. This allows users to move freely within the virtual environment.

User-generated Content (UGC) User-generated Content (UGC) refers to content created and shared online by users. This can include texts, images, videos, reviews, or comments. UGC enables users to actively participate in the exchange of information and to produce content, rather than merely consuming it passively. Platforms such as social media, blogs, and forums benefit from the diversity and engagement of users who generate UGC. This participatory approach fosters interaction, creativity, and the development of communities.

Virtual Reality (VR) The representation of a scene as a computer-generated spatial environment with the goal of achieving the highest possible level of immersion.

Fully immersive VR, or 100% VR, is considered one of the two extremes of the reality-virtuality continuum according to Milgram and Kishino.

A defining characteristic of VR is the implementation of the "direct interaction" paradigm, which enables users to interact with objects within the rendered scene. This is the key distinction from, for example, 360° photos or 360° videos, where interaction with the scene is not possible.

VR headset A VR headset is a device used to allow users to experience virtual worlds in an immersive way. It typically consists of a specialized headset worn on the head, containing two displays that present stereoscopic graphics. The VR headset tracks the user's head movements and adjusts the virtual environment accordingly to create a sense of presence.

Wearable/Wearable Computing Wearable computing refers to technology in which computers and electronic devices are integrated into clothing or accessories and worn by the user. These devices enable interaction with digital information and applications in real time. Examples of wearables include smartwatches, fitness trackers, and AR glasses. They offer convenient and practical solutions for communication, health monitoring, navigation, and much more. Through seamless integration into everyday life, wearables open up new possibilities for personal technology and digital interaction.

Wearable computing is particularly considered a distinct interaction paradigm, as the handling and use of wearable computers differ significantly from traditional computer systems.

WIMP WIMP is an acronym for "Windows, Icons, Menus, Pointer" and refers to a type of user interface for computers and applications. It is considered a paradigm that facilitates interaction between users and computers. "Windows" refers to the display of programs in separate windows, "Icons" represent files or programs, "Menus" provide access to functions, and "Pointer" is the mouse cursor used for navigation.

WIMP interfaces are a form of GUI and are widely used because they enable simple and visual interaction with the computer.

World Wide Web (WWW) The WWW is a part of the Internet and specifically refers to the system of interlinked hypertext documents that are accessed via the HTTP protocol. The WWW enables the display of web pages that are connected to each other through hyperlinks. It is one of the most well-known and widely used applications of the Internet, providing access to information, multimedia content, and interactive services.

The WWW is an important component of the Internet, but not the only one.

GPSR Compliance

The European Union's (EU) General Product Safety Regulation (GPSR) is a set of rules that requires consumer products to be safe and our obligations to ensure this.

If you have any concerns about our products, you can contact us on ProductSafety@springernature.com

In case Publisher is established outside the EU, the EU authorized representative is:

Springer Nature Customer Service Center GmbH
Europaplatz 3
69115 Heidelberg, Germany

Batch number: 09412879

Printed by Printforce, the Netherlands